SSFIPS

Securing Cisco® Networks with Sourcefire® Intrusion Prevention System

Study Guide

Todd Lammle

John Gay

Alex Tatistcheff

D0898900

A Wiley Brand

Senior Acquisitions Editor: Kenyon Brown
Development Editor: Kathi Duggan
Technical Editor: Richard Clendenning
Production Editor: Christine O'Connor
Copy Editor: Judy Flynn
Editorial Manager: Mary Beth Wakefield
Production Manager: Kathleen Wisor
Associate Publisher: Jim Minatel
Book Designers: Judy Fung and Bill Gibson
Proofreader: Josh Chase, Word One New York
Indexer: Robert Swanson
Project Coordinator, Cover: Brent Savage
Cover Designer: Wiley
Cover Image: © Getty Images Inc./Jeremy Woodhouse

Copyright © 2016 by John Wiley & Sons, Inc., Indianapolis, Indiana

Published by John Wiley & Sons, Inc. Indianapolis, Indiana

Published simultaneously in Canada

ISBN: 978-1-119-15503-4

ISBN: 978-1-119-15505-8 (ebk.)

ISBN: 978-1-119-15504-1 (ebk.)

Library of Congress Control Number: 2015951789

To my wife Shelly who has learned to live all these years with a computer nerd.
—Alex

To Jennifer and Paul Gay: Without your support through the late nights, I never would have made it! Thank you for the wonderful years, and I look forward to many more.
—John

Acknowledgments

There are many people who work to put a book together, and although as authors we dedicate an enormous amount of time to write the book, it would never be published without the dedicated, hard work of many other people.

First, Kenyon Brown, my acquisitions editor, is instrumental to my success in the Cisco world. I look forward to our continued progress together in this crazy certification world we call Cisco!

Big thanks to Kathryn Duggan, my developmental editor, who helped keep this project together, and on time. No easy feat! Thank you, Kathryn, once again!

Christine O'Connor, my production editor, and Judy Flynn, my copy editor, are my rock and foundation for formatting and intense editing of every page in this book. This amazing team gives me the confidence to help me keep moving during the difficult and very long days, week after week. I could never imagine writing a single page of a book if I didn't know that the amazing duo of Christine and Judy was behind me all the way! Thank you from the bottom of my heart.

Last listed, but certainly not least, is Richard Clendenning. Phenomenal tech editing at its best and amazing eye on details allowed the authoring team to really shine in this book. Thank you Richard!

—From Todd

Thanks to Todd for driving this entire project. If you ever meet him, you will understand right away how he could write over 60 books. Todd, you're a wild man!

And I would be remiss not to thank my Lord Jesus Christ, to whom I owe literally everything.

—From Alex

Karen Paulson, my former boss who brought me to the Sourcefire team and supported my career development and growth: I cannot thank her enough for her support over the years.

And to Ed Mendez, a co-worker who has fostered my development and been a great learning partner: thanks, man, for all the help!

—From John

About the Authors

Alex Tatistcheff is currently a network consulting engineer for Cisco Security Solutions specializing in FireSIGHT. Alex came to Cisco via the acquisition of Sourcefire, Inc., in 2013. At Sourcefire, he worked for over five years as a senior security instructor teaching the Sourcefire System, Snort, and rule writing classes. During this time, he also completed consulting engagements with several dozen customers.

Prior to coming to Sourcefire, Alex worked on the security team for a large electric utility as a Sourcefire customer and before that as a network/security consultant for numerous organizations.

Alex calls Boise, Idaho, home, where he lives with his wife, Shelly, and two Australian shepherds, Molly and Boomer. He enjoys mountain biking, traveling, and Raspberry Pi.

John Gay is a field security enablement lead with Cisco Systems. He is responsible for facilitating the learning of internal customers. Prior to Cisco's acquisition of Sourcefire, John served as director of instructional delivery, where he managed the instructor team and assisted in the creation and delivery of learning material. Since 1999, John has been in the security industry, training students around the world in IDS/IPS/NGFW/vulnerability assessment. This includes Fortune 500 companies, government agencies, and even military units in theater. Prior to beginning his career in security, John was teaching networking, routing, and back-office applications for a world-class training company. He was also tasked with giving technology presentations for high-profile partners at customer sites and conferences. John has been involved with computers and technology for over 30 years and has had over 20 years in the industry. He also holds a BS in Communication Arts and an MS in Instructional Technology.

Todd Lammle is the authority on Cisco certification and internetworking and is Cisco certified in most Cisco certification categories. He is a world-renowned author, speaker, trainer, and consultant. Todd has three decades of experience working with LANs, WANs, and large enterprise licensed and unlicensed wireless networks, and lately he's been implementing large Cisco data centers worldwide as well as FirePOWER technologies. His years of real-world experience are evident in his writing; he is not just an author but an experienced networking engineer with very practical experience working on the largest networks in the world at such companies as Xerox, Hughes Aircraft, Texaco, AAA, Cisco, and Toshiba, among many others. Todd has published over 60 books, including the very popular *CCNA: Cisco Certified Network Associate Study Guide*, *CCNA Wireless Study Guide*, and *CCNA Data Center Study Guide* as well as this FirePOWER study guide, all from Sybex. He runs an international consulting and training company based in Colorado, Texas, and San Francisco.

You can reach Todd through his website at www.lammle.com/firepower.

Contents at a Glance

Contents

Introduction

Welcome to the exciting world of Cisco certification! If you've picked up this book because you want to improve yourself and your life with a better, more satisfying, and secure job, you've done the right thing. Whether you're striving to enter the thriving, dynamic IT sector or seeking to enhance your skill set and advance your position within it, being Cisco certified can seriously stack the odds in your favor to help you attain your goals!

Cisco certifications are powerful instruments of success that also markedly improve your grasp of all things internetworking. As you progress through this book, you'll gain a complete understanding of security that reaches far beyond Cisco devices. By the end of this book, you'll comprehensively know how Sourcefire technologies work together in your network, which is vital to today's very way of life in the developed world. The knowledge and expertise you'll gain here is essential for and relevant to every networking job and is why Cisco certifications are in such high demand—even at companies with few Cisco devices!

Although it's now common knowledge that Cisco rules routing and switching, the fact that it also rocks the voice, data center, and security worlds is also well recognized. And Cisco certifications reach way beyond the popular but less extensive certifications like those offered by CompTIA and Microsoft to equip you with indispensable insight into today's vastly complex networking realm. Essentially, by deciding to become Cisco certified, you're proudly announcing that you want to become an unrivaled networking expert—a goal that this book will get you well on your way to achieving. Congratulations in advance on the beginning of your brilliant future!

> For up-to-the-minute updates covering additions or modifications to the Cisco certification exams, as well as additional study tools, videos, practice questions, and bonus material, be sure to visit the Todd Lammle website and forum at www.lammle.com/firepower.

Why Should You Become Certified in the SSFIPS Securing Cisco Networks with Sourcefire Intrusion Prevention System?

Cisco, like Microsoft and other vendors that provide certification, has created the certification process to give administrators a set of skills and to equip prospective employers with a way to measure those skills or match certain criteria.

The SSFIPS Securing Cisco Networks with Sourcefire Intrusion Prevention System (500-285) exam is designed for technical professionals who need to demonstrate their expertise and skills in deployment and management of Cisco NGIPS solutions, including Cisco FirePOWER appliances and the Cisco FireSIGHT management system.

Rest assured that if you make it through the SSFIPS and are still interested in Cisco and security, you're headed down a path to certain success!

What Does This Book Cover?

This book covers everything you need to know to pass the SSFIPS 500-285 exam.

You will learn the following information in this book:

Chapter 1: Getting Started with FireSIGHT   What is FirePOWER? What is FireSIGHT? What is Sourcefire? Understand Sourcefire by building a solid foundation in defining key, industry-wide, and Cisco-specific terms that we'll be using throughout this book. Various FireSIGHT appliance models will be discussed as well as licensing, policies, and initial system setup.

Chapter 2: Object Management   This chapter will provide you with the understanding of object types that are used by the FireSIGHT System. And as with the other chapters, this chapter includes review questions and a hands-on lab to help you build a strong foundation.

Chapter 3: IPS Policy Management   This chapter provides you with the background necessary for success on the exam as well as in the real world with a thorough presentation of IPS policy management. This in-depth chapter covers IPS policies, which precisely describe the suspicious and/or malicious traffic that the system must watch out for, and they also control how evil traffic is dealt with when it's discovered.

Chapter 4: Access Control Policy   Chapter 4 covers the heart of the FireSIGHT system. An Access Control policy acts kind of like the central traffic cop for FireSIGHT because all traffic passing through a device is processed through it. And you'll find plenty of help in this chapter as long as you don't skip the review questions and hands-on lab at the end.

Chapter 5: FireSIGHT Technologies   FireSIGHT is the name given to a technology built into the Cisco FirePOWER NGIPS to provide us with contextual awareness regarding events, IP addresses, users on the network, and even background about the hosts in the system. As with Chapter 4, plenty of help is there for you if don't skip the review questions and hands-on labs at the end.

Chapter 6: Intrusion Event Analysis   In this chapter, we'll review using the FireSIGHT System to analyze intrusion event data. We'll explore some of the workflows available when analyzing events and show you examples of how to drill into relevant event data. We'll also cover how to use the Dashboards and Context Explorer. As always, before tackling the hands-on lab in this chapter, complete the review questions.

Chapter 7: Network-Based Malware Detection   A nickname derived from the term *malicious software*, malware comes in a variety of vile flavors, from coded weapons fashioned to damage, control, or disable a computer system to reconnaissance tools for stealing data or identity theft. FireSIGHT's Advanced Malware Protection (AMP) is designed to tackle one of the worst and arguably most prevalent threat vectors today—malware! As always, don't skip the review questions and hands-on lab at the end.

Chapter 8: System Settings   This chapter will cover how to apply settings on the systems to control user preferences, time zones, and other key factors plus configuring health checks to alert you to conditions within your devices. Remember the review questions and hands-on labs at the end.

Chapter 9: Account Management   In this chapter, we're going to cover a variety of administrative functions for user account management. We'll discuss creating and managing both internal and external users. The hands-on labs and review questions will help you master this chapter.

Chapter 10: Device Management   In this chapter we'll discuss and demonstrate registering the device with the Defense Center as well as touring each of the device's properties. You'll discover the different settings for the interfaces and switch and router configurations, plus, we'll survey the different VPN and NAT types available to managed devices as well.

Chapter 11: Correlation Policy   Correlation Policy is an often overlooked but useful feature of the FireSIGHT System. The features available in this area concentrate on detection of unusual activity rather than specific intrusion or malware events. By using correlation rules, white lists, and traffic profiles, we can detect network or host behaviors that may be an indication of malicious activity.

Chapter 12: Advanced IPS Policy Settings   This chapter is the perfect time to introduce you to some essential advanced IPS policy settings, and we'll also survey important application layer preprocessor settings, network and transport layer preprocessors, and specific threat detection preprocessors. We'll also talk about the significant advantages gained via detection enhancements and performance settings.

Chapter 13: Creating Snort Rules   In this chapter, we're going to focus exclusively on the fundamentals of Snort rules, detailing their structure, syntax, and options. We'll also explore how Snort performs rule optimization for better performance and show you how rule matching takes place internally.

Chapter 14: FireSIGHT version 5.4 Facts and Features   Last, but definitely not least, this key chapter covers all the great new features in FireSIGHT Version 5.4 that launched in February 2015. Don't be fooled when you hear people refer to this release as a "point" upgrade because that's a serious understatement. Version 5.4 is a major-league upgrade with substantial new capabilities. In addition to all the bright new features, the user interface has been updated, changing the location of some configuration settings. The settings remain largely unchanged from previous versions, but they've been moved in the user interface.

Appendix A: Answers to Chapter Review Questions   This appendix contains the answers to the book's review questions.

Be sure to check the announcements section of my forum to find out how to download bonus material I created specifically for this book.

Interactive Online Learning Environment and Test Bank

We've worked hard to provide some really great tools to help you with your certification process. The interactive online learning environment that accompanies the *SSFIPS Securing Cisco Networks with Sourcefire Intrusion Prevention System Study Guide, Exam 500-285*, provides a test bank with study tools to help you prepare for the certification exam—and increase your chances of passing it the first time! The test bank includes the following:

Sample Tests   All of the questions in this book are provided, including the assessment test, which you'll find at the end of this introduction, and the chapter tests that include the review questions at the end of each chapter. In addition, there are two *exclusive* practice exams with 50 questions each. Use these questions to test your knowledge of the study guide material. The online test bank runs on multiple devices.

Flashcards   The online text banks includes 100 flashcards specifically written to hit you hard, so don't get discouraged if you don't ace your way through them at first! They're there to ensure that you're really ready for the exam. And no worries—armed with the review questions, practice exams, and flashcards, you'll be more than prepared when exam day comes! Questions are provided in digital flashcard format (a question followed by a single correct answer). You can use the flashcards to reinforce your learning and provide last-minute test prep before the exam.

Other Study Tools   A glossary of key terms from this book and their definitions are available as a fully searchable PDF.

In addition to the online test bank, the authors have provided additional study material that'll help you get the most out of your exam preparation:

Todd Lammle Bonus Material and Labs   Be sure to check the www.lammle.com/firepower web page for directions on how to download all the latest bonus material created specifically to help you study for your Securing Cisco Networks with Sourcefire Intrusion Prevention System (SSFIPS) exam.

Online Videos   Check out the online videos available at www.lammle.com/firepower.

 Go to http://sybextestbanks.wiley.com to register and gain access to this interactive online learning environment and test bank with study tools.

How to Use This Book

If you want a solid foundation for the serious effort of preparing for the Securing Cisco Networks with Sourcefire Intrusion Prevention System (SSFIPS) exam, then look no further. We've spent hundreds of hours putting together this book with the sole intention of helping you to pass the exam as well as really learn how to correctly configure and manage Firepower!

This book is loaded with valuable information, and you will get the most out of your study time if you understand why the book is organized the way it is.

So to maximize your benefit from this book, I recommend the following study method:

1. Take the assessment test that's provided at the end of this introduction. (The answers are at the end of the test.) It's okay if you don't know any of the answers; that's why you bought this book! Carefully read over the explanations for any question you get wrong and note the chapters in which the material relevant to them is covered. This information should help you plan your study strategy.

2. Study each chapter carefully, making sure you fully understand the information and the test objectives listed at the beginning of each one. Pay extra-close attention to any chapter that includes material covered in questions you missed.

3. Complete all hands-on labs in each chapter, referring to the text of the chapter so that you understand the reason for each step you take. Try to get your hands on some real equipment, or rent ASA/FirePOWER pods at www.lammle.com/firepower, which you can use for the hands-on labs found only in this book. These labs will equip you with everything you need for your SSFIPS certification goals.

4. Answer all of the review questions related to each chapter. (The answers appear in Appendix A.) Note the questions that confuse you, and study the topics they cover again until the concepts are crystal clear. And again—do not just skim these questions! Make sure you fully comprehend the reason for each correct answer. Remember that these will not be the exact questions you will find on the exam, but they're written to help you understand the chapter material and ultimately pass the exam!

5. Try your hand at the practice questions that are exclusive to this book. The questions can be found at www.sybex.com/go/firepower. And be sure to check out www.lammle.com/firepower for the most up-to-date exam prep questions, bonus material, videos, Todd Lammle bootcamps, and more.

6. Test yourself using all the flashcards, which are also found on the download link. These are brand-new and updated flashcards to help you prepare for the SSFIPS exam and a wonderful study tool!

To learn every bit of the material covered in this book, you'll have to apply yourself regularly, and with discipline. Try to set aside the same time period every day to study, and select a comfortable and quiet place to do so. I'm confident that if you work hard, you'll be surprised at how quickly you learn this material!

If you follow these steps and really study—*doing hands-on labs every single day* in addition to using the review questions, the practice exams, and the electronic flashcards—it would actually be hard to fail the Cisco exam. But understand that studying for the Cisco exams is a lot like getting in shape—if you do not go to the gym every day, it's not going to happen!

Where Do You Take the Exams?

You may take the Securing Cisco Networks with Sourcefire Intrusion Prevention System (SSFIPS) exam, or any Cisco exam, at any of the Pearson VUE authorized testing centers. For information, check www.vue.com or call 877-404-EXAM (3926).

To register for a Cisco exam, follow these steps:

1. Determine the number of the exam you want to take. (The SSFIPS exam number is 500-285.)

2. Register with the nearest Pearson VUE testing center. At this point, you will be asked to pay in advance for the exam. At the time of this writing, the exam is $250 and must be taken within one year of payment. You can schedule exams up to six weeks in advance or as late as the day you want to take it—but if you fail a Cisco exam, you must wait five days before you will be allowed to retake it. If something comes up and you need to cancel or reschedule your exam appointment, contact Pearson VUE at least 24 hours in advance.

3. When you schedule the exam, you'll get instructions regarding all appointment and cancellation procedures, the ID requirements, and information about the testing-center location.

Tips for Taking Your Cisco Exams

The Cisco exams contain about 50 to 60 questions and must be completed in about 90 minutes or less. This information can change per exam. You must get a score of about 80 percent to pass this exam, but again, each exam can be different.

Many questions on the exam have answer choices that at first glance look identical—especially the syntax questions! So remember to read through the choices carefully because close just doesn't cut it. If you get commands in the wrong order or forget one measly character, you'll get the question wrong. So, to practice, do the hands-on exercises at the end of this book's chapters over and over again until they feel natural to you.

Also, never forget that the right answer is the Cisco answer. In many cases, more than one appropriate answer is presented, but the *correct* answer is the one that Cisco recommends. On the exam, you will always be told to pick one, two, or three options; never "choose all that apply." The Cisco exam may include the following test formats:

- Multiple-choice single answer
- Multiple-choice multiple answer

- Drag-and-drop
- Router simulations

However, be advised that the current SSFIPS exam is listed as all multiple choice questions for now, but understand that this can change at any time.

Here are some general tips for exam success:

- Arrive early at the exam center so you can relax and review your study materials.

- Read the questions *carefully*. Don't jump to conclusions. Make sure you're clear about *exactly* what each question asks. "Read twice, answer once" is what I always tell my students.

- When answering multiple-choice questions that you're not sure about, use the process of elimination to get rid of the obviously incorrect answers first. Doing this greatly improves your odds if you need to make an educated guess.

- You can no longer move forward and backward through the Cisco exams, so double-check your answer before clicking Next since you can't change your mind.

After you complete an exam, you'll get immediate, online notification of your pass or fail status, a printed examination score report that indicates your pass or fail status, and your exam results by section. (The test administrator will give you the printed score report.) Test scores are automatically forwarded to Cisco within five working days after you take the test, so you don't need to send your score to them. If you pass the exam, you'll receive confirmation from Cisco, typically within two to four weeks, sometimes a bit longer.

SSFIPS Exam Objectives

Candidates will demonstrate knowledge of in-depth event analysis, IPS tuning, and configuration in addition to the Snort rules language. Exam takers will show their skills in using and configuring Cisco NGIPS technology, including application control, firewalls, and routing and switching capabilities.

This study guide has been written to cover the SSFIPS exam objectives at a level appropriate to their exam weightings. The following table provides a breakdown of this book's exam coverage, showing you the weight of each section and the chapter where each objective or subobjective is covered:

Objective/Subobjective	Percentage of Exam	Chapters
1.0 Object Management	**6%**	
1.1 Understand the types of objects that may be created and configured in object management		2
1.2 Describe the implementation of security intelligence feeds		2, 4

Objective/Subobjective	Percentage of Exam	Chapters
2.0 Access Control Policy	10%	
2.1 Describe the purpose, features, and configuration of access control policy rules		4
2.2 Describe the purpose and configuration of an access control policy		4
3.0 Event Analysis	5%	
3.1 Understand the role that geolocation can play in analysis		6
3.2 Be familiar with the interfaces for analysis, including the Dashboard, Work Flows and Context Explorer		6
4.0 IPS Policy Basics	5%	
4.1 Understand and describe the operation of the IPS policy interface		3
4.2 Describe the use of the rule management user interface in the IPS policy editor		3
4.3 Be able to implement Cisco FireSIGHT recommendations		3
5.0 FireSIGHT Technologies	12%	
5.1 Understand the discovery component inside FireSIGHT, including the policy configuration and the data collected		5
5.2 Understand the type of data collected by connection events with FireSIGHT		5
5.3 Understand the user information that is discovered with FireSIGHT		5
6.0 Network-Based Malware Detection	10%	
6.1 Describe the interface components used for analyzing malware events		7
6.2 Understand the different techniques used to identify malware		7
6.3 Describe the features of malware detection as used by the Cisco NGIPS, including communication, actions, and protocols		7

Objective/Subobjective	Percentage of Exam	Chapters
7.0 Basic Administration	**12%**	
7.1 Describe the settings contained in the system polices		8
7.2 Understand the general user preferences and system settings of the Cisco NGIPS		8
7.3 Describe the settings available for the health monitoring features of the Cisco NGIPS		8
8.0 Account Management	**5%**	
8.1 Understand the permissions available to different account roles		9
8.2 Describe the features that can use external authentication		9
9.0 Creating Snort Rules	**5%**	
9.1 Be familiar with the options used to create Snort rules inside the Cisco NGIPS		13
10.0 Device Management	**10%**	
10.1 Describe the VPN types supported and the configuration of those VPNs		10
10.2 Define the different NAT types		10
10.3 Understand the properties of the managed devices and the settings that may be configured		10
10.4 Describe the settings for configuring the virtual interface and virtual router switch types		10
11.0 Correlation Policies	**10%**	
11.1 Describe the components of a correlation policy		11
11.2 Understand the process for creating a white list		11
11.3 Describe the purpose and creation of traffic profiles		11
11.4 Be familiar with the types of responses available when dealing with correlation policies		11

Objective/Subobjective	Percentage of Exam	Chapters
12.0 Advanced IPS Policy Configuration	**10%**	
12.1 Describe the features and settings of application layer preprocessors		12
12.2 Describe the features and settings of network and transport layer preprocessors		12
12.3 Describe the features and settings for specific threat detections in the advanced section of IPS polices		12
12.4 Understand the benefits of the detection enhancements and performance settings in the intrusion policy editor		12

 NOTE Exam objectives are subject to change at any time without prior notice and at Cisco's sole discretion. Please visit Cisco's certification website (www.cisco.com/web/learning/exams/list/500-285p.html) for the latest information on the SSFIPS exam (you'll be prompted to login to your CCO account).

Assessment Test

1. You want to install a Next Generation Firewall (NGFW) and you need to license the product correctly. Which of the following license(s) will you choose?

    A. Protect

    B. Control

    C. Malware

    D. URL Filtering

2. There is a default set configured for the variable set. Which of the following is true regarding this variable set?

    A. This set is provided by Cisco.

    B. Variables in this set determine the default value for any additional variable sets.

    C. Once a variable value is edited, future Cisco updates to that variable will not be applied.

    D. All of the above.

3. You need to export a policy and provide it to your security admin. They ask you what format you'll be sending the policy in. Which of the following is your answer?

    A. Ccsv

    B. Binary

    C. Text

    D. .xls

4. You want to block the URLs for Facebook in your company; however, you want to make sure that the users understand why they were blocked so they don't bother you. How should you configure the AC rule?

    A. Create a Block rule, specify the website, and enable logging.

    B. Create an Allow rule and specify an IPS policy that contains a Snort rule blocking the website.

    C. Create an Interactive Block rule for the site, and specify an HTTP response on the HTTP Responses tab.

    D. Create a Block rule for the site, and specify an HTTP response on the HTTP Responses tab.

5. You want to view summary information of your network traffic. How would you do this?

    A. Analysis ➤ Connections ➤ Events

    B. Overview ➤ Dashboard ➤ Connection Summary

    C. Analysis ➤ Connections ➤ Hosts ➤ Network Map

    D. Overview ➤ Dashboard ➤ URL Statistics

6. You have configured the Dashboard as your default page and have also configured widgets to help you analyze your network. Which of the following are characteristics of the Dashboard? (Choose three.)

   A. Customizable widgets

   B. Flexible searching and dynamic pivoting of data

   C. Multiple searches and various event views all on one page

   D. The ability for users to add personal dashboards

7. You need to define Spero analysis to your manager. Which of the following will you use to help you define Spero?

   A. It's used to analyze a SHA-256 to determine if a file is malicious.

   B. It's a form of analysis that involves executing the file in a sandbox environment.

   C. It's a manual analysis that cannot be performed automatically.

   D. It's a method of analyzing static file attributes such as headers and metadata.

8. How often do health checks on a managed device run?

   A. Every 10 minutes

   B. Every 5 minutes

   C. Every 30 minutes

   D. Every 60 minutes

9. You want to be able to have a user escalate their user permissions if you provide them with a password. How would you accomplish this?

   A. From the System ➤ Local ➤ System Policy and choose User Interface.

   B. By changing the value of the Pluggable Authentication Module (PAM) login attribute for the user.

   C. From the User Management screen, click the User Roles tab and then click Configure Permission Escalation.

   D. From the User Management screen, click the Login Authentication tab and then click Configure Permission Escalation.

10. If an application is taking more than an allotted amount of time to pass traffic through the inline device, what feature allows traffic to pass without inspection?

    A. Automatic Application Bypass

    B. Profiling

    C. Fail-Open

    D. Automatic Application Redirect

11. You've decided to create a new traffic profile and your boss asks what the default PTW and sample rate is going to be. What do you tell him?

    A. 1 week, 1 hour

    B. 1 week, 5 minutes

C. 24 hours, 5 minutes

D. 24 hours, 30 minutes

12. Inline Normalization performs what function, which helps prevent network threats?

A. Inline Normalization–enabled IPS blocking.

B. Inline Normalization sends traffic to the IP and TCP preprocessors.

C. Inline Normalization cannot stop threats.

D. Inline Normalization removes deviations in IP, TCP, and ICMP protocol standards.

13. Which keyword is used to reduce the number of logged alerts for noisy rules?

A. byte_count

B. detection_filter

C. metadata

D. file_data

14. What are the three SSL object types added in the 5.4 code?

A. Cipher Suite List

B. TTLS

C. Distinguished Name

D. PKI

E. WPA2

Answers to Assessment Test

1. B. The Control license enables application control functionality, allowing the device to become an NGFW. See Chapter 1, "Getting Started with FireSIGHT," for more information.

2. D. All of the options are true regarding the default set. See Chapter 2, "Object Management," for more information.

3. B. Policies are exported in a binary format. This can be imported into another FSM assuming it is on the same software version. See Chapter 3, "IPS Policy Management," for more information.

4. D. While this could be done with an Interactive Block rule (C), this would also allow the user to override the block if desired. See Chapter 4, "Access Control Policy," for more information.

5. B. To view the summary of your traffic, you can go to Overview ➤ Dashboards ➤ Connection Summary. Alternately, you can go to Overview ➤ Summary ➤ Connection Summary. See Chapter 5, "FireSIGHT Technologies," for more information.

6. A, C, D. Flexible searches with multiple search criteria is a feature of the Context Explorer, not the Dashboard. See Chapter 6, "Intrusion Event Analysis," for more information.

7. D. Spero analysis involves evaluating hundreds of file attributes including headers, DLLs called, and other metadata. See Chapter 7, "Network-Based Malware Detection," for more information.

8. B. Health policies are set to run every 5 minutes by default. This can be changed in the health policy. See Chapter 8, "System Settings," for more information.

9. C. To set up a user so the user can escalate its permissions, from the User Management screen, click the User Roles tab and then click Configure Permission Escalation. Then choose the user role that the user will have its permissions escalated to. See Chapter 9, "Account Management," for more information.

10. A. Automatic Application Bypass (AAB) terminates the IPS inspection process if traffic takes an excessive amount of time to make it through the device (bypass threshold). It will generate a troubleshooting file and a health alert and restart inspection within 10 minutes. See Chapter 10, "Device Management," for more information.

11. B. The default PTW is 1 week, and the sample rate is one sample every 5 minutes. See Chapter 11, "Correlation Policy," for more information.

12. D. The purpose of Inline Normalization is to remove deviations in IP, TCP, and ICMP protocol standards. When this feature is enabled, you can pick and choose what types of normalizations will be used for the specific protocols. See Chapter 12, "Advanced IPS Policy Settings," for more information.

13. B. The `detection_filter` keyword sets a rate that, when exceeded, can generate an event. Unless the source or destination host exceeds this `detection_filter` rate, then the event won't be generated. This is used to reduce the number of logged alerts for noisy rules. See Chapter 13, "Creating Snort Rules," for more information.

14. A, C, D. The three new objects in 5.4 code are as follows:

- Cipher Suite List: A listing of cipher suites used in SSL and TLS session negotiations; these can be used for matching criteria in an SSL policy.

- Distinguished Name: Identifies the distinguished name used in a public certificate.

- PKI: These objects contain the public certificates and private keys used to either decrypt or re-sign traffic.

See Chapter 14, "FireSIGHT Version 5.4 Facts and Features," for more information.

Chapter

1

Getting Started with FireSIGHT

Let's begin our journey into the world of FireSIGHT by building a solid foundation in defining key, industry-wide, and Cisco-specific terms that we'll be using throughout this book.

We'll also introduce a variety of FireSIGHT appliance models and talk about licensing and network design.

We'll move on to tour the web-based user interface and describe Cisco FireSIGHT policy-based management; then we'll wrap the chapter up by guiding you through the new appliance initial setup process.

Industry Terminology

Let's get started by covering some important industry-wide terms that mean the same thing to Cisco as they do to the rest of the world. You're probably familiar with some of these, but they're vital for a well-built knowledge base, so make sure you thoroughly understand them all!

Firewall   Traditional firewalls work at the network/transport layer by allowing or blocking traffic based on criteria such as an IP address and/or port. Much more than a router with an access list, a firewall offers us lots of more advanced features—for example, the capacity to ensure that only packets associated with a stateful connection are allowed to pass through.

Intrusion Prevention System or Intrusion Protection System (IPS)   An IPS is a device inserted between other network components in an inline configuration. This placement forces packets to pass through the IPS, enabling it to block any traffic deemed malicious. But what equips an IPS to make that kind of judgment call? Well, an IPS is capable of *deep packet inspection*, meaning it inspects the data portion of the packets, not just packet headers. Also, most IPS systems use *rules* or *signatures*—which look for specific conditions in packets—to identify known malicious behavior. When traffic matching the signature arrives, the IPS can generate an alert, drop the offending packet(s), or both.

Intrusion Detection System (IDS)   An IDS is similar to the IPS we just talked about, but instead of being deployed inline, it's connected passively via a *network tap* or a switch's span port. The traffic that the IDS examines is actually a copy of the packets, which traverse the network. Even though the detection capabilities of an IDS are identical to those of an IPS, an IDS can't actively block traffic it considers suspect—it can only alert us to it.

Next-Generation IPS (NGIPS)   An NGIPS device provides all the traditional IPS features but packs additional powers like the ability to allow/block traffic based on specific application or user information. This expanded level of control provides more flexibility in restraining specific applications, regardless of their IP address or port. An NGIPS also gives you control over exactly who can or cannot access applications like your favorite social media site.

Next-Generation Firewall (NGFW) This device offers all the usual features that a classic firewall does, but it adds the application/user control features of an NGIPS into the mix, arming you with a firewall and NGIPS in one package!

Practically speaking, the line between an NGIPS and an NGFW is pretty fine. The main difference is the particular network layer where the two devices run. NGIPS typically operates as a "bump in the wire," meaning packets that enter on one interface of an inline interface pair always exit the other interface. The device doesn't have IP addresses assigned to the detection interfaces and it doesn't build a *CAM table* of MAC addresses either. It simply inspects packets on their way through.

Alternatively, the NGFW performs the role of a traditional firewall and adds NGIPS features. Interfaces have IP addresses assigned and the device performs Layer 3 routing of traffic.

Cisco Terminology

At this writing, Cisco is in the midst of a branding transition. Following the acquisition of Sourcefire in late 2013, Cisco retained the Sourcefire name across much of its NGIPS/NGFW product line. It was basically business as usual, with the models and product names remaining unchanged as the integration between the two companies progressed. But beginning in late 2014, the names of the various components started changing, effectively removing the Sourcefire moniker. However, given that familiar terms tend to linger, it is likely that legacy names will continue to be used for some time. The more years someone has spent using the Sourcefire IPS legacy names, the greater the odds these experienced individuals will continue to do so—if only colloquially. This means you should definitely be fluent in both the legacy and new terms to work effectively with everyone in the brave new world of Cisco FireSIGHT.

So, let's take some time now to discuss these changes and equip you with a keen ability to clearly navigate the sea of terms you must be familiar with.

FirePOWER and FireSIGHT

In early 2012, Sourcefire introduced version 5 of the *Sourcefire System*. Along with this new version came several new brands, an important one being FirePOWER, which was used to represent the advanced network interface hardware in the latest detection devices. The *Netronome Flow Processor (NFP)* included far more advanced technology than a typical network interface card. And technically, this is still the case—the power behind the detection speed of the system is still FirePOWER. But today this term has changed a bit and is used in conjunction with the Cisco Adaptive Security Appliance (ASA) software. So when you see *FirePOWER*, it's typically used to describe FirePOWER services on ASA. Furthermore, the term can refer to software services or the FirePOWER blade installed on the ASA 5585-X, which can be a little confusing.

FireSIGHT is another term introduced with version 5. Historically, meaning pre-Cisco, the term *FireSIGHT* referred to the passive detection capabilities of the Sourcefire System. In version 4.x, these capabilities were called Realtime Network Awareness (RNA) and Realtime User Awareness (RUA). When version 5 hit the scene, these two names were rebranded and combined into FireSIGHT. Prior to the Cisco acquisition, FireSIGHT never referred to the entire system. It was all about network and user awareness. These days the term *FireSIGHT* has been expanded to encompass the entire NGIPS/NGFW system—the term *FireSIGHT System* now refers to the new Cisco NGIPS.

While Cisco has expanded the sub-brand FireSIGHT to mean the entire system, this change has not filtered down to the current SSFIPS exam. When you see the term *FireSIGHT* in an exam question, it refers to only the system's network and user awareness capabilities.

A Passive IPS?

Cisco is unlikely to ever refer to the FireSIGHT System as an IDS. The term *IPS* is used almost exclusively throughout the documentation. The FireSIGHT IPS can still be deployed in a passive manner when connected to a passive tap or switch span port, but it's called an IPS.

Out with the Old...

As Cisco's integration of Sourcefire progresses, many of the previous product names are being updated. This is why it's vital to know both the older and newer terms for the various components. Table 1.1 depicts some key terminology changes, including transitional terms.

TABLE 1.1   Old and new terminology

Old	New
Sourcefire	Cisco
Sourcefire Defense Center	FireSIGHT Management Center (FMC or FSMC)
Sensor	Device
Defense Center (DC)	FireSIGHT Management Center
Sourcefire 3D System	FireSIGHT System
Sourcefire Managed Device	Managed Device

The right way to refer to the various components in Table 1.1 lies in the details. For the most part, Sourcefire avoided inner capitalization of words in its brand names. The company name itself depicts this; it's not SourceFire, but rather Sourcefire. Something else you will notice is the capitalization on other terms such as FireSIGHT or FirePOWER; the all uppercase second term is the correct way to write these brands.

How to Look Like a Noob

Spell *Sourcefire* with a capital *F*.

Spell *FireSIGHT* as *FireSight* or *Firesight*.

Appliance Models

Before we dive into talking about the many appliance models available, let's clarify a couple of related definitions.

- *Appliance* is the broad term used for any of the physical or virtual machines that make up the FireSIGHT System. This includes the Defense Center as well as the detection appliances.

- A *device* is a detection appliance. These contain the actual detection interfaces and inspect network traffic. While the Defense Center is an appliance, it is not a device. Some types of policies, such as Access Control, Intrusion Prevention, and Network Discovery, are applied only to devices.

The FireSIGHT IPS is available in a wide range of hardware and virtual appliance models, with the main difference being their bandwidth capacity. IPS throughput ratings range from 50Mbps for the lowly FS7010 up to a whopping 60Gbps for an FS8390 *stack*! It's also important to note that the Defense Center, which provides central management, event storage, correlation, and aggregation, is available in several hardware models and even as a virtual appliance.

As is typical when you're faced with picking out networking equipment, appliance selection is narrowed down by the size of your budget and the amount of bandwidth you need. The good news is that the FireSIGHT System is a really great value in terms of cost per megabit protected. Still, quality rarely comes cheap, and all that protection isn't inexpensive. Fortunately, the wide range of appliance choices helps out tremendously by offering enough options to ensure that you pay only for what you really need.

An important fact you need to remember is that the bandwidth numbers published for each appliance are guidelines based on IPS protection. Adding features such as URL filtering or file malware analysis will reduce this number, but Cisco sales engineers are equipped with sizing guidelines to help you choose the right appliance model based on the features you want.

Hardware vs. Virtual Devices

Now, as we mentioned, FireSIGHT devices come in a number of hardware models as well as a 64-bit virtual appliance. Virtual appliances are supported on VMware ESXi and VMware vCloud Director environments. An important limitation you need to keep in mind is that the virtual appliance can only perform as an NGIPS and not as an NGFW. This limitation exists because capabilities such as VPN, stacking, clustering, and switched and routed interfaces require the specialized silicon found only in hardware devices. Also, unlike hardware devices, the virtual devices do not have a web-based user interface and are accessible only via Secure Shell (SSH).

Device Models

Table 1.2 gives an idea of the various models and their throughputs.

TABLE 1.2 Device models and throughputs

Model	IPS Throughput
Virtual	150–200Mbps per core
7010	50Mbps
7020	100Mbps
7030	250Mbps
7110	500Mbps
7115*	750Mbps
7120	1Gbps
7125*	1.25Gbps
8120	2Gbps
8130	4Gbps
8140	6Gbps
8250	10Gbps
8260**	20Gbps

Model	IPS Throughput
8270**	30Gbps
8290**	40Gbps
8350	15Gbps
8360**	30Gbps
8370**	45Gbps
8390**	60Gbps

*The 7115 and 7125 use SFP interfaces and do not support bypass; these are designed for switch/firewall deployments where bypass is not desired.

**These models are stacked devices.

Defense Center Models

Although the Defense Center is the heart of the FireSIGHT System, it doesn't perform detection itself. Think of it like this: if you consider the devices to be the worker bees in the system, the Defense Center is the queen. Almost all the device configuration is performed from here, and all of the alerting and event logging from the devices is sent to it as well. This means while performing normal day-to-day operations, you only need to log in to the Defense Center's web-based UI.

Also good to know is that if the Defense Center fails for some reason or communication to a device is severed, the devices will continue to perform according to the last instructions they were given. So if they're inline, they will continue to drop traffic based on the last policies applied. However, any alerts generated will be queued on the device until connectivity is restored. Only at that point will the devices forward all queued events, which will then be processed on the revived Defense Center.

You're probably thinking, "How long will the devices queue events if the Defense Center goes down?" Well, it depends. If connectivity is lost, the device will begin to write alerts to its local storage and continue to do so until the local disk is full. How long this takes is determined by the policies applied and the volume of traffic inspected. In the real world, this is typically several weeks or more. So, barring a zombie apocalypse, you should have plenty of time to restore or replace the Defense Center before you lose any events. In the event of said zombie apocalypse, fixing the Defense Center is the least of your worries.

Deciding which Defense Center model to purchase depends on how many devices you'll be managing and what kind of event volume you expect. Taking these factors into consideration, Table 1.3 shows how the different models compare.

TABLE 1.3   Comparing Defense Center models

Model	Max Devices	Hosts/ Users	IPS Event Storage
DC750	10	2,000	30 million
DC1500	35	50,000	50 million
DC3500	150	300,000	150 million
Virtual DC	25	50,000	10 million

Note that new models are also added from time to time, such as the new FS2000 and FS4000 appliances, which begin to leverage the Cisco Unified Computing System (UCS) platform.

FireSIGHT Licensing

The FireSIGHT system has a number of detection and analysis features, and each of the physical device models is capable of performing any or all of them. To enable a specific feature, you must install the appropriate license on the Defense Center; the license can then be assigned to the devices.

And just forget about thinking you can get away with opting for the low-end devices if you want to perform multiple functions such as NGIPS, anti-malware, URL filtering and virtual private network (VPN) functions. While this is theoretically possible, if you actually try this, you're going to end up with some serious performance issues!

Here are descriptions of the different license types available:

FireSIGHT   This license is included with the Defense Center and sets the upper limit on the number of IP hosts and users that can be collected. The license count is fixed depending on the DC model and cannot be upgraded.

Protect   This is your basic, entry-level license for a device that you have earmarked to become an NGIPS. It enables intrusion detection/prevention, file control, and Security Intelligence filtering.

Control   The Control license enables NGFW features like user and application control as well as switched and routed interfaces. This license is also required for clustering or stacking supported devices.

Note that under the new Cisco sales model, the Protect and Control licenses are typically included with any device sale.

URL Filtering   URL Filtering enables allowing/blocking websites based on their URL, category, or reputation. Information such as category and business relevance is updated on the Defense Center via a cloud connection.

Advanced Malware Protection   Advanced Malware Protection (AMP) provides cloud-based malware lookup and sandbox analysis, including file trajectory and tracking across the network.

VPN   The VPN license enables site-to-site VPN capabilities between devices, and it can be used to create a secure tunnel to a remote office location without having to install separate VPN hardware.

Subscription vs. Perpetual Licenses

Each license type is available in a subscription version and a perpetual version. Subscription licenses are valid for a given period of time, and you can buy single or multiple-year licenses. The valid license period is coded into the license key. Once installed, the license key will enable the appropriate feature between the start and expiration dates. Currently, the Malware and URL Filtering licenses fall into this category.

A perpetual license has no begin or end date, and predictably, once installed, this license will enable the appropriate feature indefinitely.

License Dependencies

While licensing is somewhat of an à la carte affair, the license types are not completely independent. Some require installation of a previous license before they can be utilized on a device. Table 1.4 shows the prerequisites for each type.

TABLE 1.4   Prerequisites by license type

License Type	Requires
Protect	N/A
Control	Protect
URL Filtering	Protect
Malware	Protect
VPN	Protect, Control

Network Design

Let's take a high-level look at just how you can deploy FireSIGHT within your network. Here we'll talk about and illustrate some simplified network designs to clearly demonstrate ways you can utilize these devices.

Inline IPS

The first design we're going to cover is probably the most common. The device is installed near the perimeter of the network using an inline interface set. This means packets pass in one interface, are processed by the various policies, and then exit through a second interface. In this type of design, the device acts as the "bump in the wire" we mentioned earlier, which means the other network devices aren't actually aware of its presence. And remember, the detection interfaces have no IP addresses; the device does not build a Content Addressable Memory (CAM) table to map host MAC addresses to ports. You would expect this if the device operates at Layer 2 like a switch. However, the bump in the wire is more like a Layer 1 (physical) connection between the two inline interfaces. Inline IPS devices are often deployed just inside the Internet firewall or at other strategic choke points in the network. Figure 1.1 illustrates the placement of such a device.

FIGURE 1.1 Inline IPS

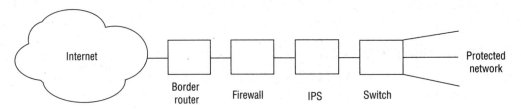

Inside or Outside the Firewall?

By definition, an IPS is not a firewall—it doesn't perform stateful inspection and typically doesn't allow/block traffic based on the port or IP address. It basically exists to inspect traffic and look for evil, so we still need an actual firewall. This is because firewalls handle the critical functions of filtering the network ports and protocols that are allowed into or out of your network. All you have to do to see just how vital firewalls are is simply execute a packet capture outside your firewall. Doing that will reveal some pretty scary stuff! Capture traffic immediately inside the firewall and you should see a much more sanitized stream.

Because of this, the best location for a perimeter IPS is *inside* the firewall. Placing your IPS outside the firewall will just result in a legion of intrusion events. Even so, most of these events won't be actionable. Many of the external attacks you see will be blocked by the firewall. This is why it's much more efficient to let your strategically placed firewall do its job and then let the IPS inspect the leftovers of what's been allowed through.

Another reason for this placement is because firewall inspection is less complex than IPS deep packet inspection, which translates to cost. Your cost per megabit protected should be less for the firewall than for the IPS. So be wise and place this expensive detection on the inside where it really belongs. You'll be rewarded with less traffic to deal with!

Finally, consider Network Address Translation (NAT) or web proxies. The IPS inspects traffic initiated from inside as well as outside your network. Many of the outbound rules are designed to detect the results of a malware infection, but the problem is correlating the event to a specific host. If your IPS is outside of your NAT firewall or web proxy, you'll only have a single source IP for all events triggered by outbound traffic. If you've got a web proxy, you might be able to cross-reference the IPS event time with the web proxy log to tie it back to a specific internal IP, but that's often a cumbersome process. And if you're dealing with NAT translation, it's likely that you just won't have a way to tie the event back to an original internal IP address at all. So here we are again, left with non-actionable intrusion events.

Everything we just talked about still won't be enough to stop some people from placing their IPS outside the firewall. Our goal here is to simply identify the trade-offs in doing so. Just know the pros and cons and that an IPS placed outside the firewall will probably need to be augmented with additional detection inside.

Passive IPS

You already know that the term *passive IPS* is really a misnomer. In reality, it's either passive, as in IDS, or it's inline, as in IPS.

As we've mentioned, in passive mode, the IPS receives a copy of the packets from a switch span port or network tap. Packets that enter the IPS are then inspected, and if they are deemed malicious, an alert is generated. An advantage to this design is that it won't impact the performance of your network, but the disadvantage is that it can only notify of attacks—it can't stop them. Figure 1.2 depicts typical device placement for passive detection.

FIGURE 1.2   Passive IPS

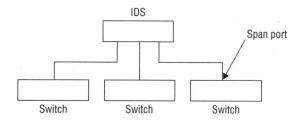

Router, Switch, and Firewall

A Cisco FireSIGHT device can be deployed as a router, a switch, or a firewall. From an intrusion detection perspective, the effect is similar to an inline IPS. Packets pass through a virtual switch or router and are inspected before being allowed to exit. In the real world, deploying the FireSIGHT System as a router/switch/firewall is uncommon because the purpose-driven switches and routers out there have more features and they're faster and cheaper than using FireSIGHT. FireSIGHT is a specifically designed security device that's just not that great at performing legacy, networking functions. Even so, the SSFIPS exam will present you with some questions about this configuration, so we'll cover it later in the book. All you need to know for now is that network locations where you would deploy a FireSIGHT device in routing or switching mode are identical to where you would deploy traditional switches, routers, or firewalls.

Policies

You will hear a lot about policies regarding the FireSIGHT system—there's a policy for everything! To help you keep your ears from bleeding, just think of policies as "settings saved in the Defense Center database." These settings control all aspects of system operation and detection on the managed devices. And know that with each new feature added to the system, there's at least one policy to manage that feature associated with it. Here's a list of all the policies available in version 5.3, with a nice little description of each.

Access Control Policy   The mother of all policies, the access control (AC) policy is the central traffic cop for packets entering the device, and it works much like a firewall rule set. Traffic is evaluated by the AC rules from top to bottom. When the traffic matches a particular rule, the selected action (block, trust, allow, etc.) is taken and processing stops. All detection features such as IPS, security intelligence, and malware detection are implemented through AC rules.

IPS Policy   This policy controls the configuration for IPS detection. If you have ever used or investigated the open source Snort IPS, you will find that most of the settings in the IPS policy correlate directly to an entry in the snort.conf. In this policy, you configure the specific Snort rules you want enabled—whether they should block or just alert—as well as myriad advanced options for preprocessors and other Snort options.

Network Discovery Policy   Think of this one as a pretty simple set-and-forget policy controlling the scope of host and user discovery for all devices.

File Policy   This policy controls the application protocol, direction of transfer, file types, and actions for file and malware detection. With it, you specify that a given type of file transfer traffic will be logged, inspected for malware, or even blocked. For instance, say you want to prevent web servers in your DMZ from uploading Microsoft executable files via HTTP. You can do this and more via the file policy.

NAT Policy   Predictably, this policy configures Network Address Translation (NAT). It supports static, dynamic IP or dynamic IP and port rules.

Correlation Policy   A policy used in conjunction with correlation rules to alert based on various event criteria. Let's say you want to receive an email when an IPS event is detected on one of your critical servers. You would first create a correlation rule to identify the IPS alert based on criteria such as the destination IP address. You then add the rule to a correlation policy, which defines the action to take when the rule triggers. In this case, the action would be to send an email to you. Don't worry if this is not clear yet; we address it in much greater detail later in this book.

System Policy   This controls a variety of device settings like local firewall, time synchronization, and so on. The system policy is applied to all appliances, meaning to the Defense Center and all devices. Much of the time, a single system policy is used for all the appliances in an organization.

Health Policy   This policy sets warning and critical thresholds for various health parameters such as disk space and CPU usage. You can also enable or disable various health checks as your heart desires.

You will find that editing and applying policies is the meat and potatoes of FireSIGHT System management!

The User Interface

Your primary method to manage the FireSIGHT System is through the web-based user interface on the Defense Center. Something we hear from the mouths of those with extensive experience with other Cisco gear is, "How do I *[insert task here]* using the command line?" Know that with FireSIGHT, there is very little command line management required. Command line access is generally reserved for troubleshooting. Most management tasks can be accomplished only within the web UI.

It's also important to remember that the Defense Center and devices do not listen on port 80. For many secure websites, you can make an initial connection on port 80 and the site will then redirect your browser to connect on port 443. This is not the case with the FireSIGHT web UI, which means when you initially connect, you must type `https://<your appliance IP or hostname>` in your web browser's URL bar.

Upon your initial connection you'll be greeted with a login splash page as shown in Figure 1.3.

FIGURE 1.3   Web UI login screen

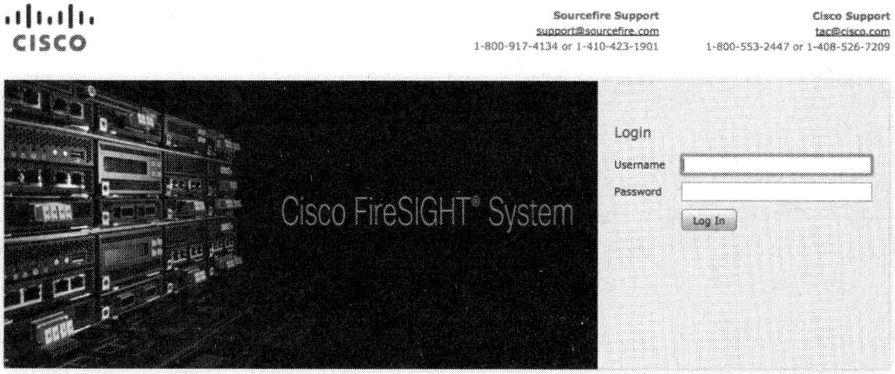

The menu system is pretty straightforward, with a top main menu bar and submenus below. Hovering over the top menu will bring up any submenu items. Clicking a submenu item takes you to the appropriate page. Top menu items are separated into left and right groupings. The left-side menu, shown in Figure 1.4, contains mostly items dealing with event analysis and detection configuration.

- Overview – Dashboards and reporting
- Analysis – View/analyze all types of events
- Policies – Configure detection behavior
- Devices – Detection device management
- Objects – Create and manage objects used in policies
- FireAMP – Manage the Defense Center malware detection cloud connection

FIGURE 1.4   Analysis and configuration items

 To quickly navigate to the left-most submenu item, you just click the corresponding main menu heading. For example, to get to the Device Management page, simply click Devices in the main menu.

The right side of the main menu (Figure 1.5) contains items focused on the care and feeding of FireSIGHT. This is where you do things like install licenses, download updates, view health status, schedule jobs, and set user preferences.

- Health – Configure and view system health status
- System – Updates, licensing, scheduling, etc.
- Help – Get help
- <username> – Log out, set user preferences

FIGURE 1.5   Operational Items

Initial Appliance Setup

Initial appliance setup includes setting the management IP address and initial connection to the web user interface.

Setting the Management IP

When a new FireSIGHT appliance arrives on the scene, one of the first steps after racking and power is to assign an IP address to the management interface. You can do this several ways:

LCD Panel   Each appliance includes an LCD front panel and four buttons, which are used to configure the management IP. Note that using the front panel requires physical access but there's no authentication. If you want, you can disable the IP management feature after the appliance's initial setup. Just follow the onscreen instructions to configure the basic IP settings.

Keyboard/KVM   Another method involves logging into the console. First, connect a keyboard and monitor; then, log in using the default credentials of admin/Sourcefire. Your next step is to run the network configuration script as root using the command sudo configure-network. This script uses an interview technique to prompt for the necessary IP configuration information.

SSH   This final method comes in handy if you want to run the network configuration script but you don't have a keyboard/monitor. Each appliance ships from the factory with a default IP address preassigned to the management interface—this IP address is 192.168.45.45. Sans keyboard/monitor, you can connect a notebook computer with an SSH client right into the management interface network port. After that, configure your notebook with an IP address in the same network and SSH to the appliance. From here, the procedure is the same as it is via the keyboard/KVM method above.

Remember, the default login credentials for all appliances are
Username: admin
Password: Sourcefire

Initial Login

After the management IP address is configured, your next step is to connect to the appliance web UI.

When you first log in, you'll see a one-time configuration web page displayed. The purpose is to gather some initial information and present the end-user license agreement prior to moving on to the standard web UI.

The Defense Center configuration page contains the following sections.

Change Password   This is a required field. You must enter a password, changing the appliance default.

Network Settings   This section contains the IP information entered via the LCD or configure-network script, but it also allows you to add more items like hostnames and DNS servers. (See Figure 1.6.)

FIGURE 1.6 Network configuration

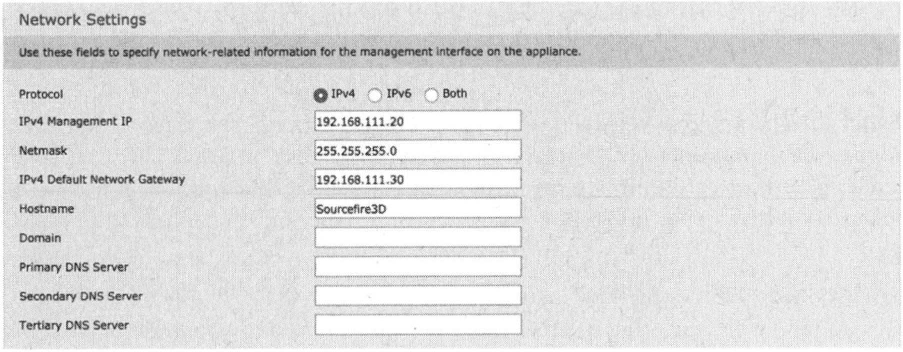

Network Settings

Use these fields to specify network-related information for the management interface on the appliance.

Protocol	◉ IPv4 ○ IPv6 ○ Both
IPv4 Management IP	192.168.111.20
Netmask	255.255.255.0
IPv4 Default Network Gateway	192.168.111.30
Hostname	Sourcefire3D
Domain	
Primary DNS Server	
Secondary DNS Server	
Tertiary DNS Server	

Time Settings This allows you to configure time synchronization from an external Network Time Protocol (NTP) source or manually. As shown in Figure 1.7, if you have multiple NTP servers, they are entered into the data field in a comma-separated format.

FIGURE 1.7 Time and update settings

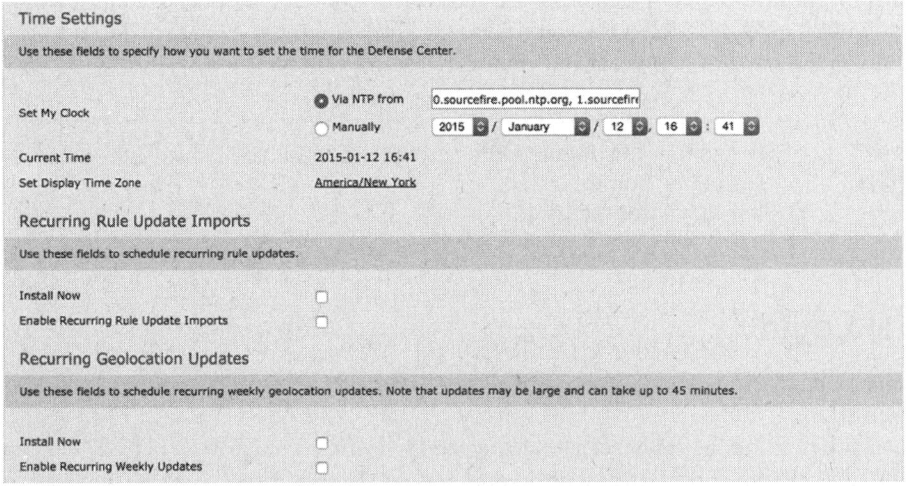

Time Settings

Use these fields to specify how you want to set the time for the Defense Center.

Set My Clock	◉ Via NTP from [0.sourcefire.pool.ntp.org, 1.sourcefir]
	○ Manually [2015] / [January] / [12] [16] : [41]
Current Time	2015-01-12 16:41
Set Display Time Zone	America/New York

Recurring Rule Update Imports

Use these fields to schedule recurring rule updates.

Install Now	☐
Enable Recurring Rule Update Imports	☐

Recurring Geolocation Updates

Use these fields to schedule recurring weekly geolocation updates. Note that updates may be large and can take up to 45 minutes.

Install Now	☐
Enable Recurring Weekly Updates	☐

Recurring Rule Update Imports Permits you to configure updating of IPS rules from Cisco on a recurring basis.

Recurring Geolocation Updates Allows you to configure updating of the IP to geographic location information from Cisco on a recurring basis.

Automated Backups Use this to configure backups of the local policy and configuration database.

License Settings   Allows you to add feature license keys.

Device Registration   Use this to register managed devices on the Defense Center.

End User License Agreement   Here's where you read and accept the Cisco software license agreement. This is a required setting.

While it is possible to configure all of these on the initial screen, most of us configure these settings later via System Policy or Local Configuration settings. The only two you have to worry about are changing the password and accepting the EULA.

Summary

Congratulations are in order! You now have a solid foundation and understand many of the terms that we'll use throughout this book. We covered some industry-wide and Cisco-specific terminology and introduced you to the various FireSIGHT appliance models. We also talked about licensing and network design. We explored the web-based user interface, described Cisco FireSIGHT policy-based management, and explained the new appliance initial setup process—you're ready to delve deeper now and build upon your knowledge!

Hands-on Lab

1.   Open your web browser and connect to your Defense Center.

2.   Log in to the Defense Center.

3.   Check your licenses on your system by going to the top-right menu bar and selecting System ➤ Licenses.

4.   Verify that the licenses are valid and that you have all licenses enabled on your Defense Center: URL Filtering, Protection, Control, and Malware.

5.   Click Devices on the main menu.

6.   Click the edit icon (the pencil icon) to make changes to a device.

7. Click the Device tab and verify that Protection, Control, Malware, and URL filtering are all set to Yes.

8. Verify that the license(s) that are enabled.

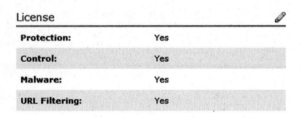

License	
Protection:	Yes
Control:	Yes
Malware:	Yes
URL Filtering:	Yes

Review Questions

You can find the answers in Appendix A.

1. The 32/64-bit device virtual appliance supports which of the following features?
   A. Switched interfaces
   B. Passive interfaces
   C. Routed interfaces
   D. All of the above

2. The default login for all appliances is username: **admin** and password: _____.
   A. **Sourcefire**
   B. **Cisco**
   C. **FireSIGHT**
   D. **password**

3. Which of the following is a valid method for configuring the initial management IP address of an appliance?
   A. Keyboard/KVM
   B. SSH
   C. LCD panel
   D. All of the above

4. Which of the following licenses is required for a device to operate as a next generation firewall (NGFW)?
   A. Firewall
   B. Control
   C. Malware
   D. URL Filtering

5. Which of the following licenses must be enabled on a device before a Malware license can be enabled?
   A. Protect
   B. Control
   C. VPN
   D. URL Filtering

6. Which license(s) must be enabled on a device before a VPN license can be enabled?
   A. Protect
   B. Control
   C. Protect and Control
   D. None of the above

Chapter

2

Object Management

THE SSFIPS EXAM TOPICS COVERED IN THIS CHAPTER INCLUDE THE FOLLOWING:

✓ **1.0   Object Management**

- ▪ 1.1 Understand the types of objects that may be created and configured in object management
- ▪ 1.1 Describe the implementation of security intelligence feeds

This chapter's focus will be on the object types that are used in the FireSIGHT System:

- Network
- Security Intelligence
- Port
- VLAN tag
- URL
- Application filters
- Variable sets
- File lists
- Security zones
- Geolocation

We're going to reveal the processes involved in creating different kinds of objects plus examine key background factors relevant to their usage in other policies. By the end of this chapter, you'll know how to create and edit these objects, and you'll get a solid briefing on how they're used within the FireSIGHT System.

What Are Objects?

Objects are reusable configurations that associate a name with a value like an IP address or port number. They handily allow you to reference their user-friendly names so you don't have to remember pesky details like which port a particular service uses. Objects also make it a whole lot easier to modify a value that has already been used in multiple rules or policies. All you have to do is modify the object and its value will automatically be changed wherever it's referenced throughout the system.

Objects are most often put to use in the access control rules. However, sometimes you'll see them employed to populate certain event search fields too. For example, if we're searching for ports in IPS events, we can just type in a port number or choose from a list of port objects.

Getting Started

The Object Management page is conveniently located in the Defense Center's primary menu. Because it only has one sub-menu item, just click on the Objects menu to navigate to Object Management, as demonstrated in Figure 2.1.

FIGURE 2.1   The Objects menu

Here's a list of the Object types:

Network   Network objects are simply IP addresses or CIDR blocks, but a single object can actually contain more than one address or block. It's pretty common to find network objects that include an organization's internal address space, such as 10.0.0.0/8 or 172.16.0.0/12.

Security Intelligence   The easiest way to remember this type of object is to think, "IP lists." *Security Intelligence* lists are really just lists of IP addresses or CIDR blocks used in the access control policy to whitelist or blacklist traffic based on the source or destination address.

Port   Network port numbers or ranges.

VLAN Tag   VLAN numbers or ranges.

URL   A URL object is an actual URL designed to match a specific URL within an access control rule. It's important to remember that this is really a substring match, meaning this type of object will match any URL containing the characters in it. This means if you've created a URL object that contains the string ign.com with the idea of matching that specific URL, know that it will also match verisign.com. Keep this behavior in mind so you don't wind up blocking or allowing the wrong URLs!

Application Filters   These objects are configured to match a specific application protocol like HTTP or POP3. And in this particular context, the term *application* includes popular sites like Facebook and ESPN, which are identified based on filters that ship with the FireSIGHT System. At this writing, FireSIGHT can identify over 2,200 applications—a number that grows with each system update—categorized by risk and business relevance from very low to very high. These are divided up further by type (application protocols, client applications, and web applications) and further still by categories (such as business, collaboration, gaming, etc.). You can use these filters to allow or block specific applications using access control rules.

Variable Set   These objects are used to configure Snort variables. We will cover these in much greater detail later on in the book. For right now, we will concentrate on how to manage the different object types.

File List   This object is a lot like the Security Intelligence object, only instead of IP addresses, it contains SHA-256 hash values which are like the fingerprint of a specific file. File list objects are used in conjunction with file policy to identify files that you want to always be considered clean or malicious. There are two file list objects available: the Clean List and the Custom Detection List. Files matching SHA values on the Clean List will be considered clean, and those with SHA values on the Custom Detection List will be considered malicious. The main objective is to override the disposition the cloud returns for a particular SHA-256 value.

Security Zones   *Security zone* is another term that has special meaning in FireSIGHT, and when you see it, think, "physical interface port." This will help a lot because the idea is to associate each physical interface with a named security zone, with the default zones being internal and external. In the real world, we usually create zone names that are more specific so that they can help identify where packets are coming from or where they're going. You can create security zones and assign them to interfaces in the Objects menu or in device configuration.

Geolocation   *Geolocation* objects contain countries or continents. For instance, we could create an object named Interesting Countries and add several countries to it. Once again, this can be employed in access control policy to customize inspection and allow or block traffic based on country or geography.

Figure 2.2 shows how these objects appear on the user interface.

FIGURE 2.2   Object types

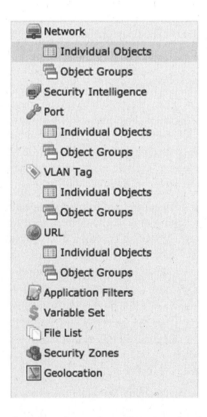

So let's move on now and get into how to configure each of these object types!

Network Objects

Network objects represent IP addresses and can be specified as individual entries or groups of entries. We'll look at both of those object types here.

Individual Network Objects

Individual objects can be entered as single IP addresses or in blocks using CIDR notation. We're going to create an individual network object by clicking Individual Objects and then clicking the Add Network button. This will display the Network Object dialog box.

Type a name in the Name field and then enter an IP or CIDR block into the Network field. Click the Add button when you're done. If you want to add multiple entries, simply enter additional addresses and click the Add button again. Keep in mind that each entry can only be a single address or CIDR block, meaning you can't just enter a comma-separated by a list of addresses.

Network Object Groups

Predictably, the grouping function allows you to combine individual objects into groups. Our example in Figure 2.3 demonstrates this nicely by showing the Corporate Network and DMZ objects grouped into a single Enterprise object group.

As with object creation, grouping objects is a pretty straightforward task. Just give your new group a name, select the existing individual objects, and click the Add button. Figure 2.3 shows the results.

FIGURE 2.3   Network object groups

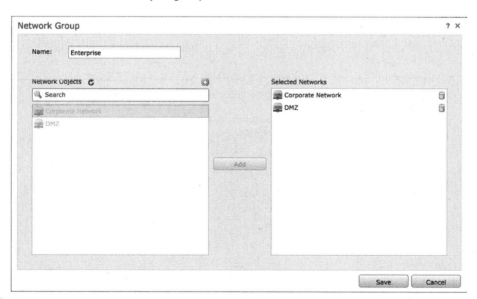

Security Intelligence

Moving down the menu from network objects we come to Security Intelligence. As mentioned previously, when you see the term *Security Intelligence*, think IP lists. When you click the Security Intelligence link, you will see that there are several objects already set up here: the global blacklist, global whitelist, and the Sourcefire Intelligence Feed.

Blacklist and Whitelist

The blacklist and whitelist are just that—lists that are intended to either block or allow traffic based on the IP address. If you click the pencil icon to the right of either of the lists, your options are fairly limited. In fact, by default, there is nothing in the list at all. These two lists are populated through the analysis view. This can be done in any one of the event views, such as connection events, IPS events, or any event view that contains an IP address.

Figure 2.4 shows the menu that appears when you right-click an IP address in an event list.

FIGURE 2.4   The IP context menu

Choosing Blacklist Now or Whitelist Now will add the IP to your target list after prompting you for confirmation. Once the IP address is added to either the blacklist or the whitelist, the new list will be pushed out to all of your devices immediately—the menu isn't kidding when it says Now! Keep in mind that once an IP is added to either the blacklist or whitelist, it stays there until you remove it. To do that, just go back to Objects ➢ Object Management ➢ Security Intelligence and click the pencil icon. Use the little trash can icon on the right to remove an entry from your list. Never forget that you can only delete entries in the blacklist or the whitelist through the object management interface!

Another key factor to bear in mind is how the global blacklist and whitelist get updated on devices. As we just said, when you use the Blacklist Now or Whitelist Now option, the list gets pushed out immediately. But if you edit either one of these objects in the object management interface and remove an IP from the list, your change takes effect only when an access control policy is applied. No worries—you'll get a message about this whenever something gets removed from one of these lists (Figure 2.5).

FIGURE 2.5   Warning dialog

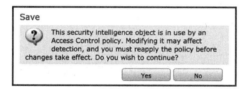

We'll dive deeper into exactly how the global blacklist and whitelist are used in Chapter 4, "Access Control Policy."

Sourcefire Intelligence Feed

Now let's talk about the Sourcefire *Intelligence Feed*. Clicking the pencil on the right side of this object reveals options for the update frequency, which defaults to 2 hours, but it can be set as high as 1 week or disabled entirely. This time period set regulates the interval in which the Defense Center will check for updates to the Security Intelligence feed from Sourcefire. The Security Intelligence feed consists of several IP address lists, and the addresses populating them are known bad actors, like spammers, botnet servers and hosts known to serve malware, and so on. These lists are constantly updated as new malware campaigns are identified or as hosts are taken offline for nefarious activities. You can also manually refresh the list with the Update Feeds button located in the upper-right portion of the screen (Figure 2.6).

And again, we'll tell you all about exactly how these lists can be utilized as well as get into more detail about the things each list contains when we get to Chapter 4!

FIGURE 2.6   Update Feeds button

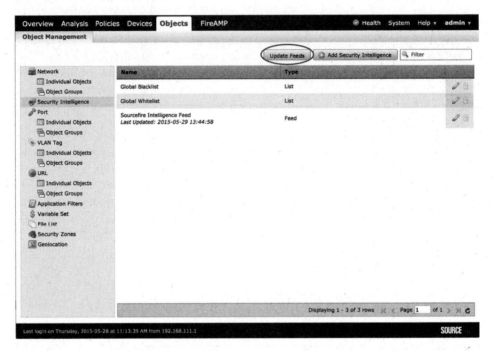

Custom Security Intelligence Objects

It's also good to know that you can add your own Security Intelligence objects. Clicking the Add Security Intelligence button near the upper-right corner opens a Security Intelligence dialog where you give your new object a name and then select its type.

There are two types of custom Security Intelligence objects you can add, with the first kind being a feed. Basically, an intelligence feed works just like the Sourcefire feed except that the source IP list comes from the custom URL that you've entered instead. Common choices include blacklist feeds on the Internet or on your local network. The second type is a static list of IP addresses, both are explained below.

Feed   The feed URL directs to a text file on a web server, which contains IP addresses. The text file itself has one IP address per line, with a maximum file size of 500 megabytes. There's an MD5 URL field below the Feed URL field (see Figure 2.7), which is actually another URL that points to the file's MD5 checksum. This provides extra protection by preventing someone from tampering with the feed URL file. The last item in this dialog allows you to select the update frequency, which is a lot like the Sourcefire feed frequency because it can be set anywhere from 2 hours to 1 week or disabled completely.

FIGURE 2.7   Custom Security Intelligence feed dialog

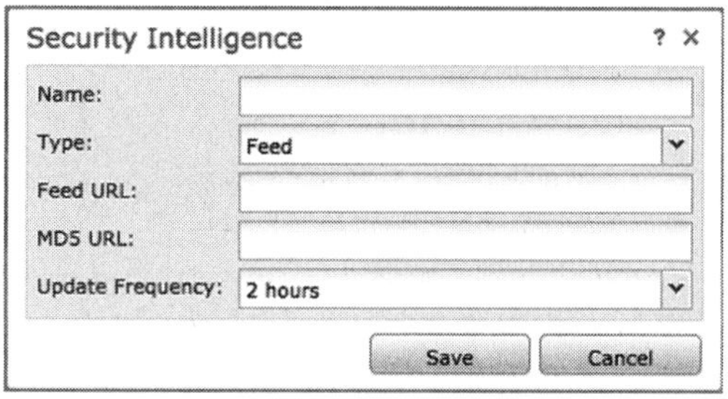

Static IP List   The second type of custom Security Intelligence object you can add is a list of static IP addresses (Figure 2.8), which is uploaded through the object management interface. The requirements for this list are the same as the custom feed—it must be a text file with one IP or CIDR block per line and a maximum file size of 500 megabytes.

FIGURE 2.8   Custom Security Intelligence list dialog

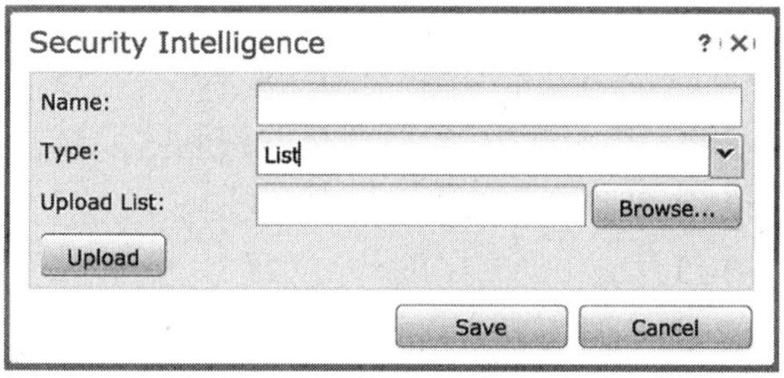

Of the two custom object types, the feed is much more flexible way to go about updating IP lists. The fact that the Defense Center will automatically query the URL, download the updated list, and push it out to all the devices is a much lower-maintenance solution. The alternative method of maintaining a static Security Intelligence list object requires reapplication of the access control policy anytime the object is updated. Also note that when a Security Intelligence list object is uploaded, it replaces the current list. This means you've got to maintain these lists yourself because they'll be overwritten when the updated objects are saved!

Port Objects

The next object type after Security Intelligence is port objects. Port objects are simply port numbers with friendly names. These can be TCP or UDP ports or even a range of ports. Clicking the Individual Objects link reveals a number of preconfigured port objects. All of the well-known ports are listed here. By using the Add button in the upper right, you can add your own custom port objects (Figure 2.9).

FIGURE 2.9 Port Objects dialog

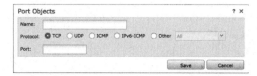

Using the Port Objects dialog, give your object a name and then select the protocol type from the radio buttons: TCP, UDP, ICMP, IPv6-ICMP, and Other. Choosing Other will bring up a list of some of the more obscure IP protocol IDs. In the Port field, you can enter a single port or a range of them, but you can't go with a comma-separated list of ports here. If you try that, you'll quickly see a bold red outline appear on the port field screaming that there's a formatting error!

Individual port objects can be placed into object groups just like network objects can. As an example, we created a new object group called Web Ports and placed both HTTP and HTTPS into this group, as shown in Figure 2.10.

FIGURE 2.10 Port object groups

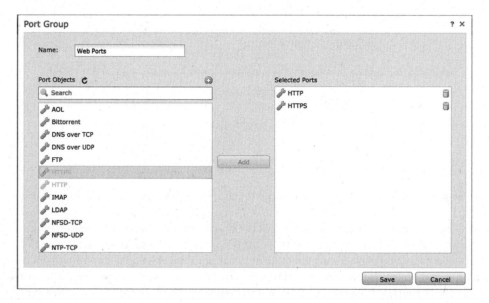

VLAN Tag

Below port objects in the menu we have VLAN tag objects, which are simply a way to give a friendly name to a VLAN ID number. Here you can create a VLAN Tag object, enter the name and the VLAN tag number(s) to assign to it. Again, VLAN tag entries can be a single number or a hyphenated range of numbers, but you can't enter a comma-separated list of VLANs.

VLAN tag groups can be used to combine objects just as with network and port object groups. In Figure 2.11, we've created a VLAN tag group named Corp VLANs and placed the various corporate VLAN objects into it.

FIGURE 2.11   VLAN tag group

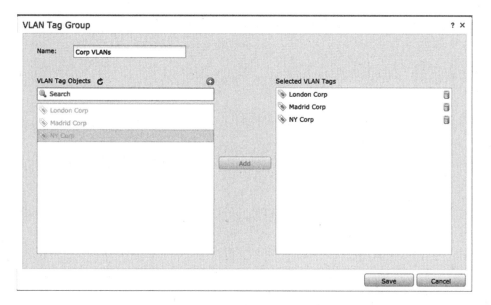

URL Objects and Site Matching

URL objects are used to identify HTTP requests by searching for the text string in the request—a simple substring match with none of the advanced features you get with regular expression or "regex" pattern matching. And as with other objects, the idea is to be able to create a friendly name for use in an access control rule.

If you want to create an individual object, follow these steps:

1. Navigate to the Objects screen by clicking Objects in the top-level menu.

2. Choose Individual Objects under the URL heading on the left.

3. Click the Add URL button in the upper right to display the URL Objects dialog.

4. Give your object a name and then enter some descriptive text into the URL field. You don't need the http:// portion of the URL because this object will match any URL that *contains* the text you've entered.

It's vital to understand how site matching happens because if you don't, you'll probably find your object matching tons more URLs than you planned or, worse, not matching enough. Let's say you want to match HTTP requests to an evil website, so you create an object: www.evilsite.com. Thing is, this site also responds to just evilsite.com, meaning your URL object is too specific; it won't match some of the requests you need it to match, so it just isn't going to work. In short, this is what is referred to as a *substring match*. There are no wildcards; the system will simply match any URL that *contains* all the characters entered.

You can also create groups of URL objects just as you would with several of the other object types. Just click the Object Groups link under URL (Figure 2.12, top), choose Add URL Group, give your new group a name, and then select one or more individual objects from the left and click the Add button to include them as shown here (Figure 2.12, bottom).

FIGURE 2.12   Creating URL groups

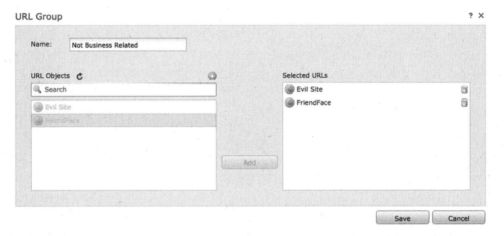

Application Filters

Application filters are tools for matching application traffic, this includes protocols, client and web applications.. The ability to identify applications based on their network traffic is really what makes the FireSIGHT System a "Next-Generation" IPS or firewall. You can create an application filter that identifies high risk and low business relevance traffic and use it to block designated applications from any or all users on your network!

Access to application filters is gained via the same Objects menu where the other object types we just covered are found. To create an application filter, click the Application Filters link on the left side of the page; doing so will get you to a menu of several preconfigured filters. You can use these in your access control rules just as they are, modify them, or even delete them if you want. If you want to create a custom application filter, just click the Add Application Filter button in the upper right to bring up the Application Filter dialog, shown in Figure 2.13.

FIGURE 2.13   Application Filter dialog

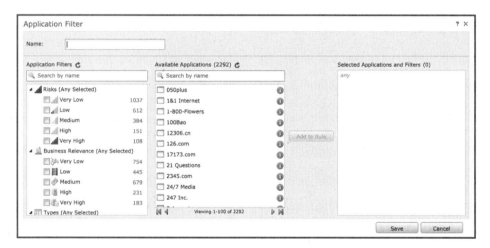

There are a number of criteria you can use to build your application filter. In the left column, you get to choose from the following options:

Via **Risk,** you can determine how likely it is that a specific application will be used to violate your company security policy with settings ranging from really low to very high.

The **Business Relevance** option allows you to deal with whether or not a certain application will probably be accessed for recreation instead of actual business needs. It can also be set from very low to very high.

The **Type** option predictably refers to the type of application you're dealing with and gives you three categories:

- Application Protocols: communications between hosts
- Clients: software running on a host
- Web Applications: the content or requested URL for HTTP traffic

Via **Category**, you get an application's general classification. Because applications can belong to more than one category, you have Tags, which allow you to get more specific about the application in question. Some good examples of application tags are evasive, high bandwidth, and open ports.

The number to the right of each filter represents the count of the applications that it matches. The center column contains a list of each of the individual, identifiable applications. The number at the top of that column in parentheses shows the count of how many applications FireSIGHT can identify in total. Once you've chosen application filter(s) on the left, the Available Applications list will update to include applications that match the filter only. Once here, you can choose the All Apps Matching The Filter entry at the top or select multiple applications from the list. Once you've done that, use the Add To Rule button and you're done!

In case you're unsure about a certain application, there is a blue information icon to the right of each of their names. Clicking it will bring up a help balloon with more details about the application, including links to several search engines you can use to investigate further (Figure 2.14).

FIGURE 2.14 Application filter balloon

A Word about Encryption

Let's talk a little bit about encryption—specifically SSL/TLS encrypted websites. From the network perspective, the use of SSL/TLS means we are not able to view the application traffic. Because the HTTP GET occurs after the session is encrypted, a typical IPS is unable to even determine the URL being requested. However, you will notice that some application detection is very specific. A prime example is Facebook. If you examine the number of applications listed for this site, you can find more than a dozen!

The challenge here is that for some time now, all Facebook traffic has been SSL encrypted, meaning that identifying these applications is impossible without using some kind of decryption technology. FireSIGHT can inspect the SSL certificate and look for the Facebook.com domain. This means you can identify the Facebook website but not the individual applications in the list. So keep these limitations in mind when you're creating your application filters and don't expect the NGIPS to work miracles!

facebook   ✕

☐ All apps matching the filter

☐ Facebook   ⓘ

☐ Facebook Apps   ⓘ

☐ Facebook Chat   ⓘ

☐ Facebook Comment   ⓘ

☐ Facebook event   ⓘ

☐ Facebook message   ⓘ

☐ Facebook post   ⓘ

☐ Facebook Read Email   ⓘ

☐ Facebook search   ⓘ

☐ Facebook Send Email   ⓘ

☐ Facebook Status Update   ⓘ

On the other hand, if you are using some type of SSL decryption device, FireSIGHT will give you visibility into all of the supported applications within encrypted sites.

Variable Sets

Variable sets are objects used to configure Snort variables found in Snort rule headers. These contain, IP address and port information constraining the rule's operation. At this point, we're going to limit the discussion to telling you how to create and edit variable sets. We'll get to a lot more detail on rules in Chapter 3, "IPS Policy Management," and explain variables more fully.

> **NOTE** You will find a number of default variables in the default variable set. These variables are used in the rules provided by Cisco. If you write your own custom rules, you may also want to add custom variables. Once you add a new custom variable, you can use it in custom Snort rules.

Variable sets are found in the Objects menu along with the rest of the object types—just click the Variable Set link on the left side of the screen. You'll be greeted by an already created default set provided by Sourcefire chock-full of defaults for all the Snort variables. This variable set gets updated by product updates and serves as a starting point for any other custom variable sets you want to create. It's important to remember that overriding a setting in the default set means it will no longer be updated by product updates from Cisco! To look at the default variable set's contents, click the pencil icon on the right to bring up the edit dialog shown in Figure 2.15.

FIGURE 2.15   Edit Variable dialog

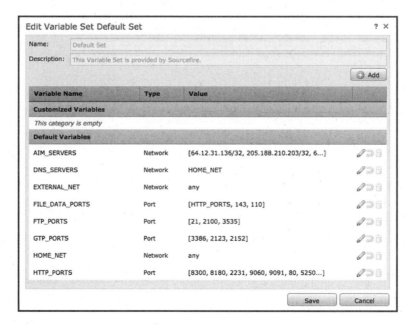

As you can see, this brings up the Edit Variable Set dialog. Clicking on the pencil icon next to HOME_NET allows you to edit the variable itself (Figure 2.16).

FIGURE 2.16   Editing the HOME_NET variable

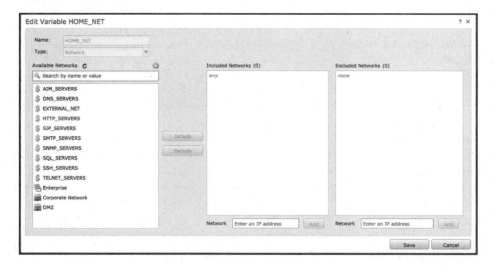

HOME_NET is an IP variable, meaning it contains IP addresses. It is one of the most important variables to consider and represents the network range that the active IPS policy protects. It can be configured to include or exclude specific IP address ranges. To include or exclude a previously created network object, just select it from the available network objects on the left and then click the Include or Exclude button. If you don't see the IP range you want shown in the Available Networks list, enter it in the Network field under Included Networks or Excluded Networks, then click the corresponding Add button. Once it's configured, click the Save button to get back to the Variable Set dialog and find your newly customized variable in the Customized Variables list (Figure 2.17).

FIGURE 2.17   Customized variable set

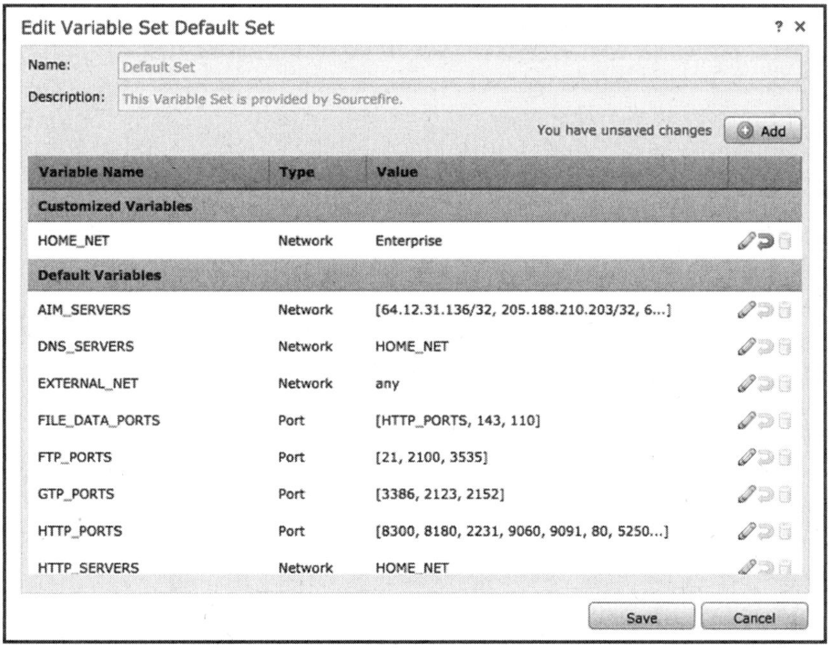

See the green reset icon just to the right of the pencil? It's telling us that the new value overrides the system default. No worries if you want to revert back to the Cisco-provided default because a click on the icon will get that done.

You can even edit port variables the same way. In Figure 2.18, notice the list of port objects in the left column. Just select one of the existing port objects or enter a port in one of the fields at the bottom of the Included Ports or Excluded Ports lists.

Keep in mind that when you're creating a custom variable set, you take the starting values for each of the variables from the default set, which gives you a layered approach to variable set configuration. You can even set HOME_NET in the default variable set to make any custom variable sets include this value. Don't forget that each custom variable set can override existing variables.

FIGURE 2.18   Edit Variable FTP_PORTS dialog

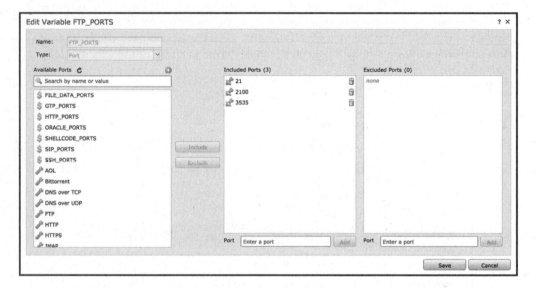

And remember—don't get upset if you still have no idea what a Snort variable is because all that will become completely clear once you've worked through Chapter 3, "IPS Policy Management." For now, just know that most of the time we modify the HOME_NET variable to match our internal network. Beyond that, modifications are generally nominal to the default variables provided.

And of course, don't forget to click the Save button when you finish editing your variable set. If the variable set is already in use by an access control policy, you'll get a warning dialog like the one in Figure 2.19.

FIGURE 2.19   Variable set warning dialog

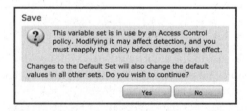

We'll show you how to use the access control policy to associate a variable set with an IPS policy in a bit.

File Lists

Moving down from Variable Set lands us at File List. From the main menu, select Objects ➢ Object Management, and then on the left side, click the File List link. When you do that, you'll find two file list items already present—the Clean List and Custom Detection List, which are the only two items permitted in this list. You can't add your own file list objects.

To understand file lists, we'll take a step back and talk about the malware detection feature of FireAMP for a minute. First, *AMP* stands for *advanced malware protection*, and it's one of the key features of the FireSIGHT system. Remember, it's a separate subscription license that must be purchased. Once you've done that, you can deploy a file policy and use the file list objects to customize your malware detection.

FireSIGHT employs several strategies to detect malware and files. We're just introducing you to the technology in this chapter, but we'll get into more detail later, in Chapter 7, "Network-Based Malware Detection." For now, let's zoom in on one method—calculate a SHA-256 hash. This a great way to begin finding out whether a file is malware or clean because every file has a distinct SHA-256 hash. The size of this hash makes it virtually impossible for two different files to have the same hash value. At this point in the history of the world, there hasn't yet been a known hash collision for SHA-256, where two different files produced the same hash value!

SHA-256 malware detection involves calculating the hash, sending it to the cloud, and then receiving back a disposition of clean, unknown, or malware. In the FireSIGHT system, this works by the device collecting a file as it passes through its detection interface. So once the entire file has been collected, the device calculates the SHA-256 hash and sends it to the Defense Center. The Defense Center then forwards the hash to the cloud and receives a disposition.

The purpose of the file list objects is to override this default behavior of the Defense Center for specific SHA-256 values, and as we've mentioned, the two file list objects available are the Clean List and the Custom Detection List. The Clean List contains SHA-256 values that will always be considered clean, so when the Defense Center receives one of these hashes from a device, it will immediately return a verdict of "clean" without checking in with the cloud. The Custom Detection List works the same way, but hashes on this list are always considered malware. This is how an administrator would override the behavior of FireSIGHT for certain files.

So clearly you would want to add a file to the clean list if it's one of your security tools that just happens to have been convicted as malicious by the Sourcefire cloud! This way you get to safely use the file and transfer it around your network without fear of generating alerts or ending up with it blocked.

To add entries to either the Clean List or Custom Detection List, again just click the pencil icon to the right to bring up the File List dialog (Figure 2.20). This dialog is the same for the Clean or Custom Detection lists—only the name is different.

There are three methods for adding entries to the file list, and clicking in the Add By field displays them (see Figure 2.21).

FIGURE 2.20   File List dialog

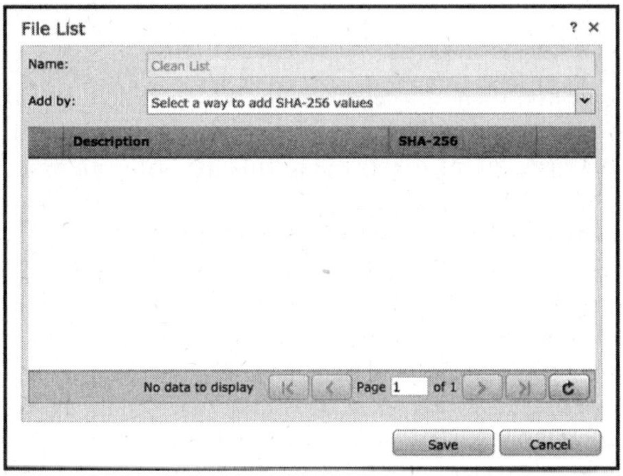

File List dialog showing:

File List   ? ×

| Name: | Clean List |
| Add by: | Select a way to add SHA-256 values ▾ |

| **Description** | **SHA-256** |
| | |

No data to display |< < Page 1 of 1 > >| ↻

[Save] [Cancel]

FIGURE 2.21   Adding file list entries

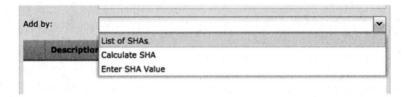

List of SHAs   When you choose List of SHAs you'll be presented with a Browse button, which allows you to upload a text file containing a list of SHA-256 values, one entry per line. You can even enter an optional description, but if you don't, the filename will be used. This method comes in really handy when you're uploading a large number of your precalculated hash values!

Calculate SHA   Another way to go is to let the Defense Center calculate the SHA value of a single file. To do this, just browse to a file that you want to be added to the list. The file will be uploaded to the Defense Center, but only for calculating its SHA-256 value—it won't be stored on the Defense Center. You can enter an optional description, but if you don't, the filename will be used.

Enter SHA Value   The third method is to enter a value manually. To do this, just enter an optional description in the Description field, then paste in a SHA-256 that you've previously calculated and click the Add button.

We used the *Clean List* to show how values can be entered in all our examples, but entering values for the *Custom Detection List* works the same way. The only difference is the name of the list, and as with the other objects, all we're doing at this stage is populating values. Again, rest assured that we'll review usage of these lists in the file policy later on in this book.

Security Zones

Next up in object management are *security zones*. In the FireSIGHT System, the term *zones* has its own special meaning. It's simply the name given to a physical interface on a device. When you create access control rules, one option is to apply your rules to traffic based on its ingress and/or egress interface. You can also gain useful insight into traffic context by understanding where the traffic entered and exited a device. This makes a great case for giving device interfaces friendly names because they go a long way in making your system a whole lot easier to use!

You can set security zones up from the Devices menu. They can also be configured in the objects interface, but it's important to remember that any changes made to security zones in either location will not take effect until these settings are applied to the device. This can only be done from the device management view.

There are several types of security zones, each corresponding to interface types like inline, passive, switched, and routed. A single zone can contain multiple interfaces, but each interface must be the same type—you can't mix inline and passive interfaces within a single zone!

So what's a strategic way to use this zone feature? Let's create a zone named Internal Passive and place all our passive inside interfaces in it. Keep in mind that these interfaces can be on a single device or on multiple ones because as long as they're all the same type, they can have the same zone name—passive in this case. Now we're going to create an access control rule and specify the source zone as Internal Passive. This means the rule will apply to traffic inbound on an interface in the Internal Passive zone. Next, we'll specify a specific IPS rule set and/or file policy in this rule. Now, when the access control policy is applied to all of our devices, any traffic in this zone would be subject to the same inspection rules.

When you click Security Zones, you'll see the current list of existing zones. By clicking the expansion triangle next to a zone name, you can see the devices where this zone exists. Below each device you'll find the interface(s) name. (See Figure 2.22)

FIGURE 2.22   Security zones

Clicking the pencil icon next to an existing zone brings up the zone edit dialog (Figure 2.23).

FIGURE 2.23   Security zones edit dialog

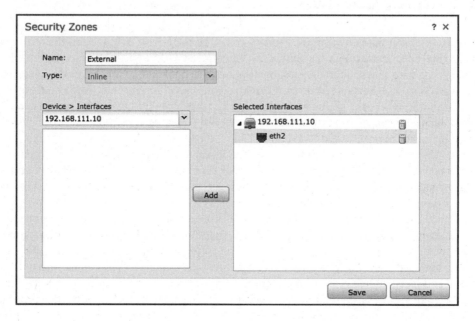

In this dialog, any interfaces that are not currently in a zone will appear on the left side. To add them to the selected zone, just select it and click the Add button. You can also rename your zone here in the Name field. And if you make changes here and click the Save button, you will see the confirmation dialog in Figure 2.24.

FIGURE 2.24   Security zone confirmation dialog

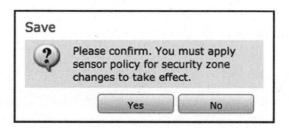

This dialog can cause a little confusion because the terminology here isn't consistent with the rest of the product. First of all, it refers to "sensor policy." Now we all know there's no such thing as a sensor in the FireSIGHT System because they're now called devices instead. Furthermore, there hasn't ever been anything called a sensor policy. No—what this dialog is really telling you is that you must go to the device configuration interface (Devices ➢ Device Management) and apply changes for the settings to take effect. Remember that this configuration is technically *not* considered a policy!

Geolocation

At the end of the object list, we finally arrive at Geolocation—an attempt to identify the country or continent in which a specific IP address is used. Of course, this doesn't apply to RFC 1918 addresses because it's limited to routable IP address space. The geolocation database that maps IP addresses to locations is updated weekly on the Defense Center, and just as it is with several other object types, this object is used to give a friendly name to a list of locations to make things easier for humans.

To add an object, click the Add Geolocation button near the top right of the screen to get to the Geolocation Object dialog. Give your new geolocation object a name—we used Interesting Locations in Figure 2.25—and afterward, you can select from all the continents and/or countries by checking the appropriate boxes.

FIGURE 2.25   Creating a geolocation object

As with all the other objects, this newly created object can be used in access control rules to selectively process traffic to or from the locations in your list.

Common UI Elements

You probably noticed that all the object management pages have two common interface elements.

Adding "On the Fly"

Whenever you see the small green "add" icon ◎ you can create objects really quickly without having to navigate back to the particular object page. For example, if you're in the process of creating groups of VLAN objects and realize you forgot to add one, you can click the "add" icon directly from the VLAN Object Groups dialog. This is true for any of the object group types.

Filter

If you went nuts and created a legion of objects, things could get ugly when you go back and try to find a particular one. If this ever happens to you, there's a field in the upper right with the word *Filter* inside. Typing a filter in this box will restrict the particular object list to items containing the string you typed. To test this, you can use the list that contains the most objects by default—port individual objects. Notice that if you select the port list and then type **HT** in the Filter box, your port list is now restricted to just HTTP and HTTPS—nice!

Summary

In this chapter, we took you on a whirlwind tour of all the object types used in the FireSIGHT System. We also covered the mechanics behind creating various object types as well as some of the background on their usage in various other policies. We covered the following object types:

- Network
- Security Intelligence
- Port
- VLAN tag
- URL
- Application filters

- Variable sets
- File lists
- Security zones
- Geolocation

Hands-on Lab

1. Open your web browser and HTTPS to your Defense Center.
2. Log in to the Defense Center.
3. Navigate to Objects ➤ Object Management.
4. Click Individual Objects under the Network heading.

5. Click the Add Network button on the right.
6. Create a network object named Corp Net and add the 10.0.0.0/8 network range.

7. Click the Add button and then the Save button.
8. Repeat steps 5 through 7 above to create an additional object named DMZ and use the 192.168.10.0/24 range. When you are finished you should have two network objects.

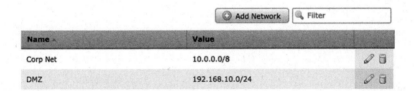

9. Click Object Groups under the Network heading.
10. Click the Add Network Group button on the right.
11. Name your new group Enterprise and add Corp Net and DMZ to this group.

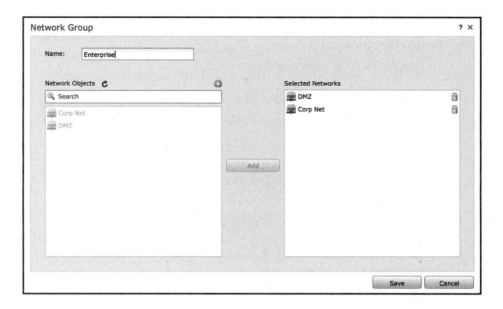

12. Click the Save button.
13. Click Application Filters.
14. Click the Add Application Filter button.
15. Name your filter High Risk Web Apps.
16. Under Risk on the left, check the High and Very High boxes.
17. Under Types on the left, check the Web Application box.
18. In the center, click on All Apps Matching The Filter (note that this is selected by default).
19. Click the Add To Rule button.

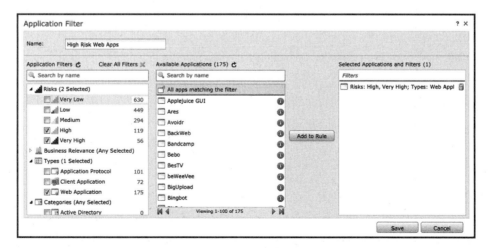

20. Click the Save button.

21. Click Variable Set.

22. Click the pencil icon to the right of Default Set.

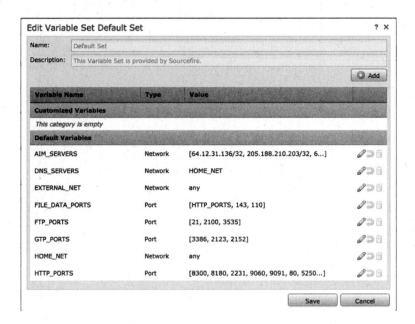

23. Click the pencil icon to the right of HOME_NET.

24. From the list on the left, select the Enterprise object group and click the Include button.

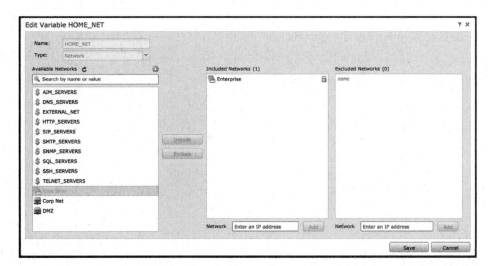

25. Click the Save button.

26. Note that HOME_NET now shows at the top under the Customized Variables heading. Click Save.

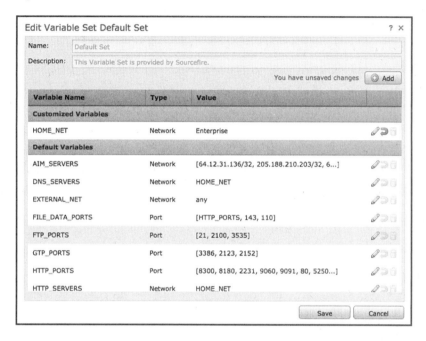

27. Note the confirmation dialog indicating that an access control policy re-apply is required for the change to take effect. Click the Yes button.

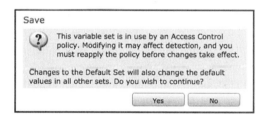

Exam Essentials

Understand the two types of variables.   Default variables are used in Snort IPS rules provided by Cisco. Custom variables can be created if desired for use with custom Snort rules.

Understand the significance of HOME_NET   The HOME_NET IP variable represents the network that the active IPS policy protects.

Understand the difference between the Clean List and the Custom Detection List. The Clean List contains SHA-256 hashes of files that are considered clean regardless of their cloud disposition. The Custom Detection List contains SHA-256 hashes of files you consider to be malware.

Know the three methods of updating IP addresses in Security Intelligence.

- Upload a list you create.
- Automatically update a list from an HTTP feed.
- Right-click on an IP address in an analysis view or Context Explorer and select Blacklist Now or Whitelist Now.

Review Questions

You can find the answers in Appendix A.

1. File list objects contain SHA-256 hash values. What method(s) can be used to add hashes to these lists?

   A. Upload a file to calculate its SHA value

   B. Enter the SHA value directly

   C. Upload a text file with a list of SHA values

   D. All of the above

2. The URL object "ign.com" would match which of the following URLs?

   A. `http://www.ign.com`

   B. `https://www.verisign.com`

   C. `http://ignite.com`

   D. All of the above

3. Network objects can contain which of the following?

   A. Individual IP addresses

   B. CIDR blocks

   C. A and B

   D. None of the above

4. Which of the following is not a valid security zone type?

   A. Forwarding

   B. Inline

   C. Switched

   D. Routed

5. Which of the following application filter criteria indicates whether the target is a web application or a client?

   A. Business Relevance

   B. Type

   C. Category

   D. Risk

6. Security zones can be configured in which of the following locations?

   A. The Objects menu

   B. The Devices menu

   C. A and B

   D. None of the above

7. What method(s) can be used to add IPs to the global blacklist and global whitelist?
   A. Right-clicking on an IP address in any analysis view
   B. Clicking the edit pencil icon next to the object in Object Management
   C. A and B
   D. None of the above

8. Which of the following is true regarding the Default Set Variable Set?
   A. This set is provided by Cisco.
   B. Variables in this set determine the default value for any additional variable sets.
   C. Once a variable value is edited, future Cisco updates to that variable will not be applied.
   D. All of the above.

9. VLAN tag objects can contain which of the following?
   A. Single VLAN IDs
   B. VLAN ID ranges
   C. Comma-separated VLAN IDs
   D. A and B only
   E. All of the above

10. Which of the following might be used to identify applications that impact employee productivity?
    A. Risk
    B. Business relevance
    C. Type
    D. Tag

Chapter

3

IPS Policy Management

THE SSFIPS EXAM TOPICS COVERED IN THIS CHAPTER INCLUDE THE FOLLOWING:

- ✓ 4.1 Understand and describe the operation of the IPS policy interface

- ✓ 4.2 Describe the use of the rule management user interface in the IPS policy editor

- ✓ 4.3 Be able to implement Cisco FireSIGHT recommendations

Get ready to hyper-focus while we dig deep into the IPS policy during this short but vital chapter. In it, you're going to learn all about this integral topic as well as a key list of the rules and settings we use in concert with it, which can be used to enable, disable, or modify the intrusion prevention system to target the exact types of malicious traffic you want it to look for on the network.

During our exploration of IPS policy, we'll talk about the *policy editor*, a key tool used to configure policies, plus policy concepts like *layers*, and finally, FireSIGHT recommendations. By the end of this chapter, you'll have a solid grasp on the important roles each of these mechanisms play in the system.

To find up-to-the-minute updates for this chapter, please see www.lammle .com/firepower or the book's web page at www.sybex.com.

IPS Policies

IPS policies precisely describe the suspicious and/or malicious traffic that the system must watch out for, and they also control how evil traffic is dealt with when it's discovered. Highly configurable IPS rules make up the bulk of the policy. These rules can be set to off or on and direct the specific actions the system takes when a match against malicious or suspicious traffic occurs. They also regulate actions taken when certain IP addresses or networks are found to be involved. Snort rules are provided via the Cisco Talos security team, but user-defined rules can also be employed. There are over 20,000 rules built into the system, so it's clearly important in terms of overhead to only enable the specific rules relevant to your environment. Dealing with 20,000+ rules is pretty overwhelming and is a huge reason why default Sourcefire-authored IPS policies come in really handy!

The Cisco Talos Security Intelligence and Research Group is a collection of leading threat researchers that are responsible for developing Snort rules, security intelligence feeds, and identifying new and emerging threats. The Talos team is comprised of the Sourcefire Vulnerability Research Team and the Cisco Security Intelligence Organization among others.

Default Policies

Default policies can fit in to many different scenarios and are great for when you first deploy the IPS. By leveraging the default policies, you gain a preset security level for your environment, but keep in mind that these policies may be configured to drop some traffic if your device is deployed inline. Legitimate traffic shouldn't have problems getting through; only the malicious stuff gets dropped. And don't forget that this policy attribute is configurable.

These four default policies provide a great starting point on which to base your own policies:

- No Rules Active
- Connectivity Over Security
- Balanced Security and Connectivity
- Security Over Connectivity

No Rules Active   The No Rules Active policy is there for anyone who wants vault-tight control over what gets enabled and disabled. All rules start out in the disabled state, and again, due to the sheer number of them, it's wise to enable only the ones that will strategically meet definite security needs.

Connectivity over Security   The *Connectivity over Security* policy is built for speed and gives the inspection engine the fastest throughput. The rules that are enabled here are intended to fend off the most insidious attacks that could possibly impact today's networks. These powerful rules rate a Common Vulnerability Scoring System (CVSS) score of 10 and must be no older than the current year plus two years prior to it. (See `https://nvd.nist` `.gov/cvss.cfm` for more on the CVSS.)

The Common Vulnerability Scoring System

The CVSS is an open framework designed to standardize the way vulnerabilities are categorized based on impact of known vulnerabilities against different types of systems. It was created to allow a metric to be put in place to rank the vulnerabilities with a consistent measure of how important they are. There is a rather complex formula used to calculate the score. This formula takes into consideration base metrics, temporal metrics, and environmental metrics, each of which is made of submetrics.

Balanced Security and Connectivity   The *Balanced Security and Connectivity* policy performs well in terms of latency and is also a good medium coverage policy. In general, it has rules enabled that have a CVSS score of 9 or higher, again from the current year or no more than the previous two. The Balanced Security and Connectivity policy has rules enabled in several key categories, like SQL-Injection and Exploit Kit.

Security over Connectivity   *Security over Connectivity* is considered the strictest of the default polices. It will have the most rules enabled with a significant number of them set to drop. When you are deployed inline, the drop action will actually discard a malicious packet to prevent an attack from succeeding. This policy's rules have a CVSS score of 8 or higher from this year or the previous three and meet requirements in a number of additional categories (SQL-Injection, Exploit Kit, and Malware CNC to name a few).

> All of the built-in policies are updated via the rule update process and controlled by the Talos team. Keep in mind that our descriptions of policy content are typical and serve as guidelines, so there will definitely be some exceptions to what you've just read in the real world. It's the Talos team who has the final say about what's enabled or disabled in the default policies!

Policy Layers

Even though you can use one of the built-in Sourcefire-authored policies, you can definitely tweak things a bit if you want to. You can turn rules on and off, set them from drop and alert, to alert only, and so on, but know that if you decide to go with a default policy, you cannot change those! So, what to do if you only mostly like a default policy? You create your very own custom policy based upon it and get exactly what you want instead! Doing this involves a concept known as *layering*. When you create a custom IPS policy, you've got to settle on what we call a base layer first. This will become your new policy's foundation, which you want to think of as pretty much permanent, much like the foundation for a building—something the rest of the structure will be built upon—but as something that you really don't want to go back and make changes to once your project is underway. To get a picture of this process, check out Figure 3.1.

FIGURE 3.1   Policy layers

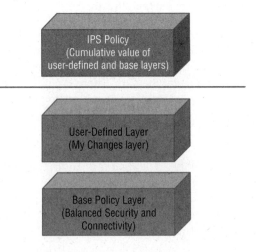

So, here you can see that the layer My Changes has been created on top of the base layer. This happens automatically. Key to understand is that any changes you make are applied to the My Changes layer and override any setting made on the base layer. One of the coolest things about this layered approach is that it makes policy management across multiple devices a lot easier. Having multiple layers on top of the base layer that can be shared across IPS policies within the Defense Center (FireSIGHT Management Center) helps tremendously!

Creating a Policy

Let's create a new IPS policy. First, inside the Defense Center navigate to Policies ➤ Intrusion ➤ Intrusion Policy, and then click Create Policy. This will bring up the Create Intrusion Policy dialog. Give the policy a name; keep in mind that although the description is optional, it's a cool feature that is handy for documentation purposes, so take a minute to say a few words describing your policy here so the next person that comes along will have an idea of the policy's purpose. Next, you're faced with the Drop When Inline check box. This one is important!

Let's first discuss what actions can be taken against malicious traffic. These actions are dependent on how the device is deployed. The two actions are either:

Drop And Generate Events—This action causes the IPS to discard the malicious traffic that matches an IPS rule. It also will send an event to the Defense Center. The events (sometimes called alerts) are what the analysts view in the Defense Center.

Generate Events (Alert)—In some cases you may not want to drop the suspected malicious traffic. This may be in scenarios where you are testing the IPS or some of the rules are used for auditing as opposed to protecting. Generate Events will cause the alert to go to the Defense Center but will not interrupt the traffic.

The Drop When Inline is a check box that controls whether the IPS rules drop traffic. The rules in the policy give you an option to drop and alert if the right type of traffic is discovered. The idea is that the IPS will save the network by discarding malicious communications, but whether or not this will actually happen depends on the following conditions:

- If the device is deployed inline and the Drop When Inline box is checked, the capability to drop is definitely there, but the network's rescue also hinges on the individual IPS policies you've put in place.

- If the Drop When Inline box is checked but the device is not deployed inline, then traffic won't be discarded.

- If the device is deployed inline and the Drop When Inline box is *not* checked, traffic still won't be discarded if there's a rule set to drop and generate events.

- If the device is deployed passively, checking the Drop When Inline box won't matter one bit.

- If the box is not checked and you've got rules set that say to drop and generate events, traffic that matches will still show in the event analysis view but will be marked as Would Have Dropped.

The last option to select when creating a new IPS policy is the base policy. There is a drop-down that lists all the built-in policies along with any previously created custom policies. You can then create and edit the policy. In Figure 3.2, you can see the Create Intrusion Policy dialog. Take note of the Name, Description, Drop When Inline, and Base Policy fields as previously described.

FIGURE 3.2   Create Intrusion Policy dialog

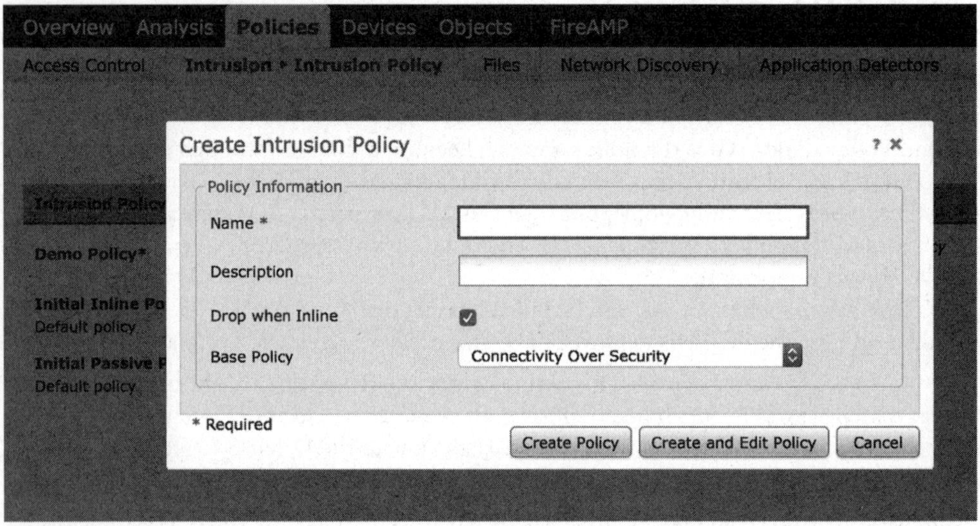

Policy Editor

When you open up the policy editor, it will display a navigation pane to the left and, on the right, the detail pane, which takes up most of the screen's real estate (Figure 3.3). Here's a list of the items you'll find in the navigation pane:

Policy Information: Displays a summary screen that lists the basic settings of the policy. This one is important because if you make any changes, you must return here to either commit the changes (save) or discard them. Understand that choosing Commit Changes here only applies the changes to the database on the Defense Center and does not actually push the settings to the managed device! You have to directly apply the policy to the device to actually push the settings.

Rules: Displays all the rules available to the policy.

FireSIGHT Recommendations: Allows FireSIGHT to recommend which rules to enable or disable based on data collected from your network through FireSIGHT.

Advanced Settings: Contain preprocessor, logging, and performance settings.

Policy Layers: Allows you to expand and view the policy layers, including the base layer and any user-defined layers.

FIGURE 3.3   The Policy Information section in the policy editor

Rules

The Rules section gets subdivided even more (Figure 3.4). Let's take a look at each section.

Filter panel: This is the vertical column toward the center of Figure 3.4. It lets you view rules associated with specific categories, classifications, priorities or rule updates. Selecting an option from the filter panel will populate the filter bar at the top of the rules list. Clicking the sections will expand or contract other sections.

Filter bar: This is in the top of the interface. Use this to manually input search criteria for rules. You also get the option to populate the filter bar by selecting items from the rules filter panel.

Rules list: This makes up the main part of the display as seen in Figure 3.4. It shows you all the rules based on the criteria specified on the filter bar.

Policy drop-down: Located below the filter bar and above the rules list. This allows you to examine a specific layer of your IPS policy. The default view shows the cumulative values of all layers.

Show Details: If you have a specific rule selected in the rules list, you'll see a Show Details button appear at the bottom of the interface. Clicking this will bring up the details of that rule, including the text of the rule itself, documentation, overhead, and reference websites.

FIGURE 3.4   The Rules section in the policy editor

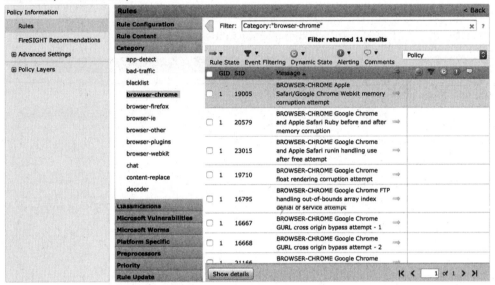

Directly under the filter bar, you'll find collections of settings that can be applied to rules individually. Settings can also be applied to multiple rules by selecting their corresponding check boxes in the rules list.

Rule State   The first menu drop-down is Rule State, which lets you specify one of three actions: Disable (turn the rule off), Generate Events (set the rule to send events to the FSM), or Drop And Generate Events (have the device discard the malicious packets). Remember that if your device is inline, you gain the ability to drop traffic provided the rules are set to drop and the policy is set to Drop When Inline.

Event Filtering   The *Event Filtering* settings allow you to specify whether you want to decrease the frequency of the alerts occurring on the Defense Center. Don't get confused—this setting has no impact on the drop actions, it only affects the alerts to the Defense Center. The choices are to adjust Threshold settings or Suppression settings.

Suppression settings are straightforward and used when you don't want any alerts generated for a specific rule, even for a rule based upon a given source or destination IP address.

Under Threshold (Figure 3.5), there are three types to choose from: Limit, Threshold, and Both. You must select one of them.

> **Limit:** Allows you to limit the number of alerts based on either the source or destination IP address as well as the number of alerts you want to trigger if the event

occurs within a selected number of seconds. Once that limit is reached, no new alerts will occur until the time period has expired. So, if you want to limit an event to 10 alerts every 5 minutes, you could use this option.

Threshold: Permits you to limit the number of alerts based on either the source or destination IP address, the number of events that must occur before you generate an alert, plus the number of seconds allotted to look for those events. For instance, let's say the count was set to 10 and the seconds set to 60. The result would be an alert for every 10 occurrences of that event within 60 seconds.

Both: A combination that lets you limit the number of alerts based on either the source or destination IP address. The count specifies the number of events that must be observed before an alert is generated. Again, the time period indicates that you don't want another alert of the same type generated within that interval. In other words, you could say alert me only if event x happens 10 times (Threshold) but only tell me every 5 minutes (Limit).

FIGURE 3.5   The Threshold dialog

Set Threshold for 1 rule   ? ✕

Type	Limit ⇕
Track By	Source ⇕
Count	
Seconds	

OK   Cancel

It's really important to remember that these settings affect only alerts and have no effect on actual traffic processing! For example, if a rule is set to block traffic and you apply a threshold to it, the rule continues to block even though the number of alerts sent to the console is reduced based on the threshold you applied. This is why these filtering options are so useful for tuning out noisy alerts. It's still hard to be proactive with these because you just never know what you'll get in your specific environment.

Dynamic State   Dynamic State (Figure 3.6) allows the device to dynamically change the state of the rule from its current one to any of the other available states: Drop And Generate Events, Generate Events, and Disabled. The state changes based upon the source or destination address as defined in the Track By drop-down. Another option that can appear in the Track By drop-down is Rule. If you specify source or destination, then the Network field must be populated. If Rule is selected in the Track By field, then the Network field does not appear. The Rate field lets you specify that the rule must fire a certain count within a given number of seconds. There's also a Timeout field that resets the rule to the previous state.

FIGURE 3.6   Dynamic State dialog

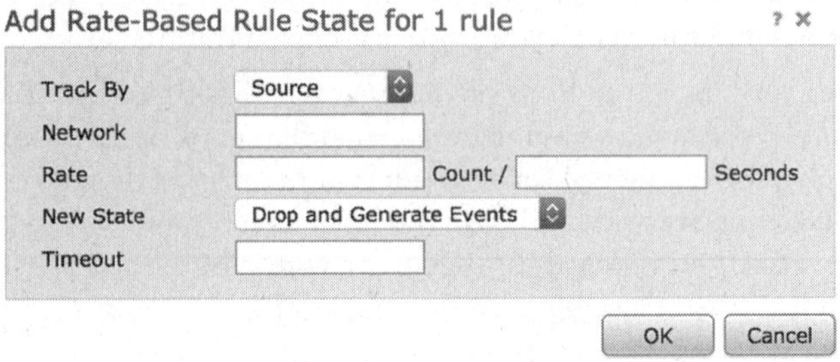

Add Rate-Based Rule State for 1 rule   ? ✕

Track By	Source
Network	
Rate	Count / Seconds
New State	Drop and Generate Events
Timeout	

OK   Cancel

Alerting   To enable or disable SNMP alerts for a specific rule, you need to use the Alerting dialog, which also comes in handy for sending data to a Security Information and Event Management (SIEM) tool or some other alerting tool. You configure the SNMP manager in the advanced settings. SNMP alerts are generated by the managed device.

Comments   You can also add comments to the individual rules that can be viewed by users of the Defense Center and analysts who inspect the traffic.

Policy   The Policy drop-down on the far right of the policy editor gives you a view of the rules based upon states set within the individual policy layers. The default view is just Policy, but you can also check out My Changes, FireSIGHT Recommendations if used, and the base policy. Colors are important indicators here:

- All rules will appear white by default.
- When you look at individual layers, pink indicates that the rule's state has been modified in a higher layer.
- A rule highlighted in yellow means its state was adjusted in a lower layer.
- Rules highlighted in orange are ones you've clicked on.

FireSIGHT Recommendations

It's not just you—there really is a massive mob of rules out there, a fact that can completely mystify the sharpest among us! This swarm of options can make figuring out exactly what you need in your particular environment a seriously overwhelming experience, but you've got to start somewhere. This is why it's such a great idea to start with one of the default policies and then enable rules that are more specific to your environment. Another super-helpful tool for clearing your path to solid choices and policies is *FireSIGHT Recommendations* (Figure 3.7). These recommendations give you a boost by inserting a policy layer between the base policy layer and the My Changes layer. These enabled rules have already been fully vetted as relevant to your environment. What determines this relevance? FireSIGHT—it's that intelligent! FireSIGHT actually learns about your network, including all its operating systems, services, applications, and potential vulnerabilities. The system uses that information to cross-reference with the rules provided from the Talos team and determines the best rules to enable—sweet!

FIGURE 3.7   The FireSIGHT Recommended Rules Configuration screen

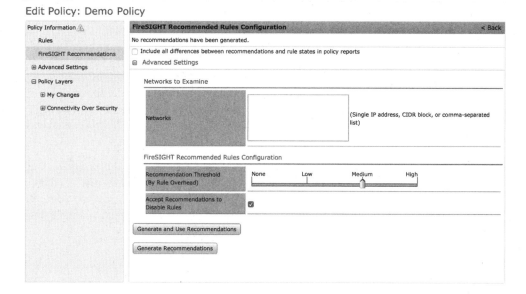

By default, the recommendations are generated for all IP addresses that have been evaluated by FireSIGHT. This can be limited by working within Advanced Settings to specify the networks to use. One reason for specifying a segment of your overall network would be for testing purposes, or maybe you want to automatically enable rules for a specific segment while manually tuning others. You'll also find a rule overhead slider pointing to the types of rules that should be enabled. There's also a check box that indicates whether or not you want to accept the recommendations to disable rules. Watch out for this—if you do not have reliable FireSIGHT data, you could end up turning off all your rules! For instance, if FireSIGHT has not seen any traffic in your network yet, it will assume that there will not need to be any rules turned on. Likewise, if it has not seen any Windows 7 traffic, it will assume that you have no Windows 7 systems and disable the rules specific to that OS.

The buttons at the bottom of the FireSIGHT Recommended Rules Configuration screen allow you to generate *and* use the recommendations or just generate the recommendations. By generating the recommendations, you can check out the changes being recommended before they're implemented. Remember that recommendations will override changes from the base policy but not changes you've made at the My Changes layer. Because of this, you could manually implement the recommended changes, but if you accept the changes, *all* the changes are accepted. Because most networks are constantly changing, it wise to update your recommendations now and then. You can see what the implemented FireSIGHT Recommendations layer looks like in Figure 3.8.

Advanced Settings

The Advanced Settings section contains many "under the hood" settings for the Snort engine. These should not be touched without a deep understanding of the consequences! As you can imagine, these settings are so detailed and in depth we're dedicating Chapter 12, "Advanced IPS Policy Configuration," to them!

Policy Layers

The Policy Layers section (Figure 3.8) shows you all the layers that have been implemented in the current policy. At the very least, you'll see the base layer and the My Changes layer. If you added any other layers, like an additional user layer or the FireSIGHT Recommendations, you'll see those actions reflected here. You'll also find a summary of the individual layers, including the number of rules in their specific states within this dialog.

FIGURE 3.8   Policy layers

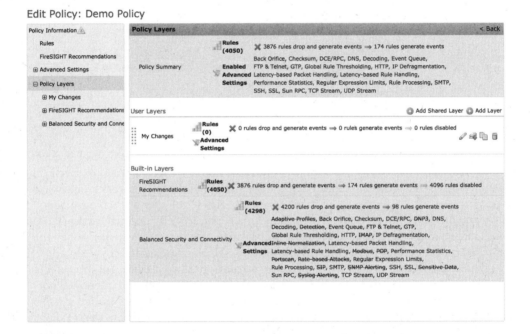

A yellow triangle will show up if you've made any changes to the policy in the Policy Information section of the navigation pane, as you can see in Figure 3.7. This is telling you that you need to either save or discard your changes by clicking the Commit Changes button or the Discard Changes button, respectively.

And just to remind you, committing changes here won't push the policy to the device; it will only commit the changes to the database on the Defense Center. You've got to add the policy to an Access Control policy so it can then be pushed to the device. We show you how to update and push the access control policy in Chapter 4, "Access Control Policy."

Intrusion Policy Repository

After you commit the changes, the intrusion policy repository will open (Figure 3.9) and you can see a list of all the intrusion policies that have been created. To the right of each policy, you'll see icons that will allow you to reapply the policy, generate a report, and export, edit or delete the policy. The report is great for documentation purposes. The export will create a binary file that can be imported to other Defense Centers provided they are running the same versions.

The Compare Policies button on this screen allows you to run comparisons between versions of the same policy and even compare different policies with each other.

FIGURE 3.9   IPS policy repository

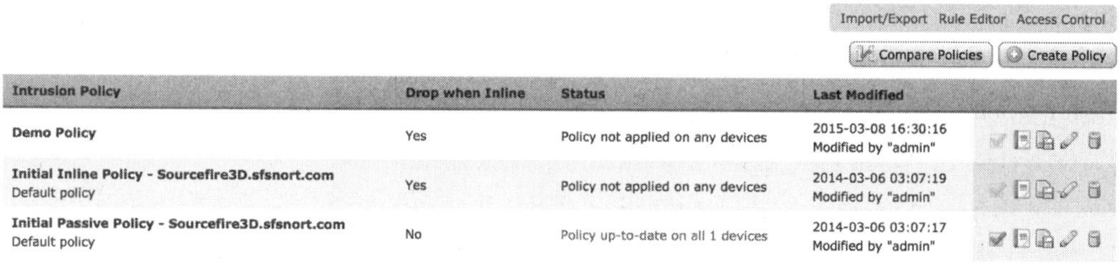

Intrusion Policy	Drop when Inline	Status	Last Modified	
Demo Policy	Yes	Policy not applied on any devices	2015-03-08 16:30:16 Modified by "admin"	
Initial Inline Policy - Sourcefire3D.sfsnort.com Default policy	Yes	Policy not applied on any devices	2014-03-06 03:07:19 Modified by "admin"	
Initial Passive Policy - Sourcefire3D.sfsnort.com Default policy	No	Policy up-to-date on all 1 devices	2014-03-06 03:07:17 Modified by "admin"	

Summary

In this chapter, you learned all about the IPS policies available to use in your system. An IPS policy contains a list of rules and settings that can be enabled/disabled or modified and tells the IPS about the types of malicious traffic to look for on the network.

We explained the IPS policies and introduced you to the policy editor, a tool used to configure policies and policy concepts like base policies, layers, and finally, FireSIGHT recommendations. Equipped with all this, you have the keys to understanding how all of these items come into play and work together within this elegant system!

Hands-on Labs

In this section, you will complete the following two labs:

Hands-on Lab 3.1: Creating an IPS Policy

Hands-on Lab 3.2: Implementing FireSIGHT Recommendations

Hands-on Lab 3.1: Creating an IPS Policy

In this lab, you will create an IPS policy.

1. Open your web browser and HTTPS to your Defense Center.
2. Log in to the Defense Center.
3. Navigate to Policies ➤ Intrusion ➤ Intrusion Policy.
4. Click Create Policy.
5. In the Create Intrusion Policy dialog, add the name **Demo IPS Policy**.
6. Verify that the Drop When Inline box is checked.
7. In the Base Policy drop-down, select Security Over Connectivity.
8. Click the Create Policy button.

Hands-on Lab 3.2: Viewing Connection Events

In this lab, you will enable the FireSIGHT recommended rules.

1. Navigate to Policies ➤ Intrusion ➤ Intrusion Policy.
2. Click the previously created Demo IPS Policy.
3. In the policy editor, navigate to the FireSIGHT Recommendations section.
4. Expand Advanced Settings in the FireSIGHT Recommendations screen.
5. Deselect the Accept Recommendations To Disable Rules option.
6. Click Generate And Use Recommendations. Note the recommendations at the top of the screen after they are generated.
7. In the navigation pane, click the Policy Layers item.
8. View the layer summaries and note the differences between them.
9. Click the Policy Information item in the navigation pane.
10. Click Commit Changes to save the policy.
11. Type in a description of the changes and click OK.

Exam Essentials

Know about the default built-in policies and what purpose each one serves.   The built-in default policies allow for a security administrator to quickly configure the IPS to protect a network. The built in policies are as follows:

- No Rules Active – All rules are off, allowing for complete customization.
- Connectivity over Security – Built for speed. Only the most severe threats are looked for.

- Balanced Security and Connectivity – Good compromise between security and speed.
- Security over Connectivity – Built to give the best default protection on typical networks.

Understand policy layers and how they allow customization.   Policy layers allow you to have a consistent base layer and then customize settings in a My Changes layer. This allows you to inherit settings from the built-in policies.

Be able to explain the Drop When Inline check box.   When an IPS policy is created, the Drop When Inline check box specifies whether or not the system will be capable of dropping traffic when deployed inline.

Be able to explain and implement FireSIGHT Recommendations   Using FireSIGHT Recommendations is a quick way to secure your network based on discovery data held in the FireSIGHT database. The implementation can be as simple as a click of the button.

Review Questions

You can find the answers in Appendix A.

1. What built-in policy is considered a good medium security policy for network inspection?
    A. Security over Connectivity
    B. Balanced Security and Connectivity
    C. Connectivity over Security
    D. No Rules Active

2. Policy layers allow you to do what?
    A. Cover multiple network attacks
    B. Control packet flow between OSI layers
    C. Have multiple configurable layers for customization purposes
    D. Have multiple layers of inspection

3. In the policy editor, what section would you select to save your policy?
    A. Policy Information
    B. Rules
    C. FireSIGHT Recommendations
    D. Policy Layers

4. What are the available rule states?
    A. Enabled, Disabled, Block
    B. Alert, Pass, Drop
    C. On, Off, Block
    D. Disable, Generate Events, Drop and Generate Events

5. Rule thresholding can be based on which of the following?
    A. Source or destination IP
    B. Attacker or victim
    C. Client or server
    D. None of the above

6. What are the layers displayed in the policy editor?
    A. Application layer and Presentation layer
    B. Host layer and network layer
    C. User layer and exec layer
    D. My Changes layer and base policy layer

7. In FireSIGHT Recommendations, what is the default setting for the Recommendation Threshold?

    A. None

    B. Low

    C. Medium

    D. High

8. When a policy is exported, what format will it be in?

    A. CSV

    B. Binary

    C. Text

    D. XLS

9. What is a way to document your policy once it's complete?

    A. Export the policy.

    B. Select the policy and choose Save As.

    C. Send it via email.

    D. Generate a report.

10. When a policy is created, there is a Drop When Inline check box. What impact will unchecking the box have in an inline deployment?

    A. Unchecking the box will prevent the system from dropping traffic.

    B. Unchecking the box allows the system to fail open.

    C. Only rules marked Drop And Generate Events will be dropped.

    D. The box only impacts normalization.

Chapter

4

Access Control Policy

THE SSFIPS EXAM TOPICS COVERED IN THIS CHAPTER INCLUDE THE FOLLOWING:

✓ **1.0   Object Management**

- 1.2 Describe the implementation of security intelligence feeds

✓ **2.0   Access Control Policy**

- 2.1 Describe the purpose, features, and configuration of access control policy rules

- 2.2 Describe the purpose and configuration of an access control policy

The *Access Control policy (AC policy)* is the heart of the FireSIGHT System and determines the types of traffic that will be logged, allowed, or blocked. It's also used to implement Security Intelligence lists, IPS rules, and file policies. An AC policy acts kind of like a central traffic cop for FireSIGHT because all traffic passing through a device is processed through it. If you have prior experience with packet filtering firewalls, AC policies will probably remind you of a traditional firewall access control list (ACL). The concepts are very similar, but the AC policy offers some very cool ways to inspect traffic more thoroughly and on a deeper level, beyond simply allowing or blocking connections based on IP address, port, and protocol.

You also gain flexibility and the ability to deploy your Access Control policies a number of ways. Create a single policy and deploy it to all your devices, or construct a separate policy for individual devices, even groups of them. Keep in mind that you are limited to applying only one AC policy to a device at a time. Also remember that applying a new AC policy will replace an existing one.

In this chapter, you're going to learn all about how Access Control policy is used in the FireSIGHT System. We'll be covering the following key skills, factors, and features:

- Getting started with Access Control policies
- Security Intelligence
- HTTP responses
- Advanced features
- Access Control rules
- Saving and applying an Access Control policy

 To find up-to-the-minute updates for this chapter, please see www.lammle .com/firepower or the book's web page at www.sybex.com.

Getting Started with Access Control Policies

To get started, look for the Access Control policy under Policies ➤ Access Control. Clicking on a top-level menu item takes you to the far-left submenu item by default, so just click Policies in the top menu to go directly to the Access Control policy management page.

The Access Control policy main page shows a list of the existing AC policies, as you can see here in Figure 4.1.

FIGURE 4.1   The Access Control policy main page

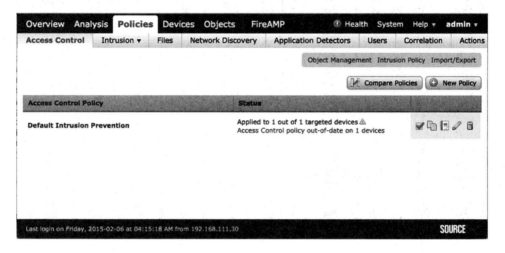

The Access Control Policy column lists the policy name. The Status column tells us how many devices the policy is applied to and whether the policy is up-to-date on these devices or not. Taking another look at the figure, see the message saying the policy has been applied to one device and is currently out-of-date? This means something in the policy has changed since the last time it was applied.

There are also five icons to the right of the policy:

The check mark icon is used to apply the policy to the targeted device(s).

Click the overlapping-pages icon to make a copy of the policy.
    Having a copy of the policy comes in really handy because it's easy to make changes to and then apply your new policy. It also means you still have the old policy in case you need to roll back!

Click the notebook icon to generate a report, which gives you a PDF of the policy rules and settings.

To get straight into editing the AC policy, click the policy name or the pencil icon.

And finally, you can totally delete the AC policy from the Defense Center with the icon shown here.

To create a new AC policy, you can either edit the preinstalled default policy or create a new one by clicking the New Policy button in the upper right. This will display the New Access Control Policy dialog shown in Figure 4.2.

FIGURE 4.2   Creating a new AC policy

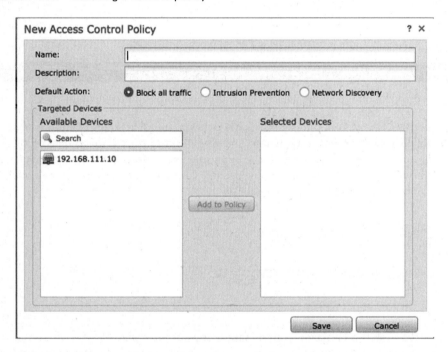

Start by giving your new policy a name and an optional description, and then choose one of these three default actions:

- **Block All Traffic:** Selecting this will cause the policy to work like a firewall rules set. If traffic doesn't match a rule in the policy, it will be blocked.

- **Intrusion Prevention:** Any traffic that doesn't match any rules in the policy will be inspected by an IPS rule set. But understand that this dialog does *not* allow selecting the IPS rule set—we'll get into that a bit later.

- **Network Discovery:** This causes any traffic not matching rules to pass through the device uninspected. You can opt to have this kind of traffic logged as connection events.

Okay—once you're done with that step, it's time to select a device for your policy to target. All the devices managed by the Defense Center are listed, and if you're in a really large environment with a legion of devices in it, use the search field to narrow down your choices. Once you have settled on one or more devices, click the Add To Policy button.

Clicking Save will predictably save the policy and take you on to the policy edit page pictured in Figure 4.3.

FIGURE 4.3   Policy edit page

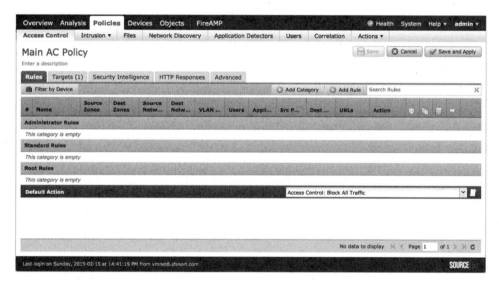

This is the page where all configuration of the AC policy happens. You can see the name of the policy there in the upper left, and right below that is the description. Click either one of these items to modify them and then depending on what you want to do, click the typical Save, Cancel, and Save And Apply buttons found on the right.

Security Intelligence Lists

Before digging deep into AC rules, it's really helpful to review some of the other configuration tabs first. A really important one that you should always consider is the *Security Intelligence* tab because it determines how you deal with traffic that matches one of your Security Intelligence lists.

Clicking on the Security Intelligence tab displays the configuration page shown in Figure 4.4.

FIGURE 4.4   Security Intelligence

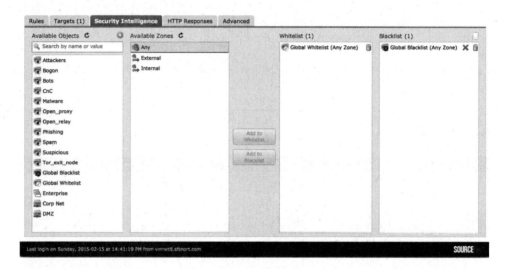

Always remember that Security Intelligence is used to block/alert on traffic solely based on its IP address. Understand that this action takes place prior to processing by any Access Control rules.

As we suggested back in Chapter 2, "Object Management," when you think Security Intelligence, think "IP lists." The main purpose of these lists is to alert or block traffic to/from specific IP addresses. For instance, and by default, any traffic to/from IP addresses on the global blacklist will be blocked. And this block action is not accompanied by an alert. Yes, you read correctly—by default, any traffic to/from IP address objects in the Blacklist column will be dropped silently—the stuff of troubleshooting nightmares. So don't doubt for a minute that we won't address how to change this not-so-charming default behavior soon!

Blacklists, Whitelists, and Alerts

The primary purpose of Security Intelligence is to alert or block traffic that's probably malicious, on par with IP address blacklisting, but we also get the option to whitelist certain traffic. Whitelists only exist to override blacklists, so by putting IP addresses into a whitelist, you're preventing them from being blocked just in case they're inadvertently added to a blacklist.

Remember from Chapter 2, the *global blacklist* can be populated by right-clicking on an IP address in an event view or by clicking on an interactive graph in Context Explorer. When this happens, the blacklist will immediately be pushed to all devices. And if the IP in question happens to be a key host or router within your environment, the results could be catastrophic! This is why it's always good to add these key IP addresses to the *global whitelist* ahead of time.

Security Intelligence Page Specifics

On the Security Intelligence configuration page, you'll find several columns:

- Available Objects
- Available Zones
- Whitelist
- Blacklist

Let's take some time to explore each of these now.

Available Objects   These are the available IP list objects. You can select one or more of these to add to the Whitelist or Blacklist column. Each one contains one or more IP addresses or ranges. You will see two broad categories of items in this list:

- Network objects and network object groups you have created
- Security Intelligence objects.

Network objects and network object groups are typically static lists or ranges of IP addresses defining parts of your network.

Security Intelligence objects include the built-in global whitelist and global blacklist, the Sourcefire Intelligence Feed, and any custom feeds or lists you have created. Assuming your Defense Center has been able to connect to Sourcefire and update its feed, you'll see the various categories of evil listed here. Each one corresponds to a list of IP addresses. All the Sourcefire objects you see, such as Attackers, Bogon, Bots, CnC, and so on, are there because the Defense Center has downloaded the latest Sourcefire Intelligence feed. We're confident that you recall that this object is updated every two hours by default.

Available Zones   Zones can be used as an additional criterion for matching one of the IP list objects. This means traffic to/from an IP will only be considered for the whitelist or blacklist if it's detected in the selected zone. The default is Any (meaning "any zone").

Whitelist   This column contains the global whitelist by default, and it's there for the singular purpose of overriding a blacklist. Any IP address found in the *Whitelist* column will not be blocked by a blacklist. But this does not mean that address gets a free ride. All traffic matching a whitelist will still be processed by the applicable Access Control rule(s).

Blacklist   Items in the *Blacklist* column will be blocked and/or generate alert notifications.

Blacklist Logging   One of the most important areas to consider on this page is the logging scroll that's found in the upper-right corner of the screen, just on top of the Blacklist column. We need to point this one out because most people overlook it because it's grayed out by default. Clicking this scroll displays the Blacklist Options dialog shown in Figure 4.5.

The image in Figure 4.5 shows that the default setting for the Blacklist is to *not* log connections. This means that if an item in the Blacklist column matches traffic, you will not receive an alert, but the traffic *will* be dropped if your device is configured as inline, switched, or routed. This is exactly why it's a superb idea to *always* enable logging for blacklisted connections. To do that, simply click the Log Connections check box, which will enable logging to the Defense Center, as shown in Figure 4.6.

FIGURE 4.5 Blacklist Options dialog

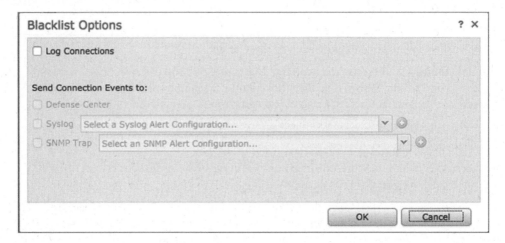

FIGURE 4.6 Blacklist logging options

 If you change nothing else on the Security Intelligence page, always enable blacklist connection logging!

Configuring Security Intelligence

Working with Security Intelligence lists is really straightforward. Just select the object under the Available Objects column, optionally choose a zone, and then click the Add To Whitelist or Add To Blacklist button.

You can place any of the objects in either the Whitelist or Blacklist column, with the exception of the global whitelist and global blacklist. These two can be added only to their respective columns.

Once you have added some items to the Blacklist column *and* enabled logging as we just recommended, you can then change the alert/block behavior by right-clicking on one of the objects. In Figure 4.7, we clicked on the Spam object.

FIGURE 4.7   Blacklist context menu

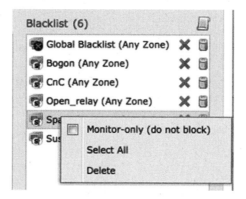

The context menu that pops up allows you to change the default block behavior of a specific Blacklist item. By clicking the Monitor-Only (Do not Block) check box, you're changing this list from a block action to an alert action. Notice that doing so turns the red X next to the list to a green arrow, as pictured in Figure 4.8.

FIGURE 4.8   Blacklist actions

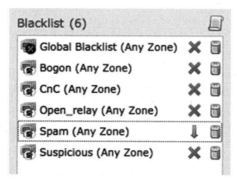

By the way, you definitely want to do this if you have lists you would like to be alerted on but just not actively blocked.

 You can't change this block action for the global blacklist. If you try right-clicking this item, you'll discover that the Monitor Only option isn't available. The global blacklist will *always* block if it's present in this column.

HTTP Responses

The HTTP Responses tab is what we use to configure the web page that will be returned when a user attempts to visit a blocked website. When using the URL Filtering feature, it's wise to present the user with a web page explaining why a particular site is blocked instead of simply dropping their HTTP request. If the latter happens, it usually just makes users think there's something wrong with their Internet connection.

And be warned—users who attempt to visit a page and experience a time-out or an unfriendly browser error message are going to get upset and call the help desk. Having the FireSIGHT System return a nice little web page notifying users that their attempts have been blocked is just so much better for everyone!

There are two available options for configuring the HTTP response on this tab—Block Response Page and Interactive Block Response Page—as shown in Figure 4.9.

FIGURE 4.9   HTTP response pages

Main AC Policy

Enter a description

| Rules | Targets (1) | Security Intelligence | **HTTP Responses** | Advanced |

Block Response Page
This page will be displayed when HTTP traffic is blocked.

| None | ▾ |

Interactive Block Response Page
This page will be displayed when HTTP traffic is blocked, but the user may choose to continue.

| Sourcefire-provided | ▾ | 🔍 |

Block Response Page

The Block Response Page will be returned anytime a user's HTTP request is blocked by a rule using either "Block" or "Block with reset actions." You have three options on this page: None, Sourcefire-Provided, and Custom, with the default being None. This means that if you use an Access Control rule to block a user's HTTP request, they won't get any information about why the page won't display. And if the rule doesn't include the reset action, the user will probably sit there watching their browser spin for a while before returning a browser-specific message telling them the site could not be loaded. These people will see a page similar to the one shown in Figure 4.10.

FIGURE 4.10   Sample browser time-out message

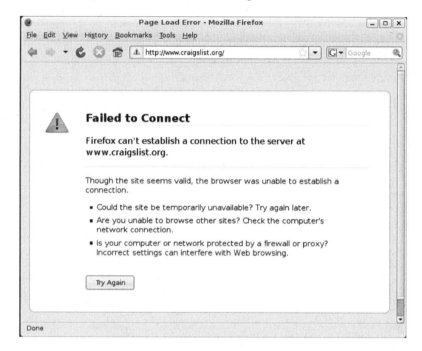

The message is saying that the site is unreachable and the user should try again later. This is just not something you want people to be greeted with. Users want to know what's going on and it just makes everyone so much happier when they receive at least a generic notification that the site was blocked—even more so when they get a nice customized response page. The default Sourcefire-provided response page is pictured in Figure 4.11.

FIGURE 4.11   Sourcefire block response

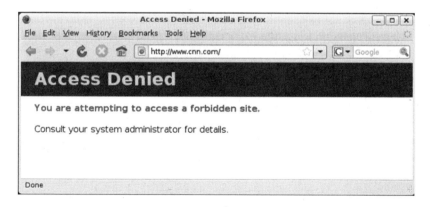

To select the standard Sourcefire response page, choose Sourcefire-Provided from the pull-down list. To view the page source, just click the magnifying glass icon next to the field.

If you want to customize the HTTP response, select Custom to load the existing page—Sourcefire-provided, by default—and edit or paste the HTML code you want. Take a look at Figure 4.12 to get a picture of this.

FIGURE 4.12 Edit Block Response Page dialog

Interactive Block Response Page

The *Interactive Block* response page is what will get returned anytime a user's HTTP request is intercepted by a rule using the Interactive Block or Interactive Block with reset action. This page functions a lot like the block response page we just talked about, with the only difference being that the Interactive Block rules give the user the option of proceeding to the site anyway. This is because Interactive Block response page includes a JavaScript-driven button that if clicked, allows the user to visit the blocked website.

The default Sourcefire-provided Interactive Block response page is shown in Figure 4.13.

FIGURE 4.13 Sourcefire Interactive Block page

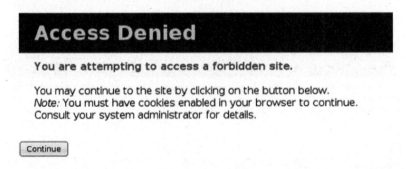

Once the user clicks the Continue button, they can load the blocked website. By default, the duration of this access is 600 seconds (10 minutes). After this period elapses, the Interactive Block page will reappear.

 Neither of the HTML response pages will work if the site blocked is using HTTPS!

Advanced Features

The Advanced tab shown in Figure 4.14 contains settings that aren't commonly modified in most installations, but we're going to go over them anyway because you just might need to use these tools at some point.

FIGURE 4.14   AC advanced settings

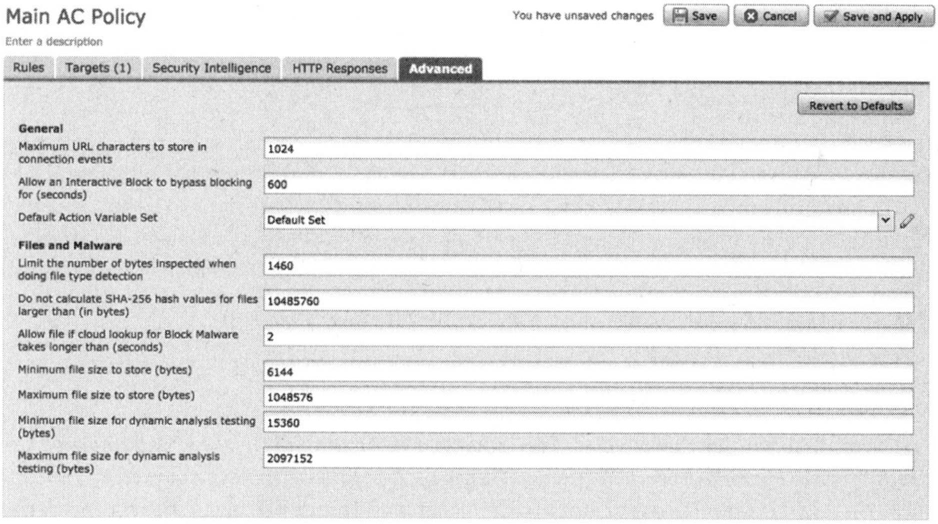

Main AC Policy
Enter a description

You have unsaved changes   [Save]   [Cancel]   [Save and Apply]

Rules   Targets (1)   Security Intelligence   HTTP Responses   **Advanced**

[Revert to Defaults]

General

Maximum URL characters to store in connection events	1024
Allow an Interactive Block to bypass blocking for (seconds)	600
Default Action Variable Set	Default Set

Files and Malware

Limit the number of bytes inspected when doing file type detection	1460
Do not calculate SHA-256 hash values for files larger than (in bytes)	10485760
Allow file if cloud lookup for Block Malware takes longer than (seconds)	2
Minimum file size to store (bytes)	6144
Maximum file size to store (bytes)	1048576
Minimum file size for dynamic analysis testing (bytes)	15360
Maximum file size for dynamic analysis testing (bytes)	2097152

The following options are under General Settings:

Maximum URL characters to store in connection events

Default: 1024

Maximum: 4096

This defines the maximum length of the field used to store URLs in HTTP connection events. Setting this value to zero disables the storing of URLs for connection events. It's good to know that reducing or disabling this setting can improve the system's performance if it's logging a huge amount of connection events.

Allow an Interactive Block to bypass blocking for (seconds)

>   Default: 600 (10 minutes)

>   Maximum: 31536000 (365 days)

This is the default time period during which a user can access a URL that triggered an Interactive Block rule. Time starts ticking when the user clicks the Continue button. Setting this value to zero requires the user to bypass the block using the Continue button for each request.

Default Action Variable Set

>   Default: Default Set

If the default action in the Access Control policy is an IPS policy, this setting will define the variable set the policy will use. You can choose any of the existing variable sets from the drop-down list. Clicking the pencil icon will load the variable set object page in a new tab and allow you to make changes or even create new variable sets.

>   The following options are under Files and Malware:

Limit the number of bytes inspected when doing file type detection.

>   Default: 1460 bytes or the maximum segment size of a TCP packet

>   Range: 0–4294967295 (4GB)

When performing file type detection, FireSIGHT looks for signatures near the beginning of the file. GIF files will always begin with the string GIF[8], and other file types like EXE or PDF also have similar telltale strings or byte patterns. This setting is used to limit the amount of bytes to be inspected, and the default size of 1460 is equivalent to the data segment of a typical Ethernet TCP packet. A value of zero completely removes the restriction.

Do not calculate SHA-256 hash values for files larger than (in bytes)

>   Default: 10485760 (10MB)

>   Range: 0–4294967295 (4GB)

This setting will prevent the system from storing, performing malware cloud lookups or blocking files larger than the specified size. This value must be greater than or equal to the settings for **Maximum file size to store (bytes)** and **Maximum file size for dynamic analysis testing (bytes)**. Setting this value to zero removes this size restriction.

At first blush, this looks like a good number to increase, right? After all, it seems like we're allowing malware larger than 10MB to prowl our network—isn't this just blowing a huge hole in our detection? The answer is yes and no... Yes in that it does mean we're not performing malware lookups on files larger than 10MB and 'no' because it turns out that 99.9 percent of all malware is actually under 10MB in size. So keeping the setting at that size helps preserve the device's detection resources by not requiring them to collect and calculate hashes for really big files. Yes, there's a risk, but statistically, really large files are extremely unlikely to contain malware, so higher settings really just drag down performance with little or no benefit to show for it.

Allow file if cloud lookup for Block Malware takes longer than (seconds)

Default: 2 seconds

Range: 0–30 seconds

This setting determines how long a device will hold on to the last piece of a file while waiting for the Defense Center to perform a malware cloud lookup on the SHA-256. It's used to prevent a long delay during a file transfer in case performing the cloud lookup holds things up. If the set time elapses with no response from the Defense Center, the device will allow the file transfer to be completed and register a disposition of Unavailable for the file's status. As with most settings, Sourcefire recommends leaving this at the default.

Minimum file size to store (bytes)

Default: 6144 (6KB)

Range: 0–10485760 (10MB)

This is the minimum file size that can be stored using a file rule. A setting of zero will totally disable file storage. Again, storing tiny files is a potential drain on system resources with dubious benefits. This field must be less than or equal to **Maximum file size to store (bytes)** and **Do not calculate SHA-256 hash values for files larger than (bytes)**.

Maximum file size to store (bytes)

Default: 10485760 (10MB)

Range: 0–10485760 (10MB)

The maximum file size that can be stored using a file rule, and again a setting of zero disables file storage. This one must be greater than or equal to **Minimum file size to store (bytes)** and less than or equal to **Do not calculate SHA-256 hash values for files larger than (bytes)**.

Minimum file size for dynamic analysis testing (bytes)

Default: 6144 (6KB)

Range: 6144 (6KB) to 2097152 (2MB)

The minimum file size the system will submit to the cloud for dynamic analysis. This field must be less than or equal to **Maximum file size for dynamic analysis testing (bytes)** and **Do not calculate SHA-256 hash values for files larger than (in bytes)**.

Maximum file size for dynamic analysis testing (bytes)

Default: 1048576 (1MB)

Range: 6144 (6KB) to 2097152 (2MB)

The maximum file size the system will submit to the cloud for dynamic analysis. This field must be greater than or equal to **Minimum file size for dynamic analysis testing (bytes)** and less than or equal to **Do not calculate SHA-256 hash values for files larger than (in bytes)**.

Access Control Rules

Congratulations—you've made it! You're now completely ready to learn all about the heart of the Access Control policy: the all-important rules. As traffic passes through the device, the Access Control policy decides whether to block it, let it pass unhindered, log it, or inspect it. Rule sets can range from very simple ones containing only a few entries to marathons of complexity comprising thousands of rules. Whether few or legion, these rules evaluate traffic from top to bottom, so keep in mind that their order is key. As traffic passes down through the rule set, it must match for any appropriate action to be taken. Most of the time, once a rule matches traffic, it won't continue diving down further into the set to match subsequent rules.

Clicking on the Rules tab will get you to the rule editing page, shown in Figure 4.15.

FIGURE 4.15   AC rules main page

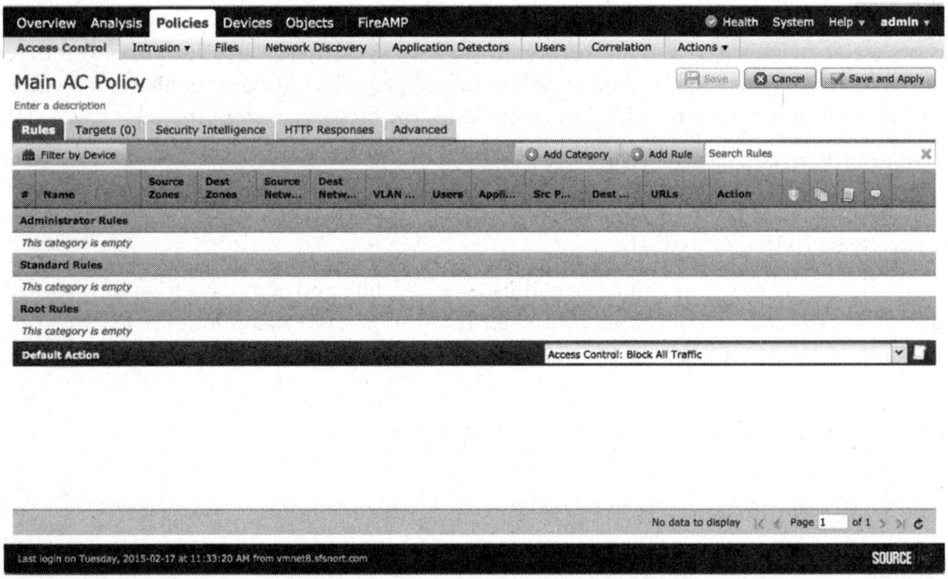

Access Control UI Elements

Okay, now let's talk about some of the buttons and features of the page displayed in Figure 4.15.

Filter by Device   This button allows you to filter the rules according to devices or device groups. This feature is helpful if you have a complex rule set because it lets you deploy the same policy to multiple devices. Filtering on a device will only reveal rules that include a zone component, which is present on the device or group selected. If the rule doesn't specify a zone, the system has no way of understanding which devices it may apply to.

Add Category   Access Control rules are placed into categories, and there are three of these by default, which we'll get to in a bit. For now you just need to know that the Add Category button allows you to add your own custom categories between the Administrator and Root categories. You can't change the default categories or modify the order of any existing categories.

Add Rule   Click this button to add a new AC rule.

Search Rules   This is another feature that comes in really handy when you're dealing with a large number of rules because it allows you to search the rule set using keywords. Rules containing the keyword search term you entered will be highlighted, and the search field will tell you how many rules match the search term as well.

Default Action   Making its appearance at the bottom of the rule set, the *Default Action* option is for configuring what the device will do if none of the Access Control rules above it match a given traffic flow. Clicking the drop-down field displays the available actions, which fall into four basic categories:

- Block All Traffic: Simply said, if traffic makes it this far, it will be blocked. This is typical for a deployment as a firewall.

- Trust All Traffic: Any traffic making it to this point gets let go with no further inspection.

- Network Discovery Only: Demands that traffic be inspected via the Network Discovery policy only.

- Intrusion Prevention: This will allow the traffic through after inspecting it with IPS and Network Discovery policies first. Depending on the IPS policy, some traffic could still be dropped if it matches an IPS rule that calls for the Drop and Generate action.

Logging Icon   Just to the right of the Default Action drop-down menu, you can see a tiny scroll. This controls the logging of traffic that matches the default action. Clicking this scroll icon displays the dialog shown in Figure 4.16.

FIGURE 4.16   AC default action logging

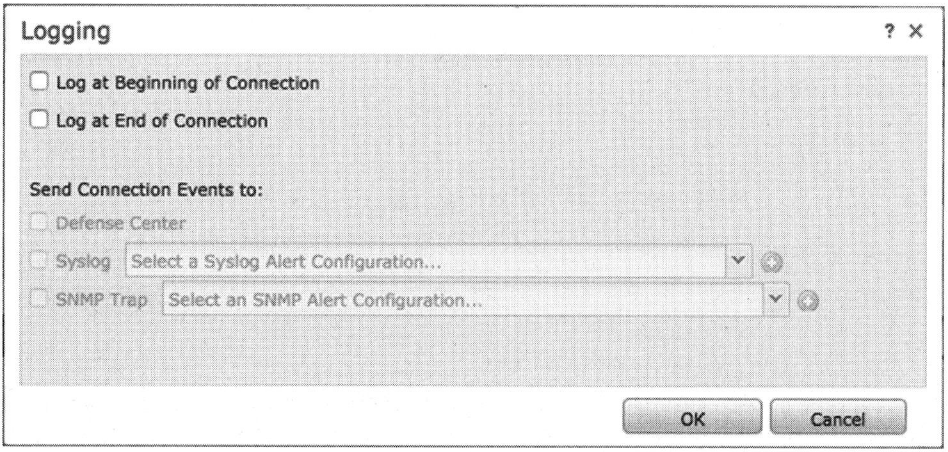

Here we're given options for logging connections to the Defense Center and, if we want to, via syslog or SNMP. The events logged as a result of checking these options are connection events. Bear in mind that in the default state, traffic that hits the default action will not generate a connection event. If you want connections logged for this traffic, you must check one or more of the options here. When you do that, the scroll icon will change from gray to blue.

Normally, you only need to log at the end of a connection. This will generate a connection event when the connection is terminated. The event will contain information like when the connection started, the number of packets and bytes, source and destination ports, IP addresses, and protocol. The Log at Beginning of Connection box is really meant for rules that block the connection. In this case, the connection is terminated prematurely by the IPS so a beginning event (the SYN in the case of TCP traffic) is all that is needed. Note that if you check both boxes, you will get two connection events for every non-blocked connection—one at the beginning and one at the end.

Rule Categories

Here's where we're going to dig deeper into rule categories because you need to be familiar with these before creating actual rules. By default, there are three: Administrator, Standard, and Root. As you're creating or editing rules, you can place them in any of these default categories with one condition—you've got to have the Administrator role to place rules in the Administrator category. Predictably, this is to prevent users without the Administrator role from inserting rules that could preempt an Administrator's rule.

Remember that regardless of their category, rules are always evaluated from top to bottom. When creating a new rule, the default practice is to put it in the Standard Rules category and if you want, you can even place all your rules there.

You can also add custom categories as mentioned earlier. To do that, click the Add Category button to reveal the dialog shown in Figure 4.17.

FIGURE 4.17 Add Category dialog

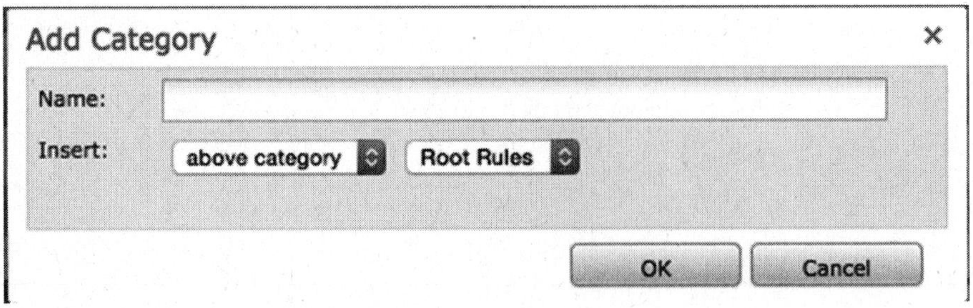

When adding a custom category, you give it a name and then choose where you want to insert it—either above a category or above/below an existing rule. Custom categories can only be placed between the Standard and Root default categories. It makes sense that the Above Rule or Below Rule option only appears if you have at least one rule in the policy already. Importantly, don't forget that once a custom category is added, it can't be moved, only renamed!

Adding Access Control Rules

To add a new Access Control rule, just click the Add Rule button to display the dialog shown in Figure 4.18.

FIGURE 4.18   AC Rule dialog

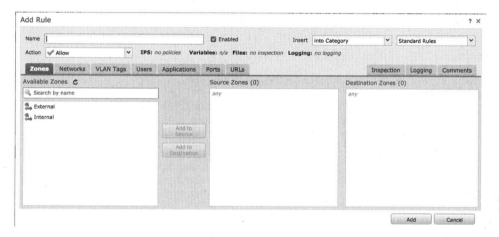

Rule Name and Action

The top portion of the dialog is where you give your rule a name, decide its execution priority, and determine the action.

Name   Enter the name of your rule, which can include any characters you want up to a maximum of 30. The Name field turns red if too many characters are entered.

Enabled   This box is checked by default, and unchecking it will leave the rule in the rule set in place but it won't be active. This comes in really handy when you want to remove a rule temporarily without completely deleting it.

Insert   This determines where the rule is placed in the rule set. As mentioned, by default, rules go into the Standard Rules category, and again, remember that once the policy contains at least one rule, you can choose to insert your rule above or below an existing one. To get this done, select Below Rule or Above Rule and enter the rule number to the right, as shown in Figure 4.19.

FIGURE 4.19 AC insert rule drop-down

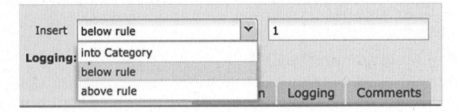

Action The rule action determines how traffic is affected. Clicking this drop-down displays the potential actions revealed in Figure 4.20.

FIGURE 4.20 AC rule actions

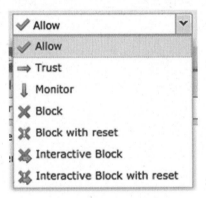

Allow: This action allows the matching traffic to pass through the device. You can optionally inspect this traffic using an IPS policy, a file policy, or both. Depending on the rules in these policies, some traffic could be blocked.

Trust: Trust allows traffic to pass without further inspection. This traffic won't be inspected by IPS, file, or discovery policy rules, but you can log connection events for it.

Monitor: This is the only action that doesn't actually affect traffic flow, meaning that matching traffic is not permitted, denied, or inspected. The only purpose of a Monitor rule is to log a connection event. Traffic matching a Monitor rule will result in a connection event and the traffic will proceed down the rule set, potentially matching another rule or the default action.

Block and Block with Reset: These two actions deny traffic without further inspection. The Block action simply stops the traffic from passing, while Block with Reset also resets the connection. Blocked traffic is not inspected via IPS, file, or discovery policy rules.

Interactive Block and Interactive Block with Reset: For HTTP traffic, these actions allow users to bypass a website block by clicking through the warning page. If the user does not bypass the block, the rule functions like a Block rule by denying traffic without further inspection. But if a user goes for it anyway and bypasses the block, the rule will work like an Allow rule, potentially performing IPS, file, and discovery inspection. These rules can be associated with IPS and file policies the same way that Allow rules can.

Rule Selection Criteria

There are seven tabs that control the criteria for matching traffic to a rule, and you can use as many of them needed to prompt the rules to match desired traffic. Each tab is treated as a logical AND operation. (Remember your CompSci 101 class where you learned about AND/OR operations?) For traffic to match this rule, it must match *all* the criteria entered in these tabs.

Zones   The Zones tab is used to limit the rule to traffic coming into or going out of specific physical interfaces. Remember—a *zone* is nothing more than a name given to one or more interfaces on a device. You can see two zones in Figure 4.21: Internal and External.

FIGURE 4.21   AC Zones tab

To select a given zone, click the zone name and add it to the Source Zones or Destination Zones column. You can specify a source or destination or even both. If you see a warning icon like the one shown here, it means the rule will be ineffective because the zone doesn't have any interfaces assigned.

Networks   This tab allows you to detail any combination of individual IP addresses, CIDR blocks, and prefix lengths. You can identify them specifically or use network objects and groups by choosing the appropriate objects and adding them to the Source Networks or Destination Networks column. You can also enter an IP address or CIDR block directly below either of these columns and click the Add button.

Clicking the Geolocation tab reveals available geolocation objects. Any combination of individual countries and continents can be used and added to the Source and Destination columns. The Networks tab is shown in Figure 4.22.

FIGURE 4.22 AC Networks tab

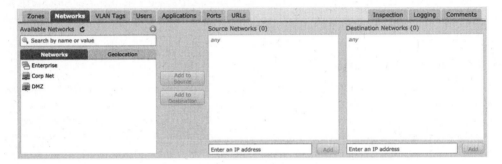

VLAN Tags This tab allows you to specify a number from 0 to 4094 to identify a network by VLAN. You can use objects you've created or enter VLAN numbers directly below the Selected VLAN Tags column, as shown in Figure 4.23.

FIGURE 4.23 AC VLAN Tags tab

Users This tab allows you to specify which users your rule should apply to, with users and groups being retrieved from a Microsoft Active Directory server. Before you can use this condition, you must configure a connection between your Defense Center and at least one Microsoft AD server. This "authentication object" contains settings and filters for populating the Available Users column on this page. This will be covered in the chapter on account management. Check out the Users tab in Figure 4.24.

FIGURE 4.24   AC Users tab

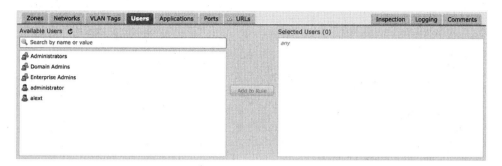

Applications   The Applications tab makes it possible to filter your rule based on applications provided by Sourcefire, user-defined applications, and any application filters you created in the Object Manager. You'll find the same application criteria—Risks, Business Relevance, Types, etc.—that were in the Object Manager plus any user-created filters previously added. The Applications tab is shown in the Figure 4.25.

FIGURE 4.25   AC Applications tab

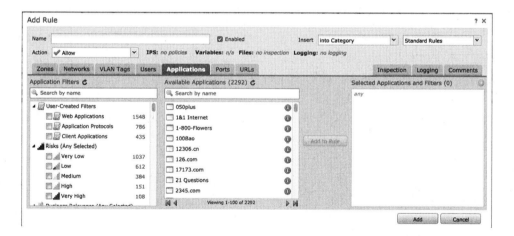

Ports   This tab is predictably used to specify the source and/or destination ports for your rule, which you can select from one of the previously created or default port objects. At the bottom of the Source and Destination columns, you can alternately select the protocol and port, as shown in Figure 4.26.

FIGURE 4.26 Ports tab

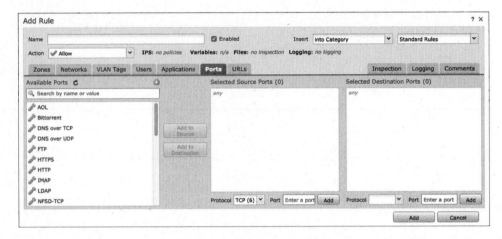

Note that the ports in the Selected Destination Ports column are different than the ports in the Selected Source Ports column because the source column allows only TCP and UDP while the Protocol drop-down under the destination column includes virtually all of the possible 255 IP protocol IDs. For some protocols, such as ICMP, you can even select additional data such as type and code, as shown in Figure 4.27.

FIGURE 4.27 ICMP types and codes

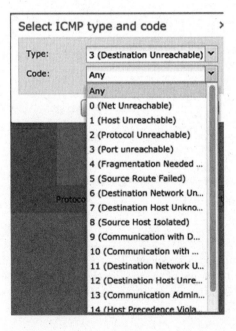

URLs   The URLs tab allows filtering based on Sourcefire-provided categories and reputations as well as user-created URL objects. You can also enter a URL in the field at the bottom of the Selected URLs column and add it here. Remember that the URLs you enter are treated as a substring match, meaning that if the text you enter is found anywhere in the URL, the rule will match. Check out the URLs tab in Figure 4.28.

FIGURE 4.28   URLs tab

Inspection, Logging, and Comments

The three tabs on the right side of the Add Rule dialog offer even more rule settings. They're used to define the type of inspection the rule provides, if connection events will be logged or not, plus you can enter additional comments.

Inspection   This is how to control how traffic that matches this rule will be inspected. Notice that all the options on this tab are unavailable (grayed out) for the rule actions: Trust, Monitor, Block, and Block with Reset. This is because these rules don't allow for IPS, file, or malware traffic inspection. The only rule actions this tab enables are Allow, Interactive Block, and Interactive Block with Reset. The Inspection tab is shown in Figure 4.29.

Use the drop-down fields to specify the intrusion policy, the variable set, and the file policy that will be employed to inspect the traffic. Bear in mind that none of these are required—you can perform file and/or IPS inspection, even no inspection at all. Selecting a file policy automatically enables and selects the File Events: Log Files check box on the Inspection tab.

Logging   The Logging tab controls the behavior of connection and file event logging. It's important to remember that the settings here will not affect logging for IPS or malware events because these will be logged based on the IPS and file policies. Generally, if an IPS rule triggers or malware is discovered, the appropriate event will be logged regardless of the settings selected here. The AC Logging tab is shown in Figure 4.30.

FIGURE 4.29 Inspection tab

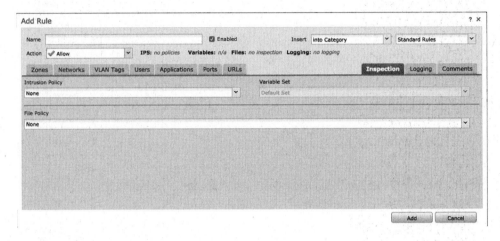

FIGURE 4.30 Logging tab

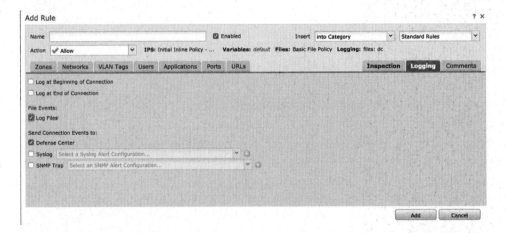

You can see that different portions of this tab are grayed out depending on the rule action and inspection criteria:

If your rule action is Allow, Interactive Block, or Interactive Block with Reset, you can select all the check boxes enabled if your rule includes IPS and file inspection.

If your rule action is Monitor, the Log At End Of Connection box will be checked and grayed out. Log Files is unavailable too, and so is Log At Beginning Of Connection.

If your rule includes a Block or Block with Reset action, the only logging option available will be Log At Beginning Of Connection.

And finally, if the rule action is Trust, you have options to log at the beginning and the end of the connection.

You probably also noticed that there are options to log connection events to the Defense Center as well as syslog and SNMP trap destinations. In most cases, only the Defense Center is selected, but sometimes you might want to add an additional logging destination. To do that, just check the syslog and/or SNMP logging options and choose a destination from the drop-down list. It's vital that you have a previously created syslog or SNMP destination to use this feature. You can also use the green plus icon to create a destination on-the-fly here. Note that syslog or SNMP messages will be generated by the device where the policy is applied.

> Throughout the Access Control policy, you'll find options for logging to SNMP or syslog. Don't forget that if these alerts are selected, they'll be sent from the device, *not* from the Defense Center.

Comments   Use this tab to add rule comments as shown in Figure 4.31. Because the rule name is limited to 30 characters, this tab comes in handy for documenting a rule's purpose. Clicking the New Comment button will get you to a dialog where you can type in a lengthy comment if you want to. Your comment will automatically be stamped with the date and user.

FIGURE 4.31   Comments tab

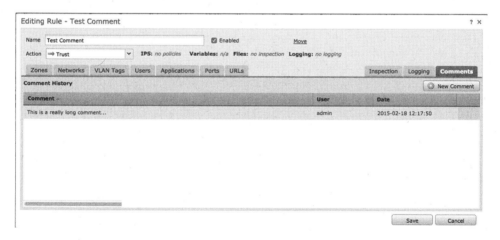

A Simple Policy

Access Control policies can contain from just a few rules up to thousands of them. We could continue with numerous examples, but doing that is beyond the scope of this book.

Figure 4.32 displays a simple policy where all connections are logged via a Monitor rule, inappropriate web apps are blocked, and all traffic is inspected by IPS and file policies via two Allow rules.

FIGURE 4.32   Access Control rules example

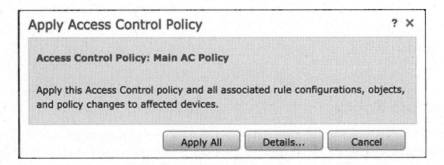

Saving and Applying

It sounds simple, but don't forget to use the Save or Save And Apply button in the upper right when your policy is ready to be saved and/or applied to a device. Choosing Save simply saves the current policy and leaves you at the edit page; clicking Save And Apply saves the policy and then displays the Apply Access Control Policy dialog, shown in Figure 4.33.

FIGURE 4.33   Apply Access Control Policy dialog

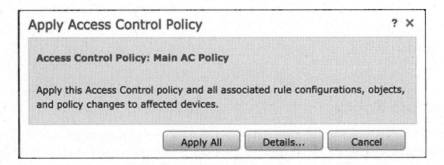

Clicking the Details button in the Apply Access Control Policy dialog will display another dialog revealing the devices and the policies that will be applied to them. It shows which Access Control or IPS policies are out-of-date and will be updated. Keep in mind that if an Access Control policy has been changed but the device already has an up-to-date IPS policy, only the Access Control policy will be applied. Optionally, you can control which policies are applied by using the check boxes in this dialog, but it's usually a good idea to let the system apply the policies automatically. See Figure 4.34 for an example of the Details dialog.

FIGURE 4.34   The Details dialog

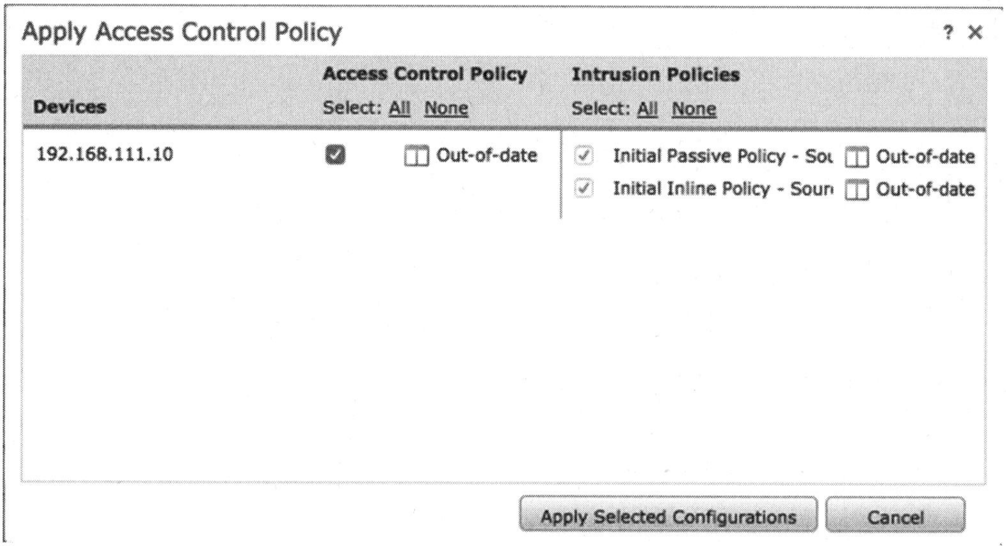

When you finally click the apply button, you'll receive a confirmation dialog with a Task Status link to monitor the apply task; it's shown in Figure 4.35.

FIGURE 4.35   Apply Policy dialog

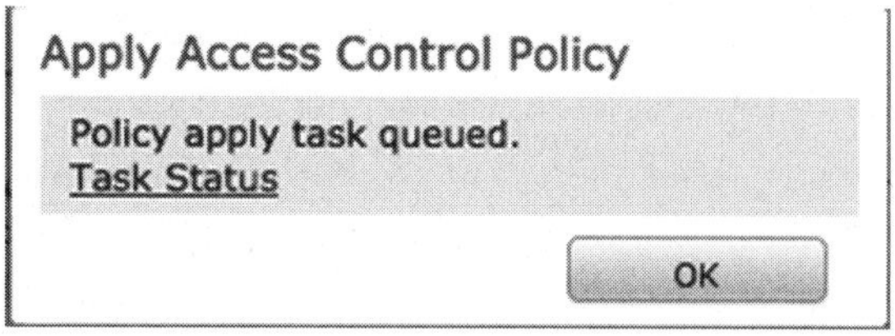

Congratulations, you have now learned how to use the "mother of all policies." Hopefully you can see now how the Access Control policy is the central rule set that dictates the inspection and logging for all packets processed by a device.

Summary

In this chapter, we covered the use of the Access Control policy in the FireSIGHT System, including the following important objectives and features:

- Access Control policy overview
- Getting started with Access Control policies
- Security Intelligence
- HTTP responses
- Advanced features
- Access Control rules
- Saving and applying an Access Control policy

If you're a little foggy about any of these items, you really need to go back to the corresponding section and make sure you've got it nailed before moving on!

Hands-on Lab

In this lab, you will create the simple Access Control policy that you saw at the end of the chapter.

1. Open your web browser and HTTPS to your Defense Center.
2. Log in to the Defense Center.
3. Navigate to Policies ➤ Access Control.
4. Click the New Policy button.
5. Name your policy (be creative).
6. Leave Default Action at Block All Traffic; you will change this later.
7. Select a target device and click the Add To Policy button.
8. Click the Save button to proceed to the Access Control Policy Editor.
9. Click the Security Intelligence tab.
10. Click the scroll icon to the right of the Blacklist column, and then check the Log Connections box.

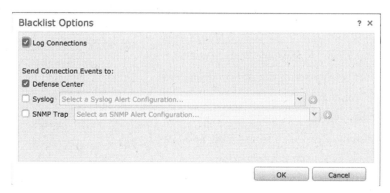

11. Click OK.

12. Click the HTTP Responses tab.

13. In the Block Response Page drop-down, select Sourcefire-Provided.

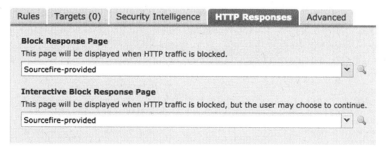

14. Click the Rules tab.

15. Click Add Rule.

16. Name this rule "Log all traffic."

17. Select Monitor from the Action drop-down. Note that the Logging tab is bold. Clicking this tab reveals that the Log At End Of Connection box is checked.

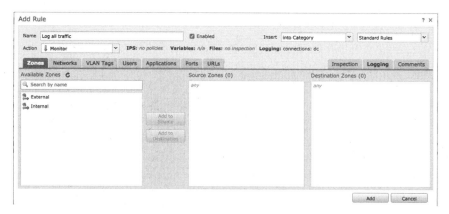

18. Click the Add button to add the rule to the policy

19. Click Add Rule again to add the Web App rule.

20. Name your rule "Undesirable Web Apps."

21. Select Block with reset in the Action drop-down.

22. Click the Applications tab.

23. Under Risks, check High and Very High.

24. Under Business Relevance, check Low and Very Low.

25. Under Types, check Web Application.

26. Under Available Applications, ensure that the line selected is "All apps matching the filter" and click the Add To Rule button.

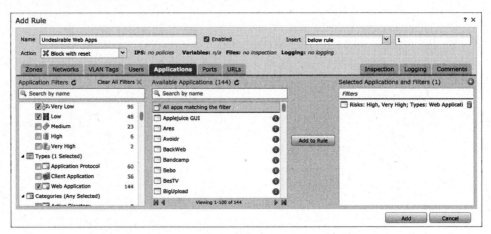

27. On the Logging tab, check Log at Beginning of Connection. Note that the Log at End of Connection check box is grayed out.

28. Click the Add button to add the rule to the policy.

29. Click Add Rule to add another rule to perform IPS inspection.

30. Name your rule something catchy.

31. Leave the Action drop-down at the default of Allow.

32. Select one of your available zones; in our example, we have zones named External and Internal. Add it to the Source Zones column.

33. Click the Inspection tab and select an intrusion policy. Optionally, if you have a file policy, select it in the File Policy drop-down.

There is no need to enable logging here because we are already logging connections with our Monitor rule.

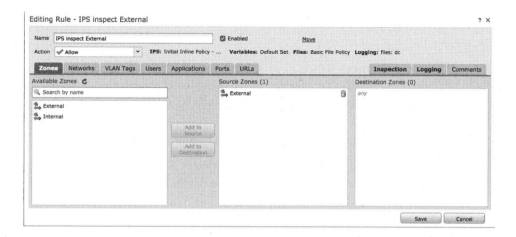

34. If desired, you can add additional Allow rules for any remaining zones

35. Under Default Action, select Intrusion Prevention, and choose either a Sourcefire or user-created intrusion policy.

NOTE   There is no need to enable the logging scroll by Default Action because we are already logging connections with our Monitor rule.

Your policy should look something like the image shown here.

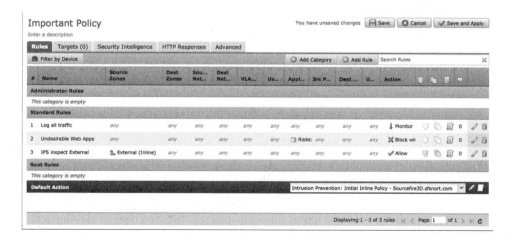

36. Click Save to save your policy.

Exam Essentials

Be familiar with the network option in an AC policy rule. You can select one or more source, destination network objects or groups. You can also enter IP address information directly into a rule if you haven't created a network object.

Understand your options for geolocation. You can use geolocation criteria to apply rules to traffic based on source or destination IP by country and/or continent.

Understand where external log events will be generated. If you enable syslog or SNMP alerting in your AC policy, these alerts will be generated by the device, not by the Defense Center.

Know your options for URL filtering. URL filtering is available via rules you create in the AC policy. Simply create an AC rule, and on the URLs tab, add the URL or URL categories you wish to block or allow.

Review Questions

You can find the answers in Appendix A.

1. When either SNMP or syslog logging options are selected, alerts are sent from
   _____.

   A. The managed device

   B. The Defense Center

   C. FireSIGHT

   D. The syslog server

2. Which rule action will permit traffic to pass through a device and optionally include intrusion and/or file inspection?

   A. Allow

   B. Monitor

   C. Trust

   D. Inspect

3. Which rule action will block an HTTP request but still allow the user to override and proceed to the site if desired?

   A. Block with reset

   B. Conditional Allow

   C. Trust

   D. Interactive Block

4. What methods are available to add IPs to the Sourcefire global blacklist or global whitelist?

   A. Edit the text file.

   B. Right-click on an IP address in an event view.

   C. Click an interactive graph in Context Explorer.

   D. B and C

   E. All of the above

5. When adding a source port to a rule, which protocols are allowed?

   A. Any IP protocol

   B. TCP only

   C. UDP only

   D. UDP and TCP

6. By default, what is the maximum number of URL characters stored for a connection event?

   A. 128

   B. 512

    C. 768

    D. 1024

7. What is the best method to ensure that access to a website is blocked and provide the user with a descriptive HTTP response?

    A. Create a Block rule, specify the website, and enable logging.

    B. Create an Allow rule, and specify an IPS policy that contains a Snort rule blocking the website.

    C. Create an Interactive Block rule for the site, and specify an HTTP response on the HTTP Responses tab.

    D. Create a Block rule for the site, and specify an HTTP response on the HTTP Responses tab.

8. Which rule action does not take any action on the traffic?

    A. Trust

    B. Allow

    C. Monitor

    D. Inspect Only

9. When configuring options on the Network tab in an Access Control rule, which of the following is true?

    A. You must enter an IP address manually.

    B. To restrict to an IP and port, use the syntax IP:Port.

    C. You can select from a preconfigured object or add an IP address manually.

    D. You cannot include multiple network objects in the source or destination columns.

10. How many Access Control policies can be applied to a single managed device?

    A. 1

    B. 2

    C. 5

    D. This is device dependent.

Chapter

5

FireSIGHT Technologies

THE SSFIPS EXAM TOPICS COVERED IN THIS CHAPTER INCLUDE THE FOLLOWING:

✓ **5.1   Understand the discovery component inside FireSIGHT, including the policy configuration and the data collected**

✓ **5.2   Understand the type of data collected by connection events with FireSIGHT**

✓ **5.3   Understand the user information that is discovered with FireSIGHT**

We've arrived at the perfect point in this book to introduce you to FireSIGHT. Once you've been acquainted with this awesome technology, we'll move on to explore discovery components like the policy, type of data collected, connection events, and host attributes associated with it. By the end of this chapter, you'll have gained sharp insight into exactly how FireSIGHT is used to powerfully enhance event analysis.

To find up-to-the-minute updates for this chapter, please see www.lammle.com/firepower or the book's web page at www.sybex.com.

FireSIGHT Technologies

FireSIGHT is the name given to a technology built into the Cisco FirePOWER NGIPS to provide us with contextual awareness regarding events, IP addresses, users on the network, and even background about the hosts in the system. It will collect information about each IP address and build a host profile that includes the operating system, services, applications users, and network connections. FireSIGHT will even include assumed vulnerabilities in profiles based upon those factors and additional data it has collected. This information is then used to automatically present an impact flag in the IPS analysis views to indicate whether or not the systems involved in the IPS events are susceptible to threats.

All of this vital intelligence is gained as a result of analyzing the packets on the wire and leveraging patented passive fingerprinting technology. For this to happen, either packets must traverse the managed device or the device must actually see the traffic itself during passive deployments.

A key benefit to this automated collection process is that it requires no additional software and doesn't probe the network. Furthermore, the more traffic that's seen moving to and from hosts, the more accurate the information entered into the database will be. And if that's not enough, you can even supplement the FireSIGHT information with active techniques.

On the other hand, when there's a limited amount of traffic to collect, we can leverage the host input API—a strategy that allows us to import data from a separated values file, Nmap, or even third-party vulnerability scanners. So during feast or famine, we're good either way!

Network Discovery Policy

The *network discovery policy* is configured on the FireSIGHT Manager and controls FireSIGHT technology. There's one discovery policy per Defense Center, and it should be specific to the environment it's being deployed in. To configure the policy, navigate to Policies ➢ Network Discovery. Figure 5.1 shows the default network discovery policy.

FIGURE 5.1 Network discovery policy

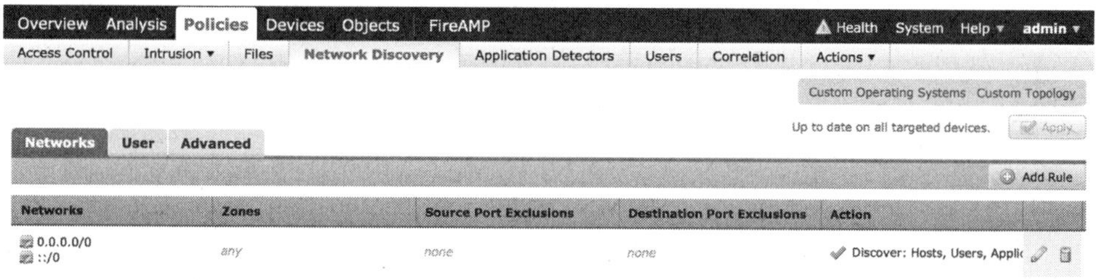

There are three main tabs across the top of the policy:

Network—Allows you to define the IP addresses on which you want to perform discovery.

User—Includes a list of protocols to discover users.

Advanced—Contains a variety of settings used to tweak the discovery settings.

Networks

The default discovery takes place on all IPv4 and IPv6 networks as noted with specified networks 0.0.0. 0/0 and ::/0. So if we see a packet originating to and from anywhere, a host profile will start being generated for the IP addresses involved. The more paranoid among us will be tempted to track absolutely everything, but understand that the Defense Center is licensed based on model type to only handle a certain number of hosts. For instance, the FireSIGHT 750 is set to a maximum of 2,000 hosts, but the FireSIGHT 4000 can handle 600,000 hosts. Considering that the clients on your internal network could easily be communicating to hundreds of web IP addresses each, your license could max out its limit pretty fast—choose wisely!

The good news here is that you can modify or delete the built-in rule and even add rules to create a specialized policy ideally suited to your particular environment's needs. Take a look at Figure 5.2. It is showing some of the options available for the rules. So if licensing worries are keeping you up at night, just create rules limiting discovery to the high-value networks in your organization. By adding rules like this, you're basically entering guidance to either discover or exclude individual IP addresses, networks, or network objects. You can also configure discovery based on zones.

FIGURE 5.2   Network discovery rule

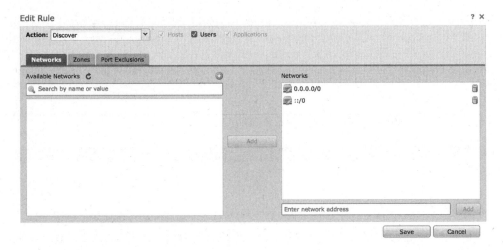

Another way to free up some resources is to exclude specific ports from discovery. You can also exclude protocols that probably aren't really that important to keep track of because they're unlikely to contain threat data.

While you can specify whether user or host information is collected, application inspection is automatically set to *on* because the FirePOWER system is designed to be application aware. So just because there's check box that makes it look like you can deselect it, you really can't. You also don't get to deselect host discovery unless user discovery is also deselected.

User Discovery

Figure 5.3 shows the User tab. This tab allows you to focus on the specific protocols on which you want to detect user logins, enabling or disabling them at will. But here again, the number of users is restricted just as it was with IP addresses based upon the Defense Center model. And restricting the protocols up for detection here is helpful for managing your license count. The following protocols are supported:

- AIM
- IMAP
- LDAP
- Oracle
- POP3
- SIP

You can also pick up users from Active Directory, but that's handled through an agent and configured elsewhere.

FIGURE 5.3 User tab

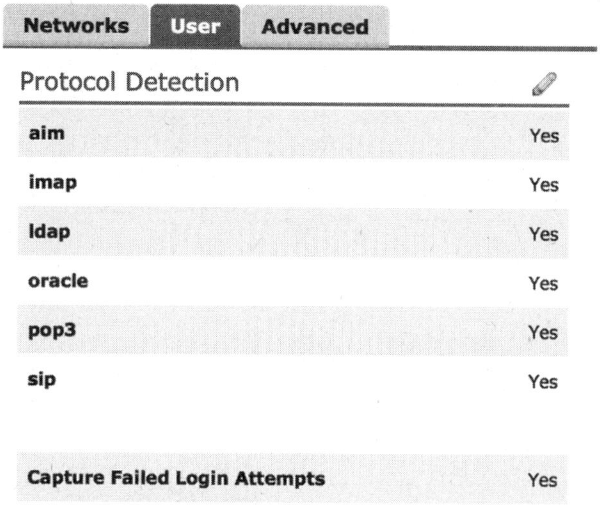

Networks	**User**	Advanced

Protocol Detection	✎
aim	Yes
imap	Yes
ldap	Yes
oracle	Yes
pop3	Yes
sip	Yes

Capture Failed Login Attempts	Yes

Advanced Discovery Settings

The Advanced tab, shown in Figure 5.4, contains settings key to tweaking the actual inspection being performed on the traffic. Here's a list of the sections into which these settings are sorted:

- General Settings
- Identity Conflict Settings
- Vulnerabilities to use for Impact Assessment
- Indications of Compromise Settings
- NetFlow Devices
- Network Discovery Data Storage Settings
- Event Logging Settings
- OS and Server Identity Sources

General Settings

In the General Settings section, you'll find the Capture Banners and Update Interval options. Capture Banners is off by default, but you can enable it to collect the protocol banners for an array of services. Update Interval is set to 3600 seconds by default and specifies how often to refresh data in the database, such as the last time an application was seen, the last time an IP address was seen, how many times a certain protocol was used, and so on. Setting Update Interval to a lower value would display more recent info on the Defense Center, but predictably, that can also result in more overhead.

FIGURE 5.4 Discovery policy advanced tab

Networks	User	**Advanced**

General Settings	✎		Network Discovery Data Storage Settings	✎
Capture Banners	No		**When Host Limit Reached**	Drop hosts
Update Interval	3600		**Host Timeout (minutes)**	10080
			Server Timeout (minutes)	10080
Identity Conflict Settings	✎		**Client Timeout (minutes)**	10080
Generate Identity Conflict	No			
Automatically Resolve Conflicts	(Disabled)			

Vulnerabilities to use for Impact Assessment	✎		Event Logging Settings	✎
Use Network Discovery Vulnerability Mappings	Yes		All events enabled.	
Use Third-Party Vulnerability Mappings	Yes			

Indications of Compromise Settings	✎
Enabled	Yes
Rules	31 / 31

OS and Server Identity Sources	✎	
Name	**Type**	**Timeout**
Nmap	Scanner	0 hours

NetFlow Devices	⊕
NetFlow Device	

Identity Conflict Settings

Identity conflicts can crop up if you're leveraging third-party data like Nmap, host input, and so on for information about the host OSs in your environment. When the data gathered with FireSIGHT conflicts with data from these third-party sources, you can generate an alert indicating that a conflict has occurred. Conflicts can be manually resolved in the host profiles or resolved automatically based on which options you select, such as Keep The Passive Information From FireSIGHT or Use The Active Information From Other Sources.

Vulnerabilities to Use for Impact Assessment

One of FireSIGHT's most beneficial features is its ability to automatically correlate vulnerability information with intrusion data. By leveraging this information, you can quickly eliminate false positives from analysis. You can choose to discontinue this feature with FireSIGHT or third-party vulnerability mappings, but we strongly recommend not doing that!

Indications of Compromise Settings

Indications of compromise (IOC) offer another way to make hosts stand out in analysis. Figure 5.5 shows some of the indications of compromise that are enabled by default. This set includes 31 different kinds of rules, which perform important correlations by analyzing data about IPS, vulnerability, file activity, security intelligence, or malware events to indicate a "compromised host." Compromised hosts will show up in any analysis view with a red icon instead of a normal, blue one, making them easy to spot. You can disable these rules individually if you want to.

FIGURE 5.5   Indications of compromise rules

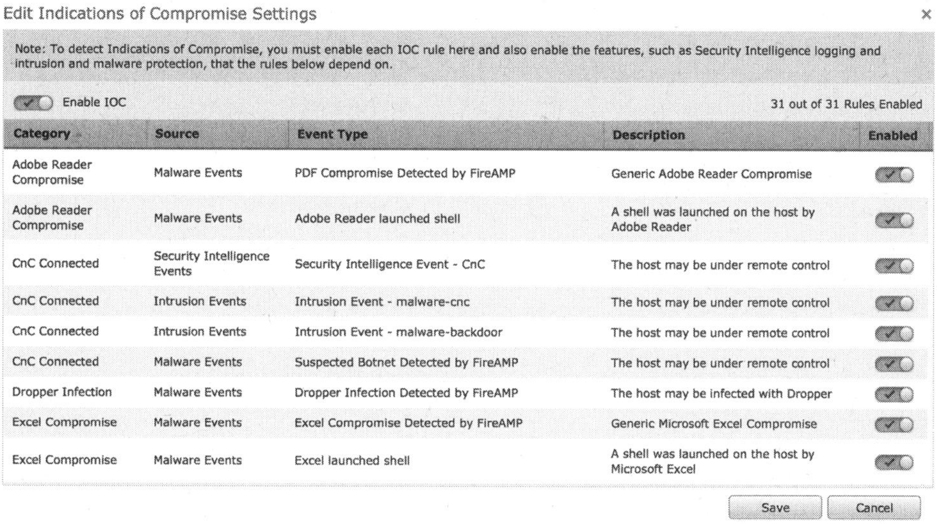

Edit Indications of Compromise Settings   ✕

Note: To detect Indications of Compromise, you must enable each IOC rule here and also enable the features, such as Security Intelligence logging and intrusion and malware protection, that the rules below depend on.

Enable IOC   31 out of 31 Rules Enabled

Category	Source	Event Type	Description	Enabled
Adobe Reader Compromise	Malware Events	PDF Compromise Detected by FireAMP	Generic Adobe Reader Compromise	●
Adobe Reader Compromise	Malware Events	Adobe Reader launched shell	A shell was launched on the host by Adobe Reader	●
CnC Connected	Security Intelligence Events	Security Intelligence Event - CnC	The host may be under remote control	●
CnC Connected	Intrusion Events	Intrusion Event - malware-cnc	The host may be under remote control	●
CnC Connected	Intrusion Events	Intrusion Event - malware-backdoor	The host may be under remote control	●
CnC Connected	Malware Events	Suspected Botnet Detected by FireAMP	The host may be under remote control	●
Dropper Infection	Malware Events	Dropper Infection Detected by FireAMP	The host may be infected with Dropper	●
Excel Compromise	Malware Events	Excel Compromise Detected by FireAMP	Generic Microsoft Excel Compromise	●
Excel Compromise	Malware Events	Excel launched shell	A shell was launched on the host by Microsoft Excel	●

Save   Cancel

NetFlow Devices

If you have NetFlow devices in your environment, you can export information from them to your FireSIGHT device to supplement connection information. Keep in mind that the IP addresses involved will deduct from your license count, so again, choose wisely!

Network Discovery Data Storage Settings

These two settings deal primarily with the retention of data in the following two ways:

When Host Limit Reached—When you reach your host license limit, you can choose to either drop newly detected hosts or overwrite older ones. The default is to drop new hosts.

Host, Server, and Client Timeout—This time-out occurs in minutes, indicating when you would like to remove information from the database. If one of the items hasn't been seen for the length of the specified time-out value, the information will be removed. The default time is 10080 minutes, or seven days.

Event Logging Settings

There are 33 different types of data that can be logged with FireSIGHT and 20 different settings that can be leveraged through the host input API. All of them are enabled by default, but these data types can be turned off or on as needed. Figure 5.6 displays these settings.

FIGURE 5.6   Event logging settings

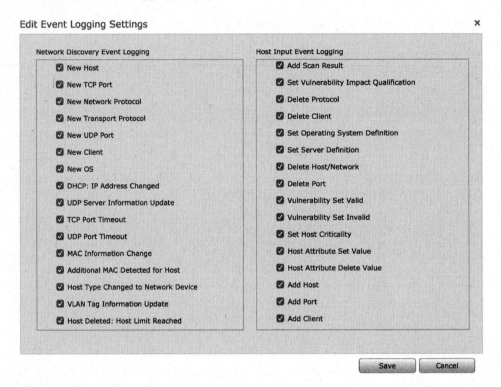

OS and Server Identity Sources

This is where you can add additional sources of host identities like Nmap or other third-party applications. You can also specify a time period after which the data becomes stale and the other identity sources take priority over it.

Keep in mind that once you have made changes to the policy, you need to click the Apply button in the upper right portion of the interface to make them stick.

Discovery Information

Once the discovery policy is created and applied, the managed devices begin sending information to the Defense Center. This information can be viewed in many different ways, but to get started, we're going to take a look at Analysis ➤ Hosts, as shown in Figure 5.7

FIGURE 5.7   Host event views

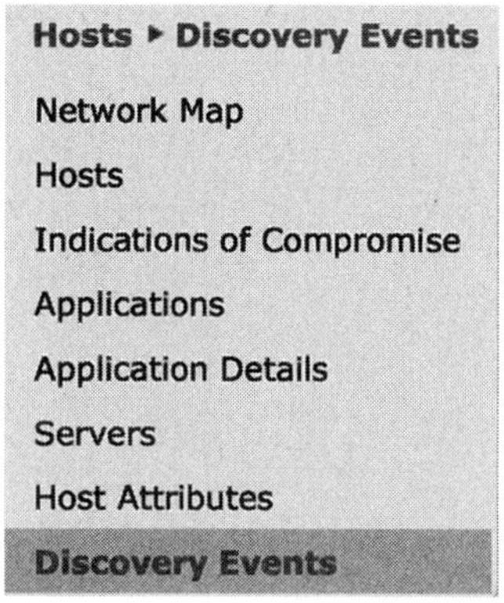

The following views are available:

Network Map—A tree view of all IP hosts discovered on the network, broken out by subnet. You can also type in an IPv4 or IPv6 address/subnet at the top of the list to view information on specific hosts/networks.

Hosts—A listing of hosts organized by operating system.

Indications of Compromise—A listing of the IOC that have been triggered by category.

Applications—A list of applications along with the number of hosts the applications have been detected on.

Application Details—An inventory of detected application client software and web applications.

Servers—An inventory of application server types along with the application vendors.

Host Attributes—An index of hosts by attribute, which are user-created definable fields. We'll describe these fields more a bit later.

Discovery Events—A list of items that were either seen for the first time (discovery events) or changed in the database (change events).

Discovery Events

Discovery events are a great way to find out exactly what's popped up on your network. You can create searches based on subnets and event types that will present you with a list of hosts based on their first appearance on the network or network segment, as seen in Figure 5.8.

Doing this would get you results like the list shown in Figure 5.9.

When you click on any of the items in this list, you're actually drilling down in a workflow. This is also restricting the view to the items you've selected. Ultimately you'll arrive at a host profile.

FIGURE 5.8 Creating an event search

Search Information

Note: If a search name is not specified, an automatically generated name will be used.

Table	Discovery Events ⌄	
Name		Search 1, My Search
Save As Private	☑	

Constraint

Event	New Host	New, Change
MAC Address		0A:BB:CD:AF:5F:07
MAC Vendor		"VMware, Inc.", Virtual_MAC_Vendor
IP Address	192.168.1.0/24	192.168.1.0/24, !192.168.1.3, 2001:db8:85a3::1370
User		jsmith
Port		1-1024, 6000-6011, !80
Description		HTTP
Device		device1.example.com, *.example.com, 192.168.1.3

[Search] [Save As New Search] [Cancel]

FIGURE 5.9 Newly discovered hosts

Host Profile

The *host profile* contains the most detail about a system, and you can get to it from any of the analysis views. Take a look at Figure 5.10 and Figure 5.11. The host profile will serve up detailed information about the IP address, hostname, indications of compromise, applications, services, attributes and potential vulnerabilities that exist on the hosts.

FIGURE 5.10   Host profile

Host Profile

| | | | | Scan Host | Generate White List Profile |

IP Addresses	**192.168.1.230**
	fe80::aabb:cfff:fe21:37ce
NetBIOS Name	MACBOOKPRO-4260
Device (Hops)	Sourcefire3D (31)
MAC Addresses (TTL)	**A8:BB:CF:21:37:CE (Apple) (255)**
Host Type	Host
Last Seen	2015-03-23 16:19:56
Current User	
View	Context Explorer	Connection Events	Intrusion Events	File Events	Malware Events

Indications of Compromise (0)   Edit Rule States

Operating System ▾   Edit Operating System

Vendor	Product	Version	Source
Apple	Mac OSX	10.8, 10.8.1, 10.8.2, Server 10.8, Server 10.8.1, Server 10.8.2	FireSIGHT

Applications (11) ▾

Application Protocol	Client	Version	Web Application		
☐ HTTP	☐ Mac App Store	1.2	☐ Apple sites		
☐ HTTP	☐ OCSPD	1.0	☐ Apple sites		
☐ HTTPS	☐ SSL client		☐ Apple sites		
☐ HTTP	☐ Safari	6.0	☐ Bing		
☐ HTTP	☐ OCSPD	1.0	☐ CR List		
☐ HTTP	☐ Safari	6.0	☐ Google Safebrowsing		

FIGURE 5.11   Host profile (continued)

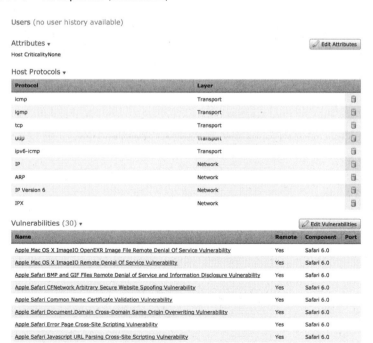

Users (no user history available)

Attributes ▾   Edit Attributes
Host CriticalityNone

Host Protocols ▾

Protocol	Layer	
icmp	Transport	
igmp	Transport	
tcp	Transport	
uup	Transport	
ipv6-icmp	Transport	
IP	Network	
ARP	Network	
IP Version 6	Network	
IPX	Network	

Vulnerabilities (30) ▾   Edit Vulnerabilities

Name	Remote	Component	Port
Apple Mac OS X ImageIO OpenEXR Image File Remote Denial Of Service Vulnerability	Yes	Safari 6.0	
Apple Mac OS X ImageIO Remote Denial Of Service Vulnerability	Yes	Safari 6.0	
Apple Safari BMP and GIF Files Remote Denial of Service and Information Disclosure Vulnerability	Yes	Safari 6.0	
Apple Safari CFNetwork Arbitrary Secure Website Spoofing Vulnerability	Yes	Safari 6.0	
Apple Safari Common Name Certificate Validation Vulnerability	Yes	Safari 6.0	
Apple Safari Document.Domain Cross-Domain Same Origin Overwriting Vulnerability	Yes	Safari 6.0	
Apple Safari Error Page Cross-Site Scripting Vulnerability	Yes	Safari 6.0	
Apple Safari Javascript URL Parsing Cross-Site Scripting Vulnerability	Yes	Safari 6.0	

Connection Events

Devices can also collect connection data, and you can check out the events by going to Analysis ➢ Connection Events. By doing that, you'll get information about protocols, applications, bytes transferred, URLs, and more, as shown in Figure 5.12. But keep in mind that the data will be found here only if the appropriate logging is enabled in the Access Control policy.

FIGURE 5.12   Connection events

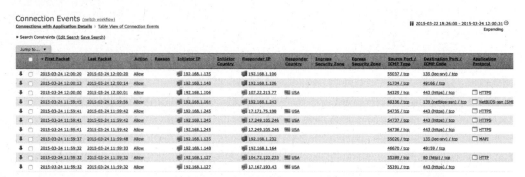

One of the very cool things you can do with this information is look at it in the context of different workflows. Choosing Switch Workflows next to Connection Events will get you the options shown in Figure 5.13.

FIGURE 5.13   Connection event workflows

Figure 5.14 shows an example of the Traffic Over Time workflow. The graphs are interactive, and you can drill down on individual elements by clicking them.

FIGURE 5.14   Traffic Over Time workflow

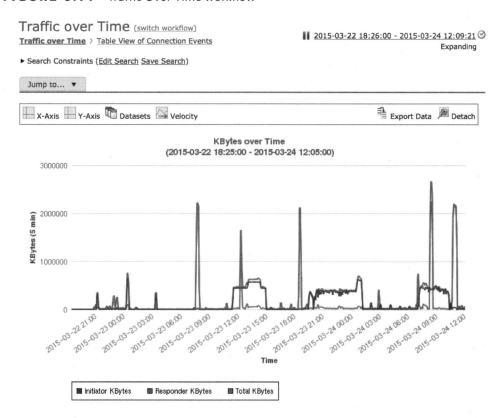

Connection Summaries

Another way to view connection information is via a dashboard. Choose Overview ➢ Dashboard ➢ Connection Summary to get the following three tabs in the summary (shown in Figure 5.15):

   Connections—Displays information on the number of connections by initiator, application, port, and responder and over time.

   Traffic—Refers to traffic bytes by initiator, application, port, and responder and over time.

   Geolocation—Displays information about the source and destination countries and continents.

FIGURE 5.15 Connection event summary

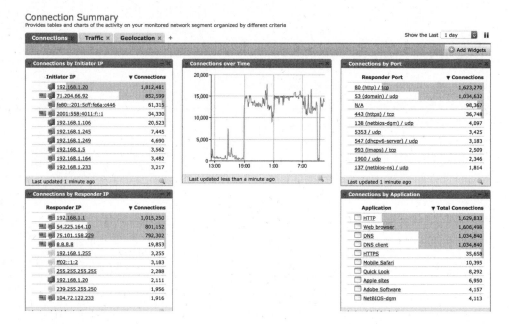

Each of these graphs is interactive, and you can use any or all of them to get even more detailed information.

User Information

User information is collected either passively, using the protocols in the discovery policy, or via an Active Directory *User Agent*. The Active Directory agent communicates with specified AD servers to collect login information based upon the audit logs. An AD agent can be installed on a Windows-based system inside your environment, but you must provide the name of an account with the capability to read the logs on the AD servers as well as a password. One AD agent can communicate with up to five AD servers.

In addition to reading the logs, you can connect with an AD server via LDAP to read other attributes on accounts. Information including the first and last name, email, department, and phone number would be included provided the data is populated in the AD server. You can also use this LDAP connection to pull user/group account information for use in AC policies.

It's also good to know that connections can be made to non-AD LDAP servers and user data can be pulled for the other discovered user types as long as there's corresponding information in LDAP.

User Agent

To configure the Defense Center to communicate with the agent, navigate to Policies ➢ Users. The screen shown in Figure 5.16 appears.

FIGURE 5.16   Users policy configuration

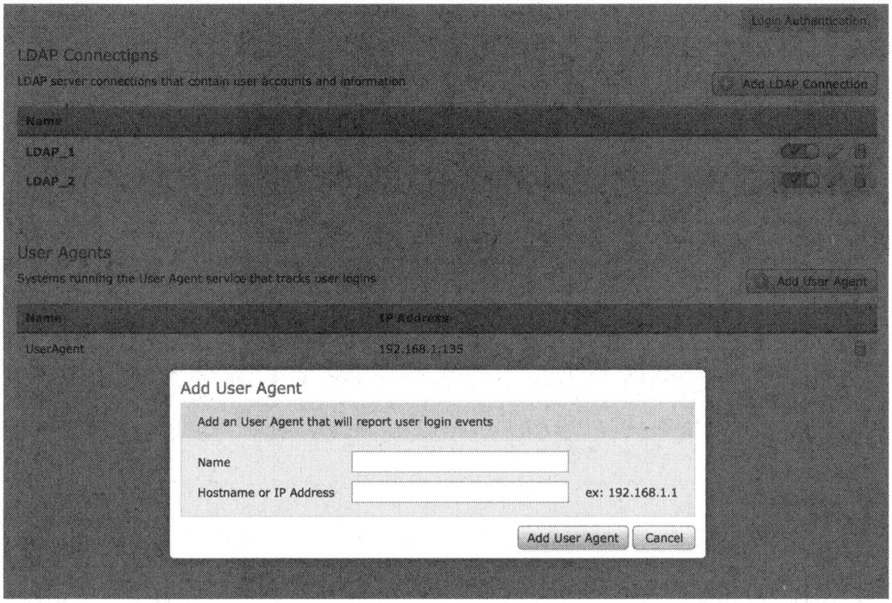

Once here, just click Add User Agent, and then enter a name for the agent plus the hostname or IP address of the system on which you want the agent to be installed.

Make sure all the key prerequisites are installed on the host on which you're installing the AD agent, including the .Net Framework and SQL CE from Microsoft. The install of the agent itself is actually really straightforward, but once it's installed, you've still got to configure it. Opening the agent reveals the dialog shown in Figure 5.17.

FIGURE 5.17   User Agent configuration

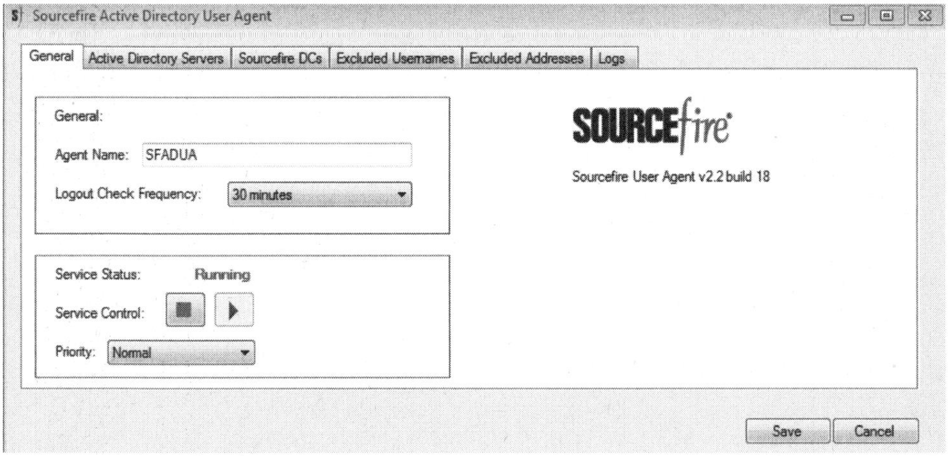

Clicking through the tabs across the top of the dialog, you can see the various settings. You will need to specify the agent name, AD servers, and Sourcefire DC (FireSIGHT Manager). Figure 5.18 shows the dialog where you add the AD server. You can also exclude names and addresses from the discovery. And if you ever hit a snag, there's a handy Logs tab for troubleshooting.

FIGURE 5.18   Active Directory server configuration

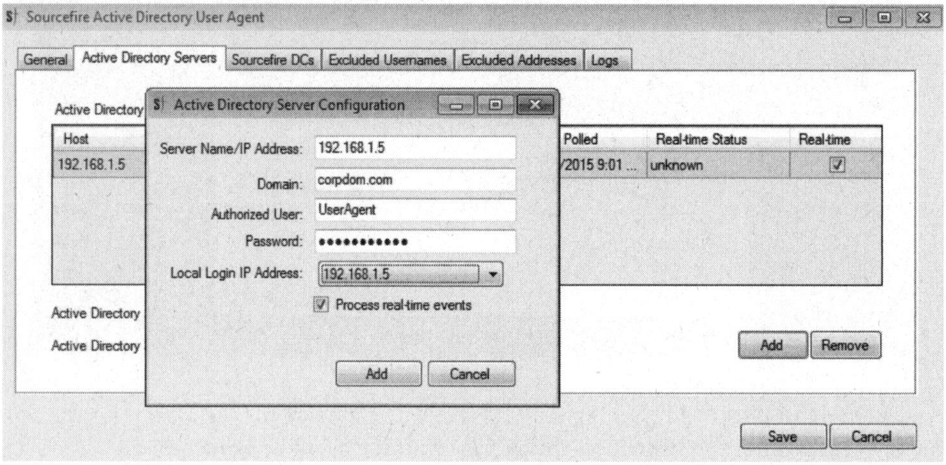

LDAP Configuration

You configure the LDAP connection on the same page that you added the User Agent. The top half of the page contains the LDAP settings. Just click Add LDAP Connection and fill out the information. Figure 5.19 shows the LDAP configuration screen. Here's a list of the key factors to remember:

Server type—Options are the MS Active Directory, Open LDAP, Oracle Directory, or Other. Select the type that matches your environment.

Primary Server and port—This should be your LDAP or AD server and port. It defaults to port 389.

Base DN—This is the starting point of the LDAP search for your users.

User name and password—A user who has the rights to read the AD or LDAP tree.

Encryption and SSL certificate upload—If you're leveraging SSL on your LDAP server, you can specify SSL or TLS as well as the certificate.

User/Group Access Control Parameters—If you enable this for your AD server, the users and groups can be leveraged in Access Control rules.

FIGURE 5.19   LDAP configuration

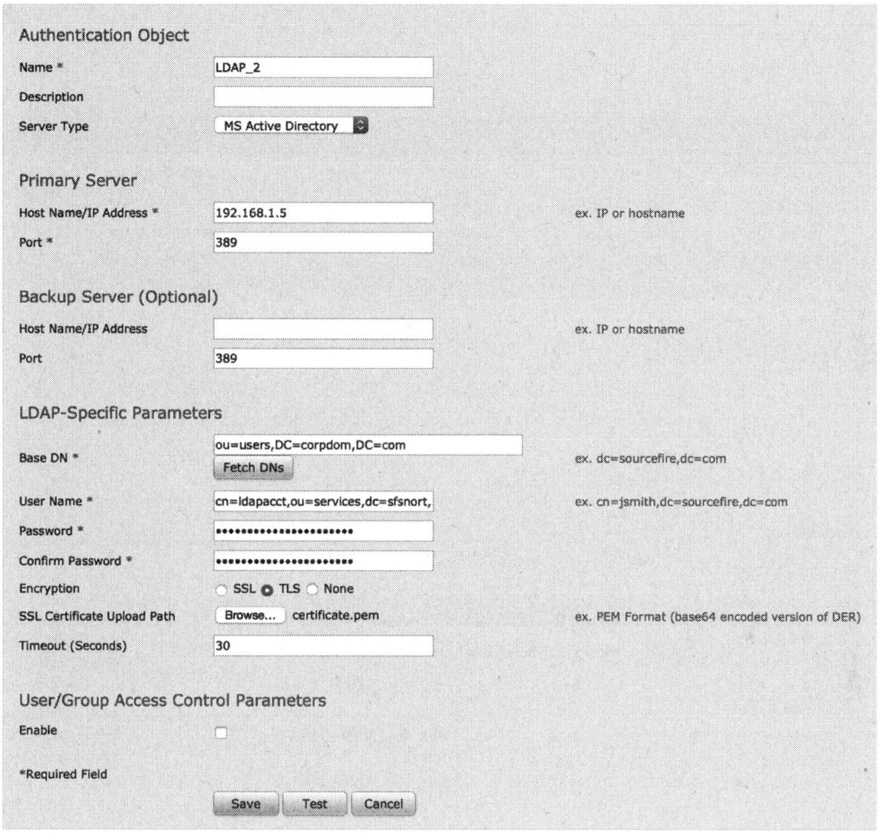

The last part of the dialog allows you to test the parameters to verify that the settings are correct.

User Analysis

Once user discovery is enabled, the users table and user activity in the database will populate. You can see their contents by navigating to Analysis ➢ Users ➢ Users; an example is shown in Figure 5.20. This will display all users that have been identified by the system.

Figure 5.21 shows the User Activity view, which is opened by going to Analysis ➢ Users ➢ User Activity. This view will reveal precisely when all those users were seen performing activities such as newly discovered, logging in, or logging out. Logouts, however, can only be seen if you are using the User Agent.

FIGURE 5.20 Table view of users

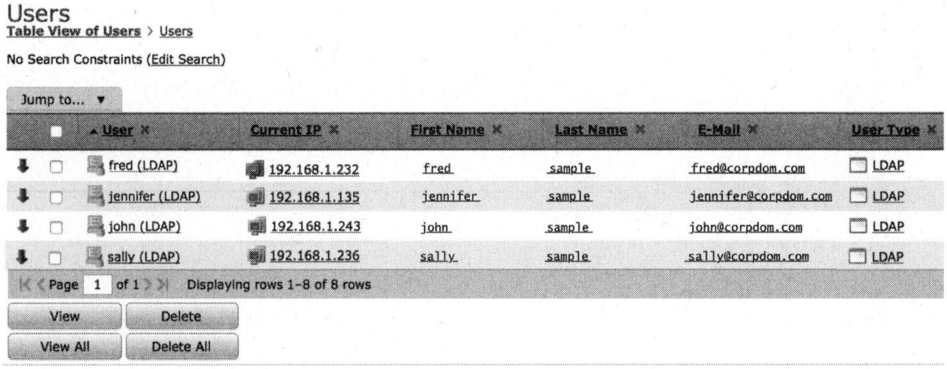

Users
Table View of Users › Users

No Search Constraints (Edit Search)

Jump to... ▼

		▲ User ×	Current IP ×	First Name ×	Last Name ×	E-Mail ×	User Type ×
⬇	☐	fred (LDAP)	192.168.1.232	fred	sample	fred@corpdom.com	☐ LDAP
⬇	☐	jennifer (LDAP)	192.168.1.135	jennifer	sample	jennifer@corpdom.com	☐ LDAP
⬇	☐	john (LDAP)	192.168.1.243	john	sample	john@corpdom.com	☐ LDAP
⬇	☐	sally (LDAP)	192.168.1.236	sally	sample	sally@corpdom.com	☐ LDAP

|◁ ◁ Page 1 of 1 ▷ ▷| Displaying rows 1–8 of 8 rows

| View | Delete |
| View All | Delete All |

FIGURE 5.21 User Activity view

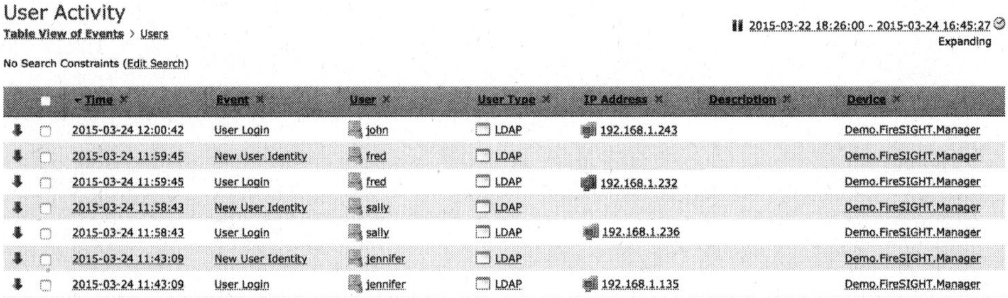

User Activity
Table View of Events › Users   ⏸ 2015-03-22 18:26:00 - 2015-03-24 16:45:27 ⊘
                                                                                              Expanding
No Search Constraints (Edit Search)

		▼ Time ×	Event ×	User ×	User Type ×	IP Address ×	Description ×	Device ×
⬇	☐	2015-03-24 12:00:42	User Login	john	☐ LDAP	192.168.1.243		Demo.FireSIGHT.Manager
⬇	☐	2015-03-24 11:59:45	New User Identity	fred	☐ LDAP			Demo.FireSIGHT.Manager
⬇	☐	2015-03-24 11:59:45	User Login	fred	☐ LDAP	192.168.1.232		Demo.FireSIGHT.Manager
⬇	☐	2015-03-24 11:58:43	New User Identity	sally	☐ LDAP			Demo.FireSIGHT.Manager
⬇	☐	2015-03-24 11:58:43	User Login	sally	☐ LDAP	192.168.1.236		Demo.FireSIGHT.Manager
⬇	☐	2015-03-24 11:43:09	New User Identity	jennifer	☐ LDAP			Demo.FireSIGHT.Manager
⬇	☐	2015-03-24 11:43:09	User Login	jennifer	☐ LDAP	192.168.1.135		Demo.FireSIGHT.Manager

Host Attributes

There's one more data type available to you in the FireSIGHT Manager. *Host attributes* are elements that you can create on your own and either automatically or manually assign to systems. These attributes can then be used as sorting and search criteria to make it easier to locate systems or tag machines that you want to flag as "special."

The attributes can be one of these four types:

Text—Creates a text box for a user to input information.

URL—Creates a field where a URL may be entered

List—Allows you to access a drop-down list with choices you create

Integer—Creates a field for a numeric value to be assigned.

To create attributes, navigate to Analysis ➤ Host Attributes and choose Host Attribute Management in the upper-right corner. You'll see a default attribute called White List there, and we'll tell you all about it later in the book. In the upper right, there will be a button labeled Create Attribute.

Clicking the Create Attribute button will open a screen presenting you with a selection of attributes you can create, as seen in Figure 5.22. Creating the URL, text, and integer attributes will cause those characteristics to appear in the host profiles of each host in your network. The list attribute also allows for the option to automatically assign the attribute based upon a network/subnet combination. First, create the list attributes and then specify which network the attributes belong to. If anything falls outside of those parameters, it would still show up in a category called Unassigned. A configured list attribute is shown in Figure 5.23.

FIGURE 5.22 Host attribute creation

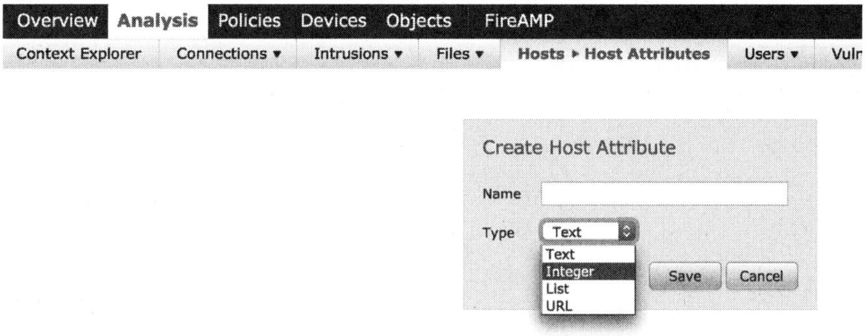

FIGURE 5.23 List attribute creation

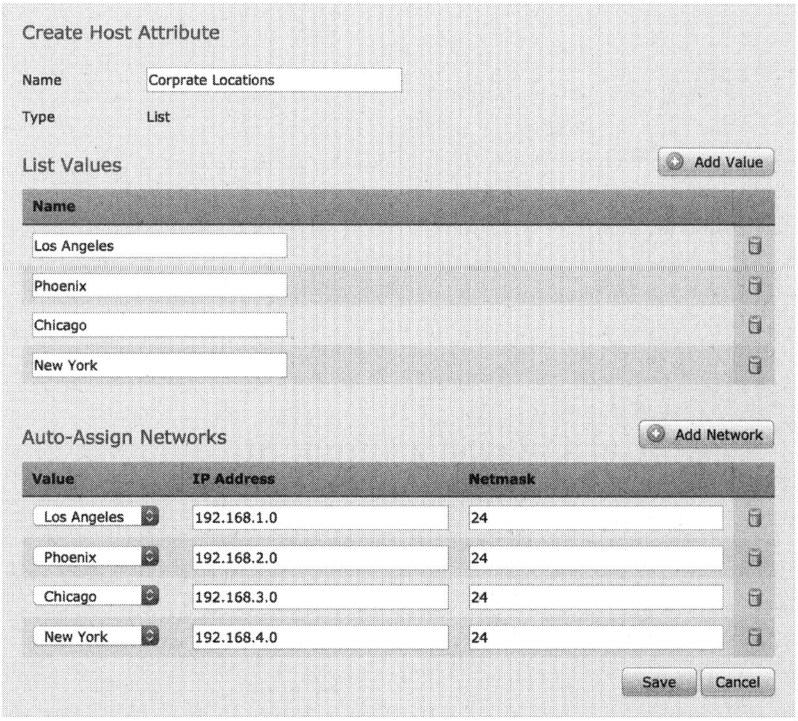

Once you've created your attributes, you can check up on them in several ways. You can use the host profile, but you can also check out the Network Map Host Attribute view seen in Figure 5.24. There's even a link on the create attribute page. If that's not enough, you can access them by going to Analysis ➤ Hosts ➤ Network Map and clicking the Host Attributes tab.

FIGURE 5.24   Network Map Host Attribute view

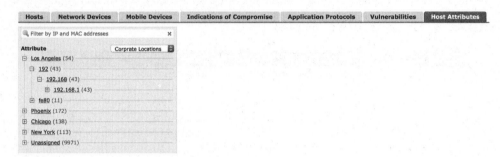

This gets you to a drop-down list where you can select any of the host attributes you or someone else created. The three attributes associated with whitelists are compliant, non-compliant, and not assigned, options that can't be assigned by an administrator. These characteristics can only be assigned based on the actual whitelist values, which we'll cover in detail in Chapter 11, "Correlation Policy."

Summary

In this chapter, you learned about the powerful and important discovery components of FireSIGHT. You were also shown how to create a policy controlling how the discovery data is collected. We then gave you a tour and viewed the discovery data in the FireSIGHT manager. After that, we discussed how user information is collected based on Active Directory and LDAP. We ended this chapter by showing you how to configure host attributes for easier analysis.

Hands-on Labs

In this section, you will go through the following four labs:

Hands-on Lab 5.1: Configuring a Discovery Policy

Hands-on Lab 5.2: Viewing Connection Events

Hands-on Lab 5.3: Viewing the Network Map

Hands-on Lab 5.4: Creating Host Attributes

Hands-on Lab 5.1: Configuring a Discovery Policy

In this lab, you will configure your discovery policy to cover internal RFC1918 addresses.

1. Open your web browser and HTTPS to your Defense Center.
2. Log in to the Defense Center.
3. Navigate to Policies ➤ Network Discovery.
4. On the Network tab, select the edit button (pencil icon) on the line with the 0.0.0.0/0 network.
5. Delete any existing networks.
6. In the Enter Network Address field, add the following items individually: **192.168.0.0/16, 172.16.0.0/12, and 10.0.0.0/8.**
7. Click the Save button to proceed to the User tab.
8. Verify that all protocols specify Yes for detection.
9. Click the Advanced tab.
10. Click the edit icon in the General Settings area.
11. Check the Capture Banners box.
12. Click Save.
13. Click Apply in the upper-right portion of the interface.
14. Click Yes in the confirmation dialog box.

Hands-on Lab 5.2: Viewing Connection Events

In this lab, you will view connection events in the Defense Center. Log in as admin before you start this lab.

1. From the main menu, navigate to Analysis ➤ Connections ➤ Events.
2. View the listing of connections displayed.
3. Scroll to the right to view all the connection information.
4. What country was the destination?
5. What URLs were accessed?
6. Click on one of the events.
7. Using the information on the screen, determine how many bytes and packets were used for the traffic?

Hands-on Lab 5.3: Viewing the Network Map

In this lab, you will view your network map. Log in as admin before you start this lab.

1. Navigate to Analysis ➤ Hosts ➤ Network Map.
2. Click the plus (+) icon to expand an available network from the network map.

3. Click on an individual IP address from the tree.

4. View the host profile in the right pane.

5. What is the OS type?

6. What servers are available?

7. What applications have been discovered?

8. Try viewing the information for other hosts.

Hands-on Lab 5.4: Creating Host Attributes

In this lab, you will create host attributes to represent different cities in your network. Log in as admin before you start this lab.

1. Navigate to Analysis ➤ Hosts ➤ Network Map ➤ Host Attributes.

2. Click the Host Attribute Management button in the upper right.

3. Click the Create Attribute button.

4. Give the attribute the name **Corporate Locations**.

5. Specify the type as List.

6. Click the Add Value button to create and add the following entries: **Los Angeles, Chicago,** and **New York**.

7. Click the Add Network button.

8. In Auto-Assign Networks section, select Los Angeles from the drop-down list. Enter the IP address **192.168.0/0/16**.

9. Click the Add Network button again,

10. In the Auto-Assign Networks section, select Chicago from the drop-down list. Enter the IP address **172.16.0.0/12**.

11. Click the Add Network button one more time.

12. In the Auto-Assign Networks section, select New York from the drop-down list. Enter the IP address **10.0.0.0/8**.

13. Click Save.

14. In the upper right, click the Host Attribute Network Map button to view the network map with the new attributes.

Exam Essentials

Understand the discovery policy.   The discovery policy is used to specify what network segments we want to retain information about in the Defense Center. Using rules, you can include or exclude IP addresses for discovery. You want to limit the discovery so you do not exceed your FireSIGHT license limits.

Know the purpose and features of the User Agent.   To facilitate Active Directory discovery, Cisco leverages the User Agent. The agent communicates with Active Directory to identify user accounts and associated IP addresses for the purpose of user awareness. The user agent can also identify user logoffs.

Be able to explain the different data types collected by FireSIGHT.   FireSIGHT collects information about hosts, services, application, users, and connections to give analysts context about your network.

Know the types of users discovered by FireSIGHT.   User discovery allows for the collection of user information for AIM, IMAP, LDAP, Oracle, POP3, SIP, and Active Directory with the use of an agent.

Review Questions

You can find the answers in Appendix A.

1. When configuring the discovery policy, you would limit the networks you want to monitor to prevent the system from what?

   A. Scanning the Internet

   B. Using all your FireSIGHT licenses

   C. Monitoring the administration traffic

   D. Reading corporate email

2. What would you implement to discover users from Active Directory?

   A. TACACS

   B. Windows Connector

   C. An Active Directory agent

   D. Log Host

3. When you're specifying network discovery address ranges, what are the available types of addresses that can be used?

   A. IPv4

   B. IPv6

   C. Both IPv4 and IPv6

   D. MAC Address

4. Host attributes allow you to assign meta information to hosts that have been discovered. What is one of the built-in host attributes?

   A. Location

   B. Time Zone

   C. Website

   D. Notes

5. What categories of information are discovered by FireSIGHT? Select the best answer.

   A. Hosts, connections, users

   B. Hosts, NetFlow, logins

   C. Traffic, IP addresses, ports

   D. Traffic statistics, IP addresses, accounts

6. Which analysis view provides the most information about a host?

   A. Detail analysis

   B. Host analysis

   C. Network map

   D. Host profile

7. What view would you use to view summary information of your network traffic?

    A. Analysis ➤ Connections ➤ Events

    B. Overview ➤ Dashboard ➤ Connection Summary

    C. Analysis ➤ Connections ➤ Hosts ➤ Network Map

    D. Overview ➤ Dashboard ➤ URL Statistics

8. Which of the following is *not* part of the configuration of the LDAP-specific parameters?

    A. Base DN

    B. UI access attribute

    C. Base filter

    D. User name

9. For which of the following protocols can user discovery take place?

    A. Yahoo IM, IMAP, POP3

    B. AIM, SMTP, POP3

    C. IMAP, POP3, RADIUS

    D. IMAP, POP3, Active Directory

10. What type of host attributes can be created?

    A. Text, URL, list, integer

    B. Text, web, list, integer

    C. Data, URL, list, integer

    D. Data, web, list, integer

Chapter

6

Intrusion Event Analysis

THE SSFIPS EXAM TOPICS COVERED IN THIS CHAPTER INCLUDE THE FOLLOWING:

✓ **3.0 Event Analysis**

✓ **3.1 Understand the role that geolocation plays in analysis**

✓ **3.2 Be familiar with the interfaces for analysis, including the Dashboard, Workflows and Context Explorer**

The world of network intrusion detection is a dynamic place where new vulnerabilities are discovered daily, new attacks are launched continuously, and networks themselves are in a constant state of flux. Vendors ceaselessly respond by creating and releasing a steady stream of software patches to address vulnerabilities, and teams like *Cisco Talos* (formerly VRT) are continuously rolling out new rules to protect against attacks. It's a never-ending battle, and network intrusion analysts on the front lines are continuously trying to separate the wheat from the chaff, at times poring over thousands of events!

In this chapter, we'll review using the FireSIGHT System to analyze intrusion event data. We'll explore some of the workflows available when analyzing events and show you examples of how to drill into relevant event data. We'll also cover how to use the Dashboard and Context Explorer.

To find up-to-the-minute updates for this chapter, please see www.lammle.com/firepower or the book's web page at www.sybex.com.

Intrusion Analysis Principles

The FireSIGHT System has several features to help analysts isolate and focus on the most critical events out of the sea of noisy ones. Over the years, updates to *Snort* as well as improvements in rule keywords and preprocessor capabilities have helped us cut to the chase. Even so, each newly deployed IPS system usually requires rule tuning.

False Positives

When we say, "tuning," we really mean noise reduction. In an IPS system the term *noise* is how we refer to events that trigger but aren't of any real value. These are often called *false positives*—a simple example of one would be when an IPS rule alerts on traffic it wasn't intended to detect. It's not that the rule is necessarily faulty or even that there's a problem with Snort itself. False positives are often simply the result of the sheer volume of packets that must be inspected. They can also occur because the rule must account for any packets where the attack *might* be present.

Here's an example: A rule looking for the string cmd.exe in an HTTP request is probably looking for some type of abuse on a Microsoft Windows host. Ancient versions of Windows had vulnerabilities where an attacker could actually execute commands through the web server by finding the path to the command processor cmd.exe. To protect against this, you could use a Snort rule to simply look for cmd.exe in an HTTP request. This rule wouldn't trigger on normal HTTP traffic, but it would detect someone trying to find the command processor.

But what if a website just happens to be hosting a graphic file named cmd.exe.gif? This would cause the rule to alert and possibly even block an HTTP request for the image. In this case, the alert would be classified as a false positive even though the rule did what it was designed to do. It's just that in this case, the cmd.exe wasn't an actual threat—it just happened to be part of an unfortunate name someone chose for an image file.

False Negatives

And of course the opposite of a false positive is a *false negative*, which happens when the rule fails to detect the attack it was designed to detect. While false positives are to be expected, false negatives are definitely something we don't want happening at all! The failure of a rule to detect an actual attack represents a failure of the IPS system as a whole and is something rule writers do their best to avoid. Understanding this objective should help you understand why we have to deal with false positives—the alternative (missed attacks) is much uglier than dealing with a bunch of noise!

So going back to our earlier example, we could have avoided the false positive for cmd.exe.gif by adding the path to cmd.exe. We could have written the rule to look for c:\winnt\system32\cmd.exe instead because doing that would eliminate the false positive for the cmd.exe.gif file. But what if the Windows host used c:\Windows for its system root? This would mean the path to cmd.exe would be c:\Windows\system32\cmd.exe. If our rule is too specific, all of a sudden we're faced with the potential for a false negative. The point we're making is that while rules must be written to avoid as many false positives as possible, they're generally written to allow zero false negatives. So in the example above, the rule would probably be written to look only for cmd.exe. and yes, it would result in an occasional false positive. But remember, our goal is to make sure we get zero false negatives.

Possible Outcomes

Of course there are two other possibilities: a true positive and a true negative. The four possible results of traffic inspection are shown in the following table.

	Traffic is malicious	**Traffic is benign**
Rule matches traffic	*True positive*	False positive
Rule does not match traffic	False negative	*True negative*

Of the possible results in the table above, an IPS system will produce any of these over the course of normal operations. The all-important exception is the false negative representing the failure to detect an actual attack, which should be avoided at all costs!

Keep in mind that the preceding table assumes that the sensor has visibility to all the traffic it's designed to inspect and that it has the necessary processing/rules/network resources to fully evaluate the traffic. Inadequate visibility or detection resources could result in some traffic bypassing inspection, again raising the possibility of a dreaded false negative.

The Goal of Analysis

Maybe you're thinking that all of this is way too complicated—why bother with all this analyzing? After all, can't we just put our devices inline, load the appropriate rule sets and trust the system to block the bad stuff? To coin a phrase, go ahead and try that and let us know how it works out for you!

Indeed, placing inline IPS devices at strategic locations within your network will provide protection against attacks and possibly hinder the effectiveness of some malware. But that approach is by no means the silver bullet that will guard against all your network security evils.

Here's why—first of all, some devices are deployed in passive mode, meaning all they can do is alert and not actually stop attacks. And we need to follow up on the events generated by these devices to address possible issues. Analysis is vital in these instances because it enables us to prioritize our responses without wasting a bunch of time on alerts that will turn out to be false positives.

While inline devices have the power to stop attacks, they also have the potential to impact legitimate traffic if the alert is a false positive. This is why we need to analyze the output of these devices to quickly identify and remediate false positives and ensure minimal impact to the business. You can clearly see that the analysis of events and effective rule tuning are critical aspects to this process.

It all boils down to a single, primary goal—to be able to determine if the event we're looking at is a true positive or a false positive. In the rest of this chapter, we'll review the features available in the FireSIGHT System user interface to analyze alerts and make this key distinction.

The Dashboard and Context Explorer

The first stop on our tour is the Dashboard. The FireSIGHT System contains a number of default dashboards, each one with multiple tabs. And each tab has multiple widgets. Figure 6.1 displays the default dashboards available.

As you can see, there are dashboards for a number of event views, and each dashboard consists of several tabbed pages. Each page contains several widgets and each of them represents a view into some aspect of the system. Most widgets display events, but some of them are better suited for system administration. These show us data like product updates, CPU load, health status, and so on. Some example dashboards are shown in Figure 6.2 and Figure 6.3.

FIGURE 6.1 Dashboard menu

FIGURE 6.2 Event oriented widget examples

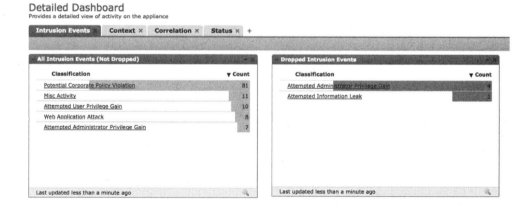

One of the most powerful aspects of *dashboard* widgets is that they give us the ability to display multiple event views on a single page. Depending on the display resolution, it's possible to have six or even nine widgets showing different event views simultaneously! The dashboard has a time range that constrains all time-based widgets, which can be set to a period as short as an hour or as long as twelve months. The dashboard provides complex and customizable monitoring of events using multiple simultaneous searches. Figure 6.4 shows the Connection Summary dashboard.

FIGURE 6.3   Status oriented widget examples

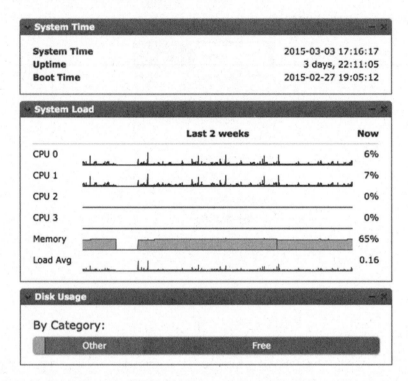

The Dashboard is highly configurable, and custom dashboards can contain multiple tabs with several widgets on each of them. You can create dashboards to show events from built-in or custom searches. Here's a short list of four ideas for custom dashboards:

- Geographic: Each widget will reveal events from devices in specific locations.

- Critical assets: Create a widget to display events from various groups of critical hosts.

- Specific event classifications: Each widget will display intrusion events from a specific classification

- Any search you have already created: Think of any custom search you have already created or one that would probably be useful. Each of these can be configured to filter the results in a dashboard widget.

By contrast, the Context Explorer also displays events using lists and graphs and probably seems pretty similar to the dashboard—at first. But instead of consisting of highly customizable components, the Context Explorer uses a set of preset visual contexts instead, as shown in Figure 6.5.

FIGURE 6.4   Connection Summary dashboard

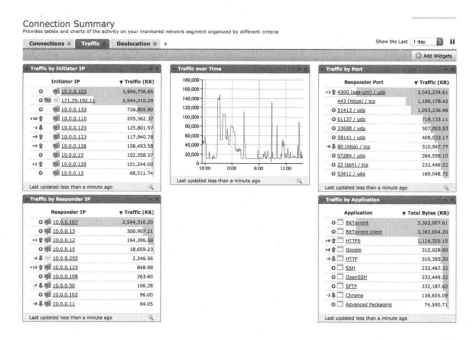

FIGURE 6.5   The Context Explorer

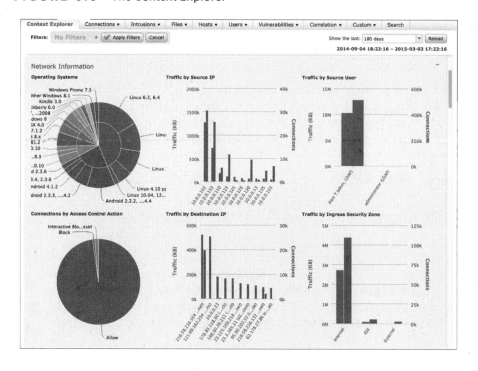

The Context Explorer uses a time window similar to the dashboard to constrain the information but it also uses filters to limit the data and assist in locating meaningful trends or activity. When you click the plus (+) icon near the upper-left corner, an Add Filter dialog appears. This allows you to filter the results on dozens of parameters. Some of the available filter parameters are shown in Figure 6.6.

FIGURE 6.6   Context Explorer filter

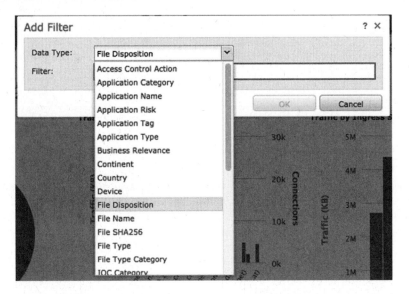

Multiple filters can be added to narrow down to the specific kind of traffic or events you are looking for. Once you've chosen your filters, click the Apply Filters button to update all the graphs and charts based on your selection, as shown in Figure 6.7.

FIGURE 6.7   Applying filters

The Context Explorer is designed for interactive searching and pivoting through the event data; it's not something you would want to use on the large screen display in your Security Operations Center. It's designed to be used interactively to ferret out useful information, and doesn't save its configuration when you're done.

Both the Dashboard and Context Explorer provide colorful, filtered views into your FireSIGHT data, but each of them has its own specialized purpose. You customize each dashboard tab and widget to zero in on and reveal only the information you want. On the other hand, you might go with the Context Explorer when you want to find out exactly how many hosts connected to country X. Next, let's dive into the depths of intrusion event analysis by exploring intrusion event workflows!

Intrusion Events

In the following sections, we'll probe the mechanics of intrusion event analysis using workflows. Entire books have been written on packet analysis, and we could truly spend the rest of this book on the subject. Instead we will focus on the use of the FireSIGHT System user interface for intrusion event analysis.

An Introduction to Workflows

To navigate to the default intrusion event workflow, go to Analysis ➢ Intrusions ➢ Events. The default workflow is called Events By Priority and Classification. Workflows are a central theme in the FireSIGHT System, and most event views include different workflows. These workflows determine how events are displayed, which columns are shown, and how they are sorted. Intrusion event workflows are all table based—they're columns of text data. You'll soon find that most of the connection event workflows are bar, line, or pie graphs.

The different workflows help analysts highlight different types of events. For example, your goal may be to find the intrusion event(s) that represent the most critical threats to your organization. However, after that you may want to find the events most likely to be false positives. By using the built-in workflows and/or creating your own custom workflows, you can quickly locate exactly the types of events you're interested in.

To switch workflows, just click the Switch Workflow link to the right of the current workflow name. In Figure 6.8, the link is just a tad to the right of Events By Priority and Classification.

FIGURE 6.8   The Switch Workflow link

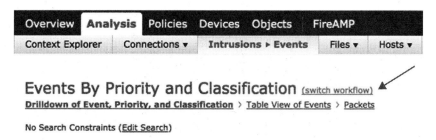

Clicking this link displays the workflows available. Figure 6.9 shows the default intrusion event workflows.

FIGURE 6.9   Default IPS workflows

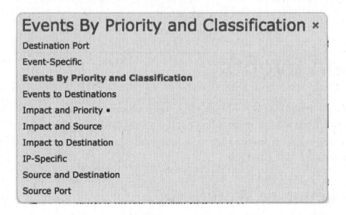

The current workflow is shown at the top and is also highlighted in red in the workflow list. We'll cover workflows in more detail later in this chapter.

The Time Window

Most data within the FireSIGHT System is time based, with data consisting of events that occurred at a certain time. So it follows that when viewing these events, you select a time window delimiting a start and stop time and date. For the events to appear in an analysis workflow, they must have occurred within this specified time window. If your time window is really huge, covering weeks or even months, you can predictably expect to see more events than if it's covering only an hour or a single day. The current time window is displayed as a start/stop date and time that you can see in the upper-right corner of the screen (see Figure 6.10).

FIGURE 6.10   Time window link

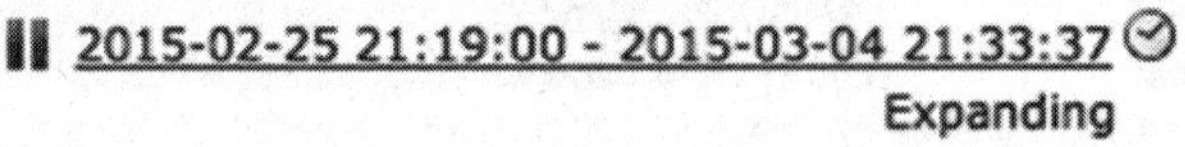

▌▌ 2015-02-25 21:19:00 - 2015-03-04 21:33:37 ⊘
Expanding

To change it, just click this link. When you do that, a new browser window will pop up as shown in Figure 6.11.

There are three types of time windows available: static, expanding, and sliding.

FIGURE 6.11 Date/time pop-up window

Static Time Window This time window has fixed start/stop times and is useful for locating events that occurred within a certain period. To use the static time window, just select it from the drop-down at the top of the pop-up window. After that, choose the start and stop time/date using the calendar and clock controls.

Expanding Time Window Like a static window, this time window also has a fixed start time, but it doesn't have a fixed stop time. It uses Now as the end time. Since the start time is fixed but the end time is constantly moving, this time window is always expanding, hence the name. If you set this time window to 60 minutes and begin analyzing events, after an hour you'll have a 120-minute window. This is the most common time window used for interactive analysis because it will always display the most current events. When setting an expanding time window, just choose the start time using the calendar and clock controls.

Sliding Time Window If you select this time window you'll see the calendar and clock controls disappear from the pop-up window. This is because a sliding window is a fixed duration, with the "front edge" always being Now. You can select the size of the time window, and once you do, it will slide as you continue to view events. For instance, if you select a time window of 60 minutes, you'll continue to see only the last 60 minutes worth of events even if you remain logged in for hours. Sliding time windows really shine for recurring reports. Let's say you have a weekly report of high-impact events. You would configure this report with a seven-day sliding time window, so each time it runs, it reports events for the previous seven days. Check out Figure 6.12 for an example of setting a sliding window.

FIGURE 6.12 Sliding time window

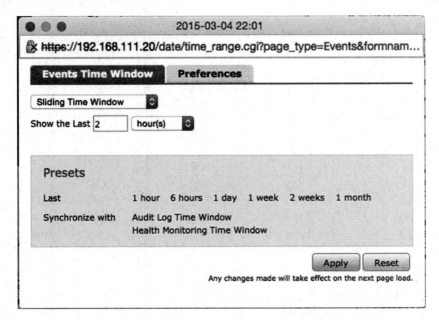

You probably noticed that there are presets available in the date/time pop-up. These come in really handy when you just want to look at some recent events. Using presets is so much faster than working with the calendar and clock controls to set a start/stop time.

Keep in mind that the default time window for the FireSIGHT System is the last hour expanding. After you've selected a new time window, it will remain for the duration of your session, but once you log out and back in, your time window resets to the default. You can change this default using the Preferences tab, clicking on it will reveal the Time Window Preferences page shown in Figure 6.13.

FIGURE 6.13   Time Window Preferences

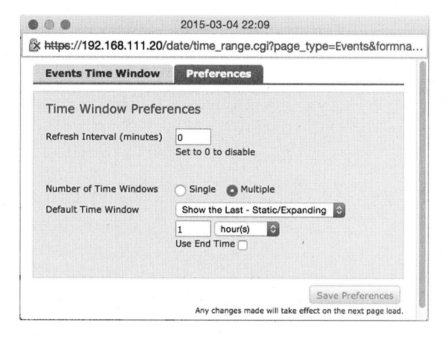

You can change your default to any of the three types and select the duration. There's also a radio button to select the number of time windows. Again, by default there are three time windows available: one for health events, one for audit events, and one for everything else. The idea behind this is to allow you to select a time window of, say, 30 days for your audit event view. This time window would not affect the time window for your health or IPS event views. Okay—once your time window is set, you can concentrate on isolating events for analysis.

The Analysis Screen

Turning our attention to the main intrusion event analysis view, let's continue our discussion of workflows. When it comes to intrusion events there are 10 built-in workflows, and you can also add additional custom workflows.

Built-in Workflows

Each of the default workflows is briefly described and illustrated in the following list.

   Destination Port: Lists the count of events for each destination port. The list is sorted with the port having the highest count of events positioned at the top, as shown in Figure 6.14.

FIGURE 6.14   Destination Port workflow

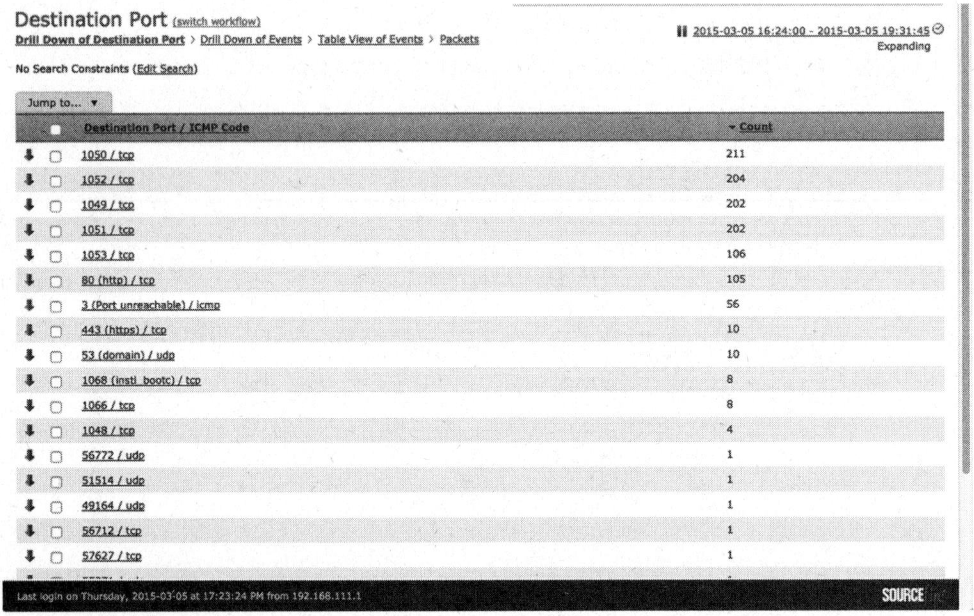

Event-Specific: Lists the events by count from highest to lowest, as shown in Figure 6.15. This workflow is helpful in looking for false positives because typically the events triggering the most are the ones most likely to be false positives.

FIGURE 6.15   Event-Specific workflow

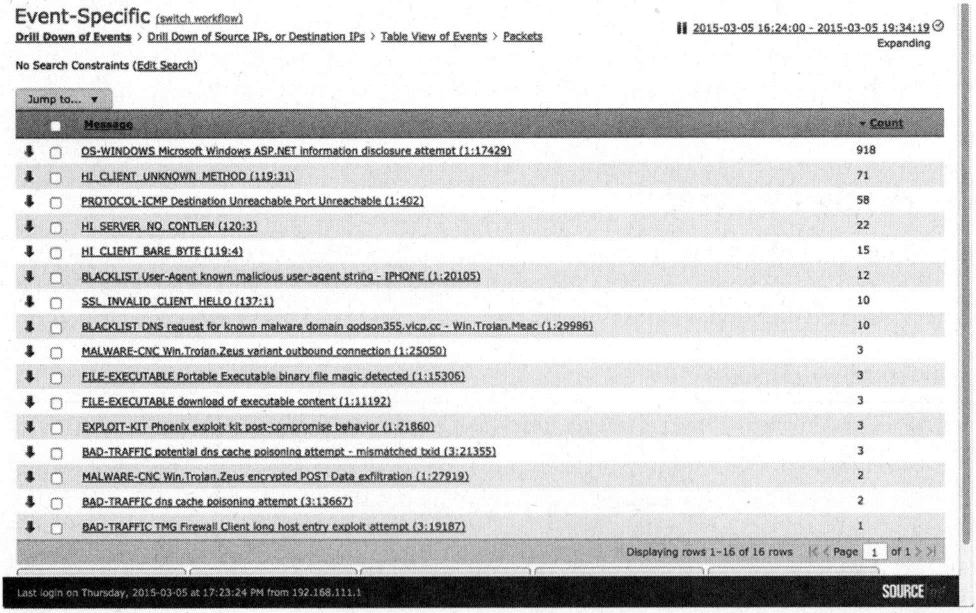

Events by Priority and Classification: This default workflow lists events by their priority and classification, with the list sorted by priority from high to low, as shown in Figure 6.16.

FIGURE 6.16   Events by Priority and Classification workflow

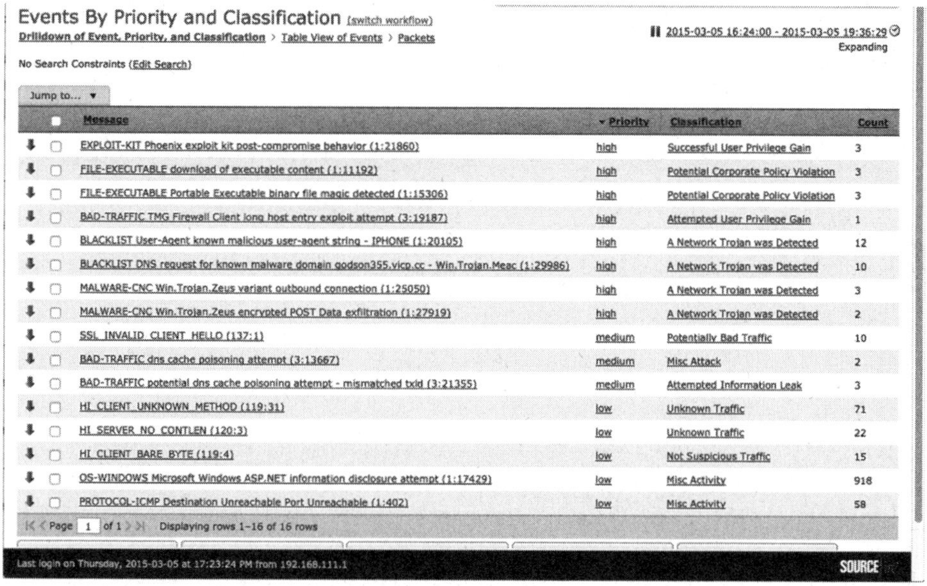

Events to Destinations: Displays which destination IP addresses are generating events, as shown in Figure 6.17. This list is sorted by a count from high to low.

FIGURE 6.17   Events to Destinations workflow

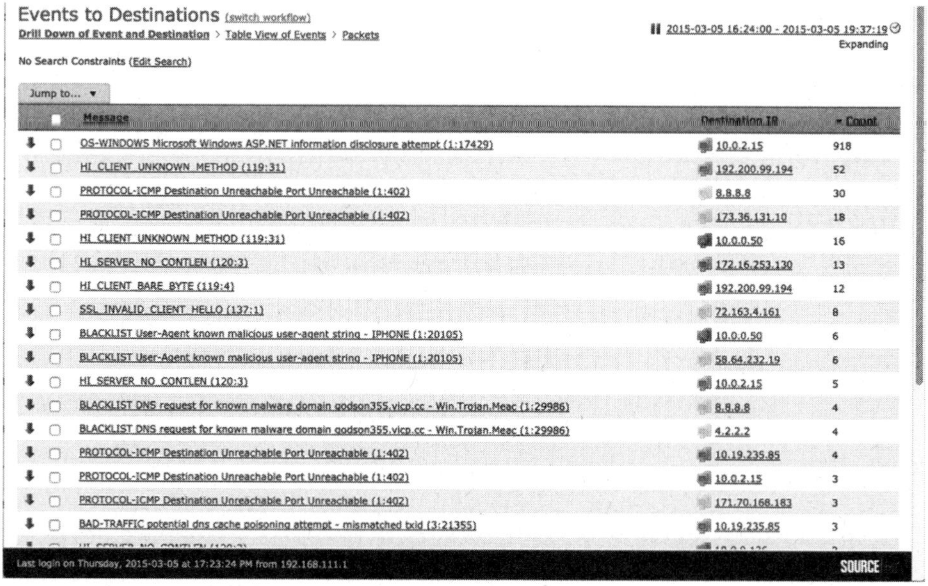

Impact and Priority: Displays six columns, which is also the maximum for a built-in workflow. Events are sorted by impact, and the view also shows the inline result, priority, and count (see Figure 6.18).

FIGURE 6.18 Impact and Priority workflow

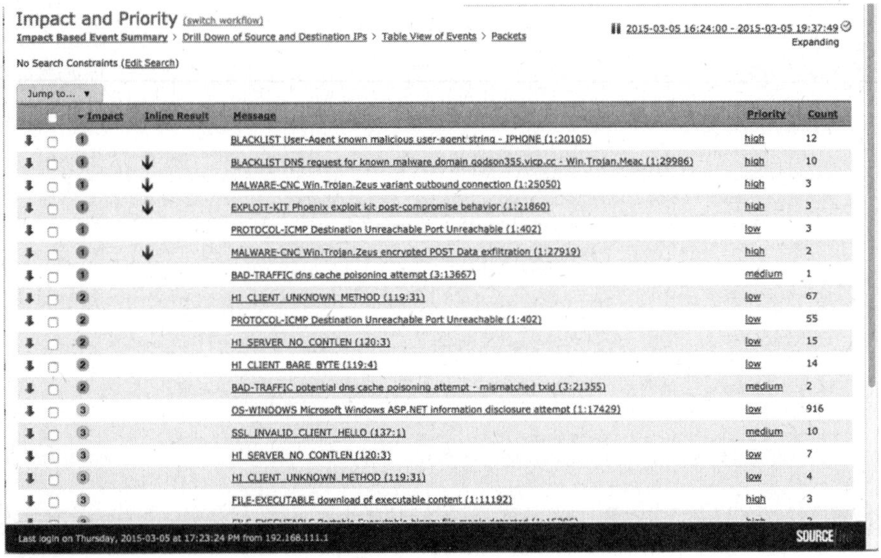

Impact and Source: This view is also sorted by impact and displays the source IP, message, priority, and count, as shown in Figure 6.19.

FIGURE 6.19 Impact and Source workflow

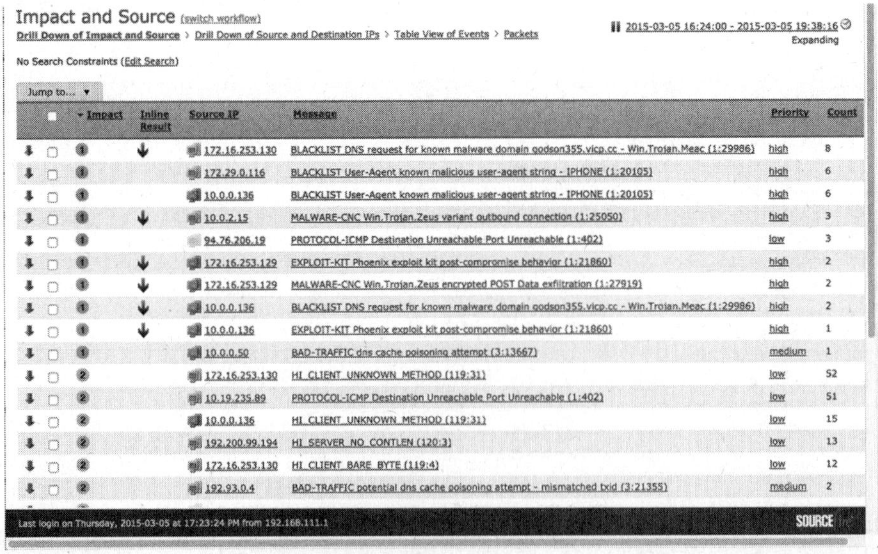

Impact to Destination: This view is the same as Impact and Source except the destination IP is also displayed, as you can see in Figure 6.20.

FIGURE 6.20   Impact to Destination workflow

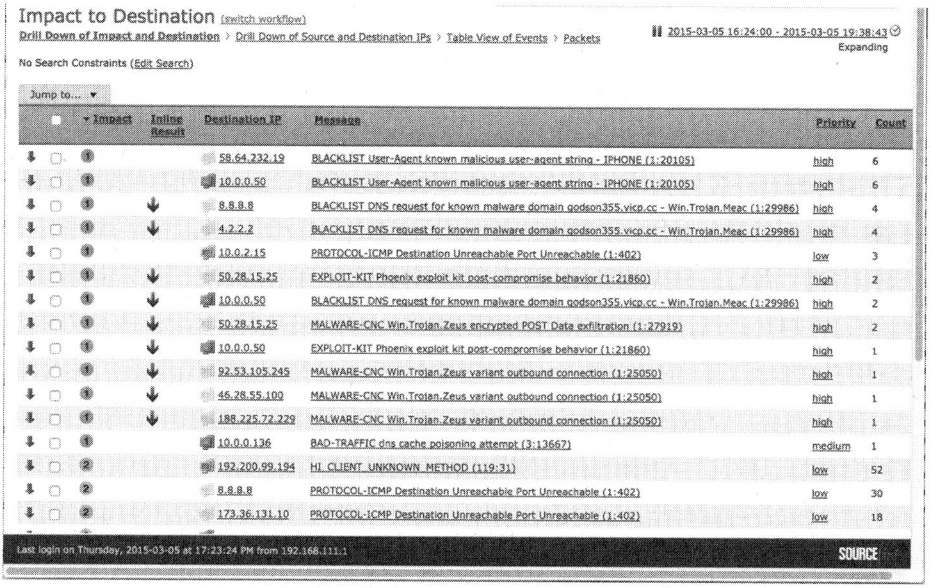

IP-Specific: This workflow is really two views in one. It lists the events by count for each source IP and the same for each destination IP, as shown in Figure 6.21.

FIGURE 6.21   IP-Specific workflow

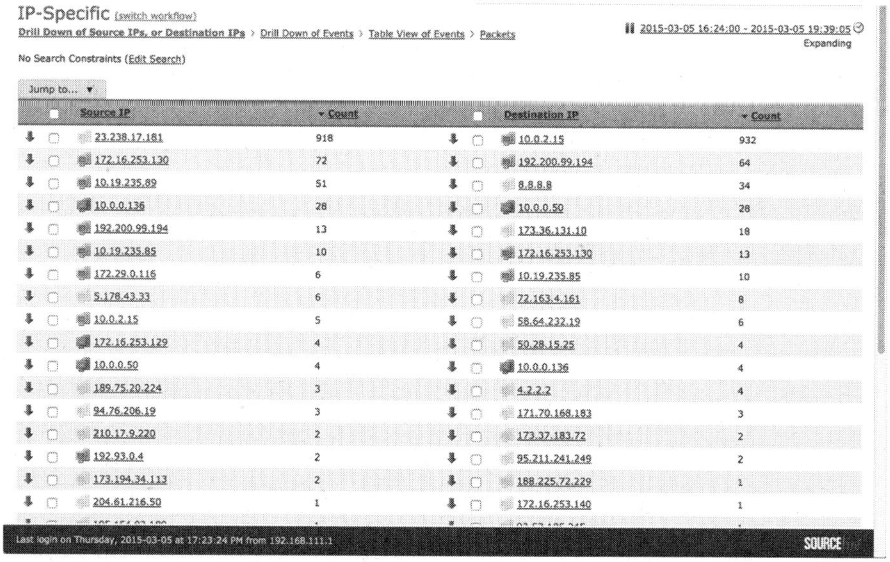

Source and Destination: As you can see in Figure 6.22, this shows the relationship between source and destination IP addresses and displays the total events between pairs of IP addresses from highest to lowest.

FIGURE 6.22 Source and Destination workflow

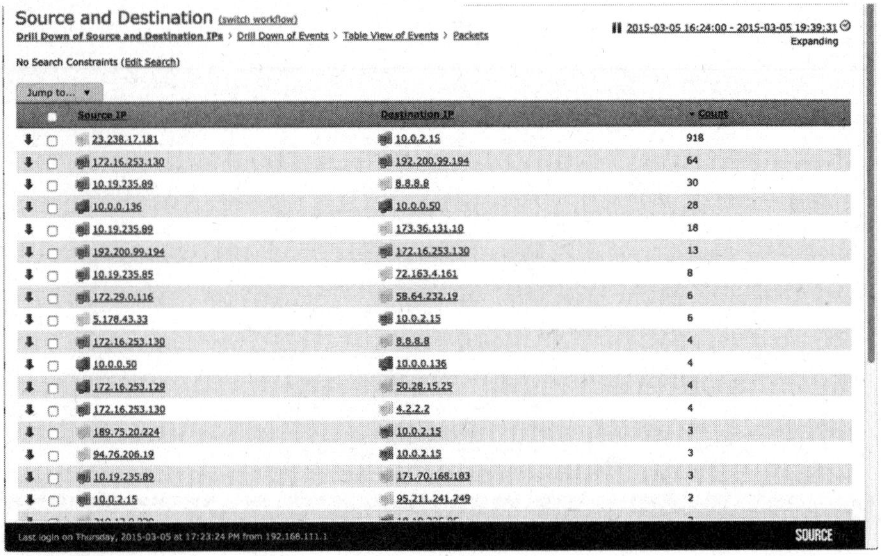

Source Port: This view shows the same information as the Destination Port workflow, but it also gives us the count of events by source port, as shown in Figure 6.23.

FIGURE 6.23 Source Port workflow

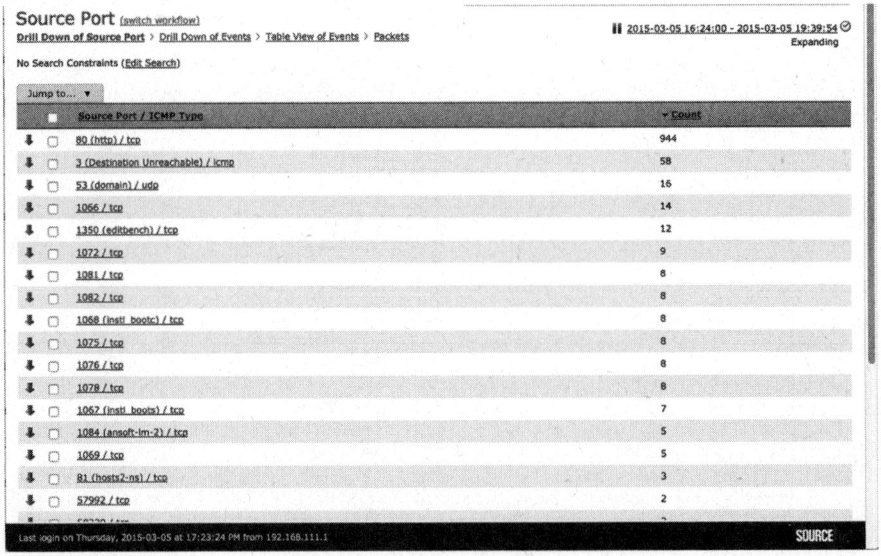

As you can see, there are quite a few default workflows to choose from. The one you choose depends on the type of events you're looking for at the moment. Looking for evidence of malware or spyware on hosts? Go with the Impact and Source workflow! This is because most of the rules written for these types of events trigger on outbound traffic. This workflow will help you quickly zero in on which of your hosts is (most) infected. Here you can see the events with the highest impact, whether or not the packet was dropped, and the source IP that generated the event.

If it's DMZ or server attacks you are looking for, the Impact to Destination workflow is just the ticket. It's similar to the Impact and Source workflow, but this one will show you the destination IP. Again, the thinking here is that rules looking for this type of attack will trigger on inbound traffic, thus the destination in this case would be the "victim."

Looking for false positives? Try the Event-Specific workflow. While this won't give you any information on the source, destination, or severity of the event, it will show which rules are triggering the most. Remember, rules that trigger thousands of times in a short period are the ones most likely to be false positives.

Navigating the Analysis Interface

There's generally one vital goal in intrusion event analysis—determining if the event represents a false positive or an actual security issue. Sometimes you can figure this out by simply looking at an event message, the meaningful text that describes the event. If the message clearly indicates that the rule is designed to detect a vulnerability that you know isn't there, then you can make a decision about the event right away. But most of the time, getting to the bottom of things will require drilling into the event detail—even the packet data—to truly know what you're dealing with.

So far, the workflows we've talked about consist of views or pages designed to help you isolate the events you're really interested in. Near the top of the screen you can see a "breadcrumb trail" showing each page in the workflow. The page you are currently viewing will be a red link. Figure 6.24 shows us the Impact and Source workflow.

FIGURE 6.24   "Breadcrumb trail" of workflow pages

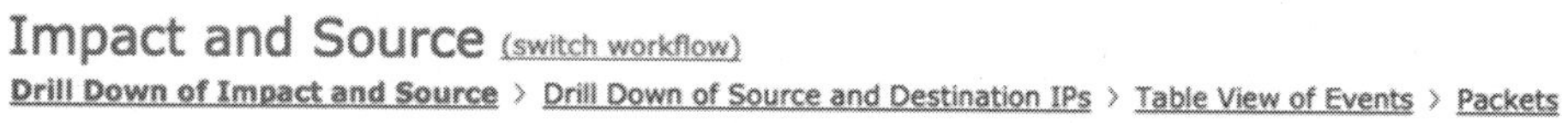

Impact and Source (switch workflow)
Drill Down of Impact and Source > Drill Down of Source and Destination IPs > Table View of Events > Packets

There are four pages in this workflow:

- Drill Down of Impact and Source
- Drill Down of Source and Destination IPs
- Table View of Events
- Packets

The page names indicate the kind of things we'll discover as we drill down into events. All the default workflows include a table view of events, which contains all of the fields in an event, although some columns are hidden by default. Whether they are built in or custom, all intrusion event workflows also include a packets view.

There are a number of ways to go deeper down to the next page, and the method you choose is a function of the particular kind of events you want to focus on. Figure 6.25 shows some of the events people would commonly want to look into.

FIGURE 6.25 Sample intrusion events

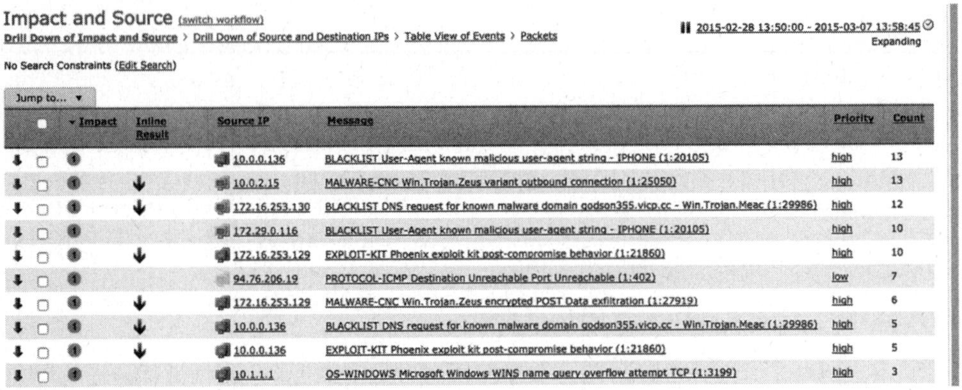

Looking at this page allows us to deduce a number of things just from the information displayed here.

First of all, these are all impact 1 events. Most of them also have a priority of high. So what's the difference?

Priority Priority is determined by the rule writer and can be set using the `priority` keyword. It can also be determined by the rule classification. Priority is Low, Medium, or High. The important thing to remember is that this simply indicates how important the rule writer felt the alert would be. For instance, a rule written for a vulnerability that could result in the complete compromise of a host will probably be high priority. On the other hand, a rule designed to alert on a simple protocol anomaly would be low priority.

Impact This is determined by FireSIGHT, which sets the different levels of impact based on what it knows about the rule, the packet, and the victim host. Figure 6.26 is taken from the FireSIGHT online help and describes how each impact level is determined.

Here are some example impact levels for different events:

- A rule triggers on a packet targeted for port 80 on a host but the target IP address isn't present within a network range defined in the Network Discovery policy. This means the host is not in the FireSIGHT database. FireSIGHT will respond by assigning an impact of 0, or Unknown, to the event.

- A rule triggers on a packet targeted for port 80 on a host. The IP address of this host is present in a discover rule in the network discovery policy, but when FireSIGHT looks in the host database, there's no entry there. This means the system has never seen traffic to or from this host before. In this case, FireSIGHT will assign an impact of 4, meaning Unknown Target, to this event.

FIGURE 6.26   Impact levels

Impact Levels

Impact Level	Vulnerability	Color	Description
0	Unknown	gray	Neither the source nor the destination host is on a network that is monitored by network discovery.
1	Vulnerable	red	Either: • the source or the destination host is in the network map, and a vulnerability is mapped to the host • the source or destination host is potentially compromised by a virus, trojan, or other piece of malicious software; see Setting Impact Level 1 for more information
2	Potentially Vulnerable	orange	Either the source or the destination host is in the network map and one of the following is true: • for port-oriented traffic, the port is running a server application protocol • for non-port-oriented traffic, the host uses the protocol
3	Currently Not Vulnerable	yellow	Either the source or the destination host is in the network map and one of the following is true: • for port-oriented traffic (for example, TCP or UDP), the port is not open • for non-port-oriented traffic (for example, ICMP), the host does not use the protocol
4	Unknown Target	blue	Either the source or destination host is on a monitored network, but there is no entry for the host in the network map.

- A rule triggers on a packet targeted for port 80 on a host. FireSIGHT responds by looking into the host database and finds a host entry there, but the host doesn't show a listening server (service) on port 80. FireSIGHT will respond by assigning an impact of 3, for Currently Not Vulnerable, to the event.

- A rule triggers on a packet targeted for port 80 on a host. FireSIGHT looks in the host database and finds a host entry and the host shows a listening server on port 80. In this case, FireSIGHT will assign an impact of 2, for Potentially Vulnerable, to the event.

- A rule triggers on a packet targeted for port 80 on a host. FireSIGHT looks into the host database and finds a host entry and the host shows a listening server on port 80. FireSIGHT then cross-references the listed vulnerabilities on the host and compares these to the vulnerability that the rule was written for based on the vulnerability ID. It finds a match—the rule was written for a vulnerability present on the host. FireSIGHT responds by assigning an impact of 1, for Vulnerable, to the event.

So as you can see, FireSIGHT is using the data it knows about the host to set an impact level for the event to help the analyst pick out the events most likely to be important. This is part of the sheer elegance of the FireSIGHT System—its ability to dynamically calculate the impact for each event relative to the hosts on *your* network!

The Caveat

While all of the power we just talked about is true, there's a key factor you've got to remember about impact—it can also be "hard-coded" into a rule. Setting the impact as described earlier is a great way to determine if a responder (server) is vulnerable to an attack, but what if a host, most likely a workstation, encounters malware? The "vulnerability" in this case is probably sitting in front of the keyboard! You'll find that rules written to look for evidence of malware will probably have the impact written into the rule, so you get an indication of the impact the event might have. In practice, the system generates very few false positive events from rules written to detect evidence of malware in outbound traffic. Because of this, hard-coding impact into the rule is a wonderful idea!

We know that was a pretty lengthy discussion about priority and impact, but hopefully it really helps you see why workflows displaying impact are so useful. The most important events are probably those with both impact level 1 and high priority. Keep in mind that we're not saying that these are the only important events. We're just pointing out that using impact and priority is a great way to start because they greatly help us narrow down events to the ones that are likely the most critical.

And we're not finished—now we need to dig into events further to find out just how bad they really are. There are several ways we can drill down to the next page in this workflow, and Table 6.1 describes what will happen for each one.

TABLE 6.1   Intrusion analysis drill-down techniques

Method	Result
Click one of the links in the table. You can click any of the items in any column except Count.	Drill to the next workflow page searching on the item. For example, clicking on an IP address will load the next workflow page, constraining the events from that particular source IP.
Click the blue down-arrow icon on the far left.	Drill to the next workflow page with only that event's row.
Select one or more check boxes and then click the View button at the bottom of the page.	Drill to the next workflow page with the selected event rows.
Click the View All button at the bottom of the page.	Drill to the next workflow page with *all* of the events
Click one of the links in the workflow pages list at the top of the page	Same as above—drill to the selected workflow page with all of the events. By the way, you can skip workflow pages using this method.

Referring back to our Impact and Source example (shown again in Figure 6.27):

FIGURE 6.27   Sample intrusion events

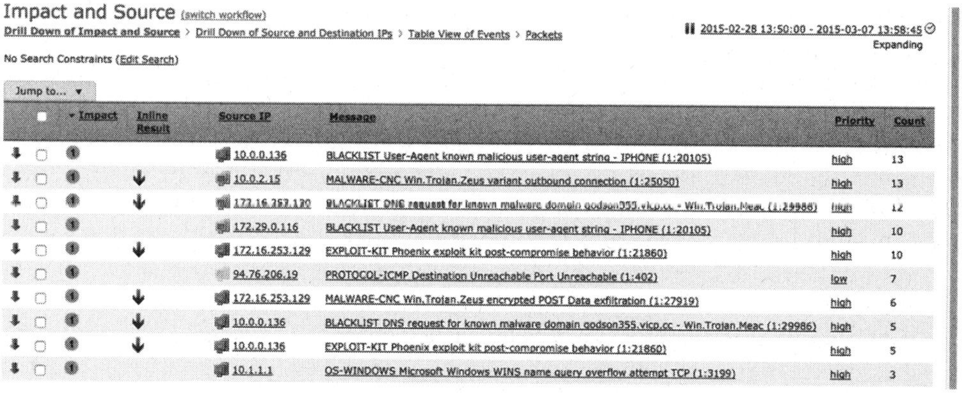

- If you wanted to drill into the next page with all the Impact 1 events, you would click any of the Impact 1 icons on the left.

- If you're interested in all the events from source IP 10.0.0.136, you would click that address in the Source IP column.

- If you're interested in a particular event type regardless of the source IP, you would click the event message.

- If you're interested in a specific event row only, you would click the blue down-arrow on the far left for the respective row.

Let's say you're interested in all the events that have been triggering for a particular source IP. Figure 6.28 shows the screen that we would get if we clicked the source IP of 10.0.0.136.

FIGURE 6.28   Event drill-down

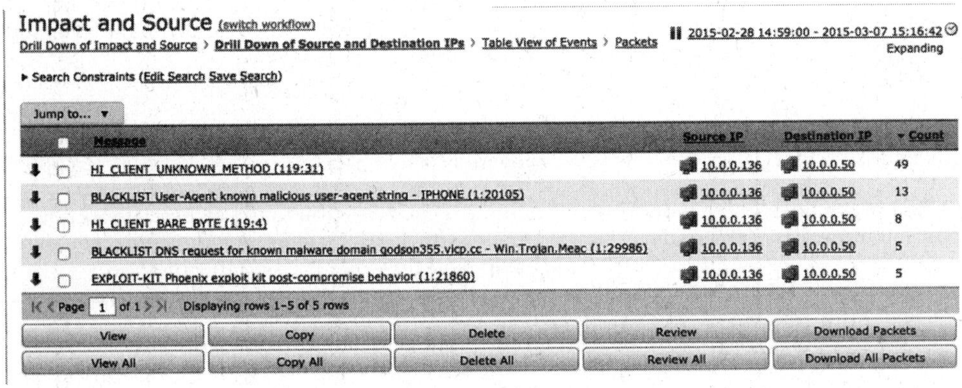

The first thing to point out here is that the workflow links at the top of the page have changed. The red bold link is now Drill Down of Source and Destination IPs, telling us that we're viewing this page.

Next, the columns have changed too because this workflow has removed some of the less relevant items and added Destination IP. Now we can see that all of the events from this source IP involve a single destination IP. Like a detective, we're gathering all of the data points, the context, around the event, and understanding that they are all between two hosts is a key piece of information! So what do we know about 10.0.0.50? Is it a proxy server? A router? And what about 10.0.0.136? It was interesting enough to drill this far, but clearly, we still need to know what this device is. Is it a server? A workstation?

To build up our context even more, we can learn about the source or destination if FireSIGHT has been collecting discovery data. Clicking on the computer icon next to an IP address reveals a pop-up with the host entry for that address. Figure 6.29 tells us what FireSIGHT knows about 10.0.0.136.

Okay, from this screen we can see that FireSIGHT believes this is a Windows host of some sort, but the traffic available so far hasn't allowed the system to make an exact determination of the host's operating system. We can also see that it doesn't appear to have anything in the way of listening services. There are two *indications of compromise (IoC)* on the system that are a bit of a concern. Check out both of these the based on the First Seen and the Last Seen columns—this host has encountered several events that fall into the categories Exploit Kit and Impact 1 Attack. We can't tell how many events have occurred between the first and last, but we do know there's been more than one.

FIGURE 6.29   Host entry

So now that we have a little more information, let's go back to the Impact and Source page of our workflow and take a closer look at one of the events for our 10.0.0.136 host. The second event in the list looks interesting because it says something about a "known malicious user-agent string." This is a common indication that a host has encountered malware, spyware, or another *possibly unwanted application (PUA)*. To drill into the next workflow page with just these events, we can either click the blue drill-down arrow at the left or click on the message in the Message column. Either one of these actions will get us to the Table View of Events screen pictured in Figure 6.30.

This view is much wider than almost any screen resolution, so you need to scroll the page horizontally to view all the fields.

When you've done that, you'll notice right away that not all the fields in an event entry are populated. Just look again at Figure 6.30 and you'll quickly see that the source and destination countries aren't listed. This is because geolocation only works on public routable addresses and the events we can see in Figure 6.30 are for non-routable private IP address ranges.

FIGURE 6.30   Table View drill-down

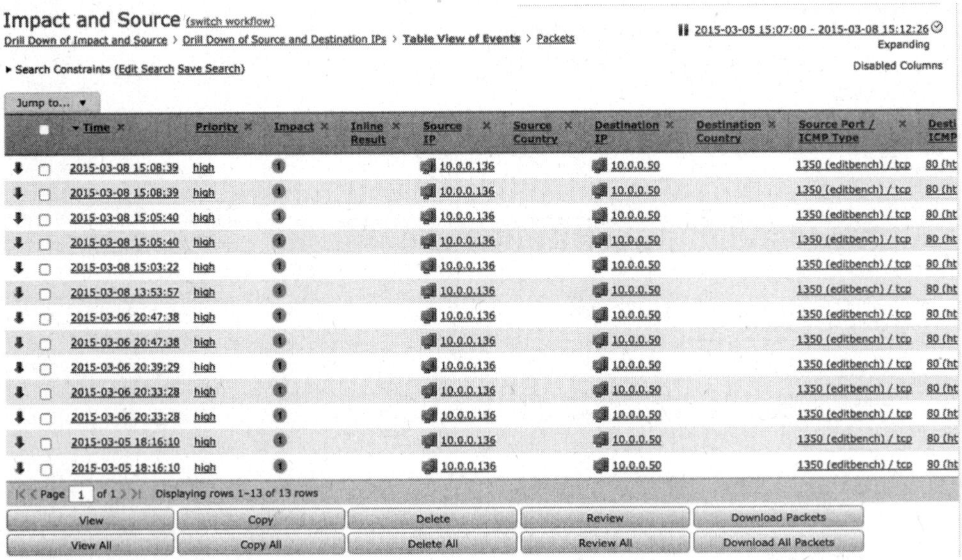

The purpose of geolocation is to identify the location of a routable IP address. The geolocation database contains IP-to-country mappings for all the IPv4 routable address space.

Table view pages contain every field available in the event. You'll see many fields such as Source and Destination Port, VLAN ID, Classification, Application Protocol, Ingress/Egress Interface, Device, and so on. Even though all that seems like a lot, it's actually not all the information available. By default, intrusion event table views still hide some information. To reveal the hidden fields, click the small black triangle to the left of Search Constraints. Once you've done that, you see the newly uncovered part of the page, shown in Figure 6.31.

As you can see, the reward for digging deeper is a nice long list of links under the Disabled Columns heading. These are the intrusion event fields that are referred to less commonly so they're disabled by default. To enable any of these columns and get it placed back into table view, just click the link. Keep in mind that this column will appear only in this particular table view. If you drill into a different intrusion event, the table view page will revert back to displaying the default columns only. If you do find a column that you would really like to see into for all events, you can create a custom workflow to include it.

FIGURE 6.31 Expanding disabled columns

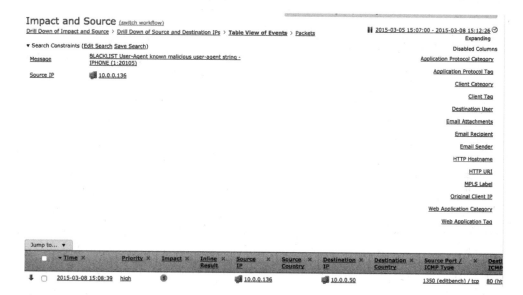

Most of the time, a table view probably won't give you all that much insight into an event because it's the packet and rule that will usually provide real understanding about why a given event triggered and what your response should be.

So let's move on and take a look at the packet view now. From the table view we have a number of options for drilling into individual packets. One of them is clicking the blue drill-down arrow, which will take you to the packet view for that individual packet. Another way is to click the Packets link near the top of the page, which will take you to the packet view and allow you to step through all the packets one at a time if you want to. Clicking either one will take you to a packet view like the one in Figure 6.32.

Clearly, the packet view page contains tons of information about the event, so we'll guide you through it one section at a time.

Event Information

Most of the information here is already available in one of the previous workflow pages. We already know what the source and destination IP are, but this does show us a few fields that are hidden in the default table view like HTTP URI. We can use this information to help us build context around the event and understand more about the type of traffic we are looking at. In this case, the fact that the source port is above 1024 and the destination port is 80 gives us a clue about what kind of packet this is because traffic destined for port 80 is almost always from an HTTP client (web browser) to a web server.

Rule

Even though the Snort rule is part of the Event Information section, it really warrants its own discussion. Because this is the actual rule that matched one or more packets, understanding what this rule was looking for will help us know how to respond to this event. We've zoomed into the rule portion in Figure 6.33.

FIGURE 6.32 Packet View page

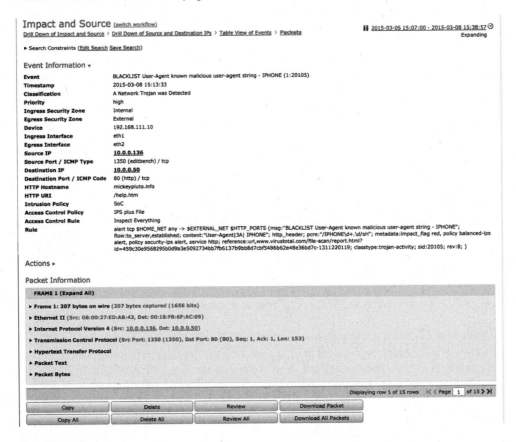

FIGURE 6.33 Snort rule

alert tcp $HOME_NET any -> $EXTERNAL_NET $HTTP_PORTS (msg:"BLACKLIST User-Agent known malicious user-agent string - IPHONE"; flow:to_server,established; content:"User-Agent|3A| IPHONE"; http_header; pcre:"/IPHONE\d+.\d/sH"; metadata:impact_flag red, policy balanced-ips alert, policy security-ips alert, service http; reference:url,www.virustotal.com/file-scan/report.html?id=459c30e9568295b0d9a3e5092734bb7fb6137b9bb8d7cbf5486b62e48e36bd7c-1311220119; classtype:trojan-activity; sid:20105; rev:8;)

We'll cover rules and rule syntax in another chapter. For now, we're going to walk through the rule to understand more about the reasons it would match a packet.

The rule header indicates that it's designed to inspect TCP traffic coming from the HOME_NET on any port going to the EXTERNAL_NET on HTTP_PORTS. In short, it's designed to inspect outbound web browsing from our network.

The message here tells us that there's a known malicious user-agent string named IPHONE.

The flow keyword restricts the rule to evaluating only traffic traveling from a client to a server. It also means only evaluates packets after the *three-way handshake*, meaning SYN, SYN/ACK, and ACK will be ignored. Understand that the flow keyword's job is to ensure the traffic qualifies for further inspection. Since you'll never see a browser user-agent in a SYN, SYN/ACK, or ACK packet and we don't care about server responses for this rule, there's no reason to waste resources inspecting them.

Next we get to a content check that's looking for the string "User-Agent" followed by a 0x3A (a colon) followed by the string "IPHONE." This search is restricted to the HTTP Header portion of the packet.

The final inspection is a "pcre" keyword. This looks for the string "IPHONE" followed by one or more digits, a single wildcard (the dot), then one more digit. The uppercase *H* following the pcre keyword is Snort specific and instructs Snort to search in the HTTP header for bytes matching this regular expression.

Packet Information

Just because the next section is Actions doesn't necessarily mean it's the next place you should look. This case is a good example—we're going to scrutinize the packet itself, first by looking at the Packet Information section below Actions, pictured in Figure 6.34.

FIGURE 6.34   Packet Information section

Packet Information

> **FRAME 1 (Expand All)**
>
> ▶ **Frame 1: 207 bytes on wire** (207 bytes captured (1656 bits)
>
> ▶ **Ethernet II** (Src: 08:00:27:ED:AB:43, Dst: 00:18:F8:6F:AC:09)
>
> ▶ **Internet Protocol Version 4** (Src: 10.0.0.136, Dst: 10.0.0.50)
>
> ▶ **Transmission Control Protocol** (Src Port: 1350 (1350), Dst Port: 80 (80), Seq: 1, Ack: 1, Len: 153)
>
> ▶ **Hypertext Transfer Protocol**
>
> ▶ **Packet Text**
>
> ▶ **Packet Bytes**

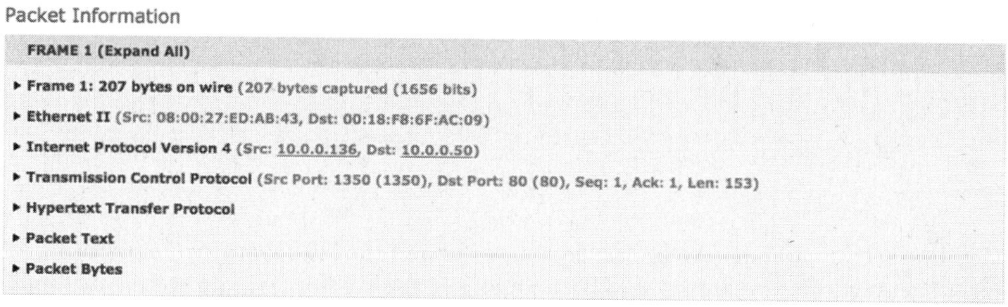

If you've ever used a packet analysis tool such as Wireshark, this section will probably look familiar. Each section of the packet is displayed from the Ethernet frame down to the data bytes. Most of the information in the packet header (source IP, destination, IP, protocol, port, etc.) has already been pulled out for us in the workflows. What we really want to examine here is the data portion, or payload, of the packet because that's where the evil is lurking.

In this example, the payload is displayed three different ways. The Hypertext Transfer Protocol, Packet Text, and Packet Bytes sections are all showing us the same data; they're just doing it in a different way. You can expand each section by clicking the black triangle at the left. In Figure 6.35, we've expanded all three sections.

FIGURE 6.35 Packet payload

```
▾ Hypertext Transfer Protocol
                                Expert Info (Chat/Sequence): GET /help.htm HTTP/1.1\r\n
                                Message: GET /help.htm HTTP/1.1\r\n
                                Severity level: Chat
                                Group: Sequence
                                Request Method: GET
                                Request URI: /help.htm
                                Request Version: HTTP/1.1

   Accept                       */*
   Host                         mickeypluto.info
   Connection                   Keep-Alive
   Full request URI             http://mickeypluto.info/help.htm

▾ Packet Text
   ...o....'..C..E...*hê.....

   ...
   ..2.F.P......[?P..=A...GET /help.htm HTTP/1.1
   User-Agent: IPHONE8.5(host:XPSP3-R93-0fc2003SP2,ip:172.29.0.116)
   Accept: */*
   Host: mickeypluto.info
   Connection: Keep-Alive


▾ Packet Bytes
   0000   00 18 f8 6f ac 09 08 00 27 ed ab 43 08 00 45 00   ...o....'..C..E.
   0010   00 c1 2a 68 40 00 80 06 bb 15 0a 00 00 88 0a 00   ..*hê...........
   0020   00 32 05 46 00 50 9a 1a 15 8f e2 f7 5b 3f 50 18   .2.F.P......[?P.
   0030   f9 3d 41 b1 00 00 47 45 54 20 2f 68 65 6c 70 2e   .=A...GET /help.
   0040   68 74 6d 20 48 54 54 50 2f 31 2e 31 0d 0a 55 73   htm HTTP/1.1..Us
   0050   65 72 2d 41 67 65 6e 74 3a 20 49 50 48 4f 4e 45   er-Agent: IPHONE
   0060   38 2e 35 28 68 6f 73 74 3a 58 50 53 50 33 2d 52   8.5(host:XPSP3-R
   0070   39 33 2d 4f 66 63 32 30 30 33 53 50 32 2c 69 70   93-0fc2003SP2,ip
   0080   3a 31 37 32 2e 32 39 2e 30 2e 31 31 36 29 0d 0a   :172.29.0.116)..
   0090   41 63 63 65 70 74 3a 20 2a 2f 2a 0d 0a 48 6f 73   Accept: */*..Hos
   00a0   74 3a 20 6d 69 63 6b 65 79 70 6c 75 74 6f 2e 69   t: mickeypluto.i
   00b0   6e 66 6f 0d 0a 43 6f 6e 6e 65 63 74 69 6f 6e 3a   nfo..Connection:
   00c0   20 4b 65 65 70 2d 41 6c 69 76 65 0d 0a 0d 0a      Keep-Alive....
```

The first section decodes the packet data according to the HTTP protocol, and the different fields within the packet have been identified and labeled. We can see the method, URI, HTTP version, and so on, but this decode doesn't include the user-agent. All that means is that this HTTP decoder isn't designed to display that data.

The next section shows the raw ASCII in the payload. Non-printable characters are displayed as dots. Here's where we can clearly see the User-Agent field and the contents:

```
IPHONE8.5 (host:XPSP3-R93-0fc200SP2,ip:172.29.0.116)
```

The Packet Bytes section also shows the data in hex and ASCII, which is really cool because it means you can see the byte value of all those non-printable characters. You can see the User-Agent in the ASCII display of the bytes on the right.

So what does all of this mean? Well, it tells us Snort found what it was looking for in the User-Agent. But how serious is the threat? Maybe it's just a new iPhone and that's what they use for a User-Agent. We still need more information, and we're going to turn to the rule documentation for it.

Actions

Now it's time to go back up the page to the Actions section. Expanding it reveals several links, as shown in Figure 6.36.

FIGURE 6.36   The Actions section

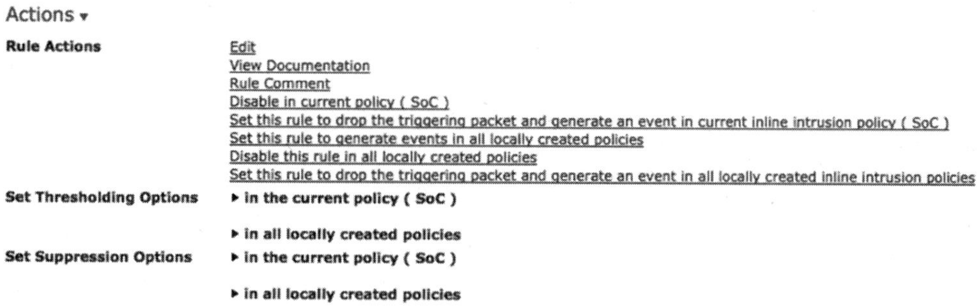

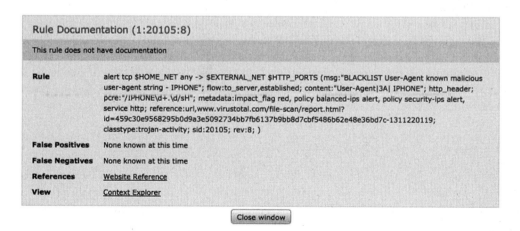

The Actions section contains a View Documentation link that will give us more insight into this rule as well as the alert. Clicking the link loads the rule documentation in a pop-up window, and you can end up getting a lot of information or none at all, depending on the rule. Figure 6.37 indicates there is not much documentation in this case.

FIGURE 6.37   Rule documentation

As you gain experience, you'll find that rules written to detect exploits against known software vulnerabilities usually have fairly decent documentation. This is because the threat vectors and methods of exploiting a particular vulnerability are usually well known.

You could say the vulnerability is a stationary target and we know what it takes to exploit it, and as a result, we can document the conditions the rule was written to detect and provide links to vendor and/or Bugtraq research on the subject. Furthermore, vulnerabilities in commercial or open-source software will have Common Vulnerabilities and Exposures (CVE) references.

On the other hand, rules written to detect malware aren't generally documented due to the lack of documentation on the malware itself. Often, we know the effect of the malware, like changing the User-Agent, but there's still not a whole lot of information available documenting what the malware actually does. In cases like this, search engines can be really useful, and for our example above, there's one Website Reference link referring to Virustotal.com. It's not a huge help because it only shows information on a particular executable, which is presumably the malware in question.

We won't try to dig into this particular rule or event much further because right now the point we want to get across is that you need enough information to treat it like a real malware event and follow up accordingly or decide it's a false positive.

Tuning False Positives

Let's talk about what you would do if this event were classified as a false positive. You have four options:

- Disable the rule.
- Suppress the alert.
- Threshold the rule.
- Create a PASS rule.

Disable the Rule

If you decide the rule is just way too prone to false positives or that it's not relevant to your environment, it's best to disable it. Doing this disables the rule in the applicable intrusion policy or policies. From the Actions view, you have two links to use to get this done: Disable in Current Policy (<policy name>) or Disable This Rule in All Locally Created Policies. Note that your user role must have the ability to edit an IPS policy to be able to use this feature.

Deciding between these two link options depends on which policies will be changed. If you only want the rule disabled in the policy that generated this alert, pick the first option. If you don't want the rule enabled on any of your policies, choose the second one. Clicking either one will result in a dialog at the top of the screen indicating what action was taken. In the example shown in Figure 6.38, we chose the first option to disable the rule only in the policy triggering the alert.

FIGURE 6.38   Disable in Current Policy

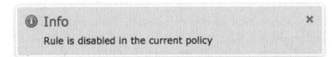

The intrusion policy has now been updated and will show up as "out-of-date" in the Intrusion Policy list view: (Policies ➤ Intrusion ➤ Intrusion Policy). The rule will continue to trigger on any matching packets until the intrusion or Access Control policy is reapplied.

Suppress the Alert

Our next option is to suppress the alert, which basically leaves the rule active while suppressing its output. This is what we normally do when we want to suppress the alert for a specific source or destination IP address. Going back to our example, what if we found that the host 10.0.0.136 was running a legitimate application using the IPHONE User-Agent? The problem is that after doing our research, we found out that there's also malware that uses this same User-Agent. But we're confident that 10.0.0.136 is the only host running the application, so we want to keep the rule active and just stop it from alerting for 10.0.0.136. This is a perfect example of when to choose suppression.

To suppress this rule for the single source IP address, we have two options: Suppress for the current policy or for all local policies. For this example we'll suppress only in the current policy by clicking the upper black triangle under Suppression Options, which displays the options shown in Figure 6.39.

FIGURE 6.39   Suppression options

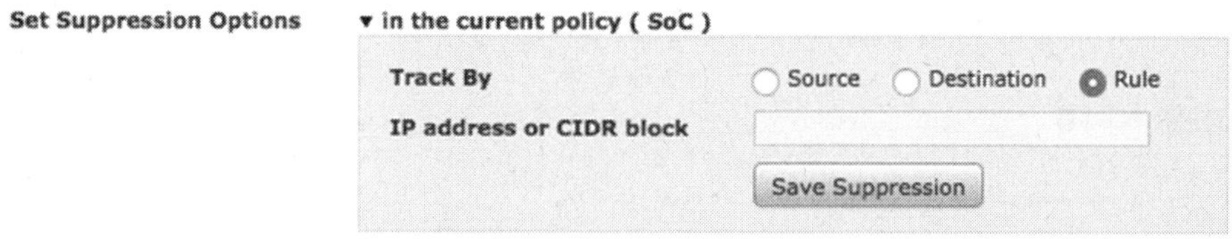

You can suppress by source IP, destination IP or by rule. To suppress a source IP, select the Source radio button and enter the IP or CIDR block into the field. Clicking Save Suppression updates the applicable policy. Remember, the intrusion or Access Control policy must be reapplied for this suppression to take effect.

A Few Notes on Suppression

While suppression is a useful tool, there are some important considerations you need to keep in mind:

Suppressing a rule does not disable the rule in the rule set; it simply suppresses the alert output. If the rule action is set to drop, the rule will *SILENTLY DROP THE PACKET, PROVIDING NO ALERT WHATSOEVER.* And yes, that was in all caps for a reason—it could be a troubleshooting nightmare! You only do this if you are absolutely sure the rule will *never* trigger a false positive alert. Suppression then is essentially useful for passive installations. For inline suppression, use a pass rule as outlined later.

If you select the "Rule" option under Track By, you will suppress the rule for all hosts, causing it to continue evaluating traffic but never alert. This is totally useless in passive installations, and for inline installations it runs the risk of dropping silently if this is a drop rule (see the all caps rant above)! It is much more common to suppress a rule based on a source or destination IP address.

You can suppress a source IP or a destination IP but not both. If you need to suppress alerts for traffic from a specific IP to another specific IP, you need a pass rule.

Threshold the Rule

Thresholding is another option for reducing the number of alerts generated by noisy rules. When you add a threshold, you are causing the rule not to alert until it matches a certain number of packets over a certain period. This is useful for rules that are designed to detect attacks like brute force password guessing. Often, rules written to detect this kind of activity will look for login failures. One or two failures from a single IP address is probably just someone mistyping their password, and we don't need to be alerted to that. But dozens of failures from the same host probably indicates something far more nefarious. To set a threshold on a rule, expand the appropriate section for current or all policies as we did in Figure 6.40 where we've expanded the current policy option.

FIGURE 6.40 Thresholding options

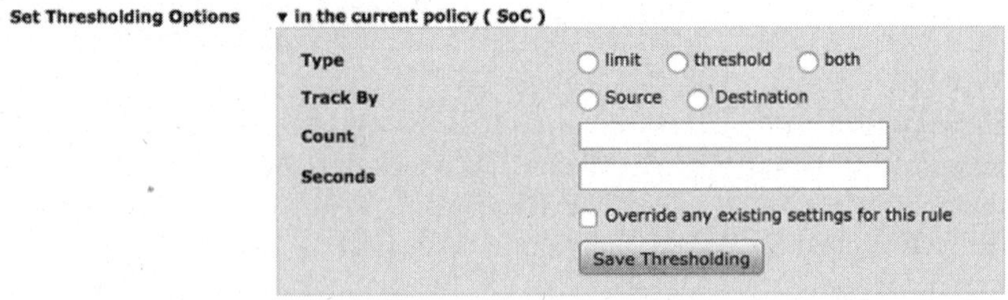

You can enter Limit, Threshold, or Both when configuring thresholding, plus a few other options.

Limit: This will limit notifications to the specified number of events set by Count per time period entered in seconds. For instance, you can limit the rule to alert no more than 5 times in 300 seconds regardless of how many packets actually match the rule.

Threshold: This will provide one alert for each number of matching packets specified by Count during the given time period. For example, you could require that one alert be generated for each 5 packets within 300 seconds.

Both: This will provide a notification once per time period after matching the specified count of packets—say, alert once per 300 seconds if you see at least 5 matching packets.

Track By: Source/Destination track matches to this rule by the source or destination IP.

Count: The count in packets matching the rule.

Seconds: A number in seconds during which the count will be evaluated.

Override existing setting: Check this box to replace any existing thresholds with the new one; otherwise, it simply adds an additional threshold.

Create a Pass Rule

The last option for rule tuning is to create a pass rule, which is great if you need to suppress a rule based on both the source *and* destination IP addresses. It's also the only real option for suppressing a drop rule in inline mode! The idea of a pass rule is to copy an existing rule, then change the action from alert to pass. You also modify the source/destination IP and/or port to match your specific suppression.

Without going too far into Snort rules, understand that a rule can have two actions in the FireSIGHT System: alert and pass. Alert is fairly self-explanatory—and means to do something when traffic is matched. But what is pass? A rule action of pass tells Snort to ignore this packet. So after matching a pass rule, Snort will "pass" the packet, skipping all the remaining the rules. Another important point is that regardless of where a pass rule appears in the rule set, Snort will always process traffic through pass rules first. This means that if you have two rules looking for the same thing and one of them is a pass rule, the pass rule will always win!

We can take advantage of this behavior to suppress certain rules. Let's say we've got a rule that's generating a false positive for specific traffic. We can respond as follows:

1. Make a copy of the rule.

2. Modify the rule header to match only the specific false positive hosts(s).

3. Change the action to pass.

Now this pass rule will only evaluate traffic between our specific hosts and look for the original rule's packet conditions. The pass rule has the same detection options as the original rule. Packets matching it will skip all the remaining rules, including the original one—effectively suppressing the original rule's alert for these packets.

Rule Comment

The last thing we're going to cover about rule actions is Rule Comment. Clicking this link will bring up the Add comment page in a pop-up window, shown in Figure 6.41.

FIGURE 6.41   The Add comment page

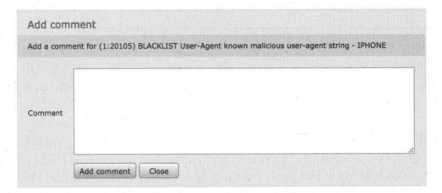

This is where we get to enter free-form text comments regarding a rule, and it's a great tool for documenting your analysis actions. When a comment is added, the system also automatically adds the user and time/date. Always keep in mind that rule comments are rule specific, not policy specific, and that comments added here will be visible regardless of where the rule is viewed on the Defense Center.

A Few More Cool Analysis Features

Finally, let's look at some of the other interesting features available for reviewing intrusion events.

Searching

The ability to search through intrusion events is a powerful feature of the FireSIGHT System. The system allows you to search any field in an event to locate the ones particularly relevant to you. From the intrusion event view, you've got three ways to navigate to the search page.

The first method is to click Search in the menu bar in the upper right, as shown in Figure 6.42.

FIGURE 6.42   Search menu

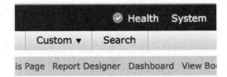

The second approach is to use the quick link located just below and to the right of the menu bar Search above. Hovering over Search here brings up your saved searches along with the built-in searches, as shown in Figure 6.43. From here you can click one of these to execute a specific search or click Search to load the search page.

FIGURE 6.43   Search quick link

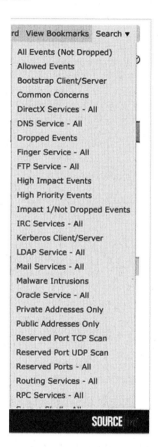

The third way to get into the search page is to click the Edit Search link on the upper left side of the screen, as shown in Figure 6.44. This also has the effect of editing an existing search query. The two prior methods won't preserve any current search condition.

FIGURE 6.44   Edit Search link

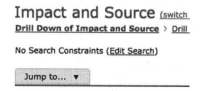

The search page itself, shown in Figure 6.45, is a pretty hefty list of all the fields you can search on in an intrusion event. On this page you'll see all of your saved searches on the left. The system comes with a number of preexisting searches by default, and you can't edit or erase these built-in items. You can however, create your own.

FIGURE 6.45   Top of the search page

Saved Searches

--- New Search---
All Events (Not Dropped) (Sourcefire)
Allowed Events (Sourcefire)
Bootstrap Client/Server (Sourcefire)
Common Concerns (Sourcefire)
DNS Service - All (Sourcefire)
DirectX Services - All (Sourcefire)
Dropped Events (Sourcefire)
FTP Service - All (Sourcefire)
Finger Service - All (Sourcefire)
High Impact Events (Sourcefire)
High Priority Events (Sourcefire)
IRC Services - All (Sourcefire)
Impact 1/Not Dropped Events (Sourcefire)
Kerberos Client/Server (Sourcefire)
LDAP Service - All (Sourcefire)
Mail Services - All (Sourcefire)
Malware Intrusions (Sourcefire)
Oracle Service - All (Sourcefire)
Private Addresses Only (Sourcefire)

[Load] [Delete]

Search Information

Note: If a search name is not specified, an automatically generated name will be used.

Table	Intrusion Events	
Name		Search 1, My Search
Save As Private	☑	

Constraint

Priority		high, medium, low
Impact		Impact 1, Impact 2
Inline Result		dropped, would have dropped
Source IP		192.168.1.0/24, !192.168.1.3, 2001:db8:85a3::1370
Destination IP		192.168.1.0/24, !192.168.1.3, 2001:db8:85a3::1370
Source / Destination IP		192.168.1.0/24, !192.168.1.3, 2001:db8:85a3::1370
Source Country		USA, United States, United*
Destination Country		USA, United States, United*
Source / Destination Country		USA, United States, United*
Source Continent		North America, *America
Destination Continent		North America, *America
Source / Destination Continent		North America, *America

To load an existing search query, select it from the list on the left and click the Load button at the bottom. After this you can modify the search criteria if you want, and when you're ready, just hit Enter or scroll to the bottom of the page and click the Search button. Figure 6.46 shows the bottom portion of the search page.

Saving searches is as easy as giving your search a name and clicking the Save or Save As New Search button. Know that if the Save As Private check box is selected, no other users will be able to use your searches.

The different search pages in the system also have sample search information to the right of each field that helps users to quickly understand what type of data is appropriate for the field. Some fields also have a green plus icon to the right, and clicking this will load any objects you've created. Figure 6.47 shows the network objects you'll get as a result of clicking the icon to the right of the Source IP field.

If you start your search name with a dash or other special character when naming custom searches, they'll be sorted above the built-in searches. This makes it much easier to locate your searches—you don't have to spend time going down the list of default searches to find them!

FIGURE 6.46   Bottom of the search page

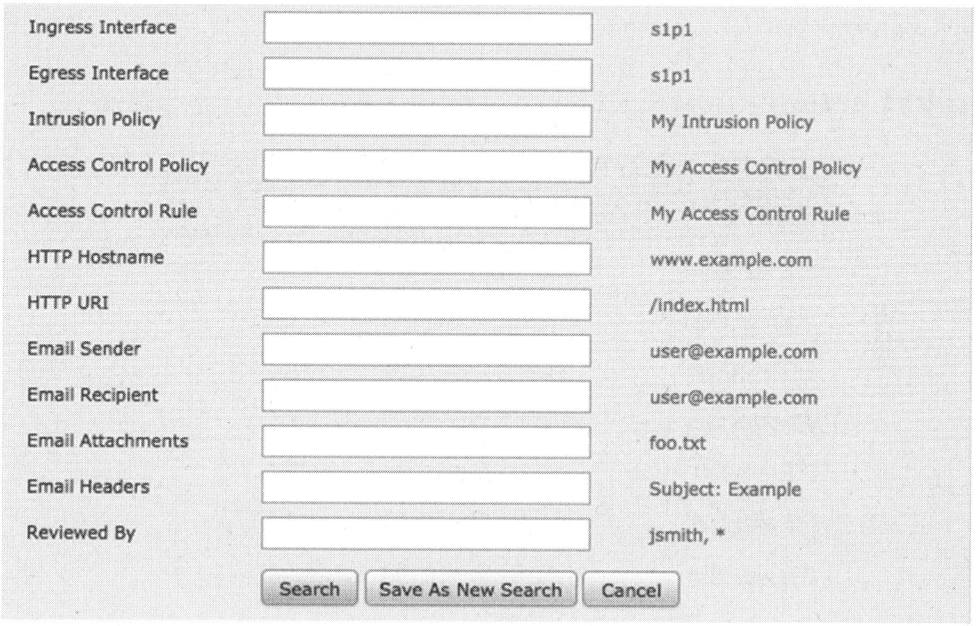

Ingress Interface		s1p1
Egress Interface		s1p1
Intrusion Policy		My Intrusion Policy
Access Control Policy		My Access Control Policy
Access Control Rule		My Access Control Rule
HTTP Hostname		www.example.com
HTTP URI		/index.html
Email Sender		user@example.com
Email Recipient		user@example.com
Email Attachments		foo.txt
Email Headers		Subject: Example
Reviewed By		jsmith, *

| Search | Save As New Search | Cancel |

FIGURE 6.47   Searching for objects

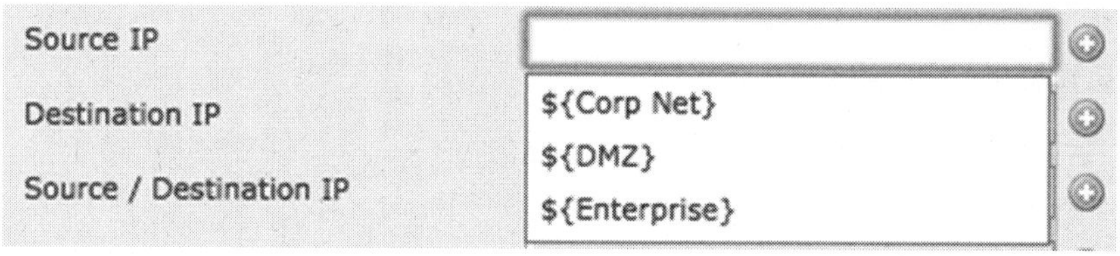

Source IP	
Destination IP	${Corp Net}
	${DMZ}
Source / Destination IP	${Enterprise}

Reviewed Events

Another FireSIGHT feature is the ability to place events into Reviewed status. To keep track of events you've already evaluated you can mark them as Reviewed. This is really helpful if you've reviewed an event, made a determination regarding its viability, and want to continue to analyze additional events because it effectively removes that event from your analysis workflow without deleting it from the database.

To review events, use the Review buttons at the bottom of the analysis view. Clicking the Review button will affect the selected events—rows with the check box selected. The Review All button will place all the events currently listed in Reviewed status. Keep in mind that this applies to *all* the events selected by the current search query and time window, not just the ones visible on the page!

Placing events into Reviewed status also marks them with the name of the reviewing user. This can be found in the Reviewed By field visible on the far right column of the table view page, as shown in Figure 6.48.

FIGURE 6.48 Reviewed status

Access Control × Policy	Access Control × Rule	Reviewed × By
IPS plus File	Inspect Everything	admin
IPS plus File	Inspect Everything	admin
IPS plus File	Inspect Everything	admin
IPS plus File	Inspect Everything	admin
IPS plus File	Inspect Everything	admin
IPS plus File	Inspect Everything	admin
IPS plus File	Inspect Everything	admin

Figure 6.49 shows a portion of the search page where you can also search by name for events reviewed by a particular user or search for all reviewed events by using a * in the Reviewed By search field.

FIGURE 6.49 Reviewed By search

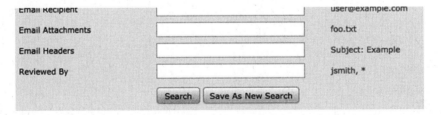

Email Recipient		user@example.com
Email Attachments		foo.txt
Email Headers		Subject: Example
Reviewed By		jsmith, *
	Search Save As New Search	

Placing an event into Reviewed status removes it from intrusion event workflows for all users!

Okay, once events have been placed into Reviewed status, you can view them two ways. One is to use the Reviewed By search and the other is to select Analysis ➤ Intrusions ➤ Reviewed Events. Figure 6.50 shows this is actually just a shortcut to loading the Reviewed By * search, as you can see if you expand the Edit Search link on the left.

FIGURE 6.50   Reviewed events menu

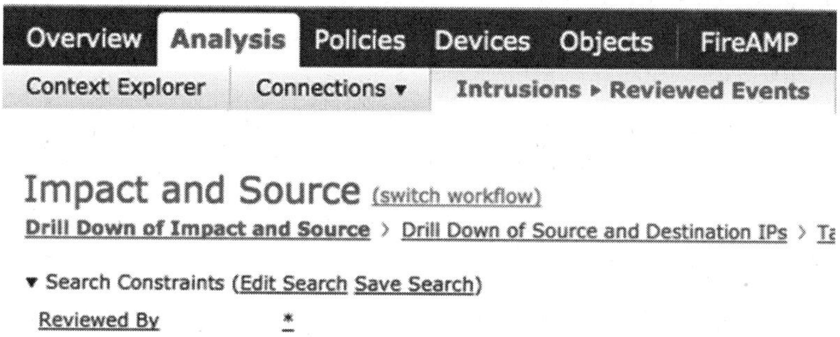

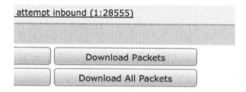

Packet Downloads

By default, when an intrusion event is triggered, Snort saves the packet. During event analysis, these packets can be downloaded to the analyst workstation for archival or for further analysis. Each workflow page contains a Download Packets button in the row of buttons at the bottom, as shown in Figure 6.51. Clicking this will download the selected event packets. As with the other buttons in this row, the Download All Packets button works for all the packets returned by the time window and search query.

FIGURE 6.51   Packet download buttons

When you're drilled into the packet view, the top row button changes slightly, from the plural *Packets* to the singular, *Packet*. There's also a difference in the downloaded file.

> **NOTE**   FireSIGHT captures the single packet or sometimes the reassembled frames that caused an event to trigger. It does not capture the entire session.

When the page shows multiple packets or when you use the Download All Packets button, you get a zip archive containing multiple pcap format files. But when you are drilled down to the packet view, clicking the Download Packet button downloads a single file in pcap format. In this case, you can often just select Open With and select an application like Wireshark to view the packet contents. If you're downloading multiple packets, you'll have to unzip the archive first.

If you want to keep a long-term record of packet data, the download feature is really helpful. Due to the circular nature of event storage, intrusion events will eventually be purged from the Defense Center and along with them the packet data.

Incidents

The FireSIGHT System contains a "rudimentary" incident handling function that you can use to keep track of noteworthy events. The features are admittedly limited, and most organizations will have a more full-featured incident management system, but it does offer the ability to keep track of intrusion event incidents within the security team.

To create an incident, first select the event(s) you would like keep track of by checking the boxes on the left. Then click the Copy or Copy All button at the bottom of the page. You'll see a message at the top of the page confirming the copy operation, as shown in Figure 6.52.

FIGURE 6.52   Copy dialog

Navigate to Analysis ≻ Intrusions ≻ Incidents and click the Create Incident button to bring up the new incident screen, shown in Figure 6.53.

FIGURE 6.53   Create New Incident

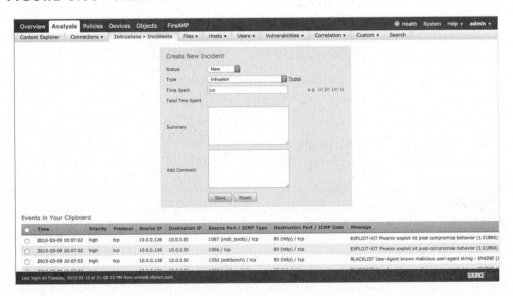

Now you can complete the incident information. The events you copied will be shown below the incident. Once you've entered the information, you can click the Save button or scroll down to the bottom of the screen and click the Add To Incident or Add All To

Incident button. Clicking the first button will add only the checked events, while the second button will add all the events.

> When you add the events to an incident, you're not adding the packets. In fact, you're not even adding all the event metadata to the incident. The only fields from the intrusion event that will be are stored are Time, Priority, Protocol, Source/Destination IP, Source/Destination Port, and Message, so if you need to save the packets as part of your incident, be sure to download them manually. Otherwise, if and when events are purged from the intrusion event database, you'll be left with only this subset of event metadata!

Summary

You now know how to use of the FireSIGHT System to analyze intrusion event data. You're familiar with some of the workflows available for analyzing events, and you learned from many examples how to drill into the relevant event data you're after. You also have a pretty good idea of some strategic actions to take when confronted with certain intrusion events. We also introduced you to the Dashboard and Context Explorer.

Hands-on Lab

In this lab, we will run through some of the common tasks you'll perform when analyzing intrusion events. It should be noted that for this lab to work, you must have some intrusion events to analyze.

1. Open your web browser and HTTPS to your Defense Center.

2. Log in to the Defense Center.

3. Navigate to Analysis ➤ Intrusions ➤ Events.

   You should see the default workflow. If it has not been customized, it will be Events by Priority and Classification.

4. To customize the workflow default, navigate to <your login name> ➤ User Preferences.

5. Click the Event View Settings tab.

6. Under Default Intrusion Workflow, select Impact And Source.

7. Scroll to the bottom of the screen and click the Save button.

8. Return to Analysis ➤ Intrusions ➤ Events and note that you now have a new default workflow.

9. From your list of intrusion events, choose one with a count higher than 1. Click the blue drill-down arrow at the far left of the screen. This will bring you to the second page in this workflow, showing the count of events between each source and

destination IP. You may see a single row or multiple rows if there is more than one source/destination pair generating these events.

10. Return to the main workflow page by clicking the Drill Down Of Impact And Source link in the upper left. Notice that instead of seeing all the events, you still see only the row you drilled into earlier. This is because the search is still in effect.

11. To view the current search, click the small black triangle to the left of Search Constraints in the upper left. Notice you have a link named Compound Constraints with several search constraints.

12. Click the Compound Constraints link to remove the search. This will clear the search and once again display all the events in your time window.

13. Edit the existing time window by clicking the time/date range link in the upper-right corner. This will bring up the Time Window dialog in a new browser window.

14. Select a time window larger or smaller than your current time window. You can do this by using the calendar and clock controls or clicking one of the presets.

15. Click the Apply button. Note the change in your event counts.

16. Choose an event with a blue or red computer icon in the Source IP column and click the icon. This will bring up the host profile in a new browser window.

17. Review the host information. When you're finished, close the Host Profile window.

18. Right-click on the blue drill-down arrow at the left of one of your events. Note the context menu and the actions available. Click on a blank area of the screen to allow the list to close.

19. Select several events by clicking on the selection check boxes. Then click the View button. This will take you to the next page in the workflow, with all of the selected events.

20. Click the Table View of Events link. You are now viewing a table view with one row for each packet of your selected events.

21. Click the X to the right of the Priority column. A list of all the available columns will appear. Note that you can enable or disable multiple columns using this method. Select some disabled columns and deselect some enabled columns. When you are finished, click the Apply button.

    Note that you have customized this table view and have added and/or removed columns.

22. Click the Packets link.

23. From the Packets screen, review the event information and the Snort rule. If your rule contains a "content" keyword, expand the appropriate packet section and look for the string and/or hex bytes in the content match. Note that this will probably be easiest to find in the Packet Text section.

24. Expand the Actions section. Review some of your options for this rule, including disabling, suppression, and thresholding.

25. Click the View Documentation link and review any documentation for the rule. When you're finished, click the Close Window button.

26. Click the Download Packet button at the bottom to download the pcap file.

27. Click the Drill Down of Impact and Source link in the upper left to return to the main workflow page. Notice that your search is still in effect; you are seeing only the events you selected previously.

28. Select one or more rows by clicking the check boxes at the left.

29. Click the Review button. Notice that these events are no longer visible.

30. Reset the search by navigating to Intrusions ➤ Events. Note this is another method of removing the current search criteria.

31. View your reviewed events by navigating to Analysis ➤ Intrusions ➤ Reviewed Events.

Exam Essentials

Understand the basics of geolocation.

Geolocation maps routable IP addresses to geographic locations.

Be able to describe key dashboard features:

- Customizable widgets
- Tabbed pages
- Event-based as well as operational information
- Ability to create custom dashboards and pages

Be familiar with the Context Explorer:

- Interactive searches and pivoting
- Fixed preset visual contexts
- Extensive filter capability
- Resets to default upon exit

Understand time windows:

- The default time window is the last hour expanding.
- The static time window has a fixed start and stop date/time.
- The sliding time window is useful for reporting.
- There are three time windows by default.
- The default time window is customizable per user.

Review Questions

You can find the answers in Appendix A.

1. The default FireSIGHT intrusion event workflow is _____ .
   A. Events by Priority and Classification
   B. Impact and Source
   C. Event Specific
   D. Packet view

2. Which of the following represents a time window that becomes longer as an analyst continues to sift through events?
   A. Static
   B. Expanding
   C. Sliding
   D. Stretch

3. What is the result of clicking on a source IP address in a table view?
   A. Load the host entry
   B. Ping the IP address
   C. Perform a Whois search
   D. Load the packet view

4. Which of the following is not a characteristic of the Dashboard?
   A. Customizable widgets
   B. Flexible searching and dynamic "pivoting" of data
   C. Multiple searches and various event views all on one page
   D. Ability to add personal dashboards

5. An Orange Impact 2 (Potentially Vulnerable) indicates what?
   A. The source or destination is potentially compromised by a worm or malware.
   B. For port-oriented traffic, the port is not open.
   C. For port-oriented traffic, the port is running a server application protocol.
   D. There is no entry for the host in the network map.

6. Which of the following would probably not be appropriate to reduce noise from a drop rule in an inline environment?
   A. Pass rule
   B. Suppression
   C. Threshold
   D. Disable rule

7. Which of the following can be used to cause a rule to trigger only if it matches a predetermined number of packets?

   A. Pass rule

   B. Suppression

   C. Threshold

   D. Disable rule

8. What is the file format when downloading multiple packets?

   A. libpcap

   B. zip

   C. ASCII

   D. LZH

9. What is the purpose of the Copy and Copy All buttons?

   A. Events can be pasted to a local folder.

   B. Copying packets makes them easier to analyze.

   C. For packet playback using tcpreplay.

   D. To save the event data in an incident.

10. What is a false positive?

   A. An event that should be avoided at all costs

   B. Something that can be expected from time to time

   C. A result of a poorly written rule

   D. A total failure of the IPS

Chapter

7

Network-Based Malware Detection

THE SSFIPS EXAM TOPICS COVERED IN THIS CHAPTER INCLUDE THE FOLLOWING:

✓ 6.0 Network-Based Malware Detection

✓ 6.1 Describe the interface components used for analyzing malware events

✓ 6.2 Understand the different techniques used to identify malware

✓ 6.3 Describe the features of malware detection as used by the Cisco NGIPS, including communication, actions, and protocols

FireSIGHT's Advanced Malware Protection (AMP) is designed to tackle one of the worst and arguably most prevalent threat vectors today—malware! Nicknamed from the term *malicious software*, malware comes in a variety of vile flavors, from coded weapons fashioned to damage, control, or disable a computer system to programs that perform reconnaissance and steal data (identity theft). Basically, malware's purpose is to carry out some kind of nefarious act on its victim that often goes undetected—at least for a while. Even worse, most of the time, the exploited vulnerabilities are users themselves, even though malware can take advantage of software bugs and weaknesses too.

Cisco has two versions of its AMP product—one for endpoints and one for networks—and they have a lot in common when it comes to their detection methods. In this chapter, our focus is going to be on the AMP network version.

To find up-to-the-minute updates for this chapter, please see www.lammle .com/firepower or the book's web page at www.sybex.com.

AMP Architecture

Modern networks make communicating, sharing information, and collaborating with other users and businesses a breeze. We take for granted being able to download and run software with a click, spiriting through barriers that existed not so long ago like birds through mist. But all these convenient virtual amenities come teeming with significant risks. As it's said, "With great power comes great responsibility," and far too many users are unaware of or naïve to the fact that there's really no way to tell what a binary program will actually do before install. When we execute software, we're taking a huge leap of faith, totally trusting the application/attachment/file to behave and do only what it's supposed to—nothing more. In reality, the program can generally do anything within the context of the user's permissions, meaning that if that user happens to have admin or even root privileges, then the sky is pretty much the limit and the software can do nearly anything on the system!

A key component of AMP is cloud intelligence. *The Collective Security Intelligence cloud* continuously processes samples of files received from many sources. The files gathered are then run through a series of checks comparing them to known malware, at times executing them in a sandbox environment. These files are then assigned a proper disposition.

AMP uses this cloud intelligence to block and/or alert on known malicious software before it reaches the endpoint target via these techniques:

- SHA-256 hash

- Static file fingerprint (Spero)

- Dynamic analysis

SHA-256

The first technique is to calculate the *SHA-256* hash for the file in question. Each file has a unique SHA-256 hash value that the FireSIGHT device calculates and transmits to the Defense Center, which in turn transmits it to the Cisco Intelligence cloud. If the hash matches a known file, the appropriate disposition is returned. It's important to understand that the file itself never leaves the device in this case—only the SHA-256 hash is transmitted.

Spero Analysis

The second strategy is a static file analysis known as *Spero*. It examines several hundred file attributes, including file header information, DLLs called, and other static metadata information and generates a hash of these values. The idea is that even if the file isn't exactly the one we're looking for, signs within the file indicating it's malware can be identified anyway. The Spero hash is analyzed in the Cisco Intelligence cloud and, along with dynamic analysis, results in a malware score. If this score is high enough, the file can be convicted as malware. Spero analysis doesn't require that the file itself be transmitted to the cloud.

Dynamic Analysis

The third technique differs from the other two we just talked about in several ways. First of all, it takes time, sometimes 20 minutes or more, to return a disposition. Also, *dynamic analysis* requires the file to be uploaded to the cloud. It involves executing the file in a "sandbox"—a virtual machine environment—and as the file executes, its actions are analyzed, including behaviors like the ones in this list:

- Host IPS/firewall/operating system protection evasion

- Persistence and installation behavior

- Anti-debugging

- Boot survival

- Data obfuscation (packer)

- Remote access functionality

- Virtual machine detection

- What network connections are made

So if the analysis score is high enough, the file is considered malware. Yet once the analyzed file has already passed through the device, the window to block it has clearly closed. But even though it can no longer be blocked, at least the file's hash has been classified as malware, so any future detection events of its kind will immediately return a malware verdict.

Retrospective Events

Another cool feature of AMP is known as a *retrospective event*. This occurs when the malware disposition for a previously detected file changes and almost always means a file previously assigned the disposition of "unknown" has since been exposed as malicious. This after-the-fact detection generates a special, retrospective event, which can happen anywhere from minutes to days after a file is first detected. The change is reported to the Defense Center from the Cisco Intelligence cloud, which then updates all previous detections of this SHA-256 value with its new disposition.

As you can imagine, retrospective detection is a powerful feature of the AMP product because it means that even if a new piece of malware escapes detection initially, once its true evil nature is known, you'll be alerted. And once you've been made aware of the threat, you can go back and locate anyplace it has traversed your network.

Communications Architecture

To get a picture of what the AMP communications architecture looks like for this process, check out Figure 7.1. This snapshot was taken from the actual FireSIGHT System help screen.

FIGURE 7.1   AMP communications architecture

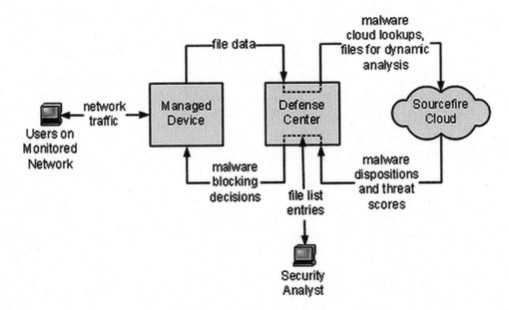

The diagram is pretty straightforward—the managed device inspects the file transfer traffic, collects files, and calculates the SHA-256 and Spero hashes. These hashes are then sent to the Defense Center, which first checks its cache and then forwards them to the Sourcefire (Cisco) cloud. The disposition is returned in real time, and the Defense Center advises the device whether to block or allow the file. If Dynamic Analysis is configured in the file policy and the disposition of the file is unknown, the device then uploads the file directly to the cloud for analysis.

File Dispositions

By now you probably understand that the purpose driving these techniques is to arrive at a correct file disposition. Here's a brief on the five, potential returned dispositions:

Clean—Tells us that the file is benign and indicates it's a known good file. It might be digitally signed by a known vendor or have been vetted another way.

Unknown—Means that a definitive disposition could not be determined. It's possible that this file hasn't been seen anywhere else or that a sandbox analysis shows the file is low risk.

Malware—The file is known to be malicious.

Unavailable—This isn't actually a disposition returned from Cisco, but it definitely means something prevented the cloud lookup.

Custom Detection—The user added the file to the custom detection list.

File Disposition Caching

To minimize the number of cloud lookups, file dispositions are cached on the Defense Center. Once a file disposition is returned from the cloud, it is cached so that subsequent lookups of this same hash value do not result in repeated cloud communications. The cache time-to-live values are listed here:

- Clean: 4 hours
- Malware: 1 hour
- Unknown: 1 hour

File Policy

Advanced Malware Protection is configured through the file policy that controls which application protocols will undergo file inspection, the direction of file transfer, the type of files to inspect, and the action. A file policy is applied to traffic via an Allow rule in the Access Control policy instead of directly to devices. Interestingly, this is the same rule you would typically use to implement IPS inspection through an intrusion policy. Figure 7.2 offers a review of where the file policy is configured in an Access Control rule.

FIGURE 7.2   Allow rule Inspection tab

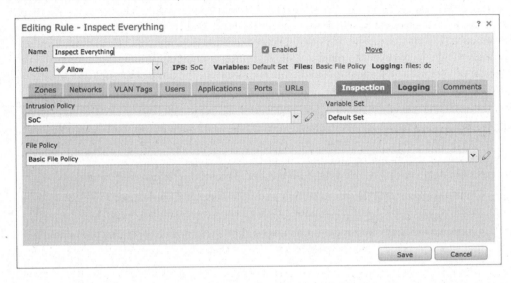

To create a file policy, navigate to Policies ➢ Files. Remember—there's no default file policy, so to create one, click the New File Policy button. Once you've done that, give your policy a name in the dialog, as shown in Figure 7.3.

FIGURE 7.3   New File Policy dialog

Advanced Settings

First, let's take a look at the Advanced tab, where we've got several options:

Enable Custom Detection List—You would check this box to use your custom detection list object. It contains a list of SHA-256 values that will be considered malware.

Enable Clean List—Selecting this box enables your clean list object. These SHA-256 values will always be considered clean regardless of their cloud disposition.

Mark files as malware based on dynamic analysis threat score—This option has four subsettings:

> **Disabled**—Files that will not be considered malware based on dynamic analysis
>
> **Medium**—A score of 26 or above
>
> **High**—A score of 51 or above
>
> **Very High**—A score of 76 and above

The last three items represent the Dynamic Analysis scores that will result in marking a file as malware. This applies to any files analyzed in the Cisco Intelligence cloud.

The File Policy Advanced tab is shown in Figure 7.4.

FIGURE 7.4   File Policy Advanced tab

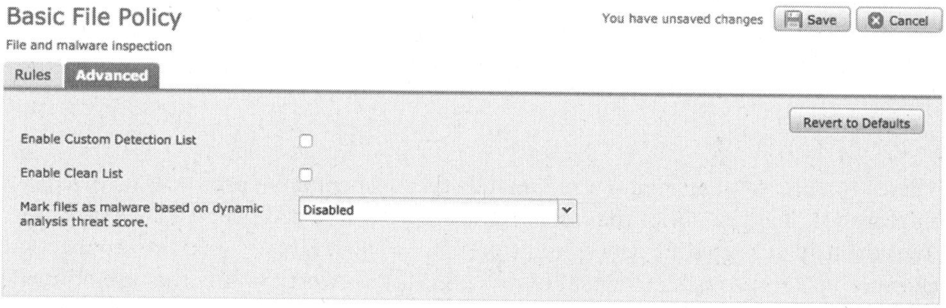

File Rules

File policy rules are configured on the Rules tab. To create a rule, just click the Add File Rule button, which will bring up the Add File Rule dialog, shown in Figure 7.5.

FIGURE 7.5   Add File Rule dialog

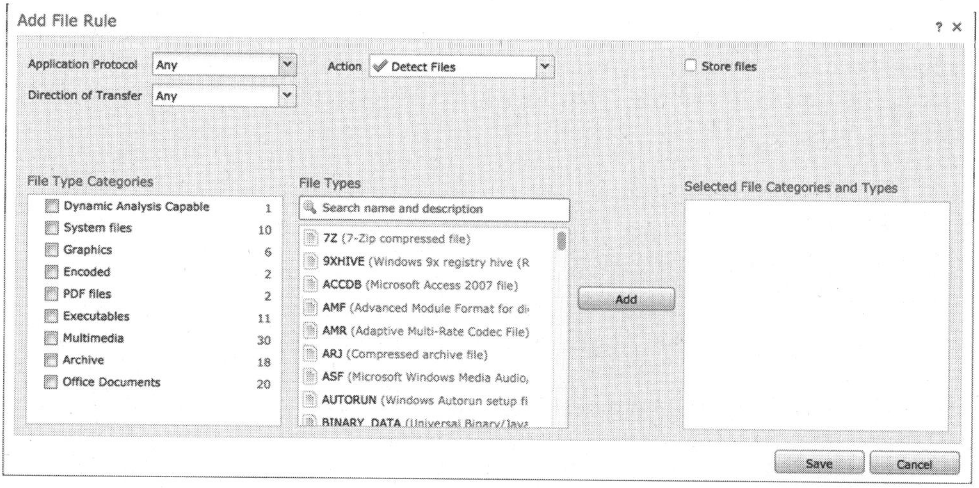

Application Protocol

The first item on this screen is Application Protocol. Clicking this drop-down reveals the protocols available for file inspection, as shown in Figure 7.6.

FIGURE 7.6 File application protocols

These are fairly self-explanatory and include the most common protocols involved in file transfers. Did you notice that all of these are clear-text protocols? That's because without the help of a separate decryption solution, FireSIGHT can't peer into connections using encrypted protocols like SSH, SSL, or TLS. It's also worth noting that even though NetBIOS (SMB) is listed, this is version 1 of the protocol. Because all Windows operating systems since 2006 (Windows Vista) use SMB 2.0 or higher, this may mean you can't inspect SMB files as they traverse your internal network.

We'd also like to point out that all application protocols are not treated equally—some are restricted in the direction of file transfer supported.

Direction of Transfer

Below the Application Protocol drop-down, you'll find the Direction Of Transfer option. The values available in this drop-down depend on what you selected in Application Protocol. For instance, if you chose Any for a given protocol, then you have the following options:

- Any
- Upload
- Download

Still, if certain protocols have been selected, then the options for Direction Of Transfer will be limited. Table 7.1 shows the directions that are supported for each protocol.

So bear in mind that certain protocols, especially those used for email, allow analysis in only one direction.

TABLE 7.1   Table of protocols for inspection and direction of transfer

Application Protocol	Direction of Transfer
Any	Any, Upload, Download
HTTP	Any, Upload, Download
SMTP	Upload
IMAP	Download
POP3	Download
FTP	Any, Upload, Download
NetBIOS-snn (SMB)	Any, Upload, Download

Action

Next to the transfer direction, we find the Action drop-down, where we determine the action to take on the traffic matching the rule. The default is Detect Files, but there are several other options available:

Detect Files—Will log the movement of files while still allowing them to pass.

Block Files—Will block the files.

Malware Cloud Lookup—Will calculate the SHA-256 hash value and use the cloud lookup process to determine the malware disposition. Once that's determined, this option will log the malware disposition of files while still allowing them to pass.

Block Malware—This is the same as Malware Cloud Lookup only this rule will actually block transfer of files that represent threats.

Figure 7.7 shows the Action drop-down in a file policy rule.

FIGURE 7.7   File rule actions

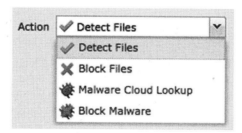

In Figure 7.8, we can see that each of the actions selected will display additional option check boxes. The Detect Files action offers us the option of storing the files, and if it's checked, files matching the rule are stored on the device.

FIGURE 7.8   Detect Files option

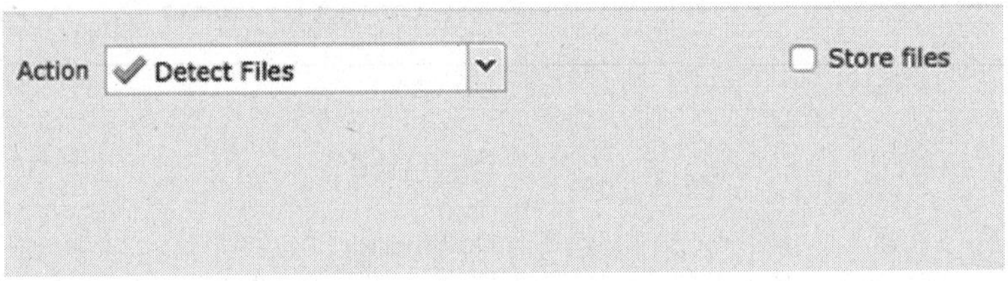

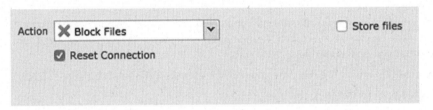

The Block Files action also allows for storing the file and offers the option to reset the connection, as you can see in Figure 7.9.

FIGURE 7.9   Block File options

The Malware Cloud Lookup action adds the three options revealed in Figure 7.10.

FIGURE 7.10   Malware Cloud Lookup options

Spero Analysis for MSEXE—Checking this box will cause the device to send the Spero hash to the Defense Center if the initial SHA-256 comes back as unknown. This only applies to MSEXE file types.

Dynamic Analysis—Checking this box tells the device to upload the file to the cloud for dynamic analysis. This is only for unknown MSEXE files that haven't been previously analyzed.

Store Files—This option allows for the storage of files on the device based on their disposition.

The Block Malware action is very similar to Malware Cloud Lookup, but it adds the option to reset the connection, as shown in Figure 7.11.

FIGURE 7.11   Block Malware options

File Types and Categories

The final criterion for a file rule is the file type, and there are three columns in the rule related to file types, as you can see in Figure 7.12.

FIGURE 7.12   File Type selection

The File Types list is in the center column, it shows all the supported file types that can be inspected with a file rule. If you know the specific file type(s) you want to inspect, you can select one or more from this column and click the Add button to add them to the Selected File Categories And Types column. However, the File Type Categories column on the left is there to make this selection easier for you. By checking the boxes on the left, you can select all the file types matching a given category. The number to the right of each category indicates how many file types are currently in this category. Keep in mind that there may be some overlap with File Type Categories; for instance, the MSEXE file type is present in both the Dynamic Analysis Capable and Executables categories.

Once you have selected the criteria for the rule, you're ready to add it to your policy. The rule shown in Figure 7.13 is configured to inspect all supported protocols and directions for executable and system files for malware. It will perform Spero and Dynamic Analysis if required. Any files exceeding the Spero score or those that return a malware status will be blocked and the connection reset. Depending on the Access Control policy, a file/malware event will also be logged to the Defense Center.

FIGURE 7.13 Example file rule

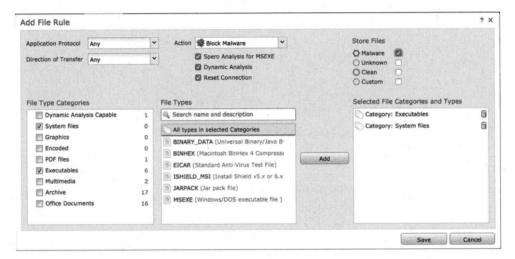

Rule Precedence

Unlike Access Control rules, file rules are unordered. They'll be placed into the policy in the order they're created and their order has no effect on how they operate. Be warned that it's still possible to have conflicting file rules. This means that if a file policy includes a rule to inspect a given file type plus another rule blocking the same file type, one of these rules will not work as expected. For an example of this kind of file policy, take a look at Figure 7.14.

See those warning triangles to the left of the rules? The problem with this policy is that executable files will be blocked, preventing them from being analyzed as malware! This behavior has to do with the way the device identifies file types versus the technique used for malware analysis.

File type analysis only requires the first packet of the file. By examining the file header, FireSIGHT can determine the type of file that's being transferred, which is enough to make the decision to block a file based on file type. Once the transfer is blocked, the rest of the file won't pass, meaning we can't calculate the SHA-256 for malware analysis. So basically, you can't block a file and analyze it for malware too!

FIGURE 7.14   Conflicting file rules

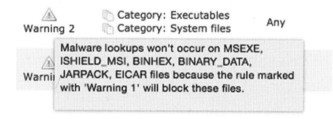

Hovering over the warning icons brings up a help balloon that explains this conflict, as shown in Figure 7.15.

FIGURE 7.15   Rule conflict help

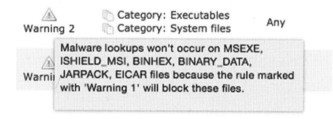

Once the file policy is created and saved, it can then be applied to traffic via an Allow rule in the Access Control policy.

File and Malware Event Analysis

There are several views available for analyzing the events generated by file policy rules found under Analysis ➢ Files:

- Malware Events
- File Events

- Captured Files
- Network File Trajectory

Malware Events

The Malware Events view lists all the malware detections and is a time-based table view similar to other views like Connection or Intrusion Events. There are also several workflows available, as you can see in Figure 7.16.

FIGURE 7.16   Malware event workflows

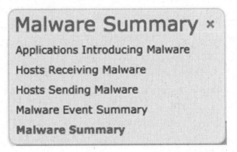

The default workflow is Malware Summary, which shows an overview of the threats detected sorted by count. An example of this workflow is shown in Figure 7.17

FIGURE 7.17   Malware Summary workflow

Malware Summary (switch workflow)
Malware Summary > Table View of Malware Events

2015-02-21 11:44:00 - 2015-03-21 11:54:09
Expanding

No Search Constraints (Edit Search)

Jump to... ▼

	Threat Name	File Name	File SHA256	File Type	▾ Count
⬇ ☐	W32.Generic:Mydoom.17m1.1201	message_part2.exe	de9bf315...30d0cfb5	MSEXE	16
⬇ ☐	W32.Generic:Mydoom.17m1.1201	Details.exe	de9bf315...30d0cfb5	MSEXE	13
⬇ ☐	W32.Generic:Mydoom.17m1.1201	nothing.exe	de9bf315...30d0cfb5	MSEXE	11
⬇ ☐	W32.Generic:Mydoom.17m1.1201	Zip.scr	de9bf315...30d0cfb5	MSEXE	10
⬇ ☐	W32.Generic:Mydoom.17m1.1201	information_4116.scr	de9bf315...30d0cfb5	MSEXE	10
⬇ ☐	W32.Generic:Mydoom.17m1.1201	part2.cmd	de9bf315...30d0cfb5	MSEXE	8
⬇ ☐	W32.Generic:Mydoom.17m1.1201	info_9290.exe	de9bf315...30d0cfb5	MSEXE	8
⬇ ☐	W32.Generic:Mydoom.17m1.1201	for_you.exe	de9bf315...30d0cfb5	MSEXE	8
⬇ ☐	Lovgate-tpd	\hamster.exe	6870cfb7...46a7aa36	MSEXE	8
⬇ ☐	Lovgate-tpd	\My Pictures\tamagotxi.exe	6870cfb7...46a7aa36	MSEXE	7
⬇ ☐	Lovgate-tpd	\My Pictures\Sample Pictures\tamagotxi.exe	6870cfb7...46a7aa36	MSEXE	7
⬇ ☐	Lovgate-tpd	\My Pictures\joke.exe	6870cfb7...46a7aa36	MSEXE	7
⬇ ☐	Lovgate-tpd	\My Pictures\docs.exe	6870cfb7...46a7aa36	MSEXE	7
⬇ ☐	Lovgate-tpd	\My Music\hamster.exe	6870cfb7...46a7aa36	MSEXE	7
⬇ ☐	Lovgate-tpd	\My Music\SETUP.EXE	6870cfb7...46a7aa36	MSEXE	5
⬇ ☐	Lovgate-tpd	\My Music\Sample Music\searchURL.exe	6870cfb7...46a7aa36	MSEXE	5

The Hosts Receiving/Sending Malware workflows are a really good way to discover hosts that might be badly infected and/or spreading malware! Figure 7.18 shows the Hosts Receiving Malware workflow.

FIGURE 7.18   Hosts Receiving Malware workflow

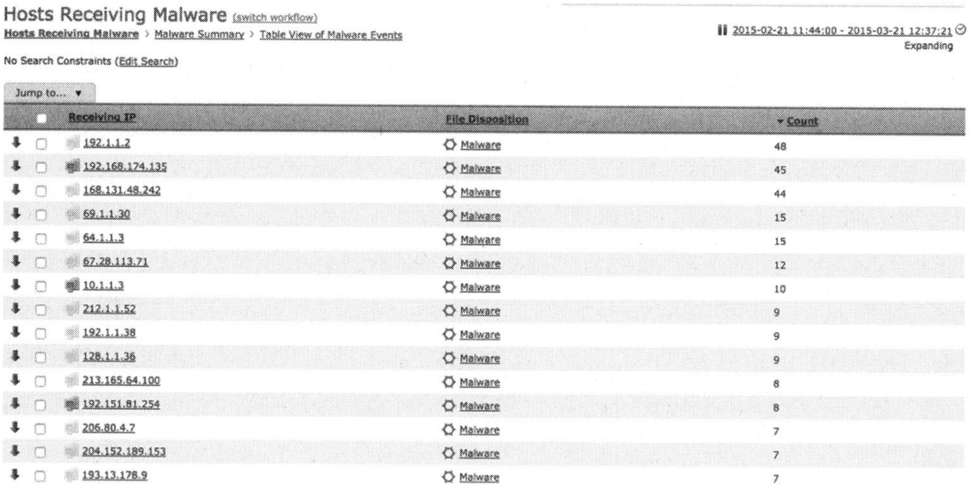

As with the other analysis views, the time window determines the scope of the events that will be displayed. Clicking a specific column link has the effect of drilling into the next workflow page using the link as a search criterion. Looking back at the previous example, if we clicked on the second IP address in the list, it would take us to the next workflow page—Malware Summary, which only reveals events involving this host, as shown in Figure 7.19.

FIGURE 7.19   Malware Summary page

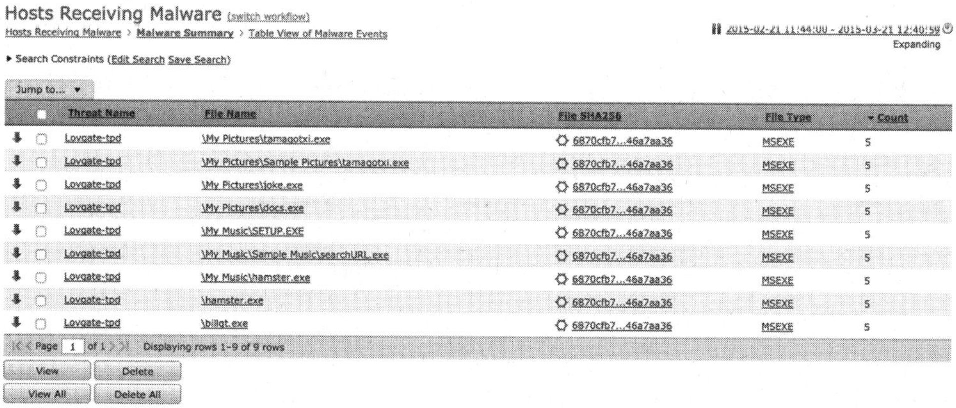

The table view is the most detailed workflow page, and it's also the final page in all of the default malware workflows. It contains every field available in a malware event, as shown in Figure 7.20.

FIGURE 7.20   Malware table view

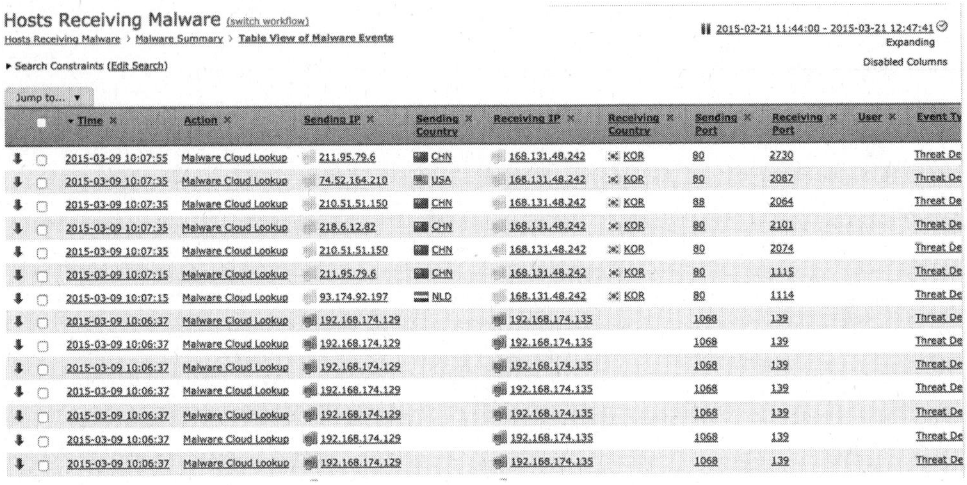

File Events

The File Events view (Figure 7.21) displays all the file events, whether they resulted in a malware detection or not. The default workflow is File Summary and shows files sorted by disposition.

FIGURE 7.21   File Summary workflow

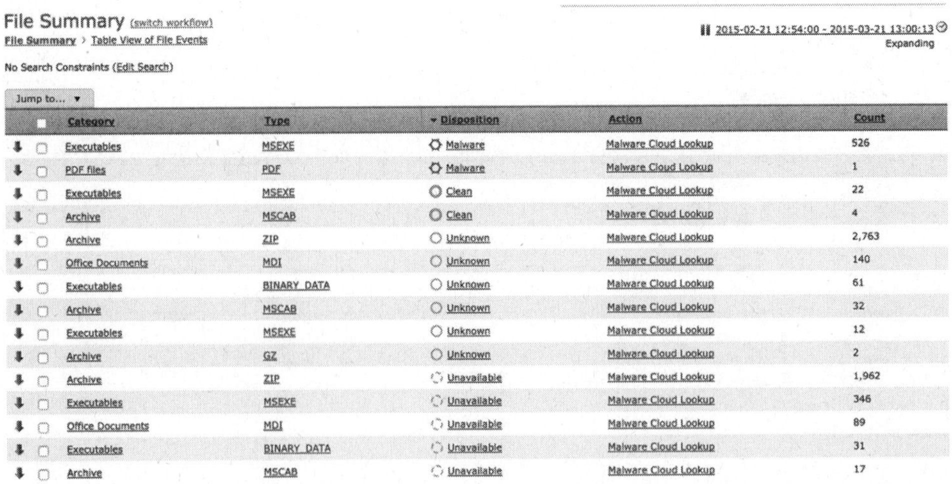

There are also workflows showing files sent and received by each host. These pages are similar to the host views available in the Malware Events workflows that we previously discussed.

Captured Files

The Captured Files view shows us the files that were captured as they traversed the network, with two workflows available:

- Captured File Summary
- Dynamic Analysis Status

The Captured File Summary workflow reveals captured files sorted by their threat score, as shown in Figure 7.22.

FIGURE 7.22   Captured File Summary workflow

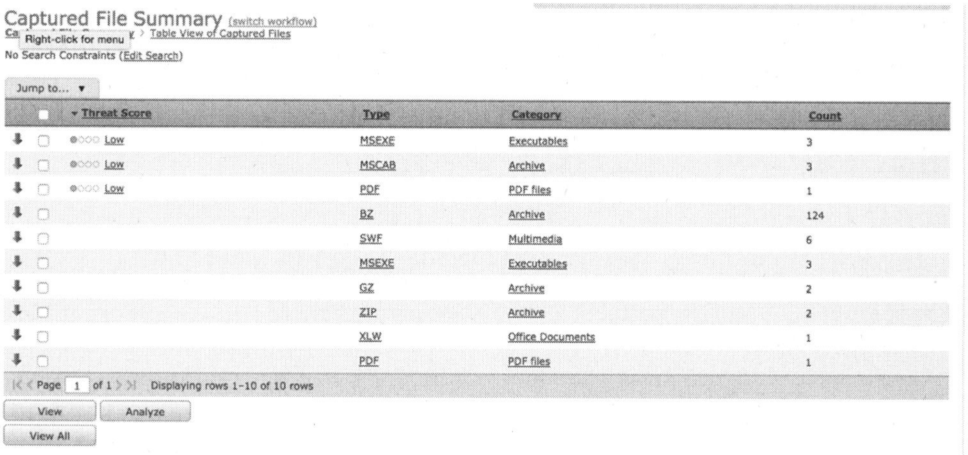

Drilling in from this workflow gets us to the table view of captured files, shown in Figure 7.23.

FIGURE 7.23   Captured files table view

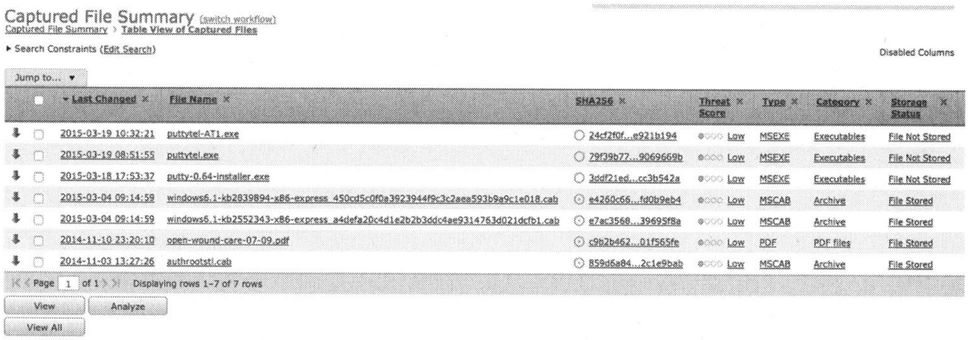

If the file has a threat score listed you'll see an icon representing the score as well as the score name: Low, Medium, High, or Very High, as seen in the Threat Score column in Figure 7.24.

FIGURE 7.24   Threat score

SHA256 ✕	Threat ✕ Score	Type ✕
○ 24cf2f0f...e921b194	●○○○ Low	MSEXE
○ 79f39b77...9069669b	●○○○ Low	MSEXE
○ 3ddf21ed...cc3b542a	●○○○ Low	MSEXE

Clicking the Threat Score icon itself loads the Dynamic Analysis Summary in a pop-up window, as shown in Figure 7.25.

FIGURE 7.25   Dynamic Analysis Summary dialog

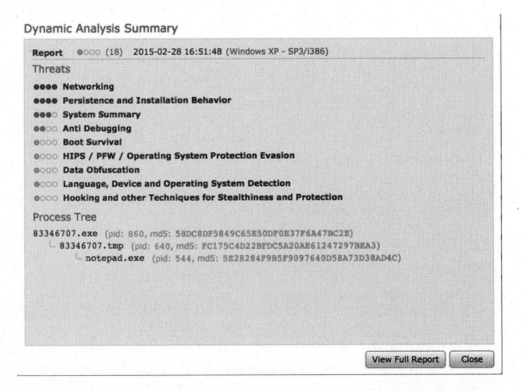

This summary reveals the threats evaluated for the file plus their rating. Clicking one of these threats will expand that section for even more detail, as shown in Figure 7.26.

FIGURE 7.26   Dynamic Analysis details

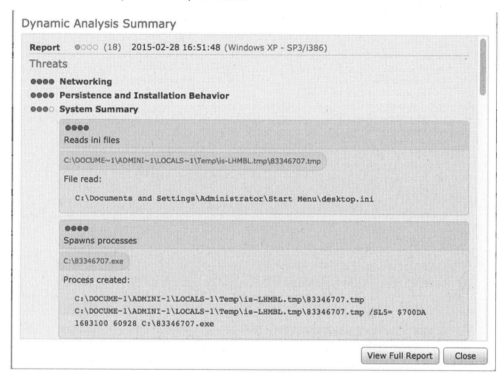

You can also click the View Full Report button at the bottom of the Dynamic Analysis Summary dialog to be directed to the full analysis report for the file, as shown in Figure 7.27.

Network File Trajectory

The *Network File Trajectory* view is a powerful tool for determining the extent of a malware infection. It allows you to see the hosts that have encountered a particular file and can even help you locate *"patient zero"*—the initial entry point for the infection.

The initial page (Figure 7.28) shows recently viewed files and recent malware detections. You can also enter a SHA-256, IP address, or filename in the search field at the top of the screen.

FIGURE 7.27 Detailed file analysis

FIGURE 7.28 Recent malware

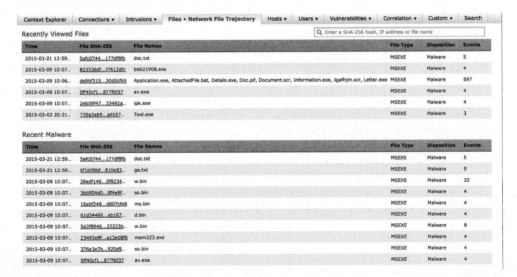

Clicking on one of the SHA-256 values brings you to the Network File Trajectory screen, as shown Figure 7.29.

FIGURE 7.29   Network File Trajectory

This page is a virtual treasure trove of file information! The page elements are described here:

File SHA-256—This reveals the SHA-256 hash of the file. Clicking on this field expands the text so it can be copied if you want.

Download icon—Immediately to the right of the file hash is a download icon. If the file has been stored on the device, this arrow will be bright green and clicking the icon will download the file to your local workstation. If the file has an unknown or malware disposition, you'll get a warning like the one pictured in Figure 7.30.

FIGURE 7.30   Download warning

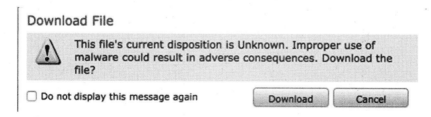

Files are encoded as a password protected zip archive prior to downloading. The default password is "infected" and is configurable in user preferences.

File Name—The filename.

File Type—The file type as configured in the file policy.

File Category—The file category from the file policy.

Current Disposition—The file's current disposition: clean, unknown, or malware.

Pencil icon—The pencil icon to the right of Current Disposition can be used to add the SHA-256 hash to your clean or custom detection list.

Threat Score—If the file was uploaded for dynamic analysis, the threat score is shown here.

Dynamic Analysis icon—Just to the right of Threat Score is a small cloud-like icon. Clicking this will upload the file to the cloud for dynamic analysis, but understand that if the file isn't stored on a device, the icon will be grayed out.

First/Last Seen—This indicates when the file was first and last detected.

Event Count—Reveals the number of events involving this file.

Seen On—Tells us the number of unique hosts that have encountered this file.

Seen On Breakdown—Gives us a breakdown of how many hosts have sent/received this file.

Trajectory—This section uses icons to give a graphical representation of where the file has gone in your environment. The key below the graph indicates the action taken, such as transfer or block, and includes the disposition. The combination of the shape and color of icon tells us exactly what occurred on each host. You can see that some of the events are specific to the Endpoint AMP product. Network AMP cannot detect if a host created, moved, executed, or quarantined a file. These events are generated by the endpoint product and pulled from the cloud by the Defense Center.

Hovering—Hovering over a specific trajectory event icon brings up details about that specific event. This is shown in Figure 7.31.

FIGURE 7.31   Trajectory Information

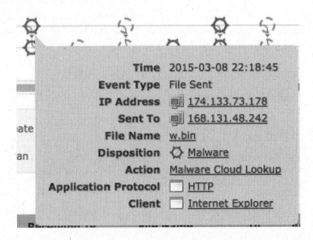

Events—The table view at the bottom reveals the event source for the Trajectory view pictured above it.

As you can see, Network File Trajectory is extremely useful for tracking down and identifying hosts that just might require remediation for malware!

Context Explorer

You can navigate directly to the Network File Trajectory view from any file or malware event table view by clicking the disposition icon next to the File SHA256 value. You can also go directly to the Network File Trajectory page from the File Information section of the Context Explorer as shown in Figure 7.32.

FIGURE 7.32   Context Explorer

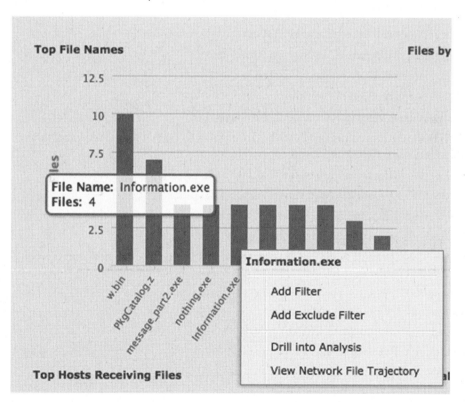

Summary

In this chapter, you learned all about the many techniques the FireSIGHT System uses to identify malware. We looked at the features of malware detection, including communication, actions, and protocols, and we described the elements of the file policy and rules to you. Finally, you learned about the interface components used to analyze malware and file events.

Hands-on Lab

In this lab, we will cover creating and implementing a sample file policy.

Create the File Policy

1. Open your web browser and HTTPS to your Defense Center.
2. Log in to the Defense Center.
3. Navigate to Policies ➤ Files.
4. Click the New File Policy button.
5. Give your new policy a name and click Save.
6. Click the Advanced tab, and use the drop-down to mark files as malware if their dynamic threat score is 51 and above (High).
7. Click the Rules tab and then the Add File Rule button.
8. Select HTTP from the Application Protocol drop-down.
9. Under Action, select Block Malware. Note the new check boxes that are now available.
10. Check the Spero Analysis For MSEXE box.
11. Select System Files, PDF Files, Executables, and Office Documents from the File Type Categories column.
12. Make sure the All Types In Selected Categories option is selected in the File Types column, and then click the Add button.
13. Click the Save button to save the rule.
14. Click Add File Rule to add a second rule.
15. Leave the application protocol and direction as Any.
16. Under action, select Block Files.
17. Select the System Files and Executables check boxes, and add those file types to the Selected File Categories And Types column.
18. Click the Save button to save the rule.

19. Notice that you have warning icons by each of the rules. Hover over the yellow triangle to view the help text explaining the conflict.

20. Delete the second rule blocking files.

21. Save your policy.

Implement File Policy

1. Navigate to Policies ➤ Access Control.

2. Edit your existing Access Control policy.

3. If you have an Allow rule, edit the existing rule. If not, add a new rule and set the rule action to Allow.

4. Click the Inspection tab in your Allow rule.

5. Under File Policy, select your newly created file policy.

6. Click the Logging tab. Note that you have a Log Files check box that is now selected by default.

7. Save your rule, and then save your Access Control policy.

Exam Essentials

Understand Spero analysis.   The system analyzes certain file characteristics such as metadata and headers to determine if a file is malicious.

Understand file policy rule limitations for upload or download:

HTTP: Upload and download

SMTP: Upload only

IMAP: Download only

POP3: Download only

FTP: Upload and download

NetBIOS-ssn: Upload and download

Know your options for determining the network trajectory of a file.   You can navigate to Analysis ➤ Files ➤ Network File Trajectory or use the Context Explorer.

Know your options for searching for files using Network File Trajectory.

You can search on the following:

SHA-256 hash

IP address

Filename

Review Questions

You can find the answers in Appendix A.

1. On the Network File Trajectory page, which of the following search options can you enter in the search text box?

   A. SHA-256

   B. IP address

   C. Filename

   D. Any of the above

2. When you click an event icon in a Network File Trajectory map, a context box opens. Which of the following is *not* an element of this box?

   A. SHA-256

   B. Disposition

   C. File Name

   D. Application Protocol

3. Spero analysis is _____.

   A. Used to analyze a SHA-256 to determine if a file is malicious

   B. A form of analysis that involves executing the file in a sandbox environment

   C. A manual analysis that cannot be performed automatically

   D. A method of analyzing static file attributes such as headers and metadata

4. Which statement is true regarding malware inspecting via POP3?

   A. It can only be performed on downloaded files.

   B. It can only be performed on uploaded files.

   C. In can be performed on uploaded and downloaded files.

   D. POP3 is supported for inspection but not blocking.

5. The policy controlling file and malware inspection is _____.

   A. Access Control policy

   B. IPS policy

   C. Discovery policy

   D. File policy

6. On the Network File Trajectory page, which of the following search options can you enter in the search text box?

   A. SHA-256

   B. IP address

   C. Filename

   D. Any of the above

7. Which of the following methods is a valid way to access the Network File Trajectory page?

   A. From the Hosts menu

   B. From Context Explorer

   C. From the Connections menu

   D. From the Files dashboard

8. File Policy is applied to traffic by _____.:

   A. Applying the policy directly to the target device

   B. Calling the policy from an intrusion rule.

   C. Configuring the Inspection tab on an Access Control rule

   D. Applying the policy to the device through the system policy

9. File dispositions returned by the cloud are _____.

   A. Clean, suspect, malware

   B. Malware, unknown, trusted

   C. Malware, signed, unknown

   D. Clean, unknown, malware

10. Which statement regarding Dynamic Analysis is true?

   A. It requires uploading the file to the cloud.

   B. It returns a real-time malware disposition for a file.

   C. Files are uploaded to the cloud from the Defense Center.

   D. It supports all file types.

Chapter

8

System Settings

THE SSFIPS EXAM OBJECTIVES COVERED IN THIS CHAPTER INCLUDE THE FOLLOWING:

✓ 7.1 Describe the settings contained in the system policies

✓ 7.2 Understand the general user preferences and system settings of the Cisco NGIPS

✓ 7.3 Describe the settings available for the health monitoring features of the Cisco NGIPS

There is more to configuring the system than creating strategic policies to direct the way your devices detect network activity. You can apply settings to the system such as user preferences, time zones, audit logging, and other key factors like health checks to alert you to conditions within your devices.

So let's get started by going over the system settings and user preferences. We'll also guide you through system policy and health settings.

To find up-to-the-minute updates for this chapter, please see www.lammle. com/firepower or the book's web page at www.sybex.com.

User Preferences

Each user inside the FireSIGHT Manager can set their own preferences. The preferences control your default views and time zone and dashboard settings. When you click your username in the upper-right corner of the Defense Center web interface, it will bring up a menu that allows you to log out or navigate to the *User Preferences* page. Here's a list of the tabs available on the User Preferences screen:

Change Password   Allows the user to change their current password

Home Page   Lets the user specify the page that's displayed on initial login.

Event View Settings   This tab has many settings that deal with the analysis views. It allows you to specify if you want to resolve IP addresses or not, what your time window preferences are, and the default workflows you want to display in various analysis views.

Time Zone Preferences   Event times are always stored in the database in Coordinated Universal Time (UTC). This setting allows users to choose to view the events in UTC or another time zone if they prefer. This allows anyone analyzing events to view the events in their own time zone and avoid constantly converting back to UTC to determine when an event actually occurred.

Dashboard Settings   Specifies which dashboard is displayed by default. If you create your own custom dashboard, this is where you would make this new dashboard your default.

Most of the settings on the different tabs are self-explanatory except the Event View Settings tab, so we're going to go over that one with you now.

Event Preferences

Under *Event Preferences*, seen in Figure 8.1, you have controls that help adjust how analysis data is seen. For example, the Confirm 'All' Actions setting gives you a pop-up confirmation window anytime you take an action that would affect 'All' events. This is handy so you don't inadvertently delete all your intrusion events—an action that cannot be reversed!

Resolve IP Addresses will add the hostname in the event views alongside the IP address. You specify the DNS server to use in System ≻ Local ≻ Configuration. Note that this will generate a fair amount of traffic to the DNS server as event view pages load. This can also cause the event views to load more slowly if there are issues with your DNS lookup settings. The other settings in this section allow you to define the number of rows to display per page and an automatic refresh interval for your event data. The default is 0, which means auto refresh is off.

FIGURE 8.1   Event Preferences

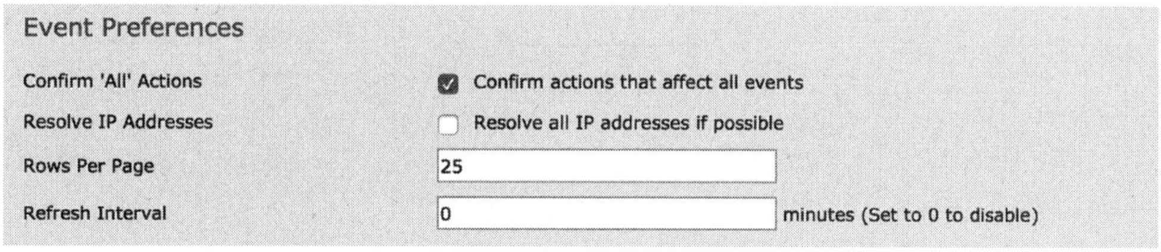

Event Preferences	
Confirm 'All' Actions	☑ Confirm actions that affect all events
Resolve IP Addresses	☐ Resolve all IP addresses if possible
Rows Per Page	25
Refresh Interval	0 minutes (Set to 0 to disable)

File Preferences

The *File Preferences* (Figure 8.2) handle some of the settings when you're using the malware detection capabilities of the system. One nice feature is the ability to capture files, which can then be downloaded for offline analysis in a password protected zip format. You can specify the password here.

FIGURE 8.2   File Preferences

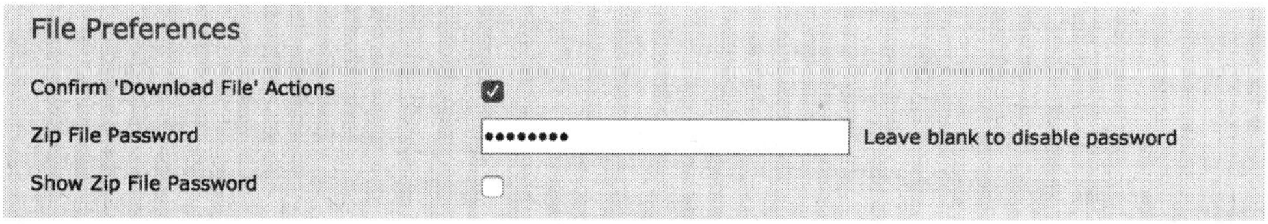

File Preferences	
Confirm 'Download File' Actions	☑
Zip File Password	•••••••• Leave blank to disable password
Show Zip File Password	☐

Default Time Windows

The system allows for a single time window or multiple *time windows*. Multiple allows for three unique settings; one for Audit, one for Health, and one for the rest of the event views as shown in Figure 8.3. When viewing different data types, you have four choices for time views.

Show the Last – Static/Expanding: This setting lets you specify a certain number of seconds, minutes, hours, days, weeks, or months to show. It will default to showing one hour prior to the users login until the current time. The time window will expand with the current time and can be optionally set to static in the analysis view where the user explicitly sets a start and stop time for it.

Show the Last – Sliding: The Sliding window will always show the previous data collected during the specified time window. The time line shows the previous hour's worth of information by default. Unlike with the expanding time window, the "width" of the sliding time window does not change.

Current Day - Static/Expanding: Shows data from midnight on the current day.

Current Week - Static/Expanding: Shows data from midnight Sunday of the current week.

FIGURE 8.3   Default Time Windows

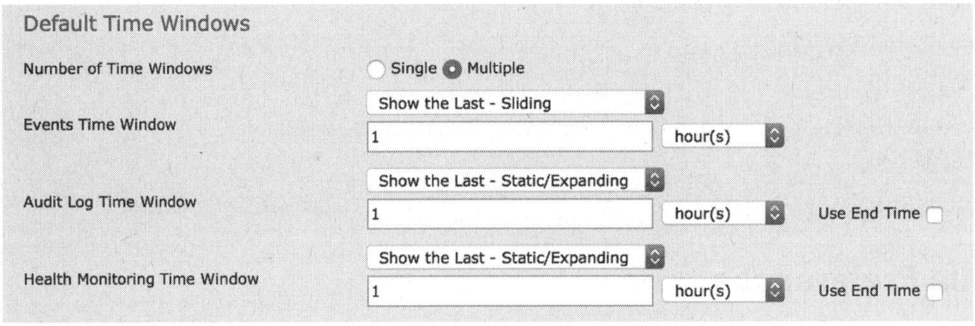

Default Workflows

A *workflow* essentially steps you through the analysis of your data. You begin with a very broad view and then drill into interesting data, getting into more and more detail. There are a number of built-in workflows for the different analysis views that can be leveraged to view the data in different ways. Your default workflows can be selected as part of your user preferences. The dialog for this is shown in Figure 8.4. The ability to select your preferred workflow is especially helpful when you're analyzing intrusion data. However, not all event views have multiple workflows. Discovery Events is an example of one of these views.

Users also have the ability to create their own workflows based on their own needs.

System Configuration

There are a variety of settings that must be configured during the initial setup of the system. These include the management IP address, gateway, DNS, and proxy settings. If you need to revisit any of these, just go to System ➢ Local ➢ Configuration (Figure 8.5).

FIGURE 8.4   Default workflows

FIGURE 8.5   System configuration

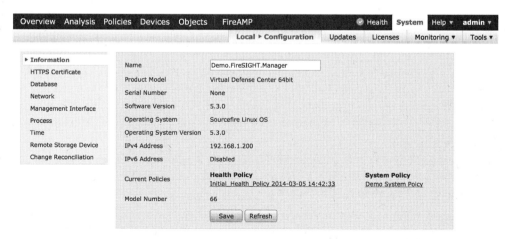

Information   The first section that appears is Information, which displays information about the appliance, including the hostname that's shown, the serial number if it's a physical device, the version, and IP and policy information.

HTTPS Certificate   The HTTPS Certificate section allows you to generate a certificate signing request (CSR) and also import a certificate. If your organization has its own certificate server, then you can import your own signed certificate instead of using the built-in self-signed certificate.

Database   The Defense Center allows for external database connectivity. This connectivity is done by a Java Database Connectivity (JDBC) connector in a read-only format. This is very useful for connecting external reporting tools.

Network   This section contains the network settings for the appliance, including IPv4 and IPv6 configurations. Other settings include DNS servers, MTU size, and the management port. The management port is 8305 and should not be changed.

There's also a section that deals with network proxies. Management of the system is much easier if the Defense Center can communicate to the Internet. Connection to the Internet means simplified updates and also allows the Security Intelligence feed, URL Filtering, and Advanced Malware Protection (AMP) lookups. If you're not allowed to connect directly to the Internet, you can also specify proxy information here.

Management Interface   Interface settings allow you to adjust duplex and speed settings of the management interface.

Process   The Processes section allow you to carry out these three tasks:

> **Shut Down Defense Center**   This is a graceful way to shut down and power off the system. Just make sure you have someone around to turn it back on or that you've set up lights out management!
>
> **Reboot Defense Center**   This will reboot the Defense Center.
>
> **Restart Defense Center Console**   This will restart the web server processes.

Time   The current time will be displayed here and if the time setting found in the system policy specifies that the time is set manually, then you'll be able to adjust the system time. If the time setting is set to NTP, you can view the current time and view the NTP properties.

Remote Storage Device   Remote Storage Device lets you specify a remote storage type. Remote storage is disabled by default, but if it's enabled, you can store backups and reports remotely. The protocols supported are NFS, SMB, and SSH. A common question is whether events can be stored remotely. The answer is no—remote storage is used for backups and reports only.

Change Reconciliation   Change Reconciliation is a great feature for auditing. When enabled, it will email a report every 24 hours showing any changes that have taken place in the Defense Center's configuration.

There are many features in System Configuration, but for the most part it's a good idea not to change things unless you really need to.

System Policy

The *system policy* can be applied to the Defense Center or the managed device. The DC can hold several system policies, and unique ones can be applied to each device. However, in most installations you will see the same system policy deployed across multiple—or all—devices. To navigate here, go to System ➤ Local ➤ System Policy. The system policy contains the following settings:

Access Control Preferences   ACL settings specifying the IP addresses allowed to communicate with the appliance. These are the local host firewall settings.

Audit Log Settings   Allows you to send audit events to a syslog server in addition to storing them locally.

Authentication Profiles   Lets you specify an external LDAP or RADIUS server for login authentication. The default is to use local accounts (more on this later).

Dashboard   Lets you disable the dashboard custom analysis widgets.

Database   Allows you to modify some of the database sizing properties. It also allows you to specify an email address to notify when the database is being pruned.

DNS Cache   DNS caching is automatically enabled and defaults to 300 seconds.

Email Notification   This is where you would configure the SMTP mail relay you want alerts and notifications sent through. TLS and SSLv3 are supported along with clear text.

Intrusion Policy Preferences   Determines if detailed IPS policy changes will be written to the audit log. It also lets you to specify if the user is required to enter a comment when an intrusion policy is saved.

Language   Sets the language preference. The supported options are US English and Japanese.

Login Banner   Enter your legal text here. It will be displayed when SSH or HTTPS is used to access the appliance.

SNMP   Enables read-only SNMP access to the appliance. Supported options are SNMP v1, v2, and v3. The reporting MIBS can be found on the appliance in /etc/sf/DCEALERT. MIB. Note that you must enable the SNMP port in the Access Control Preferences or the SNMP Manager will not be able to connect to the appliance.

STIG Compliance   There's a check box in here to enable STIG (Security Technical Implementation Guide) compliance. A documentation guide is available on the support site that lists the changes made.

STIG compliance can impact performance and can't be undone without re-imaging the system!

Time Synchronization This section lets you specify how times should be set on the Defense Center and the managed devices. They can be set manually or via NTP. The DC can also be used as an NTP server for managed devices. The dialog for Time Synchronization is shown in Figure 8.6.

FIGURE 8.6   System policy time settings

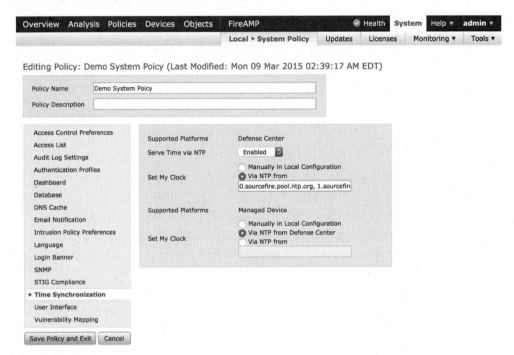

User Interface Lets you adjust the browser session time-out and the shell time-out. Valid values for this range are from 0 to 1440 minutes. There's also a check box for disabling expert access to the managed device CLI. This locks shell users at the Cisco CLI and disables the "expert" command. After selecting the check box, this there is no way to load a normal Linux (bash) shell.

   Once you disable this access, it requires opening a TAC case to re-enable it.

Vulnerability Mapping This configures something known as version-less vulnerability mappings. Basically, it means disassociating versions from specified applications. This is used when application versions can't be discerned from traffic. You should leave this at the default (no impact flag mapping for the listed applications).

Once a system policy is created, it must be applied to the device targets. You can apply a single system policy to some or all devices, to just the DC, or only to managed devices. You can also compare, export, and delete policies here. Figure 8.7 displays a list of system policies.

FIGURE 8.7   System policy list

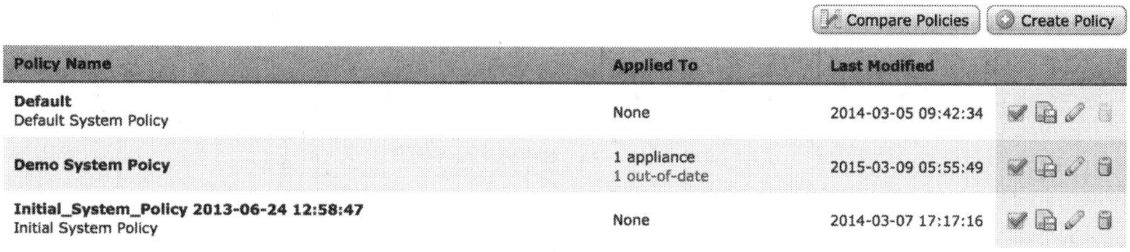

Health

Good health is always key, so clearly, keeping an eye on the health of your system is a seriously important job. There's a tab at the top of the screen and an icon that will display the current health status of the Defense Center and all managed devices. You will see a green circle with a check mark in it when things are healthy.

Health Monitor

Clicking the Health tab brings up the *Health Monitor*, which reveals details about the health of your system. There are several different status messages that can be displayed, with Normal being optimal for all systems. Critical indicates just what you'd think—that there are issues that probably require immediate attention, and Warnings definitely indicates that there are things to keep an eye on too. Recovered indicates that a health check was in a problem condition but is now okay. Disabled indicates that there's no health policy loaded, and Error tells you that there's an issue with the health system itself.

The Count column next to a status shows the number of appliances in that specific state. Notice in Figure 8.8 that there's a small triangle to the right of the number for the Normal status. Clicking it will expose details of the devices.

FIGURE 8.8 Health Monitor

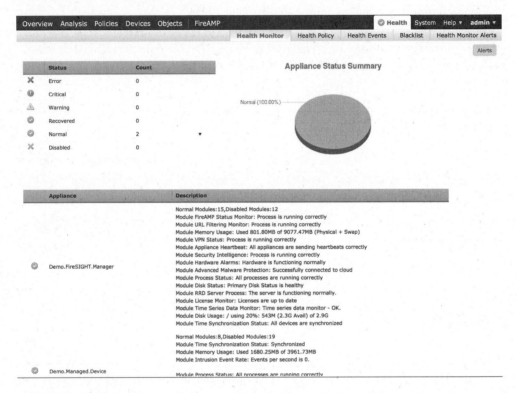

Health Policy

Data for the Health Monitor comes from the *health policy*, which is a collection of checks that are executed every 5 minutes by default. You can modify the health policies to meet the needs of each environment. Health checks can also be disabled. To edit or create a new health policy, navigate to Health ➤ Health Policy and either click the edit icon or click Create Policy. When creating a new policy, you get the option to copy an existing health policy.

There are many different checks in a list to the left of the policy. Each setting can be enabled or disabled and some allow you to specify thresholds for warnings or critical alerts (Figure 8.9). Most of the default settings work just fine, but if you make any changes, be sure to use the Save Policy And Exit button on the bottom and then reapply the policy.

Health Events

To view current and past health events, click the Health Events tab. The health events will be displayed from all your devices. If you're looking for a specific health event, use the Search feature and specify your search criteria. You can also adjust the time window to a specific range, as shown in Figure 8.10.

FIGURE 8.9   Health policy settings

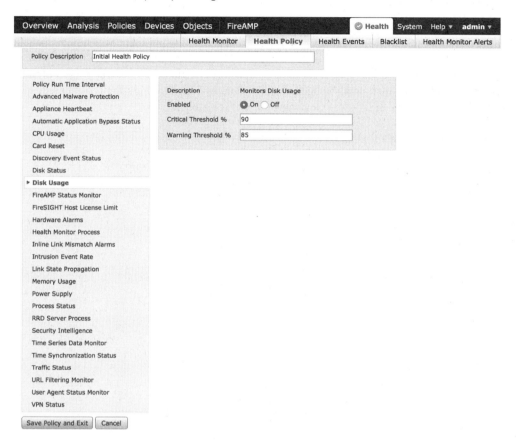

FIGURE 8.10   Health events

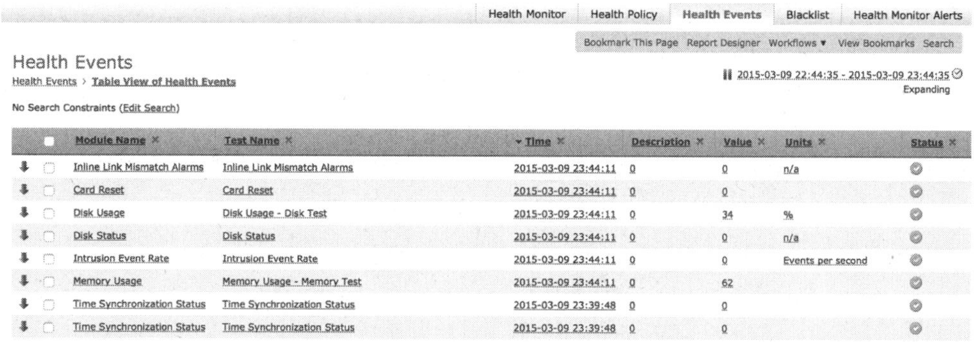

Blacklist

The *Blacklist* tab allows you to set up exclusions to health checks. You can blacklist an entire device or just individual counters. This can be helpful when there's a known issue but you don't need alerts nagging you about it every 5 minutes. A good example is when you've had a power supply fail but you've contacted Cisco for a replacement. Here, you would just blacklist the power supply health check for the appliance until you get the replacement. Figure 8.11 shows the dialog for selecting elements for a blacklist.

FIGURE 8.11 Blacklisting health events

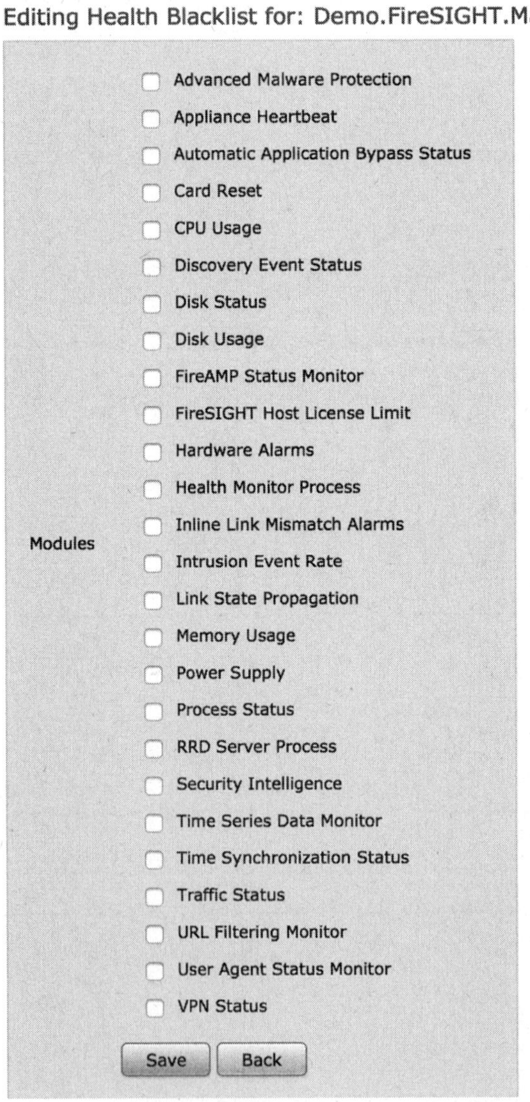

Editing Health Blacklist for: Demo.FireSIGHT.Manager

Modules

- Advanced Malware Protection
- Appliance Heartbeat
- Automatic Application Bypass Status
- Card Reset
- CPU Usage
- Discovery Event Status
- Disk Status
- Disk Usage
- FireAMP Status Monitor
- FireSIGHT Host License Limit
- Hardware Alarms
- Health Monitor Process
- Inline Link Mismatch Alarms
- Intrusion Event Rate
- Link State Propagation
- Memory Usage
- Power Supply
- Process Status
- RRD Server Process
- Security Intelligence
- Time Series Data Monitor
- Time Synchronization Status
- Traffic Status
- URL Filtering Monitor
- User Agent Status Monitor
- VPN Status

Save   Back

Health Monitor Alerts

In some environments, the Defense Center console may not be manned 24/7. In these situations, it's a good idea to have external alerts set up to notify people immediately to any health conditions that crop up. This is where *Health Monitor alerts* come in—with them, you can send email, SNMP traps, or syslog messages. To configure the Health Monitor alerts, you must first set up the responses known as alerts. Clicking the Health Monitor Alerts tab will display the configuration page. In the upper-right corner is the Alerts button for setting up the responses. You can also access the Alerts dialog by going to Policies ➢ Action ➢ Responses ➢ Alerts. Click Create Alert and add one of the three alert types, as shown in Figure 8.12.

FIGURE 8.12   Creating an alert

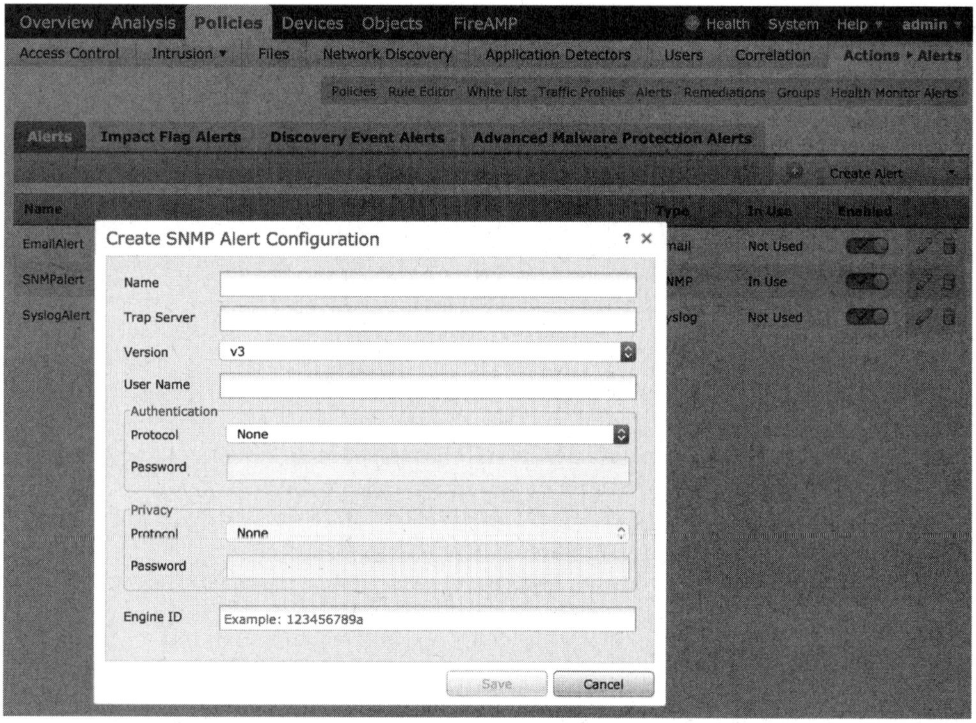

Once the alert(s) are created, go back to the Health Monitor Alerts screen. To create the Health Monitor alert, select a severity based on when you want the alert to occur, the module to monitor, and finally, the alert you want generated. Specify the health alert name at the top and click Save. Keep in mind that you can opt to include multiple severities, modules, and alerts as shown in Figure 8.13.

FIGURE 8.13   Health Monitor alerts

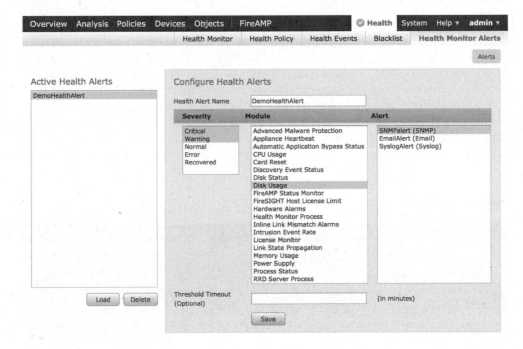

Summary

This was a quick, succinct chapter that lead you through various system settings, user preferences, and system policy and health settings.

We demonstrated the User Preferences settings, which allow users to customize their analysis views and other personal settings.

We moved on to cover system configuration as it relates to the Defense Center and then guided you through the settings inside the system policy. We wrapped the chapter up by covering health policy settings.

Hands-on Lab

In this section, you will go through the following two labs:

Hands-on Lab 8.1: Creating a New System Policy

Hands-on Lab 8.2: Viewing Health Information

Hands-on Lab 8.1: Creating a New System Policy

In this lab, you will create a new system policy that will present a login banner and enable NTP settings.

1. From the main menu, navigate to System ➤ Local ➤ System Policy.
2. Click Create Policy.
3. In the Create Policy window, copy the default policy and name the new policy **Demo System Policy.**
4. Click Create.
5. Navigate to Login Banner and enter the following information: **This System is for authorized use only.**
6. Select Time Synchronization.
7. In the Set My Clock section of the Defense Center settings, click the Via NTP From button.
8. Enter the following information for the NTP servers: **0.sourcefire.pool.ntp.org** and **1.sourcefire.pool.ntp.org**.
9. In the Set My Clock section of the Managed Device settings, click the Via NTP From Defense Center button.
10. Click the Save Policy And Exit button.
11. Click the green check mark to apply the system policy.
12. Apply the system policy to your Defense Center and managed device.
13. Log off and then log back in to view your login banner.

Hands-on Lab 8.2: Viewing Health Information

In this lab, you will view health information about your systems

1. From the main menu, click the Health tab to view the Health Monitor.
2. Click the small triangle next to the Count column to expose information about your managed device and Defense Center.
3. Notice the values of the health setting counters.
4. Click the Health Events tab.
5. View the events. Notice that the events repeat every 5 minutes.

Exam Essentials

Understand the system policy. The system policy allows the user to configure settings that will be used across your devices and/or Defense Center. These would include things like device access, time settings, language preferences, and audit log settings.

Describe the User Preferences settings.   The users of the system can set preferences for their event workflows, time zone preferences, and dashboard settings.

Describe the system settings.   The system settings allow a user to adjust things specific to the device or Defense Center. This would include network settings and database settings and would even allow you to shut down or restart the system.

Be able to analyze and configure the health settings of the Defense Center.   The health of the system is monitored via an applied health policy. These can be user configured and should be applied to all devices. The health events can be viewed in the Defense Center by clicking the health icon. Noisy health events can be silenced by using a blacklist.

Review Questions

You can find the answers in Appendix A.

1. Where in the interface would a user change their password?

    A. System ➢ Local

    B. Device ➢ Device Management

    C. User Preferences

    D. Overview ➢ Management

2. To permit external users to connect to the database, the user must have external database access enabled. What else is required?

    A. JDBC must be installed on the Defense Center.

    B. Allow External Database Access should be enabled under Local Configuration.

    C. Allow External Database Access should be enabled in the system policy.

    D. Enable database access in the tools menu.

3. What function provides for daily emailed reports about changes in configuration?

    A. Change Reconciliation

    B. Audit Report

    C. Administrative Summary Reporting

    D. Recovery Logging Report

4. What types of remote storage are available to store backups and reports?

    A. FTP, HTTP, and SSH

    B. NFS, SMB, and SSH

    C. TFTP, TFTP, and SSH

    D. NFS, SMB, and SSL

5. Besides English, which languages preferences are available in the FireSIGHT Manager?

    A. Chinese

    B. Russian

    C. Japanese

    D. French

6. Time on the managed devices may be set using what method?

    A. NTP from an external server

    B. Manually

    C. NTP from the Defense Center

    D. All of the above

7. What is the default interval for the health checks to run?

   A. 10 minutes

   B. 5 minutes

   C. 30 minutes

   D. 60 minutes

8. In the Health Monitor, what does red indicate?

   A. Danger

   B. Warning

   C. Fail

   D. Critical

9. What is the mechanism to prevent health events from displaying?

   A. Blacklist

   B. Exclusions

   C. Disabling

   D. None of the above

10. Health Monitor alerts provide what type of output?

   A. Email, SNMP, and syslog

   B. Netflow, SNMP, and syslog

   C. Pop3, SNMP, and syslog

   D. IMAP, SNMP, and syslog

Chapter

9

Account Management

In this chapter, we're going to cover a variety of administrative functions for user account management. For instance, having a user account with administrator access allows you to create, manage, and delete other user accounts.

As we progress, you'll learn all about internal and external user account management, how to describe various user roles, and how to create custom user roles. We'll demonstrate how to configure both internal and external user accounts and show you how to permit a user to escalate their account privileges. You'll discover that user authentication can be achieved locally through the internal database or via an external authentication server like LDAP or RADIUS.

To find up-to-the-minute updates for this chapter, please see www.lammle .com/firepower or the book's web page at www.sybex.com.

User Account Management

When you log in to the FireSIGHT GUI interface with a username and password, the appliance first looks for the user ID in the local database. Users in the local database will predictably be authenticated locally on the appliance, but even if the user account that's asking for access requires external authentication, the system will still try the local database first. If it can't find a local user that corresponds, it will move on and look into an external server for a match. These external servers can either be a Lightweight Directory Access Protocol (LDAP) directory server or a Remote Authentication Dial In User Service (RADIUS) authentication server. Both types can provide a database list of users.

It's good to know that you can completely control user permissions for anyone no matter if they're trying to authenticate internally or externally. Unless you change the user permissions manually, externally authenticated users receive their permissions via these three ways:

- Through the group or access list they belong to
- Based upon the default user access role you've set in the server authentication object
- Through a system policy on the managing Defense Center

Internal versus External User Authentication

So, by default, the appliance will go with the internal database for authentication to check for users' credentials when they log in. But though internal authentication is definitely the simplest way to manage users, it's just not at all an efficient or even a feasible option for really large networks. This fact makes being able to specify whether a given user you're creating will be internally or externally authenticated a very cool feature!

Still, understand that when using internal authentication, all user credentials are managed in the internal database and local authentication won't take place until the username and password are verified against the internal FireSIGHT System database. Since you manually create each user in the local database to be authenticated there, you set the user role and access setting for that user at that time as well. This means you don't need to deal with any default settings for users attempting to authenticate.

External authentication occurs when the FireSIGHT Management Center (FMC) or a managed device tries to authenticate users from either an external LDAP or RADIUS server database, but you can't use both methods. And if you choose to go with external authentication, you must create an authentication object for each server to specify the exact location from which you want to authenticate users. The authentication object contains your settings for connecting to and checking the user database from that particular server. Once this is done, you've got to enable that object in a system policy on the managing FMC, then apply that policy to an appliance to enable authentication. The appliance will then check each configured authentication server in the order in which they're listed in the system policy when attempting to find the user in the database.

An internal user will be automatically converted to external authentication if the same username and password exists on an external server. Once the user has been converted to external authentication, it cannot revert back to internal authentication.

User Privileges

You can create users using predefined roles or create custom roles to assign to individuals or even a group of users. Let's say you want to create a group of users that only gets access to data to analyze the security events of the monitored network, but you don't want this group to ever gain access to the administrative functions of the FireSIGHT system itself. This is where the ability to create custom roles really shines—you can easily use predefined roles like Discovery Admin and Security Analyst, which allow the users to view network events without being able to change any configuration settings. Creating custom roles provides even more detail on what a particular user or a given group of users can and cannot do—nice!

Another benefit to configuring external users is that you can set a default access role for all users that are externally authenticated in the system policy. We'll explore this in detail later in the section called "Configuring External Authentication." For now, it's important for you to remember that once the user logs in externally for the first time and receives the default access role, you'll be able to find this user on the User Management page and add or remove access rights for them. You can opt to not modify the rights, which will grant the user the rights via the default access role. And remember, when you create internal users, you assign the role manually as you create them.

The default access role for an externally authenticated user can be overridden by the configured management of access rights. You can do this through either the LDAP or RADIUS groups or objects, where the permissions for users originate from the default access rights assigned to their specific group—assuming they belong to one. If they don't belong to an LDAP group or RADIUS object, they'll assume the default role.

Predefined User Roles

Here's a list of the FireSIGHT System predefined user roles, depending on the features you've licensed:

Access Admins can view and modify access control and file policies, but they can't apply their policy changes.

Administrators can set up the appliance's network configuration, manage user accounts and Collective Security Intelligence cloud connections, and configure system policies and system settings. Users with the Administrator role have all the rights and privileges of all other roles, with the exception of lesser, restricted versions of those privileges.

Discovery Admins can review, modify, and delete network discovery policies, but they can't apply their policy changes.

External Database users can query the FireSIGHT System database using an external application that supports JDBC SSL connections. On the web interface, they can access the online help and user preferences.

Intrusion Admins can review, modify, and delete intrusion policies and intrusion rules, but they can't apply their policy changes.

Maintenance Users can access monitoring functions such as health monitoring, host statistics, performance data, system logs, and maintenance functions, including task scheduling and backing up the system. Note that Maintenance Users do not have access to the functions in the Policies menu and they can access the dashboard only from the Analysis menu.

Network Admins can review, modify, and apply device configurations as well as review and modify access control policies, but they can't apply their policy changes.

Security Approvers can view and apply policy changes, but they can't create configuration and policy changes.

Security Analysts can review, analyze, and delete intrusion, discovery, user activity, connection, correlation, and network change events. They can review, analyze, and when applicable, delete hosts, host attributes, services, vulnerabilities, and client applications. Security Analysts can also generate reports and view health events, but they can't delete or modify these.

Security Analysts (Read Only) enjoy all the same rights as Security Analysts, except that they cannot delete events.

Custom User roles allow you to customize exactly what users with a designated role can access. They also allows you to place precise restrictions on exactly what information users can view.

Note that any role can be the default access role for externally authenticated users and that you set this in the system policy.

Creating New User Accounts

Now would be the perfect time for us to demonstrate exactly how to create internal user accounts. To do that, just follow this procedure.

From the menu options, on the right side of the menu bar, choose System ➤ Local ➤ User Management, as shown in Figure 9.1

FIGURE 9.1   Access User Management

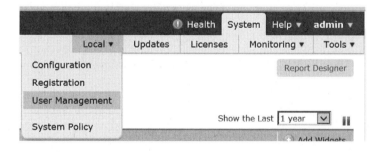

This will display the User Management page, which lists the information on existing user accounts. Figure 9.2 shows the User Management page.

FIGURE 9.2   User Management page

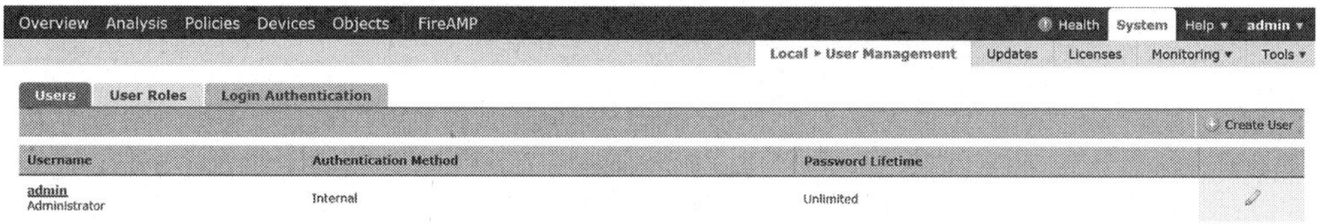

There are two things you should focus on in Figure 9.2. First, there's a default admin user, which uses an internal authentication method, and second, there are those three tabs at the top: Users, User Roles, and Login Authentication. We're going to focus on these tabs throughout this section.

Okay—so let's create a new user and assign it a role. From the User Management screen, on the right side, click Create User. You'll receive the screen shown in Figure 9.3, called the User Configuration options page.

FIGURE 9.3   User Configuration options page

User Configuration

User Name	
Authentication	☐ Use External Authentication Method
Password	
Confirm Password	
Maximum Number of Failed Logins	5 (0 = Unlimited)
Minimum Password Length	8
Days Until Password Expiration	0 (0 = Unlimited)
Days Before Password Expiration Warning	0
Options	☐ Force Password Reset on Login ☐ Check Password Strength ☐ Exempt from Browser Session Timeout

User Role Configuration

Sourcefire User Roles

☐ Administrator
☐ External Database User
☐ Security Analyst
☐ Security Analyst (Read Only)
☐ Security Approver
☐ Intrusion Admin
☐ Access Admin
☐ Network Admin
☐ Maintenance User
☐ Discovery Admin

[Save] [Cancel]

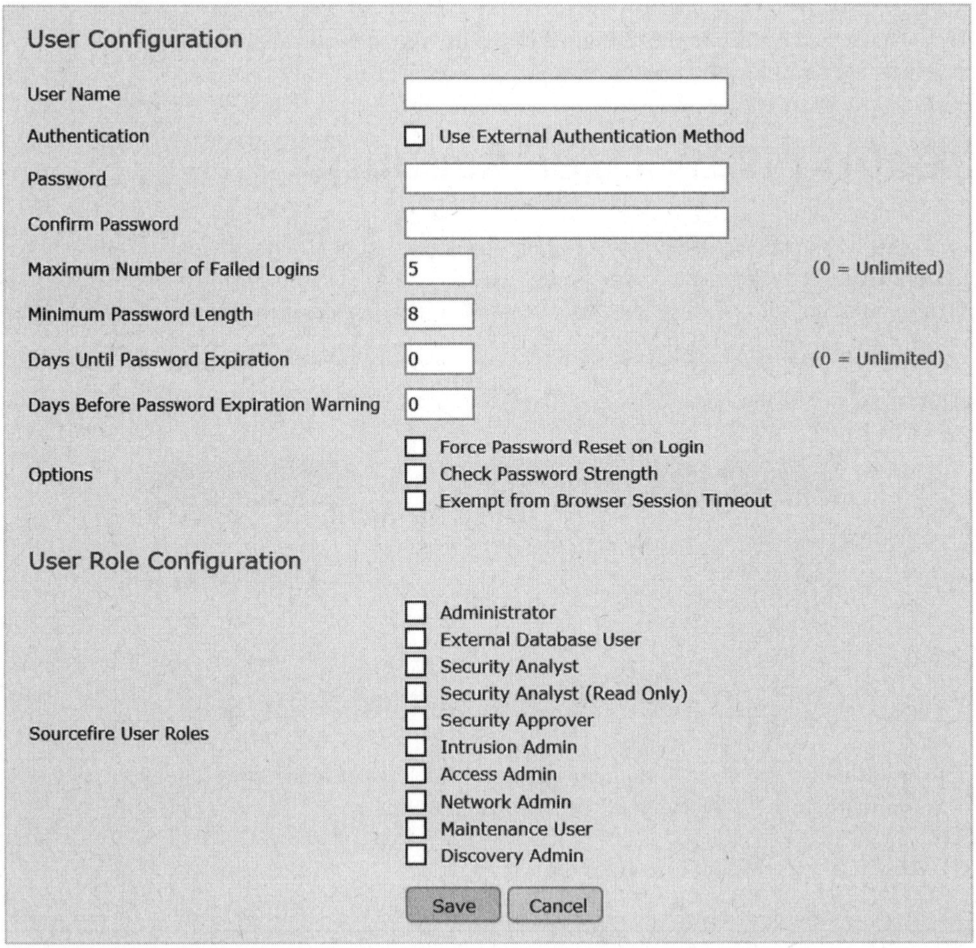

If you create a user here, know that you are creating a local user account. If you click Use External Authentication Method instead, most of the options on this page will disappear and you'll only be able to pick the user role from the screen pictured in Figure 9.4.

FIGURE 9.4   Choosing an external authentication option

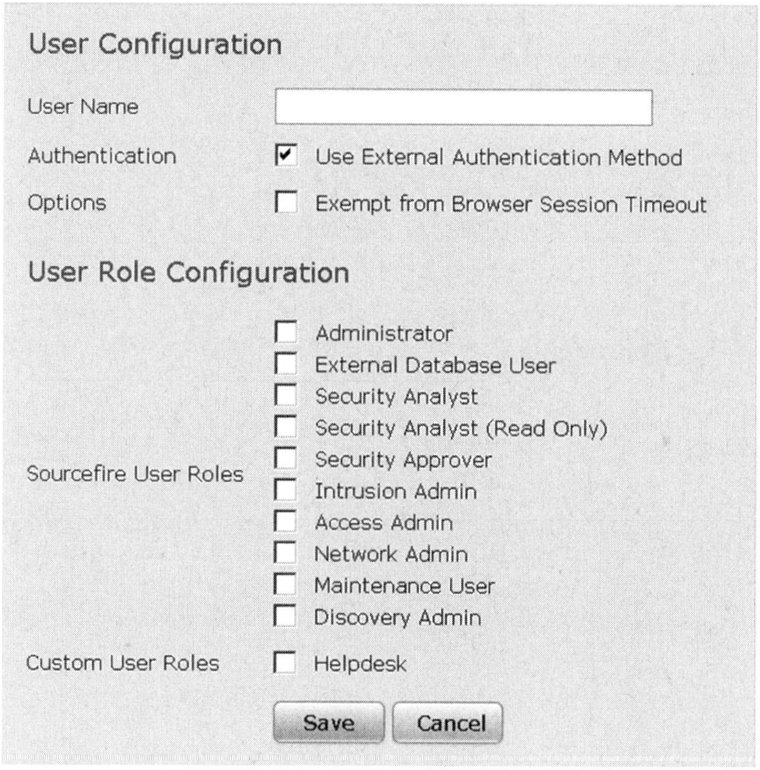

For now, we're just going to create a simple internal user with a Security Analyst (Read Only) role. Figure 9.5 illustrates how to create an internal user.

Look at Figure 9.5 again... did you notice we created a user named Todd and that we could have forced the password to be reset on first login? Good! We also left the defaults for the maximum number of failed logins at 5 and a minimum password length of 8 characters, and we didn't set the password to expire either.

FIGURE 9.5   Creating an internal user

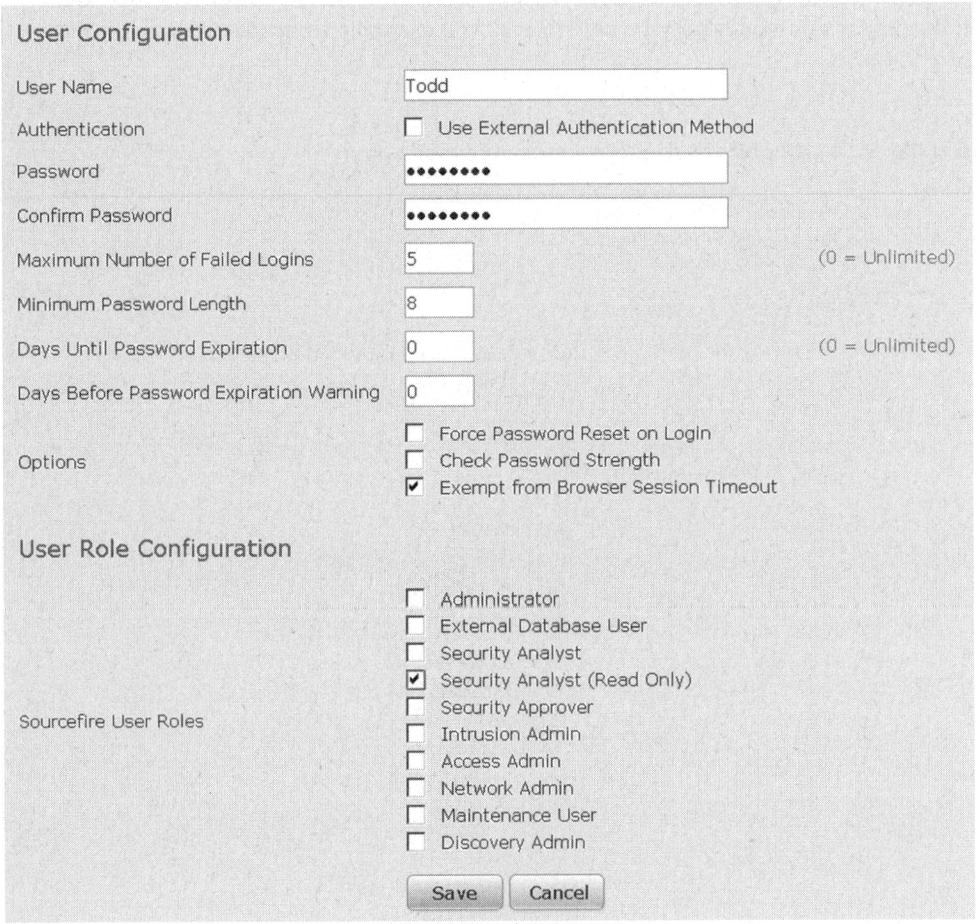

User Configuration

User Name	Todd
Authentication	☐ Use External Authentication Method
Password	••••••••
Confirm Password	••••••••
Maximum Number of Failed Logins	5 (0 = Unlimited)
Minimum Password Length	8
Days Until Password Expiration	0 (0 = Unlimited)
Days Before Password Expiration Warning	0
Options	☐ Force Password Reset on Login ☐ Check Password Strength ☑ Exempt from Browser Session Timeout

User Role Configuration

Sourcefire User Roles
- ☐ Administrator
- ☐ External Database User
- ☐ Security Analyst
- ☑ Security Analyst (Read Only)
- ☐ Security Approver
- ☐ Intrusion Admin
- ☐ Access Admin
- ☐ Network Admin
- ☐ Maintenance User
- ☐ Discovery Admin

[Save] [Cancel]

Another thing you can do when creating a user is to opt for checking password strength, which will require strong passwords, meaning they'll have to be at least eight alphanumeric characters—uppercase and lowercase, including at least one numeric character. The password cannot appear in a dictionary or include consecutive, repeating characters.

We chose not to have the browser session time-out since the user role is a read-only analyst. You probably wouldn't want a user to timeout if they were logged into a screen in a large network operations center (NOC), where the browser is displayed in all its glory on the NOC's huge screen, right?

We then clicked Save, and Figure 9.6 shows that the user was created and that it is active.

FIGURE 9.6 Verifying that the new user is active

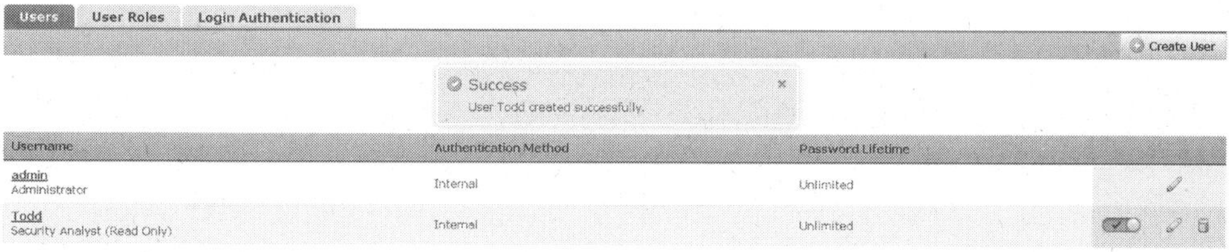

So, now that we've created a user using a predefined role and verified that the user is active, let's create a custom user role and assign Todd to that role. Look at Figure 9.7 and notice all the available menu items on the left side of the screen, from Overview to FireAMP.

FIGURE 9.7 Verifying the current user rights and logging out

Now check out the right side and notice that I'm choosing to log out as admin. Once I log in as Todd, we get a look at the options I obtain as System Analyst (Read Only). Figure 9.8 shows the menu items after I logged in as Todd.

FIGURE 9.8 Logging in and verifying the new user's rights

Focus on the top left and notice that I now only have the options for Overview and Analysis. On the right side I no longer have the System menu option. I'm going to log back in as admin and then create a custom user role.

Figure 9.9 shows the predefined user roles available. Notice that while they can be disabled, they're all enabled by default.

FIGURE 9.9   Verifying the default user roles

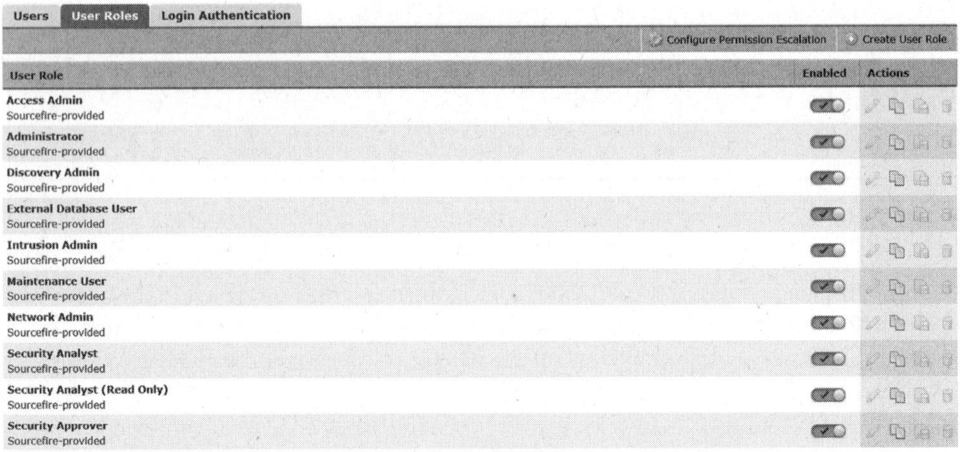

These predefined roles can be edited, but when you try to save the changes, you will be asked to name the new custom role. So basically, you can edit an existing role, but you can't save them as a predefined role—only as a new role.

Okay, so on the top right side, I'm clicking Create User Role, and as shown in Figure 9.10, I'm going to create a user role named Helpdesk and assign some individual custom options for this role.

FIGURE 9.10   Creating a custom user role

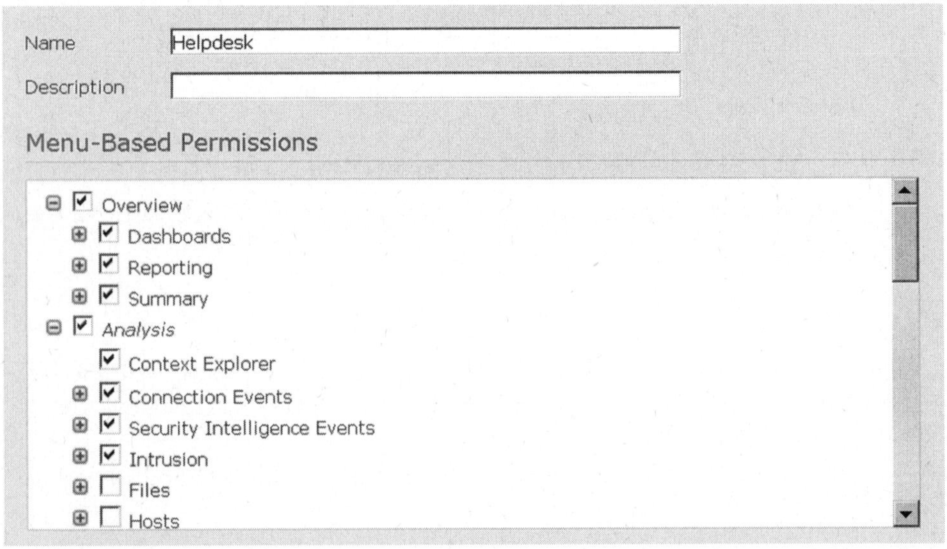

Now once I created the custom user role, I'm allowed to assign a user to it. Look at Figure 9.11 and notice that when I edit user Todd, the custom user role of Helpdesk is now available at the bottom.

FIGURE 9.11   Assigning a custom user role

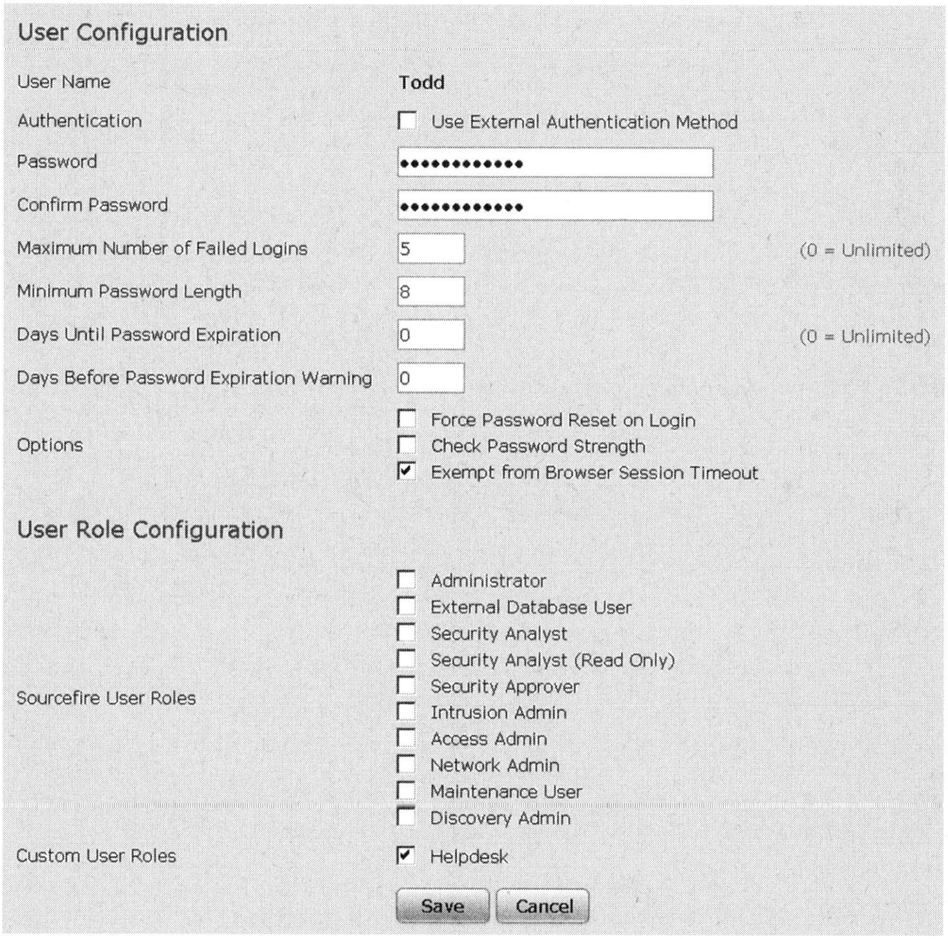

User Configuration

User Name	**Todd**
Authentication	☐ Use External Authentication Method
Password	••••••••••••
Confirm Password	••••••••••••
Maximum Number of Failed Logins	5 (0 = Unlimited)
Minimum Password Length	8
Days Until Password Expiration	0 (0 = Unlimited)
Days Before Password Expiration Warning	0
Options	☐ Force Password Reset on Login ☐ Check Password Strength ☑ Exempt from Browser Session Timeout

User Role Configuration

Sourcefire User Roles	☐ Administrator ☐ External Database User ☐ Security Analyst ☐ Security Analyst (Read Only) ☐ Security Approver ☐ Intrusion Admin ☐ Access Admin ☐ Network Admin ☐ Maintenance User ☐ Discovery Admin
Custom User Roles	☑ Helpdesk

[Save]   [Cancel]

Once I click Save, user Todd is now using only the newly created, custom role of Helpdesk.

Managing User Role Escalation

Let's say that user Todd was working alone on a holiday and something really serious goes wrong. The user Todd calls you in a panic saying, "What do you want me to do? All I can do is verify information!" This is a perfect example of when you would use permission escalation. Take a look back at Figure 9.9 and notice the Configure Permission Escalation button up there at the top. Clicking that button will get you to the next screen, depicted in Figure 9.12.

FIGURE 9.12   Configuring permission escalation

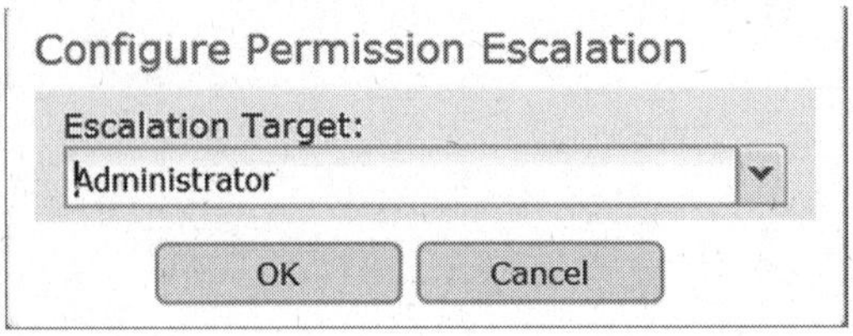

As you can see, you can choose to escalate to any predefined or custom user role that you've created. I'm going to choose Admin. Now, go back to User Roles and edit the role you want escalated. In Figure 9.13, I am going to edit that Helpdesk custom role I just created.

FIGURE 9.13   Configuring permission escalation part II

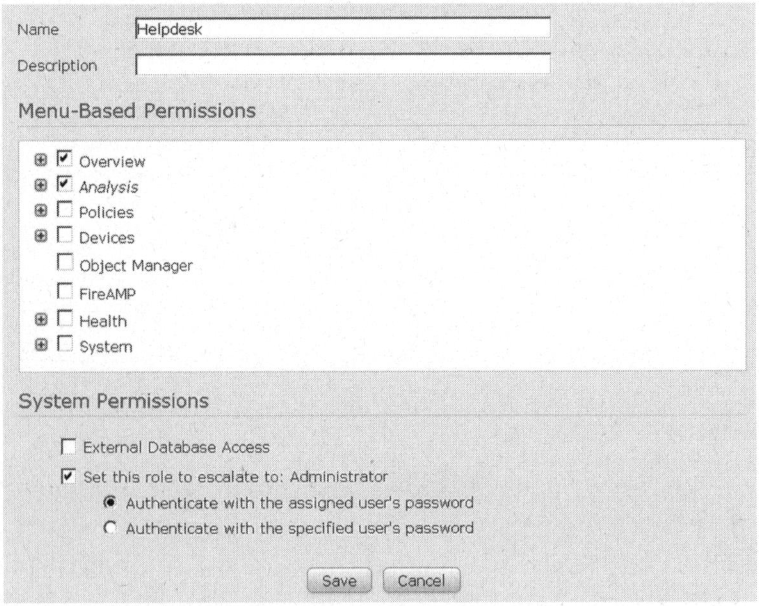

As you can see in Figure 9.13, I chose the Helpdesk role and then set the role to escalate to Administrator, using the assigned user's password. This is an awesome feature that gives you the power to escalate a user's privileges on a temporary basis!

Okay—so now I'm going to log out as Admin, as shown in Figure 9.14.

FIGURE 9.14   Logging out as Admin

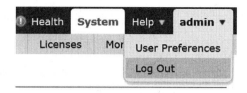

Once I log out as Admin and log back in as Todd (shown in Figure 9.15), notice that I get a new option under the user Todd. That's right—Escalate Permissions!

FIGURE 9.15   Escalating permissions

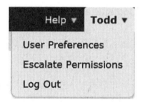

Now if I were to choose the Escalate Permissions options, and I enter Todd's password when prompted, then user Todd would be escalated to Administrator. To stop user Todd from escalating using his own password, you would want to choose the radius button Authenticate With The Specified User's Password instead of using the Authenticate With The Assigned User's Password radius button.

Configuring External Authentication

The reason we would opt to have an external authentication method over an internal authentication method for users logging into the FMC is because doing this allows you to set up a directory on your network to organize different objects like user credentials in a handy, centralized location. If you ever need to change a user profile, you don't need to go to each network device; you just make changes in one location and it will affect the user's rights across the network.

Authentication objects are server profiles for external authentication servers and contain the settings for the connection as well as authentication filter settings for your external servers. When you create an authentication object, you define settings that let you connect to an authentication server. These objects are created, managed, and deleted on the FMC, not on the managed devices themselves. Using an external authentication method allows a user to log in to any FMC or managed device with a single login by applying a system policy on the managed device, because when you apply the policy, the object is copied to the device—sweet!

Creating Authentication Objects

Make a mental note that in order to create an authentication object, you must first make sure you have a solid IP connection through the network from your FMC to the authentication server(s) you'll be using.

From the menu options, on the right side of the menu bar, choose System ➢ Local ➢ User Management, just like back in Figure 9.1, and then choose the Login Authentication tab located in the main panel of the screen, as shown in Figure 9.16.

FIGURE 9.16 Login Authentication tab

In the upper-right corner, click the Create Authentication Object button and you'll receive the screen shown in Figure 9.17. The first option to choose is what type of authentication object you want to create: LDAP or RADIUS.

FIGURE 9.17 Choosing LDAP or RADIUS

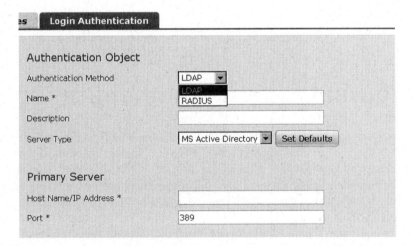

After you choose your object type, you'll need to set your server type as well as the primary server. You can have a backup server, but that's optional in the configuration. Figure 9.18 shows an LDAP server that I've got running on the local network. I've configured the name, server type, and primary server information, including the port number.

FIGURE 9.18   Configuring LDAP server options

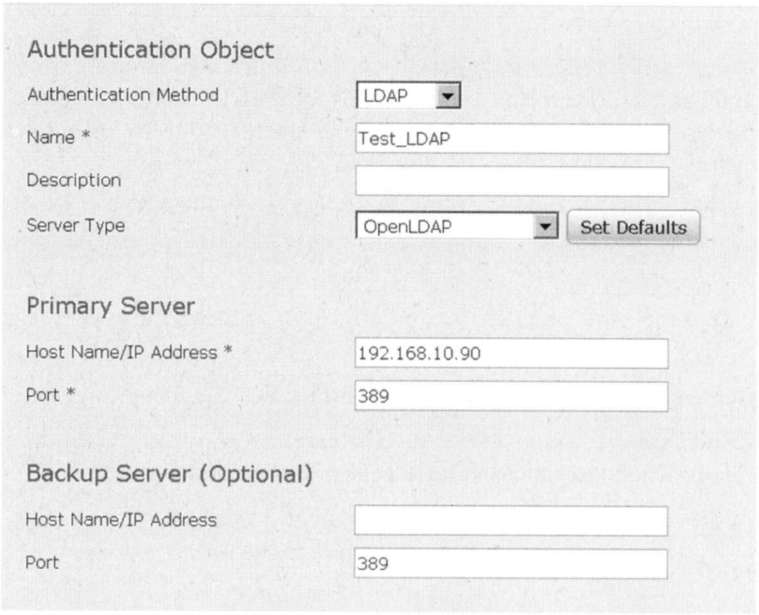

In the Server Type field, you can choose OpenLDAP, MS Active Directory, Oracle Directory, or Other. Choosing MS Active Directory, Oracle, or OpenLDAP populates the page with some default values used with those servers. Choosing the Other option populates the page with no default values whatsoever.

From here, you want go down the page and configure LDAP-specific parameters as shown in Figure 9.19.

FIGURE 9.19   LDAP-specific parameters

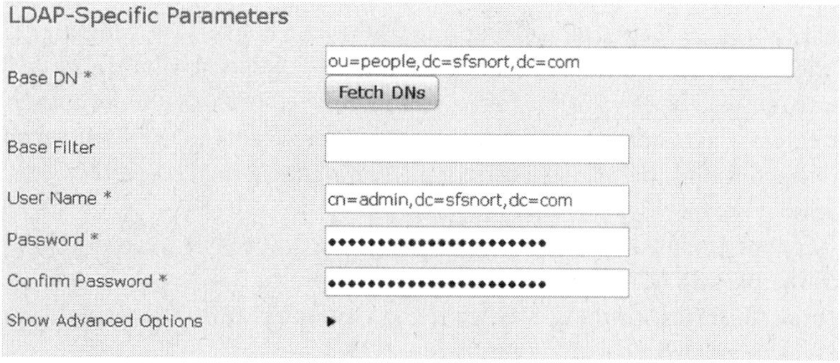

Really—the hardest part of the LDAP configuration is getting the right information in order to configure the LDAP-specific parameters in the first place. Figure 9.19 shows the information you need to know in order to configure LDAP.

Base DN   Sets a starting point for searching the LDAP directory tree. If you filled out the User Name and Password/Confirm Password fields for the LDAP admin account, you can use the Fetch DNs button and it will use the configured credentials to log in to the LDAP server and fetch the DN value.

Base Filter   Sets a filter that retrieves only the objects in the BASE DN that has the characters you configured in the filter. You need to use parenthesis when defining the characters!

User Name   Type the name of a user that is authorized to access the objects in the LDAP directory.

Password / Confirm Password   Type the password for the user name you entered.

After you have configured your LDAP-specific parameters, you can click the Show Advanced Options icon to expand that field, as demonstrated in Figure 9.20.

FIGURE 9.20   Show Advanced Options field

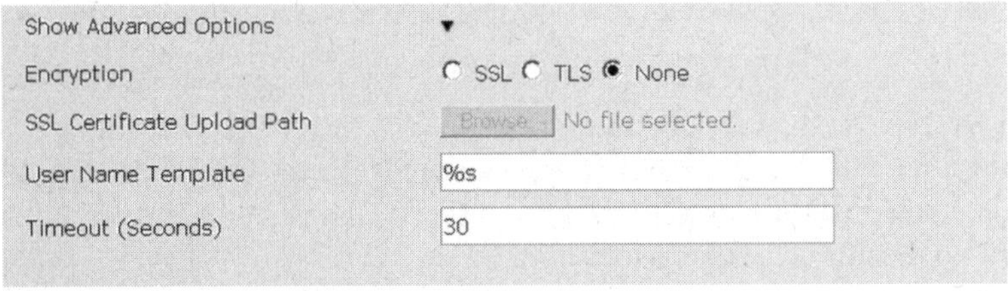

From here, you can configure an encryption method if your LDAP server is configured to support it. Plus, it lets you set a path to the location of the TLS or SSL authentication certificate, if you're using one.

The User Name Template option allows you to specify how user names entered in the user login field should be formatted by mapping the string conversion character (%s) to the value of the *Pluggable Authentication Module (PAM)* login attribute for the user. This user name template is the format for the distinguished name used for authentication. When a user enters a user name into the login page, the name is substituted for the string conversion character, and the resulting distinguished name is then used to search for the user credentials.

Last, the timeout field is used to allow you to set the amount of time the appliance takes to fail over to the backup LDAP server if one is configured.

After you have finished with the Show Advanced Options portion of the page, then configure the Attribute Mapping options as shown in Figure 9.21.

FIGURE 9.21   Attribute Mapping options

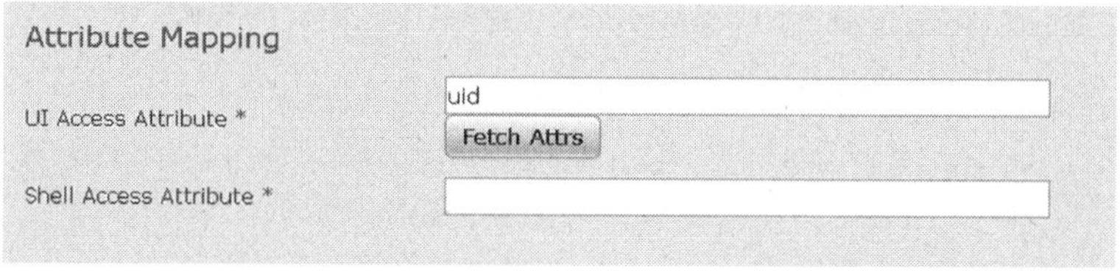

Different types of LDAP servers use different attributes to store user data. For an LDAP server that uses the PAM, as my server does, use the login attribute of uid. If the PAM login attribute for the target server is something other than uid, set it here. For a Microsoft Active Directory server, use a UI Access attribute of userPrincipalName or sAMAccountName to enable the retrieval of users.

The Fetch Attrs button, which provides the output shown in Figure 9.22, will allow you to access the LDAP server by way of the impersonation account login credentials to obtain UI access and/or shell access attributes—if they exist.

FIGURE 9.22   Fetch Attrs output

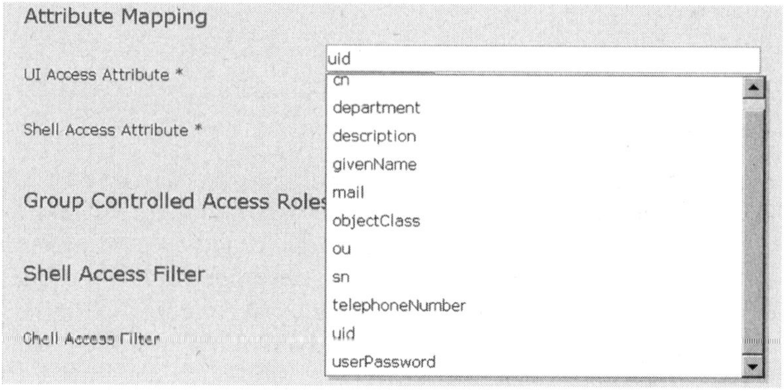

Selecting a server type and setting defaults prepopulates a shell access attribute that's usually appropriate for that specific type of server. You can use any attribute, if the value of the attribute is a valid user name for shell access. Valid user names are unique and can include underscores (_), periods (.), hyphens (-), and alphanumeric characters.

If you prefer to base access permissions on a specific user's membership within an LDAP group, you can specify distinguished names for existing groups on your LDAP server for each of the access roles used by your FireSIGHT System. Do this from the Group Controlled Access Roles configuration screen, as shown in Figure 9.23.

FIGURE 9.23 Group Controlled Access Roles configuration

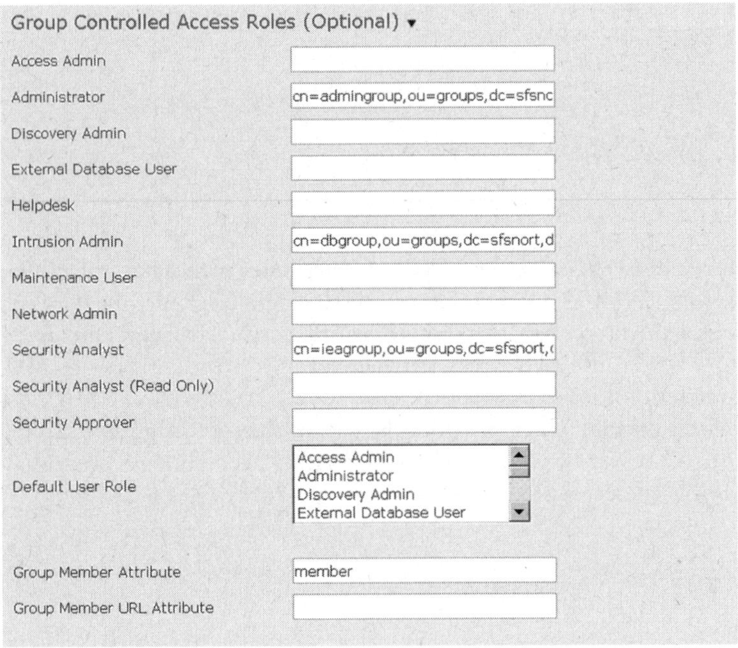

You can also configure a default access role for those users detected by LDAP that do not belong to any specified groups. When a user logs in, the FireSIGHT System dynamically checks the LDAP server and assigns access rights according to the user's current group membership. It's really important to remember that you can also add roles to users in the User Management interface, but you cannot assign privileges lower than what is already granted to the user by the Group Controlled Access Roles settings!

Check out Figure 9.23 again...in it, you can see that the Default User Role field lets you define the default role for users retrieved that don't fall into any of the groups you've defined. If the LDAP server is using static groups, then enter the attribute in the Group Member Attribute field. If the LDAP server is using dynamic groups, then enter the attribute in the Group Member URL Attribute field.

Figure 9.24 shows the Shell Access Filter and Additional Test Parameters settings.

By configuring the Shell Access Filter settings, you can allow LDAP-authenticated users shell access, but to stop anyone from having shell access, you need to check the Same As Base Filter box.

FIGURE 9.24   Shell Access Filter and Additional Test Parameters settings

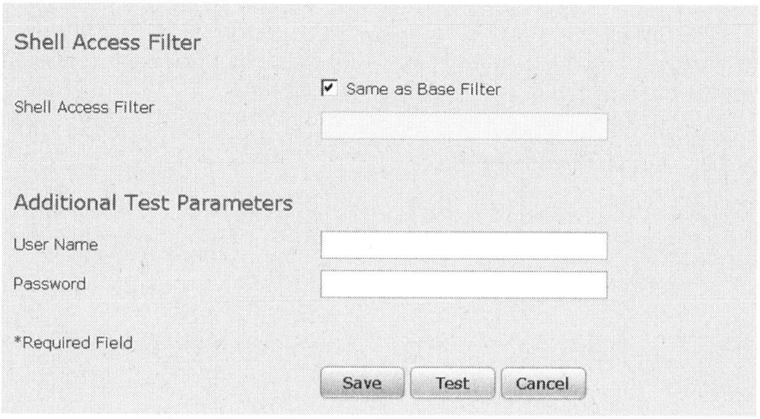

Shell Access Filter

☑ Same as Base Filter

Shell Access Filter

Additional Test Parameters

User Name

Password

*Required Field

[Save] [Test] [Cancel]

Last, as shown at the bottom of Figure 9.24, you can test your server settings with the Test button. You can also test specific user credentials on the server from there by entering the user name and password. I'm going to test my server setup by pressing the button. Figure 9.25 shows the output I received once I tested my server connectivity and authentication.

FIGURE 9.25   Server test results

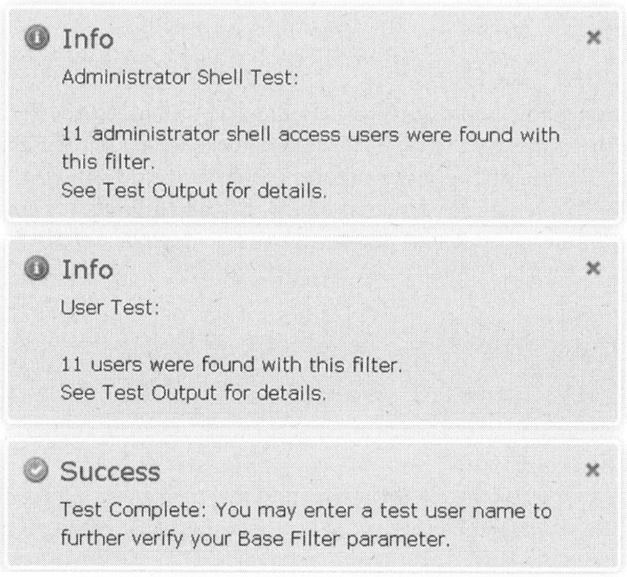

ℹ **Info**   ✕

Administrator Shell Test:

11 administrator shell access users were found with this filter.
See Test Output for details.

ℹ **Info**   ✕

User Test:

11 users were found with this filter.
See Test Output for details.

✅ **Success**   ✕

Test Complete: You may enter a test user name to further verify your Base Filter parameter.

After you set up your server and test your connectivity and authentication, click the Save button at the bottom of the screen to save your configuration. At this point you need to enable the object in the system policy and apply the system policy to your devices. To do this, go to System ≻ Local ≻ System Policy. Edit the policy you want to use, and then navigate to Authentication Profiles, as shown in Figure 9.26.

FIGURE 9.26   Authentication Profiles

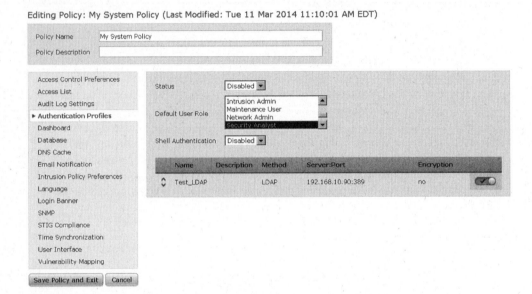

From here you can enable and disable your servers as well as set the default user role. Be sure to notice that the status on the top is disabled. For external authentication, this must be enabled in order to authenticate external users. A default user role can be chosen for the user if they didn't have a local user group assigned. Be careful here! It's super easy to set the default user role to Administrator and not realize you've done it.

Summary

In this chapter we covered user authentication and the differences between internal and external authentication methods.

We also described how to create a local user and assign the user a predefined role. We created a custom role and assigned the role to the user that we created. We then configured permission escalation and showed you how a user can escalate their rights.

After that, we demonstrated configuring an external authentication method and finished the chapter by going step-by-step through setting up an LDAP authentication object.

Hands-on Lab

In this section, you will go through the following two labs:

Hands-on Lab 9.1: Configuring a User in the Local Database

Hands-on Lab 9.2: Configuring Permission Escalation

Hands-on Lab 9.1: Configuring a User in the Local Database

In this lab, you will create an internal user account.

1. From the main menu, navigate to System ➤ Local ➤ User Management.
2. Click Create User.
3. In the User Configuration section, enter *your name* in the User Name field.
4. Enter a password that you will remember.
5. In the Options section, select Exempt From Browser Session Timeout.
6. Go down to the User Role section and choose Security Analyst.
7. Click the Save button to create the new user.
8. Since the new user will not timeout when in the browser, change the value of the browser time-out session. Go to System ➤ Local ➤ System Policy and choose User Interface.
9. Set the time-out of the browser session to 2 minutes.
10. Click the Save Policy And Exit button.
11. Apply the system policy to your FMC.
12. Log in as your new user and verify that the GUI does not log out after 2 minutes. Also, notice the rights you have and which rights you no longer have since you are not an administrator.

Hands-on Lab 9.2: Configuring Permission Escalation

In this lab, you will create a custom user role and configure the user to have the ability to escalate permissions. Log in as admin before you start this lab.

1. From the main menu, navigate to System ➤ Local ➤ User Management.
2. From the User Management screen, click the User Roles tab.
3. Click the Create User Role button and enter the name **Helpdesk**.
4. Click Save and then OK.
5. From the User Management screen, click the User Roles tab and then click Configure Permission Escalation.
6. Set the target to Administrator.

7. Edit the Helpdesk role you created and select the check box that says "Set this role to escalate to: Administrator."

8. Set the role to authenticate with the assigned user's password.

9. Click Save.

10. Edit the user you created in lab 9.1, and select Helpdesk as the custom user role.

11. Click Save.

12. Log out as Admin and log in as the user you created in lab 9.1.

13. Notice that you no longer have rights to all menu items.

14. Go to the upper right and click your username, and then choose Escalate Permissions. Type in the password for the user you created in lab 9.1 when prompted.

15. Notice that even though you are logged in as the user you created in lab 9.1, you now have administrator rights.

Exam Essentials

Understand internal authentication.   When you log in to the FireSIGHT GUI interface with a username and password, the appliance first looks for the user ID in the local database. Users in the local database will predictably be authenticated locally on the appliance, but even if the user account that's asking for access requires external authentication, the system will still try the local database first.

Understand external authentication.   External authentication occurs when the FireSIGHT Management Center or a managed device tries to authenticate users from either an external LDAP or a RADIUS server database.

Remember how to configure permission escalation.   From the User Management screen, click the User Roles tab and then click Configure Permission Escalation.

Remember the LDAP-specific parameters.   The LDAP-specific parameters are Base DN, Base Filter, User Name, and Password / Confirm Password.

Review Questions

You can find the answers in Appendix A.

1. When you configure permission escalation, which user role can you escalate to?

  A. Only System Analyst

  B. Only a user role configured as Read Only

  C. Only an external authenticated user role

  D. Only a user role with Administrator rights

  E. Any user role

2. When configuring external authentication, which of the following is optional?

  A. Primary server

  B. Backup server

  C. LDAP-specific parameters

  D. Attribute mapping

3. Which of the following preconfigured user roles can review, modify, and apply device configurations as well as review and modify Access Control policies?

  A. Network Admins

  B. Security Approvers

  C. Security Analysts

  D. Security Analysts (Read Only)

4. Which of the following preconfigured user roles can view and apply, but not create, configuration and policy changes?

  A. Network Admins

  B. Security Approvers

  C. Security Analysts

  D. Security Analysts (Read Only)

5. Which of the following preconfigured user roles can review, analyze, and delete intrusion, discovery, user activity, connection, correlation, and network change events?

  A. Network Admins

  B. Security Approvers

  C. Security Analysts

  D. Security Analysts (Read Only)

6. Which of the following preconfigured user roles can have all the same rights as Security Analysts, except that they cannot delete events?

  A. Network Admins

  B. Security Approvers

    C. Security Analysts

    D. Security Analysts (Read Only)

7. How is permission escalation configured?

    A. From System ➢ Local ➢ System Policy, choose User Interface.

    B. From the User Management screen, click the User Roles tab and then click Configure Permission Escalation.

    C. By changing the value of the Pluggable Authentication Module (PAM) login attribute for the user.

    D. From the User Management screen, click the Login Authentication tab and then click Configure Permission Escalation.

8. Which of the following is *not* part of the configuration of the LDAP-specific parameters?

    A. Base DN

    B. UI Access attribute

    C. Base Filter

    D. User Name

9. Which is the path you take to configure an internal or external user?

    A. From the main menu, navigate to System ➢ Local ➢ Configuration.

    B. From the main menu, navigate to System ➢ Local ➢ System Policy.

    C. From the main menu, navigate to Health ➢ Local ➢ User Management.

    D. From the main menu, navigate to System ➢ Local ➢ User Management.

10. Which preconfigured user role can view and modify access control and file policies but cannot apply their policy changes?

    A. Access Admins

    B. Administrators

    C. Discovery Admins

    D. External Database

Chapter

10

Device Management

THE SSFIPS EXAM OBJECTIVES COVERED IN THIS CHAPTER INCLUDE THE FOLLOWING:

- ✓ **10.1** Describe the VPN types supported and the configuration of those VPNs

- ✓ **10.2** Define the different NAT types

- ✓ **10.3** Understand the properties of the managed devices and the settings that may be configured

- ✓ **10.4** Describe the settings for configuring the virtual interface and virtual router switch types

As the name suggests, managed devices need management, so we're going to guide you through exactly how to do that in this chapter. We'll discuss and demonstrate registering the devices with the Defense Center as well as touring each of the device's properties. You'll discover the different settings for the interfaces and switch and router configurations, plus we'll survey the different VPN and NAT types available to managed devices as well.

By the time we've finished this chapter, you should be well equipped with a solid awareness of how these elegant devices can be configured. You'll also be well versed about the features available regarding their properties.

To find up-to-the-minute updates for this chapter, please see www.lammle.com/firepower or the book's web page at www.sybex.com.

Device Management

Anyone who's experienced waiting eagerly for a device to arrive knows that it's just the beginning when you finally get it. As usual, you'll have to start your relationship with some initial configurations. It's no different for managed devices—you'll need to set the management IP address on the system, specify a detection mode, and register it with a Defense Center. And once your device is registered with a DC, you're free to do all kinds of wonderful things with it! You can modify the detection method—inline or passive—and opt to set up virtual routers or switches if it's a physical appliance. You can also work with NAT or VPN configurations.

The guides can be downloaded from the Cisco support portal.

When you turn on your brand-new managed device, it will boot to a login prompt that will lead you to a series of configurations screens (Figure 10.1). The devices have a default IP address of 192.168.45.45 with a user name of *admin* and a password of *Sourcefire*. To access the device, you can either connect a monitor and keyboard or SSH to the default IP address (you can also assign a new IP address through the front panel

LCD). The first thing to appear will be an end-user license agreement that you'll need to page through.

FIGURE 10.1 Managed device console login

```
login as: admin
Sourcefire 3D7120 v5.3.0.1 (build 66)
Using keyboard-interactive authentication.
Password:
Last login: Fri Apr 10 10:25:11 2015 from 192.168.45.1

Copyright 2001-2013, Sourcefire, Inc. All rights reserved. Sourcefire is
a registered trademark of Sourcefire, Inc. All other trademarks are
property of their respective owners.

Sourcefire Linux OS v5.3.0 (build 63)
Sourcefire 3D7120 v5.3.0.1 (build 66)

You must accept the EULA to continue.
Press <ENTER> to display the EULA:
```

Next, we're going to walk you through the initial setup (Figure 10.2). First thing on your checklist is to change the password for the admin account and make sure you pick a strong one here. Keep in mind that this changes the GUI password on the device too. Then comes the network configuration. The system can be managed over IPv4 or IPv6, and you'll be asked to provide an IP address, netmask, gateway, hostname, DNS server, and search domain. Once these items are confirmed, you've got to reconnect to the newly configured IP address.

FIGURE 10.2 Initial device settings

```
Please enter 'YES' or press <ENTER> to AGREE to the EULA:YES

System initialization in progress.  Please stand by.
You must change the password for 'admin' to continue.
Enter new password:
Confirm new password:

You must configure the network to continue.
You must configure at least one of IPv4 or IPv6.
Do you want to configure IPv4? (y/n) [y]: y
Do you want to configure IPv6? (y/n) [n]: n
Configure IPv4 via DHCP or manually? (dhcp/manual) [manual]:
Enter an IPv4 address for the management interface [192.168.45.45]:
192.168.1.22
Enter an IPv4 netmask for the management interface [255.255.255.0]:
Enter the IPv4 default gateway for the management interface []:
192.168.45.1
Enter a fully qualified hostname for this system [Sourcefire3D]: 3D7120
Enter a comma-separated list of DNS servers or 'none' []: 192.168.1.1
Enter a comma-separated list of search domains or 'none' [example.net]:
none
If your networking information has changed, you will need to reconnect.
```

If you think you'll want to change the IP settings in the future, you can log in to the device and type expert at the prompt. After entering expert mode, type the following command:

    sudo /usr/local/sf/bin/configure-network

Doing this launches a network configuration script that allows you to set your IP address and netmask.

You'll also be asked about whether or not to allow the front panel to configure the device and be prompted to select one of these four detection modes:

Inline: Allows the device to function as an IPS.

Passive: Allows the device to function as a passive IDS.

Network Discovery: Allows the device to perform only FireSIGHT functions.

Access Control: Allows the system to control traffic with an AC policy.

Keep in mind that you can modify the mode you choose later on.

Once you have the networking configured, you need to join the device to the Defense Center. This is a two-step process that requires action on both the device and the DC. On the managed device, you'll need to specify the name or IP address of the DC and a registration key. This registration key is a user created one-time passphrase that will also need to be entered in the DC. The registration key is used to authenticate the DC to the managed device for the initial connection. Once the connection has been established, authorization is handled via certificates.

To complete step 1 of the process, type the following on the command line as shown in Figure 10.3:

    configure manager add <IP Address> <Registration Key>

Voilà—you're ready to add the device to the DC!

FIGURE 10.3 Specifying the Defense Center

```
> configure manager add 192.168.1.100 1qaz2WSX
Manager successfully configured.

>
```

Configuring the Device on the Defense Center

To continue with step 2, log in to the Defense Center's web interface and click Devices in the main menu. This will take you to the Device Management screen. Once there, click Add in the upper right and select Add Device.

This will load the Add Device dialog, shown in Figure 10.4. You must enter either the hostname or IP address of the managed device here as well as the registration key that was entered on the device. Then select an Access Control policy and specify the licenses to be enabled.

FIGURE 10.4   Add Device dialog

When the device has been successfully added, it will appear on the devices tab in your Device list as seen in Figure 10.5. Here's a short list of some other options under the Add menu:

Add Group: Use this to organize devices, making it easier to perform certain management tasks.

Add Cluster: A cluster allows for the sharing of state and connection data in case of a failover between routing devices.

Add Stack: A stack is two or more managed devices connected together with a special kit that allows the devices to increase their throughput by sharing CPU and memory. Use this option to stack two supported devices together.

FIGURE 10.5 Devices tab

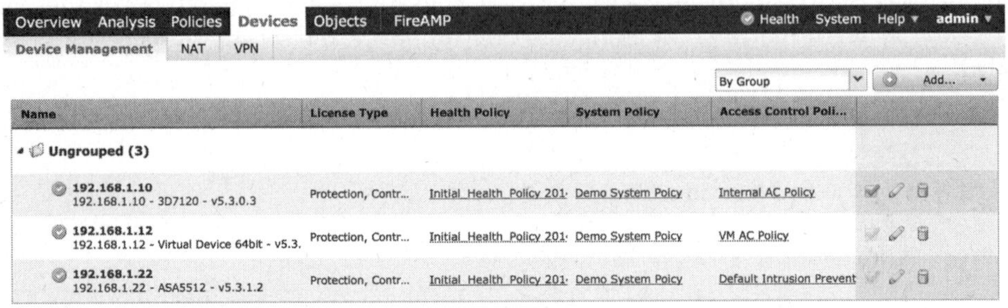

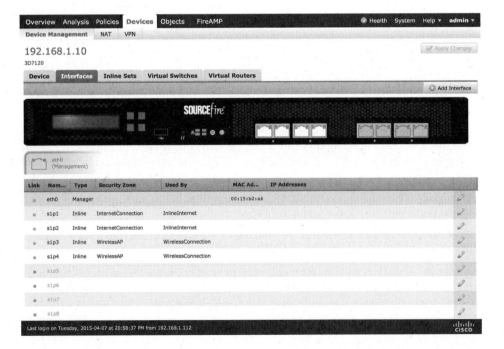

To carry out most configuration tasks, you don't need to go directly to the managed device CLI or GUI. Nearly all of the configuration can be done from the Defense Center. To view or edit the properties of your device, either click the device name itself or click the edit icon that's shaped like a pencil.

The Device Management screen opens to a graphical representation of your managed device (Figure 10.6). If you have a virtual device or an ASA running FirePOWER Services, then there will be no graphic here. The device's graphic will show the ports that are enabled and active, and if you hover your mouse over one of these ports, it will reveal additional information about it.

FIGURE 10.6 Device management

Device Tab

We will get back to the interfaces more in a bit. For now, let's look at the Device tab, where we can see and modify some of the more generic properties of the device. Under this tab, you can see these six categories, as shown in Figure 10.7:

FIGURE 10.7 Device settings

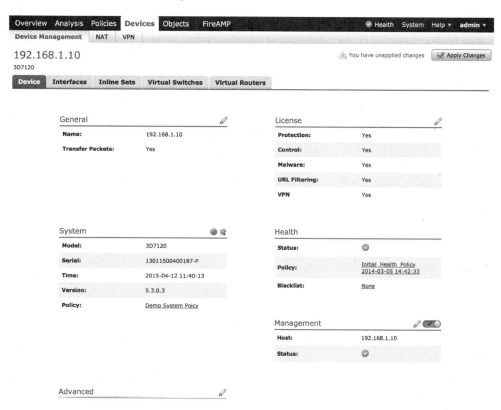

General: Lets you modify the name of the device as seen in the interface. This also controls whether or not packets from the IPS events will be sent to the Defense Center so they can be viewed by event analysts. It defaults to on.

License: Allows you to enable or disable feature licenses on the device. If a license for a feature is disabled, then that particular feature will not be permitted on the device.

System: Displays information about software versions, serial number, current time on the device, model number, and the system policy that has been applied. There are also two icons here. Clicking the red octagon shuts down the device, and the other one allows you to restart it.

Health: Details the current status, the health policy applied, and any blacklisted items.

Management: Displays the current IP address and management status. There's also a slider to disable management if needed.

Advanced: Allows you to enable Automatic Application Bypass (AAB). Use this to set the threshold for AAB and whether or not to inspect local router traffic. In the 8000 series models, you also have fast-path rules, which you can use for directing traffic to bypass inspection. On the other devices (non-8000 series models) you can tell the system to not inspect traffic via the Access Control policy. It is a best practice to put all your exclusions in the AC policy.

Automatic Application Bypass

Automatic Application Bypass (AAB) is a managed device feature that's really designed for inline systems, even though it can be used in passive deployments too. AAB terminates the IPS inspection process if traffic takes too long to make it through the device and exceeds the bypass threshold. If that happens, it will generate a dump file and a health alert and restart inspection within 10 minutes. The idea here is that if the IPS hasn't been configured efficiently and begins to have an impact on your network throughput, then the IPS automatically terminates. Of course, there's a downside—now there's no inspection occurring. The good news is that there's another way of achieving similar results without the ugly consequences and that is via a feature called Latency-Based Packet Handling (along with Based Rule Handling), which we'll tell you all about a bit later, in Chapter 12, "Advanced IPS Policy Configuration"!

 Know that if changes are made to any of the properties of the device, they won't take place right away because the administrator must click the Apply Changes icon in the upper right of the interface. Still, you'll be given the opportunity to see what those changes are prior to the final application.

Interfaces Tab

As we mentioned earlier, the Interfaces tab displays the interfaces of the managed devices. You can adjust the properties of the interfaces by either double-clicking on the interface or clicking the edit icon. The interfaces can be configured into one of these six modes:

None Disables the interface.

Passive Allows the interface to be used in a passive manner for detection.

Inline Allows the interface to be used in an inline interface set. Inline interfaces need to be configured in pairs.

Switched Allows the interface to be used as part of a virtual switch. Clicking Add Interface at the top of the screen can create sub-interfaces, which need to be assigned to separate VLANs.

Routed Allows the interface to be used as part of a virtual router.

HA Link Allows the connection to be used to exchange High Availability (HA) information between configured devices. HA is beyond the scope of this book, but if you're curious, consult the user guide.

Passive

As you can see in Figure 10.8, passive interface configuration is pretty straightforward. There are the typical settings that should match the network that you're placing the device on: the modes, MDI/MDIX settings, and MTU size.

FIGURE 10.8 Passive interface configuration

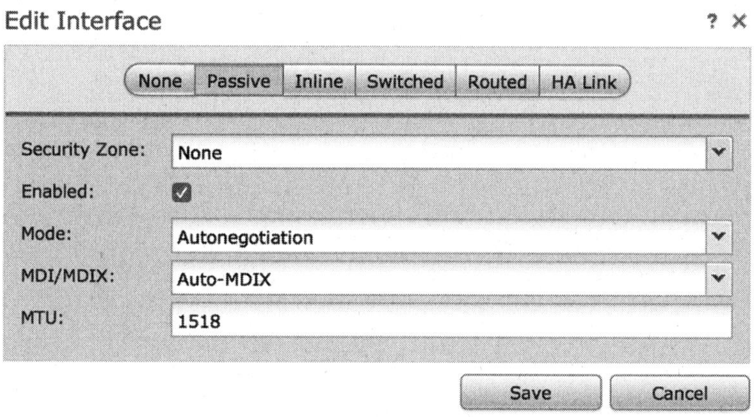

The Security Zone options allows you to specify the zone you want to assign this interface to. You can even create a completely new zone if you want to. Remember, zones can be configured as objects, as you learned in Chapter 2. These zones can be used to control how traffic is inspected through the interface via the Access Control policy.

Inline

The inline interface configuration (Figure 10.9) adds another option as an alternative to passive configuration—the inline set, which is a collection of inline interfaces that are treated as an entity within the device. When an inline interface is enabled, the adjacent interface will be enabled as well, making it possible for the device to be placed inline. The interfaces can fail open or closed, meaning they'll allow traffic to pass or not if the device is down; this depends on the actual hardware and inline set configuration.

FIGURE 10.9   Inline interface configuration

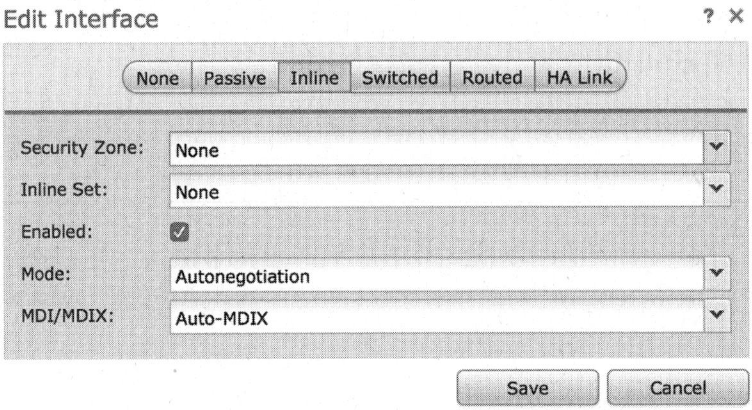

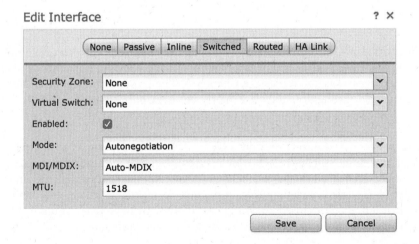

Switched

Another option is to configure the interfaces in switched mode. Using this feature, you can create one or more virtual switches. They operate in the same manner as any other Layer 2 network switch. This feature is only available on the Series 3 hardware, not virtual or ASA. Keep in mind that traffic inspection—including FireSIGHT, IPS, and malware—will still work for the traffic moving through the switch. The switched interface configuration is shown in Figure 10.10.

FIGURE 10.10   Switched interface configuration

Routed

Routed interfaces can be joined together in a virtual router and will route traffic between network segments. Like the traffic moving through the virtual switch, routed traffic is subject to inspection based on the rules in the Access Control policy.

The additional settings on the routed interface (Figure 10.11) include whether or not to allow the interface to respond to ICMP pings or traceroutes, IPv6 router advertisement options, and IP address and static ARP entries.

FIGURE 10.11   Routed interface configuration

Inline Sets Tab

Interfaces that are configured inline must be made part of an *inline set*. There are some configuration options you can apply to this set to control what happens to traffic in a variety of circumstances. Editing the properties of an inline set will bring up the dialog shown in Figure 10.12.

FIGURE 10.12   Inline set configuration

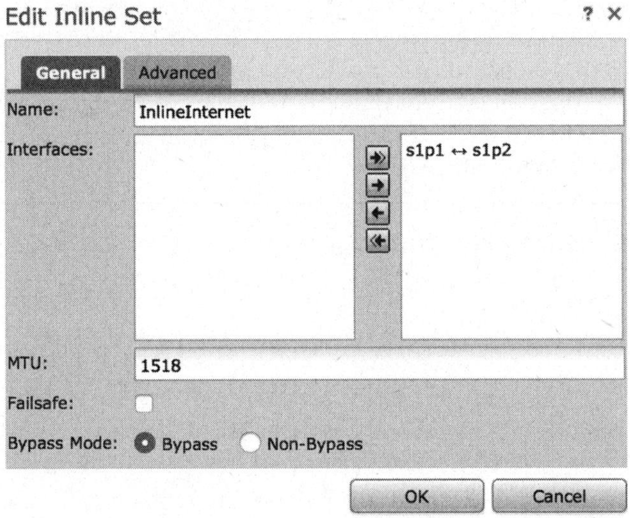

You can configure these properties:

Name A user-friendly name for the set.

Interfaces Refers to the interfaces included in the set. These interfaces are added in pairs.

MTU This should be based on your network's largest packet size. The values range from 576–10172 for Series 3 inline sets.

Failsafe If Failsafe is enabled, traffic will continue to flow even if the interval inspection buffers are full. Note that even though the traffic will still flow, some of it won't be inspected.

Bypass Mode Specifies what happens if there's a problem with the device. Bypass lets traffic flow even when the detection processes are stopped. Non-Bypass causes the traffic flow to stop unless the inspection processes are running. The bypass mode is also dependent on the type of network modules installed on the device. Some contain magnetic switches or prisms to allow traffic to pass even when power is lost to the device. However, some network modules only allow "software bypass," meaning if power is lost or the device is rebooted, traffic will not pass even if Bypass is enabled.

There's also an Advanced tab offering four more settings that are enabled or disabled with check boxes:

Tap Mode In tap mode, the real traffic is not being sent through the device for inspection; it's being passed straight through the inline interfaces. Only a copy will be sent through the system for inspection. No blocking happens in tap mode.

Propagate Link State This will ensure that if the link state changes on one interface in the set, it will change for the other interface as well. This is helpful in cases where you have redundant network paths and want to ensure a clean failure in case one side of the inline set fails.

Transparent Inline Mode This allows the system to function as a transparent device. Any packet that touches one interface is passed to the second in the set. If this is disabled, the device actually functions as a Layer 2 bridge. Note that this option is only available in the virtual device; it is grayed out in FirePOWER hardware models.

Strict TCP Enforcement This setting will block traffic when the system doesn't witness the three-way handshake as well as a few other abnormal TCP conditions. Be very careful with this setting because no alert is generated if these "abnormal" TCP handshake packets are blocked.

Virtual Switches

What you're actually doing with the *virtual switch* is joining multiple configured switch ports together to become a switch. This can be deployed as a network switch, where inspection takes place on the traffic passing through. Aside from adding a name and interfaces, there's also a setting called Hybrid Interface, which is really a switch that's assigned as part of a router. If traffic is destined for an adjacent host, it will stay in the switch, but if it's headed for a remote network, it will be passed to the router. Figure 10.13 shows the General tab of the virtual switch configuration dialog.

FIGURE 10.13   General virtual switch configuration

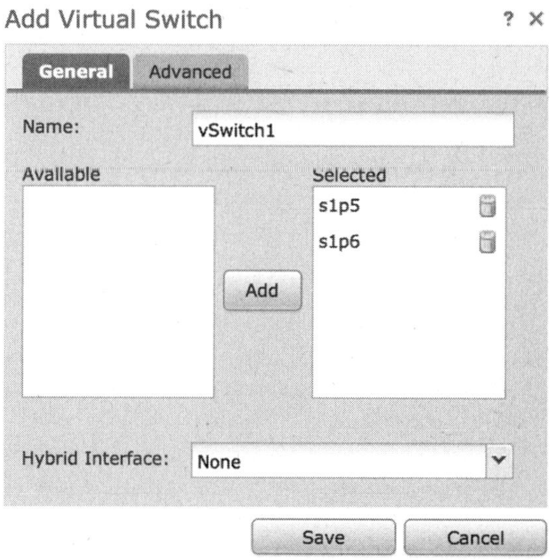

In Figure 10.14, we see the Advanced tab. You can specify static MAC entries and also enable or disable the following three items:

Enable Spanning Tree Protocol Doing this will allow the virtual switch to participate in Spanning Tree Protocol (STP) activity on the network to prevent networking loops and facilitate networking redundancy.

Strict TCP Enforcement Will block traffic if the system doesn't witness the three-way handshake as described previously.

Drop BPDUs Removes Bridged Protocol Data Unit (BPDU) information from packets, allowing traffic to be sent between VLANs on the switch. This requires multiple sub-interfaces on a single physical interface to accept the traffic and is known as One-Armed IPS or IPS on a Stick.

FIGURE 10.14   Advanced virtual switch configuration

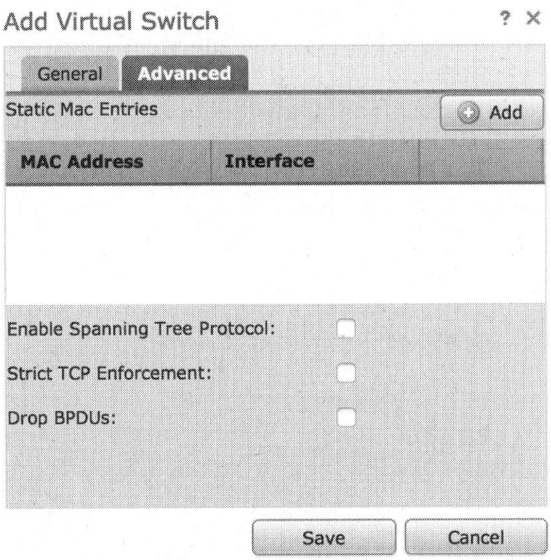

Virtual Routers

If you have a Series 3 device, it can function as a *virtual router*. When you configure the router, you must define the name and specify the interfaces to use. Other settings available on the General tab (Figure 10.15) include enabling IPv6 support, strict TCP enforcement, and the ability to relay DHCP traffic.

Directly connected networks will be automatically added to the routing table of the device. Other routes can be added statically or via the dynamic RIP or OSPF protocols (RIP and OSPF are not covered in this book). To create a static route, you would complete the dialog in Figure 10.16.

FIGURE 10.15   Virtual router configuration

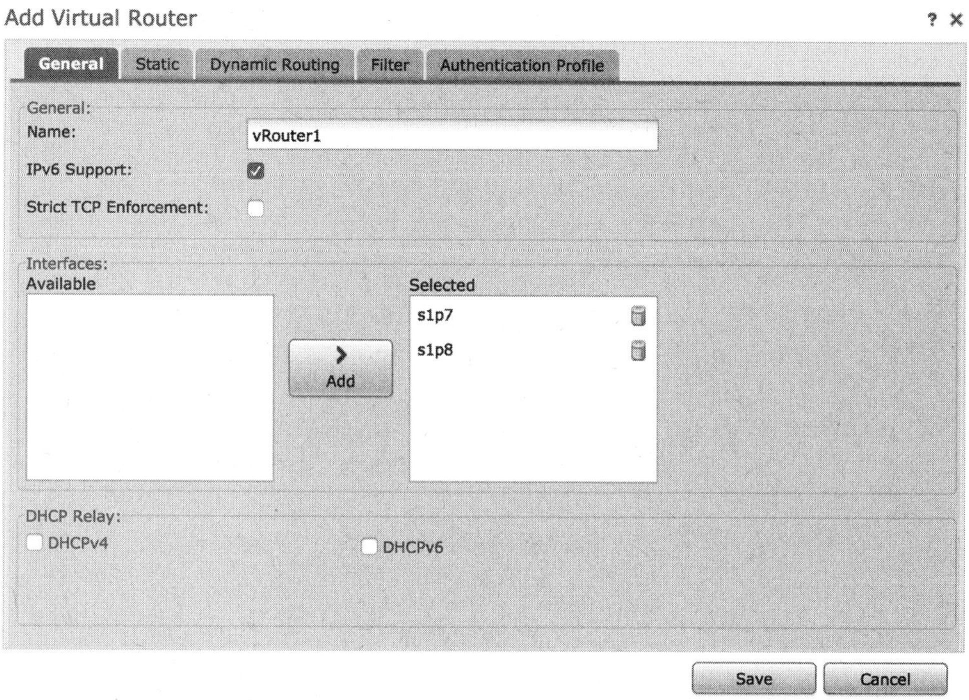

Add Virtual Router   ? ✕

| **General** | Static | Dynamic Routing | Filter | Authentication Profile |

General:
Name: vRouter1

IPv6 Support: ☑

Strict TCP Enforcement: ☐

Interfaces:
Available   Selected

                                         s1p7   🗑

                          >   s1p8   🗑
                          Add

DHCP Relay:
☐ DHCPv4   ☐ DHCPv6

                                        Save   Cancel

FIGURE 10.16   Static route configuration

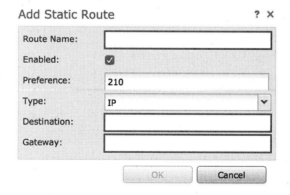

Add Static Route   ? ✕

Route Name:

Enabled: ☑

Preference: 210

Type: IP   ▾

Destination:

Gateway:

              OK   Cancel

To view the routing table of the device, you can enter the following command at the CLI of the device:

```
show routing-table
```

When changing any of the interface configurations, be sure to click the Apply Changes button!

NAT Configuration

Network address translation (NAT) is implemented within the system via a NAT policy. You can have one NAT policy active on a device at any given time. If you ever want to do away with NAT on a device, just create an empty NAT policy and apply it.

To create a NAT policy, simply navigate to the Devices tab and click New Policy. Give the policy a name and specify what device it should apply to (Figure 10.17).

FIGURE 10.17   New NAT policy

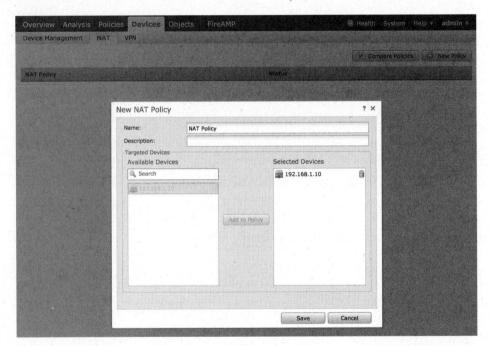

There are three NAT varieties that are supported in the policy, as seen in Figure 10.18:

Static   Static allows the translation of IP to IP. Ports can also be translated through the configuration as well. You need to specify the destination network and translated destination network.

Dynamic IP   Dynamic is a many-to-many translation wherein you need to specify a source network, a translated network address, and a destination network for the traffic. The ports stay the same across the translation.

Dynamic IP and Port   This option is a many to one, or a many to many translation. You need to specify the source network, a translated network address and a destination network for the traffic along with the original port.

FIGURE 10.18 NAT rule configuration

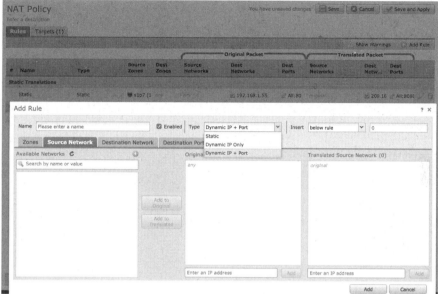

And of course, once you've created the NAT policy, make sure to apply it to the managed device!

Virtual Private Networks

You can configure VPN connectivity between managed devices that are configured as routers, which will encrypt all traffic flowing between the devices. It's a nice way to secure inter-office communication or site-to-site communication that's available with Series 3 hardware and the VPN license.

There are currently three VPN types supported:

- Point-to-point
- Star
- Mesh

Let's take a closer look at each one of these now.

Point-to-Point VPN

The *point-to-point VPN* deployment allows you to encrypt data being exchanged between two endpoints. If you have two managed devices configured as routers with a collection of hosts behind each that need to intercommunicate, this is a really great solution!

To configure the connection, click the VPN tab under devices. Click Add, provide a name, click PTP, and enter a pre-shared key. Once you've done that, define your endpoint nodes as shown in Figure 10.19.

FIGURE 10.19   Point-to-Point VPN configuration

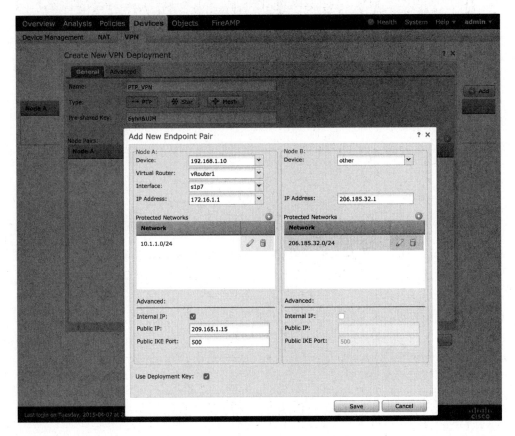

For this to work, you've got to specify both endpoints in the VPN. Node A would be one of the virtual routers you had configured in your network. Specify the interface and network that would be facing Node B and indicate the protected networks. Do the same for Node B. But, if the Node B device is managed by another Defense Center, you would specify "other" and populate the available fields. For the shared secret, the system will use the pre-shared key specified when you first configured the VPN. Alternately, you can clear the Use Deployment Key check box and provide a unique entry for each point-to-point pair.

Star VPN

The *star VPN* refers to when you have a central location known as a hub node. In this case, you would have multiple remote sites known as leaf nodes. Some other vendors still call this a hub and spoke VPN.

The configuration here is a lot like point-to-point only you have multiple sites. To get started, add the VPN and specify Star. The next screen is where you define the hub and then the leaf nodes. Just as you did before, select your virtual router, interface, and IP address from the available drop-downs, plus specify the networks to protect. You configure the leaf nodes the same way, except if the leaf nodes aren't managed by the same Defense Center, you need to select Other in the drop-down, as shown in Figure 10.20.

FIGURE 10.20   Star VPN configuration

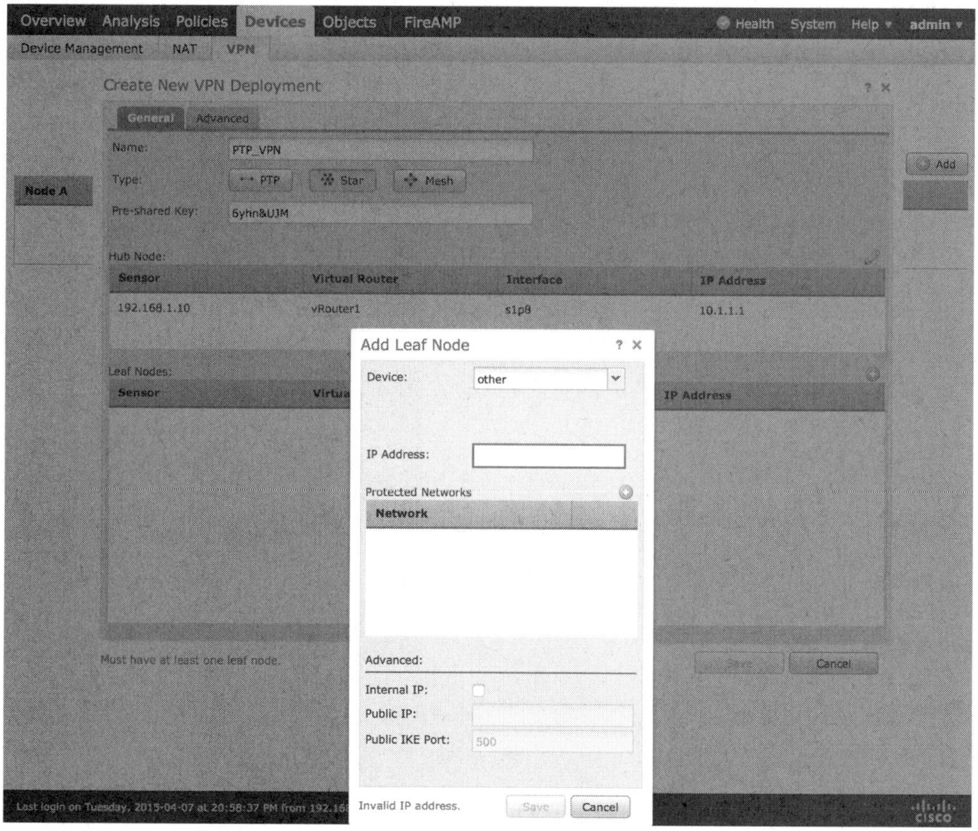

Mesh VPN

The *mesh VPN* paves the way for redundant connectivity between multiple sites. Configure this by adding each of the nodes into the dialog. You need to choose from the drop-down options for any of the members that are being managed by the Defense Center. If the devices are managed by others, then you need to select Other and add the information as required. The result is that each VPN endpoint will have a connection to each of the other endpoints. Figure 10.21 shows the configuration screen.

FIGURE 10.21 Mesh VPN configuration

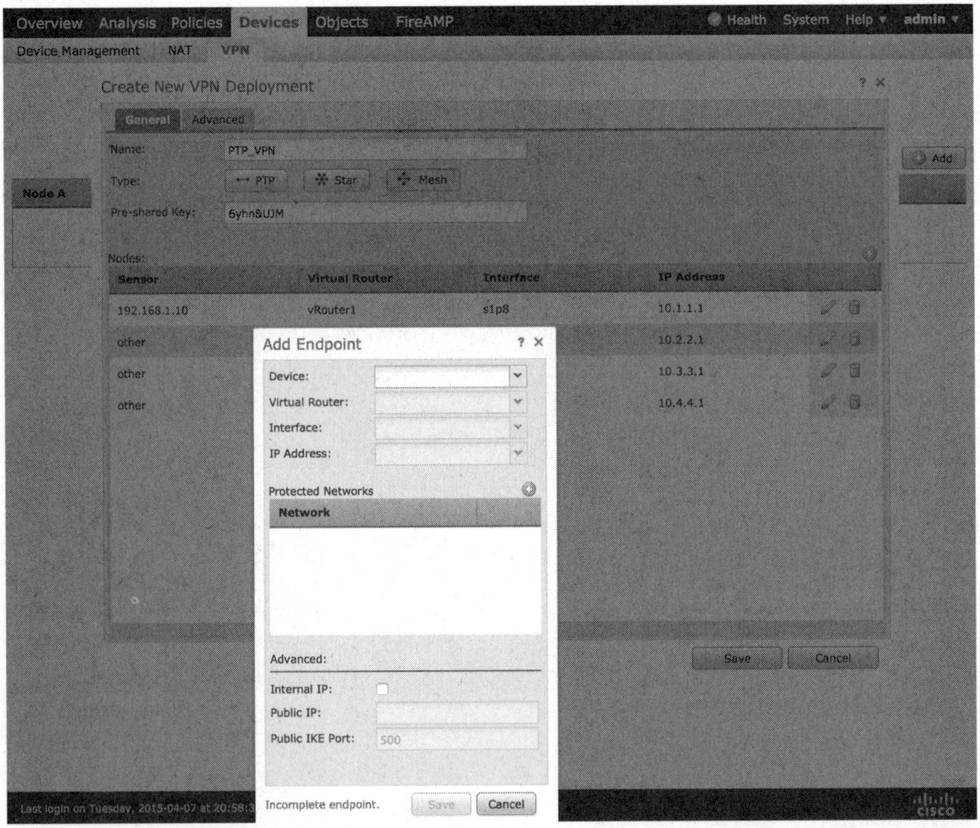

Advanced Options

There's an Advanced tab containing information about the IKE and IPSec configurations for each of the VPN configurations (Figure 10.22). If you really need to customize these, you've got to make sure that the customization is done for all endpoints!

FIGURE 10.22   Advanced VPN configuration tab

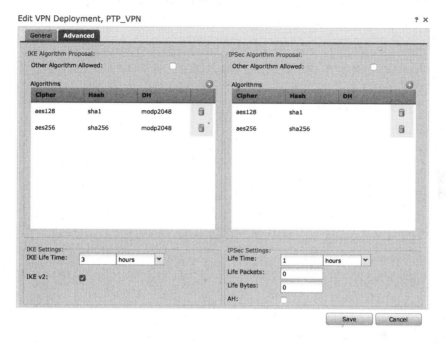

Once the VPN options have been configured, don't forget to apply the configuration by clicking the check mark. Once you've done that, you can view the status and statistics of the VPN by clicking the status icon next to the VPN.

Summary

You learned all about how to configure managed devices in this chapter. We guided you through how to manage the managed devices, including registering the device with the FSM and looking at properties of the device. You also learned about the different settings for the interfaces and for switch and router configurations and explored the different VPN and NAT types available to the managed device.

Hands-on Labs

In this section, you will go through the following three labs:

    Hands-on Lab 10.1: Creating a Device Group

    Hands-on Lab 10.2: Renaming the Device

    Hands-on Lab 10.3: Modifying the Name of the Inline Interface Set

Hands-on Lab 10.1: Creating a Device Group

In this lab, you will create a group to place your device in.

1. Open your web browser and HTTPS to your Defense Center.
2. Log in to the Defense Center.
3. Navigate to Devices.
4. Click the Add drop-down button in the upper right and select Group.
5. In the name field, enter **My Network Devices**.
6. In the Available Devices column, select your device and click Add.
7. Click OK.
8. Notice the newly created group containing your device.

Hands-on Lab 10.2: Renaming the Device

In this lab, you will rename your device.

1. Open your web browser and HTTPS to your Defense Center.
2. Log in to the Defense Center.
3. Navigate to Devices.
4. Expand the group My Network Devices that you created earlier.
5. Click on your device.
6. Click the device sub-tab.
7. Click the edit icon for the General section.
8. In the name field, type **InlineDevice**.
9. Click Save.
10. Click Apply Changes.

Hands-on Lab 10.3: Modifying the Name of the Inline Interface Set

In this lab, you will modify the name of the inline interface set.

1. Open your web browser and HTTPS to your Defense Center.
2. Log in to the Defense Center.
3. Navigate to Devices.
4. Expand the group My Network Devices that you created earlier.
5. Click on your device.
6. Click the Inline Sets tab.
7. Double-click on the inline set called Default Inline Set.

8. In the name field, enter **DMZ Inline Set**.

9. Click OK.

10. Click Apply Changes.

Exam Essentials

Identify the different types of VPN topologies supported.   There are three types of site-to-site VPNs supported inside the FireSIGHT system:

- Point to Point: Allows a site to communicate directly with another

- Mesh: Allows multiple sites to connect to other systems directly

- Star: Has a site act as a central hub with multiple leaf sites

Describe the different NAT types supported by the FireSIGHT System.   There are three types of NAT types supported in FireSIGHT:

- Static: Allows the translation of IP to IP.

- Dynamic IP: A many-to-many translation wherein you need to specify a source network, a translated network address, and a destination network for the traffic.

- Dynamic IP and Port: This option is a many-to-one or a many-to-many translation.

Be able to view and modify device properties.   When a device is first initialized, you must go through basic configuration steps and add the device to a Defense Center. Once it's in the Defense Center, you can edit the device to configure the interfaces and view other properties. You can view the health of the device, remove licenses, configure automatic application bypass parameters, or even restart or shut down the device.

Describe the interface configuration properties.   The individual interfaces of the managed device can be configured to detect traffic in the following modes: passive, inline, switched, and routed. If the interfaces are in switched or routed mode, then a virtual switch or virtual router must be created.

Review Questions

You can find the answers in Appendix A.

1. When configuring a managed device, what is the default IP address?
   - **A.** 192.168.0.1
   - **B.** 172.16.1.1
   - **C.** 192.168.1.1
   - **D.** 192.168.45.45

2. What is the default password of the managed device?
   - **A.** admin
   - **B.** Cisco
   - **C.** Sourcefire
   - **D.** default

3. What does a stacked device allow the system to do?
   - **A.** Maintain state and session data for routed devices for failover
   - **B.** Share CPU and memory to increase inspection throughput
   - **C.** Increase port density
   - **D.** Support multiple VPN encryption types.

4. Which of the following are VPN types that the FireSIGHT System supports?
   - **A.** SSL and mesh star
   - **B.** PTP, SSL, and web
   - **C.** PTP, hub and spoke, and remote
   - **D.** PTP, mesh, and star

5. What is the NAT type that translates many to many called?
   - **A.** Dynamic IP
   - **B.** Dynamic IP and Port
   - **C.** Static
   - **D.** Dynamic PAT

6. Which interface type allows you to monitor traffic only?
   - **A.** Inline
   - **B.** Routed
   - **C.** Switched
   - **D.** Passive

7. The registration key that is required when adding a new device to the FireSIGHT Manager
_____.

   A. Is provided by Cisco as part of your license

   B. Is a one-time passphrase used for initial authentication

   C. Must be obtained prior to installation

   D. Can be recovered if lost

8. If a device fails and traffic continues to flow, how is the system likely configured?

   A. Stacked with fail-open (bypass)

   B. Inline with fail-closed (non-bypass)

   C. Inline with fail-open (bypass)

   D. Stacked with fail-closed (non-bypass)

9. Which feature allows the system to stop detection if traffic is taking an excessive amount of time to pass through the device.

   A. Automatic Application Redirect

   B. Profiling

   C. Fail-Open

   D. Automatic Application Bypass

10. What type of dynamic routing protocols are supported on managed devices?

   A. RIP and OSPF

   B. BGP and OSPF

   C. RIP and IGRP

   D. OSPF and EIGRP

Chapter 11

Correlation Policy

THE SSFIPS EXAM TOPICS COVERED IN THIS CHAPTER INCLUDE THE FOLLOWING:

- ✓ **11.1** Describe the components of a correlation policy
- ✓ **11.2** Understand the process for creating a white list
- ✓ **11.3** Describe the purpose and creation of traffic profiles
- ✓ **11.4** Be familiar with the types of responses available when dealing with correlation policies

Correlation policy is an often overlooked but useful feature of the FireSIGHT System. The features available in this area concentrate on detection of unusual activity rather than specific intrusion or malware events. By using correlation rules, white lists, and traffic profiles, we can detect network or host behaviors that may be an indication of malicious activity. In this chapter, we will review the options available for creating *correlation rules*, white lists, and *traffic profiles* to identify unusual activity even when there are no Snort rules available to detect a specific threat.

To find up-to-the-minute updates for this chapter, please see www.lammle.com/firepower or the book's web page at www.sybex.com.

Correlation Overview

Correlation focuses on identifying network behaviors. Correlation rules are written to identify network traffic or other events that would be considered something worth alerting on. The rule identifies the condition we want to know about—for example, a particular intrusion event or an unusually large HTTP file transfer. However, the rule by itself simply identifies the condition; the response is the action taken as a result of the rule triggering. The response is generated by the Defense Center and can be any one of the built-in notification types: syslog, SNMP, or email. It can also be a *remediation*: a script or program that runs on the Defense Center. The rule and response are linked together with the correlation policy. This relationship is shown in Table 11.1. The left column shows all of the types of activity that a correlation rule can detect. The right column shows the responses available. The function of the correlation policy is to link the response to the rule.

TABLE 11.1 Correlation policy links the rule with the response

Event Types	Response
Intrusion event	Syslog
Discovery event	SNMP
User activity	Email (SMTP)

Event Types	Response
Host input event	Built-in remediation
Connection event	Custom remediation
Traffic profile change	
Malware event	
White list*	

* A white list is slightly different because it operates like a rule.

Correlation provides a powerful, flexible alerting mechanism. But there's even more to it than that. By using the remediation feature, you can trigger a built-in or custom script in response to a correlation rule. This means the Defense Center can respond with either a custom alert or whatever action you can write a script to perform. We will discuss remediation in more detail later.

Correlation Rules, Responses, and Policies

When you set out to create a custom response to an event, you might be tempted to start with the correlation policy. However, the policy simply links the correlation rule with the response. This means before you can create the policy, you need to have both the rule and the response already completed.

Correlation Rules

Let's start with a simple rule example. Suppose we want to be alerted whenever there is an HTTP connection that transfers more than 5MB total. Suppose we found that almost all HTTP connections from our network are less than 5MB in total size. In fact, a connection over 5MB typically indicates either malicious or unauthorized activity. Rather than try to create a Snort rule that might look for specific data in a packet, we need a way to identify anytime an internal host initiates an HTTP connection that transfers more than 5MB of data. Assuming we are already logging connection events, this is a perfect application for a correlation rule.

To begin, navigate to Policies ➤ Correlation, and then click the Rule Management tab. On your first visit, you will see an empty rule list as shown in Figure 11.1.

FIGURE 11.1 Rule Management tab

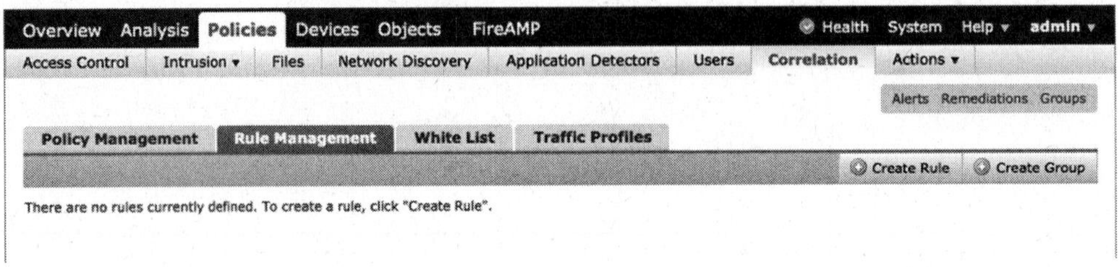

Clicking the Create Rule button on the right takes you to the Rule Information screen, shown in Figure 11.2.

FIGURE 11.2 Rule Information screen

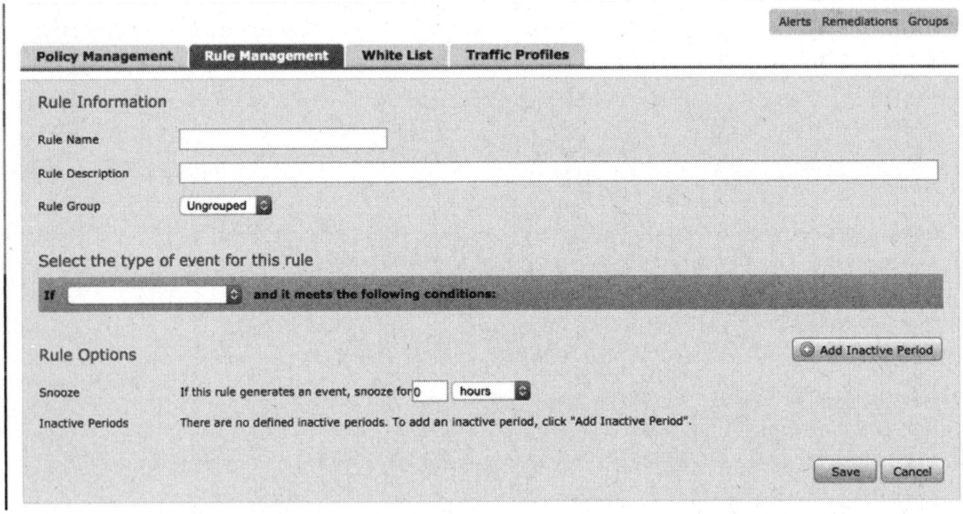

The Rule Name and Description fields are self-explanatory. The Name field is required, while the description is optional.

Below this is the Rule Group option. Initially you will see just the Ungrouped option available. Rule groups are similar to folders. They are a good way of keeping your rules organized, especially if you write quite a few. By default, all of your rules will exist in a single flat list. Groups can be added on the Rule Management tab by clicking Create Group.

Next is the meat of the correlation rule: selecting the event. In this section, you create a sentence structure that defines what type of activity the rule is designed to detect. The sentence starts with *If* and then contains the criteria. Clicking the drop-down displays the types of events we can write rules for:

- Intrusion events
- Discovery events
- User activity

- Host input events
- Connection events
- Traffic profile changes
- Malware events

The drop-down list is shown in Figure 11.3.

FIGURE 11.3   Event types

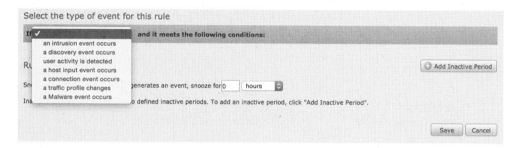

In our example rule, since we are looking for a specific type of HTTP connection, we will select "a connection event occurs."

After an event type is selected, a second drop-down list may appear. The contents of this list depend on the type of event selected. In the case of a connection event, the drop-down contains the options shown in Figure 11.4.

FIGURE 11.4   Event criteria

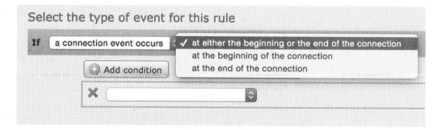

Note that this second drop-down may contain just a few items or numerous items or—in the case of intrusion events—is not displayed at all. Deciding what to select here is fairly intuitive because we are simply building a sentence describing the type of activity we want to detect.

In our example, we are looking for large HTTP connections. For most connection rules, leaving the default setting of "at either the beginning or the end of the connection" will suffice. That option will work for our example as well. However, we might as well be as specific as possible. Since we are looking for large connections, this information will only be available at the end of the connection. Because of that, we will select "at the end of the connection" for this rule.

Next we add conditions to the rule. Our example mentioned several criteria for connections that we will include in this rule:

- Application protocol is HTTP.
- Initiator IP is on our internal network.
- Larger than 5MB.

As a general rule, you want to make your conditions as specific as possible to reduce or eliminate false positives. We don't want this rule matching connections unless they meet all our criteria. Adding these conditions is just a matter of selecting the options and connecting them with the proper operator (either AND or OR). Depending on the event type selected, the drop-down of criteria will change. Figure 11.5 shows all the criteria available for a connection event.

FIGURE 11.5   Connection event criteria

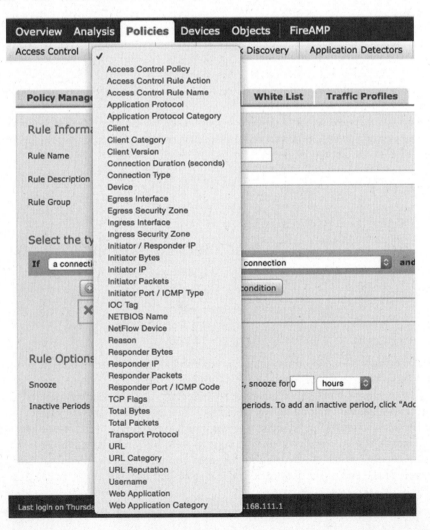

For our example, we will start with Application Protocol. Once this is selected, the rest of the options in the condition are populated. We then select "is" or "is not" and choose a protocol. This is shown in Figure 11.6.

FIGURE 11.6   More event criteria

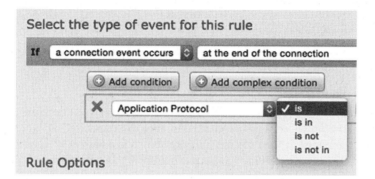

As you can see in Figure 11.7, the list of application protocols available is quite lengthy; the figure shows less than a 10th of the entries in this particular list.

FIGURE 11.7   Application protocols

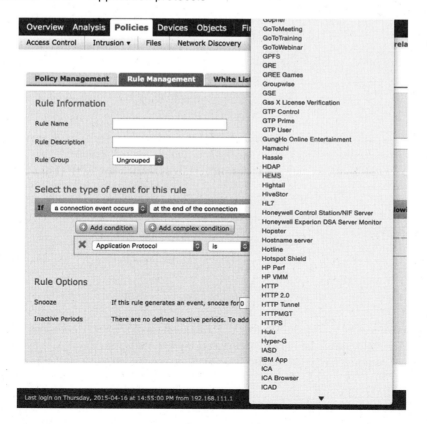

When we are finished with this first condition (Figure 11.8), it is quite descriptive and easy for anyone to read and understand what this rule is doing.

FIGURE 11.8 Rule condition

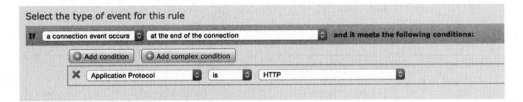

From here, we can continue to add additional criteria. By using the operators AND and OR to connect the criteria, we can make our rule broader (by using OR) or more specific (using AND). The completed criteria for our rule are shown in Figure 11.9. Notice that we have added the initiator network and total bytes using the AND operator to make the rule more specific.

FIGURE 11.9 Completed rule criteria

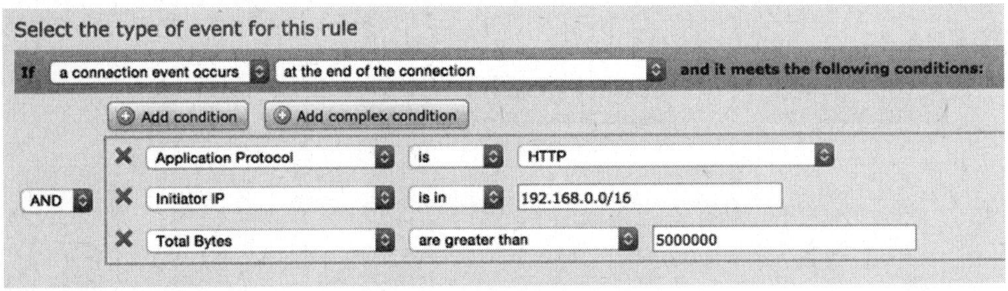

Note that the terms *source* and *destination* are not used with connection events. Instead, you will see *initiator* and *responder*. This is analogous to *client* and *server*. Clients initiate connections, so they are initiators, while servers respond to connection requests.

Rule Options

Below the rule criteria, there are options for Snooze and Inactive Periods. These may be desirable for some rule types.

Snooze

Snooze has the effect of reducing the number of times a rule will trigger. In our example rule, what if there are multiple large HTTP connections initiated from the same host in a very short period of time? The result would be the rule triggering multiple times. If the rule is linked to an email response, this could result in a flood of email messages. A single email message is probably sufficient to alert us that this host should be investigated; we don't need a spam storm from the Defense Center.

To prevent this, you can snooze the rule for a user-defined period of time. This will cause the Defense Center to trigger this rule only the first time it matches during the snooze period. This effectively suppresses subsequent notifications during this period.

Figure 11.10 shows a sample snooze period.

FIGURE 11.10   Rule Snooze settings

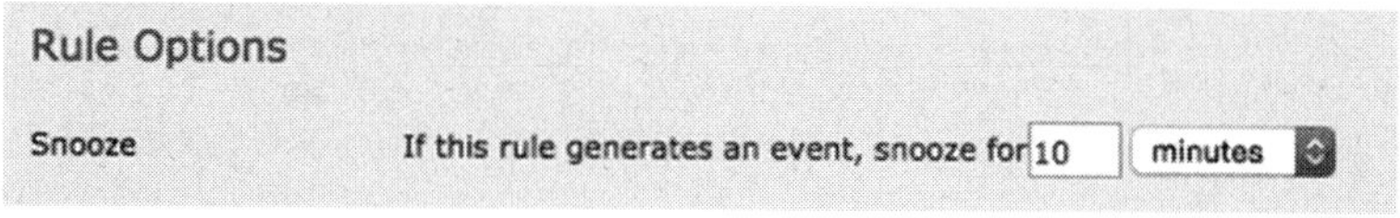

Rule Options

Snooze   If this rule generates an event, snooze for 10   minutes

Inactive Periods

Similar to Snooze, Inactive Periods also has the effect of reducing the number of alerts generated by a rule. Again, using our rule example, what if this large HTTP connection behavior was normal during business hours? Maybe the intention is to detect this traffic only outside of normal business hours. To do so, we could add inactive periods, making this rule inactive during the workday.

To add an inactive period, click the Add Inactive Period button on the right. Then select the period: daily, weekly, or monthly. Then continue with the day of the week, start time, and minutes of inactivity. In our example (Figure 11.11), we would create five different inactive periods, one for each day of the workweek.

FIGURE 11.11   Inactive periods

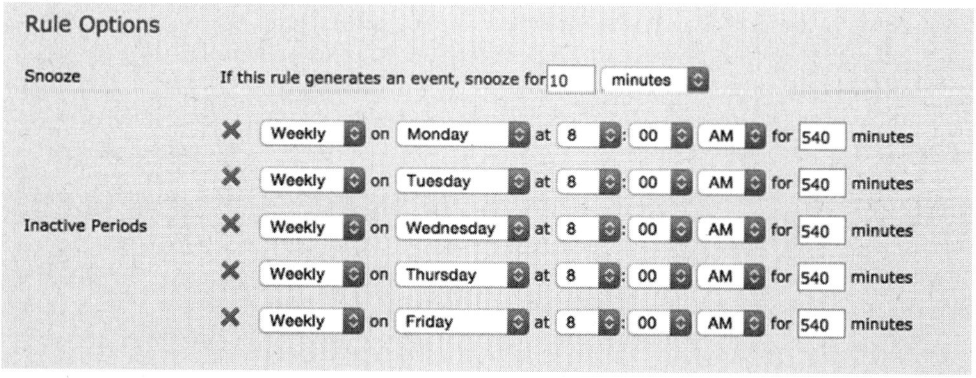

Rule Options

Snooze   If this rule generates an event, snooze for 10   minutes

                ✖ Weekly on Monday   at 8 : 00 AM for 540 minutes
                ✖ Weekly on Tuesday   at 8 : 00 AM for 540 minutes
Inactive Periods ✖ Weekly on Wednesday at 8 : 00 AM for 540 minutes
                ✖ Weekly on Thursday   at 8 : 00 AM for 540 minutes
                ✖ Weekly on Friday   at 8 : 00 AM for 540 minutes

Once your rule is finished, clicking the Save button will save the rule and return you to the rules list.

Responses

The next step is to ensure that we have the proper response created. A response is simply an action performed on the Defense Center when a correlation rule triggers. A response can be as simple as an email message or as complex as a customized remediation script that executes an action on a remote device or system. Responses fall into two broad categories: alerts and remediations. Both types can be found on the main menu under Policies ➤ Actions (Figure 11.12).

FIGURE 11.12   Responses menu

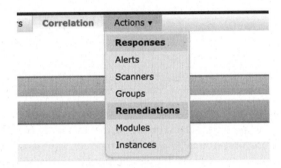

Alerts

Alerts are simply notifications generated by the Defense Center. There are three built-in alert types available:

Email—SMTP message sent via the mail relay configured in the system policy.

SNMP— SNMP versions 1, 2, and 3 are supported.

Syslog—Standard syslog sent to UDP/514.

To configure these alerts, navigate to Policies ➤ Actions ➤ Alerts. Once here (Figure 11.13), you can click the Create Alert button on the right. This will display the drop-down to create any of the three alert types.

FIGURE 11.13   Alert options

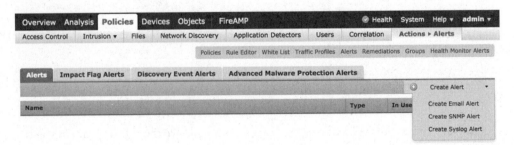

Creating an alert is simply a matter of giving it a name and completing the fields for the alert type. Once an alert is created, you can use it when a correlation rule is triggered. The example in Figure 11.14 shows an email alert.

FIGURE 11.14   Sample email alert

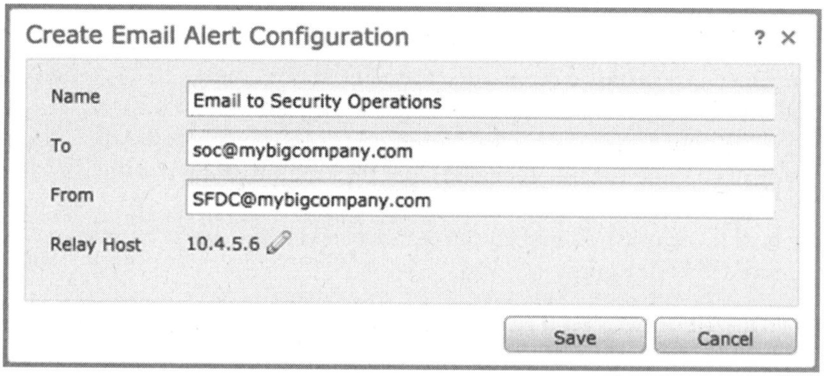

Create Email Alert Configuration	? ×

Name	Email to Security Operations
To	soc@mybigcompany.com
From	SFDC@mybigcompany.com
Relay Host	10.4.5.6

Save   Cancel

Remediations

A remediation is another type of response. It is a script or program that runs on the Defense Center in response to the triggering of a correlation rule. This is a very powerful capability, allowing the Defense Center to perform an action in response to a correlation event. There are several built-in responses included. Custom responses can also be created and then uploaded to the Defense Center.

To get an idea of what type of responses are available, navigate to Policies ➢ Actions ➢ Modules. You will find Modules under the Remediations heading on the menu. This brings up the screen shown in Figure 11.15.

FIGURE 11.15   Built-in remediation modules

There are four built-in remediation modules:

Cisco IOS Null Route—Add a null route entry to a remote Cisco IOS router.

Cisco PIX Shun—Add a shun to a remote Cisco PIX (or ASA) firewall.

Nmap Remediation—Perform an Nmap scan from a device or the Defense Center.

Set Attribute Value— Set the value of a host attribute.

These built-in remediations come unconfigured. To use them, you must create at least one instance. An instance represents a specific set of configuration values for the remediation. For example, if you have four Cisco IOS routers you want to use with the Cisco IOS Null Route remediation, you would create four instances. After you create an instance, you can add specific remediations; these can then be used in the correlation policy.

To show how this works, we will go through setting up one of the built-in remediation modules: Cisco IOS Null Route.

Setting up the Cisco IOS Null Route Remediation

First, we will navigate to the modules page at Policies ➤ Actions ➤ Modules as shown previously in Figure 11.15. Then click the magnifying glass icon to the right of the Cisco IOS Null Route remediation module. This brings up the configuration page for this module, shown Figure 11.16.

FIGURE 11.16   Cisco IOS Null Route remediation module

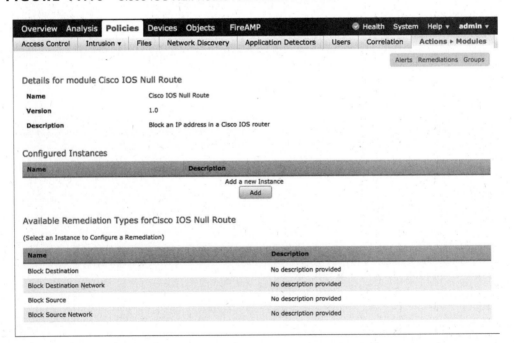

From here, click the Add button to create a new instance. Remember, in this case we will need an instance for each router we wish to control. This brings up the edit page for this remediation, as shown in Figure 11.17.

FIGURE 11.17   Cisco IOS Null Route configuration

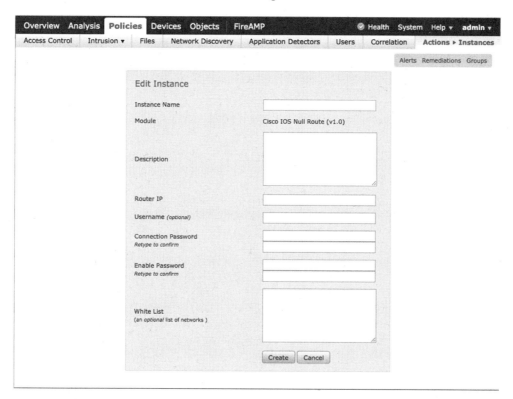

This configuration page is built from an XML file created by the author of the remediation module. The page contains information the module needs to function. To configure this instance, you would fill in the applicable values on the form. Note that this is one of the few places in the FireSIGHT user interface where you cannot use spaces in the name field.

Once you complete the required fields and click the Create button, the Configured Remediations section will appear at the bottom of the page, as shown in Figure 11.18.

Notice that for this particular instance, we have four remediation types:

- Block Destination
- Block Destination Network
- Block Source
- Block Source Network

FIGURE 11.18   Configured Remediations

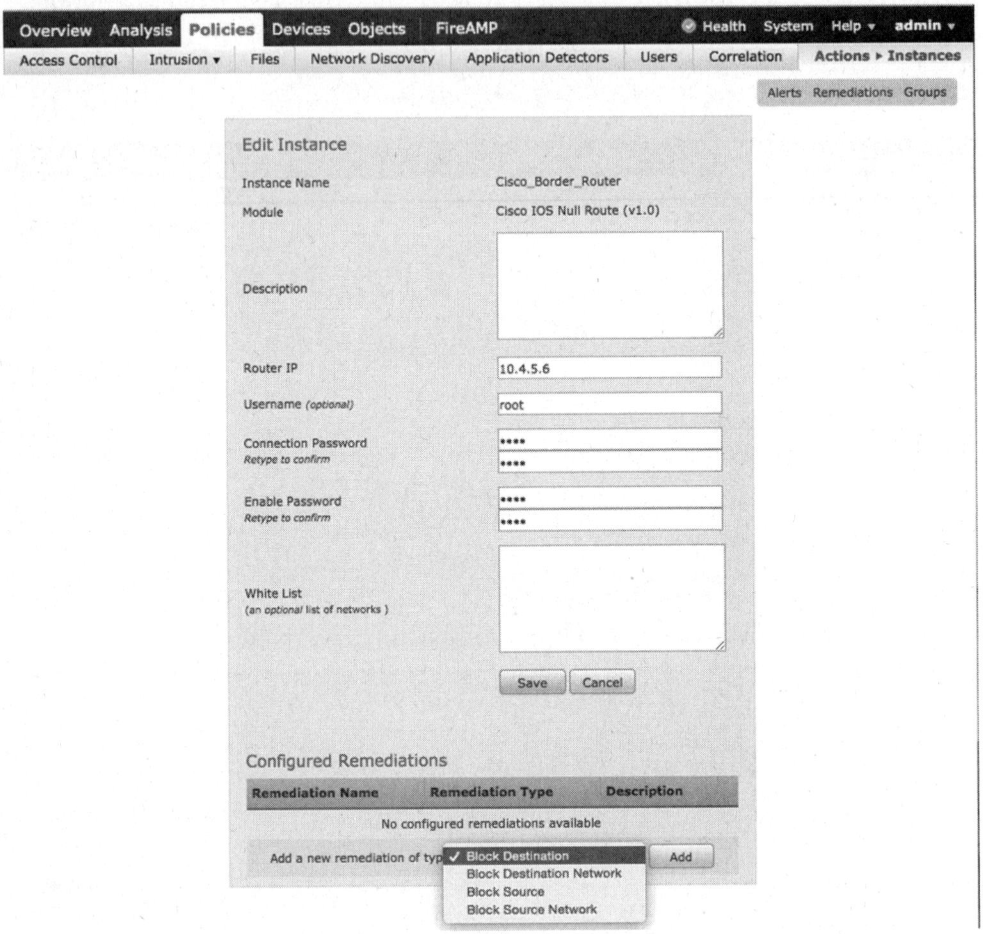

These were built into this remediation by the author. Some remediations may have more or fewer actions they can perform. It all depends on how they were designed.

For our example, we will pick the Block Source remediation type and click the Add button. This takes us to the Edit Remediation page shown in Figure 11.19.

Here we have to give our remediation a name. This name is what you will see when you are selecting remediations in the correlation policy. With that in mind, you should pick one that is descriptive enough so you know what you are selecting. Again, you will see an error if you try to enter a name with spaces in it. Figure 11.19 demonstrates a descriptive name for a remediation.

The last step is to click the Create button to save your new remediation.

FIGURE 11.19   Edit Remediation page

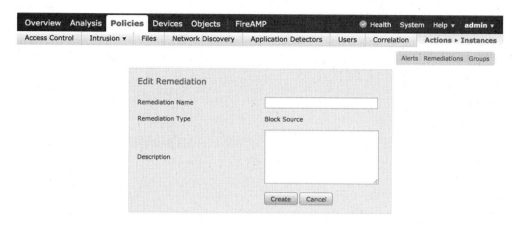

Creating Custom Remediations

One of the powerful features of remediations is the ability to create and upload your own. By following the *FireSIGHT System Remediation API Guide*, you can create a custom remediation to perform whatever function you want. The remediation runs on the Defense Center. You can code your remediation using one of several techniques, including the following:

- Perl
- Shell script
- Precompiled, statically linked C program

A custom remediation consists of an XML file called module.template and the remediation program itself. You can also optionally provide a help file with your remediation. If you're using Perl, you can also include any required Perl modules not already present on the Defense Center. The remediation files are packaged into a gzipped tarball (.tar.gz or .tgz) and uploaded to the Defense Center from the main module page. For more information, refer to the *FireSIGHT System Remediation API Guide*.

Correlation Policy

Now that you have correlation rules and responses, you need to implement them with a policy. To create a policy, navigate to Policies ➢ Correlation. Policies are on the Policy Management tab, as shown in Figure 11.20.

FIGURE 11.20 Policy Management tab

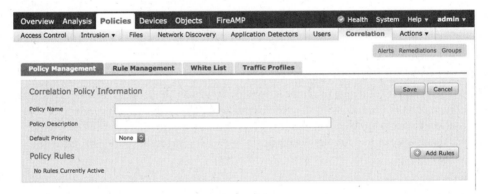

As you can see, we have no policies by default. To create a new policy, click the Create Policy button. This loads the page shown in Figure 11.21.

FIGURE 11.21 Create a correlation policy

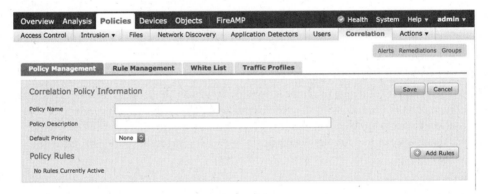

The policy requires a name and optional description. Click the Add Rules button to load the list of existing correlation rules, shown Figure 11.22.

FIGURE 11.22 Add correlation rule

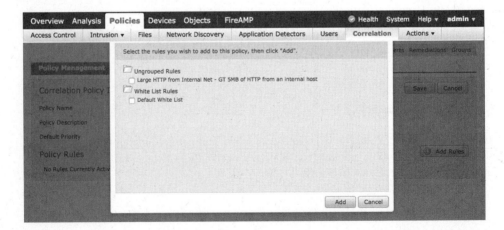

To add a rule, click the rule's check box and click the Add button. For this example, we added the HTTP rule created earlier, as shown in Figure 11.23.

FIGURE 11.23   Policy with rule added

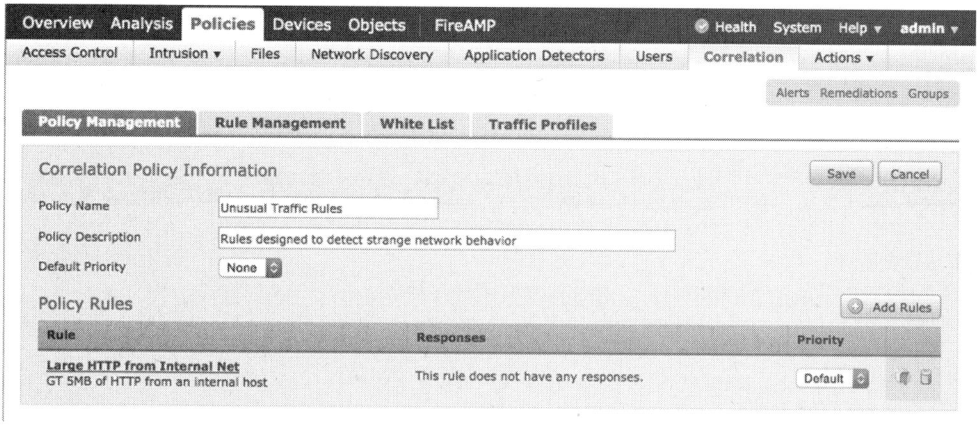

Notice under the Responses column we have not selected anything yet. While you can create a correlation policy without configuring responses, most users find that the additional notifications or remediations are quite useful. Configuring a rule with no response will still generate a special type of event called a *correlation event*. For our example, however, we will add some more interesting responses.

By clicking the red flag icon to the right, you can add responses to your policy as shown in Figure 11.24.

FIGURE 11.24   Assigned responses

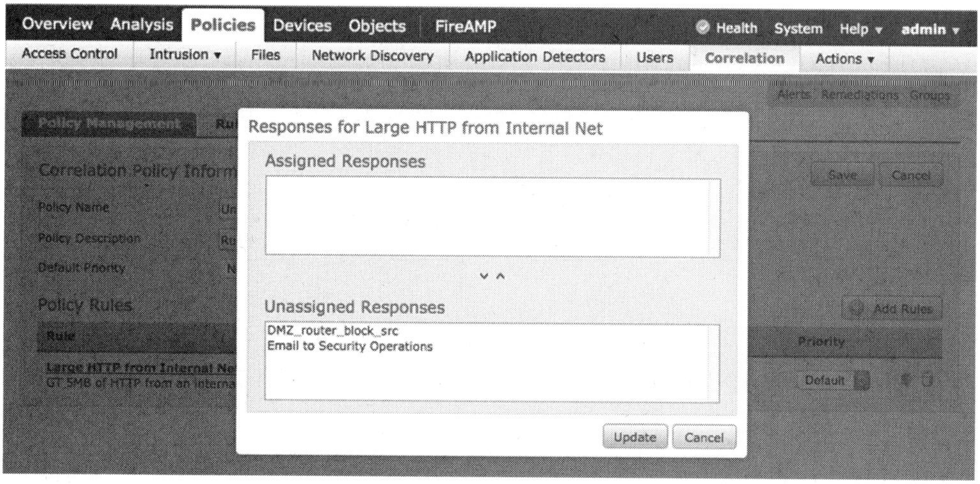

Clicking the red flag icon loads the responses dialog. By selecting an unassigned response and clicking the ^ symbol, you can assign one or more responses to your rule. When you are finished, the Update button updates the policy with the new settings. As shown in Figure 11.25, we added both the email response and the Cisco IOS remediation configured earlier. This also illustrates the importance of giving your rules/alerts/remediations descriptive names because the policy and responses are now fairly self-explanatory. If we had named our SMTP alert "Email alert," we would have no idea *who* is receiving emails.

FIGURE 11.25 Policy with a rule and responses

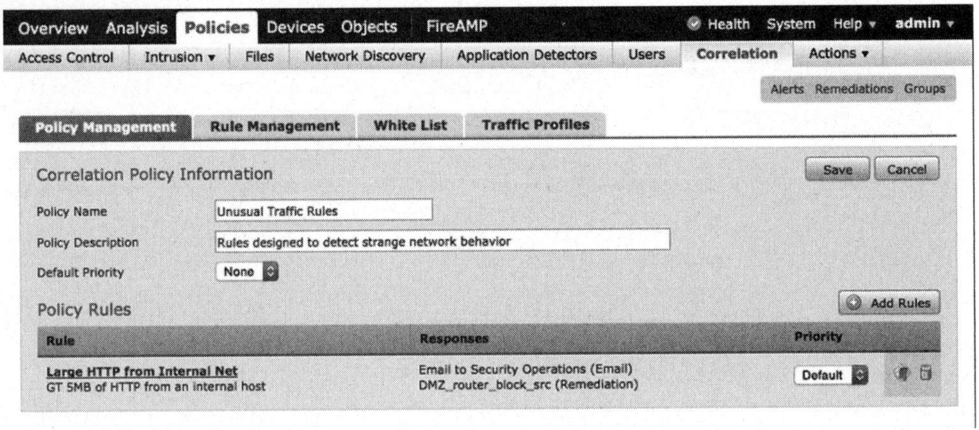

You can add multiple rules to your correlation policy, and each rule can have its own specific responses assigned.

When you are finished editing the correlation policy, click the Save button. This will return you to the Policy Management tab, as shown in Figure 11.26.

FIGURE 11.26 Updated policy

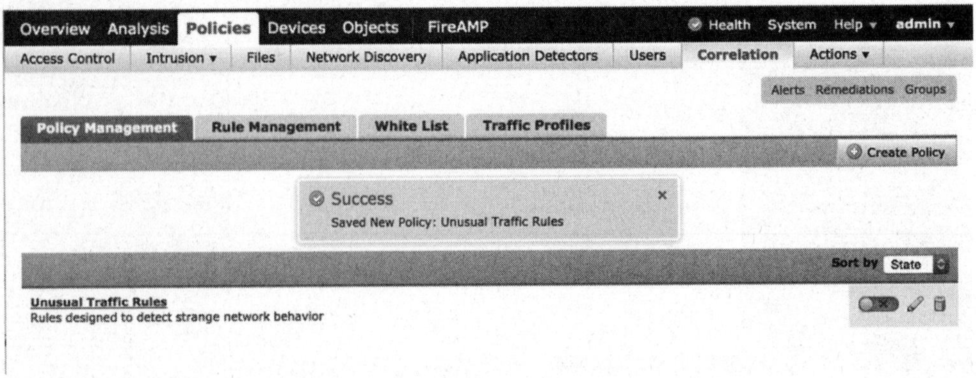

There is still one important step to remember before you are finished. When creating a new correlation policy, the default state will be disabled. For the policy to actually do anything, you must enable it by clicking the switch icon on the right. Once you do, you will see the confirmation message, and the switch icon will change, indicating the policy is enabled, as shown in Figure 11.27. From this point forward, your policy is active, and you should start seeing notifications when correlation rules trigger.

FIGURE 11.27   Active correlation policy

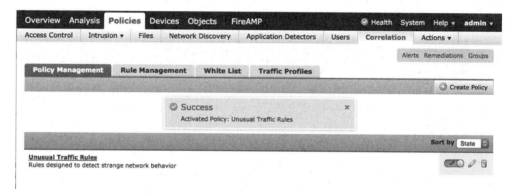

The policy only needs to be enabled once. If you subsequently edit the policy and update or add to your rules/responses, these will go into effect as soon as the policy is saved.

White Lists

Another FireSIGHT feature that falls under correlation is white lists. This is not the same as a Security Intelligence whitelist. In this context, a white list is a set of criteria you can use to define operating systems, client/server apps, and protocols that are allowed to run on your network. If you think of correlation rules looking for something undesirable, then white lists are designed to look for what is desirable. While a correlation rule will trigger when it finds an event matching a certain criteria, a white list will trigger if it finds a condition that is *other than* what is allowed.

A simple white list might only specify a single criteria such as operating system. For example, if you only allow Linux operating systems on a given network segment, by creating a white list that contains only these operating systems, you can be alerted if FireSIGHT detects any other OS on that segment.

A white list consists of two main parts: targets and host profiles. The targets are the IP addresses or ranges that are to be evaluated by the white list. In the example we've been using in this chapter, your target would be the IP range where you only allow Linux systems.

The second part is the host profile. The profile contains the operating systems, client or server applications, protocols, and web applications allowed. The host profile can be simple, such as just operating system, or it can contain several criteria. You can even add specific applications to your white list. By doing so, if a host is discovered with an application that is not included, it will generate a violation.

We will create a sample white list to help flesh this out.

As with the other correlation items, it all starts by navigating to Policy ➤ Correlation. From here, click the White List tab. This brings us to the currently available white lists. By default, only Default White List is displayed, as shown in Figure 11.28.

FIGURE 11.28   White List page

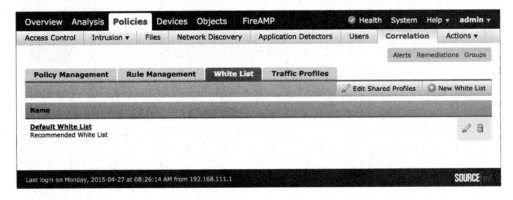

The default white list contains numerous operating systems and applications. For our example, we will create a new white list to apply to a selected network segment. Clicking the New White List link on the right brings up the Survey Network screen shown in Figure 11.29.

FIGURE 11.29   Survey Network screen

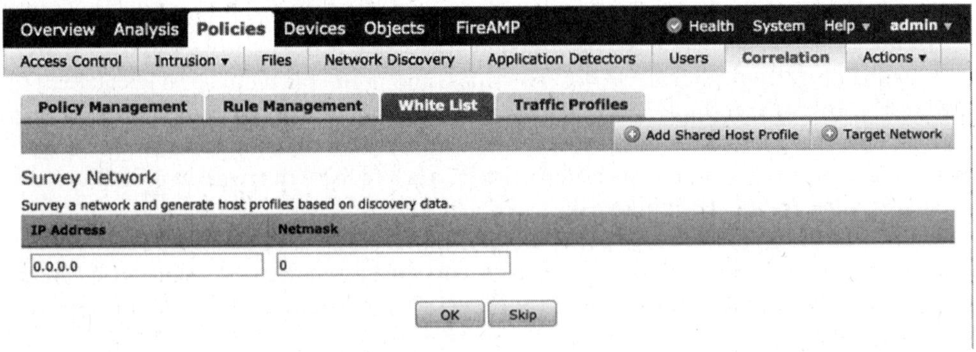

This is where we select an IP address range that our white list will apply to. We could leave it at 0.0.0.0/0, which would mean this list applies to all hosts in the FireSIGHT database. However, most often you will want to restrict this to a specific network segment.

The process of surveying a network actually scans through the existing FireSIGHT database and populates a host profile based on what is found there. By entering a survey network on this page, you are limiting the scope of this activity. The result will be a host profile that contains all the operating systems, applications, and protocols that were discovered for hosts within this range. It's important to note that we are not actually scanning the network range in this step. All we are doing is querying the existing host database to build the profile.

For this example, we will enter the IP range of 192.168.174.0/24. This means the resulting host profile will represent hosts found in the FireSIGHT database within this range. The result is shown in Figure 11.30.

FIGURE 11.30   Survey results

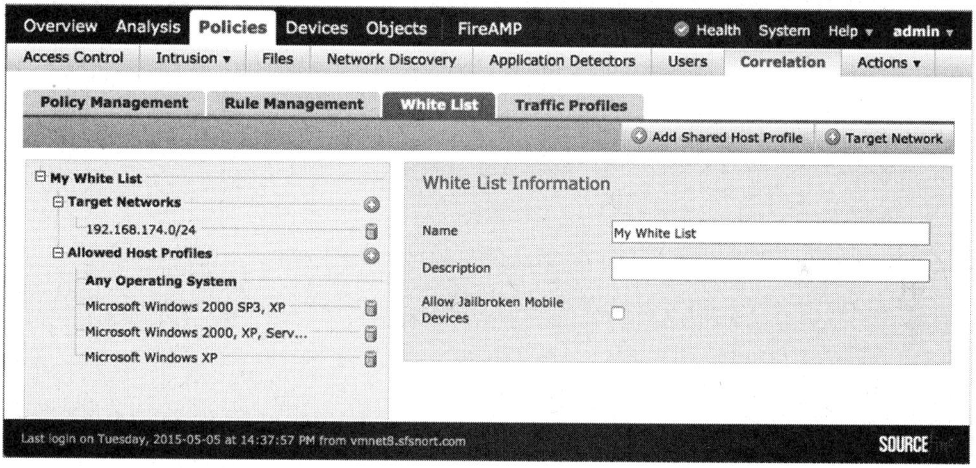

One of the first things to do is change the default of My White List to a more meaningful name. A description is also optional but may be helpful. Notice that FireSIGHT has discovered three different operating system types in this part of the network.

Clicking on one of the operating systems on the left reveals the details of the operating system, application protocols, clients, web applications, and protocols. This is shown in Figure 11.31.

What we are seeing here is the criteria that will be used for the white list. At this point, you would verify that the details discovered for these hosts correspond to your organizational policies. Any items discovered that are not relevant would be removed. For example, if your organization policy doesn't limit client applications, you can check the Allow All Clients box. You can also add an item to one of the categories by clicking the green plus icon in the category heading. The result is a "white-listed" set of host criteria that you can then apply using a correlation policy. When finished, click the Save White List button. This will return you to the main White List tab as shown Figure 11.32.

FIGURE 11.31 Host Profile details

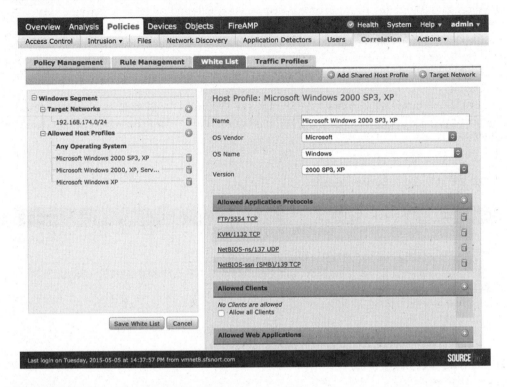

FIGURE 11.32 Newly added white list

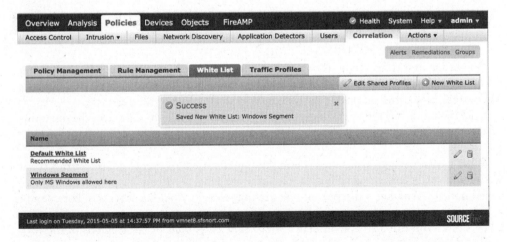

Once the white list is created, it is treated in the same manner as a correlation rule. That is, it must be implemented via a correlation policy. Returning to the Policy Management tab, we will create a new policy for our white list rules. As shown in Figure 11.33, we've added a new policy and given it a name.

FIGURE 11.33   NEW CORRELATION POLICY

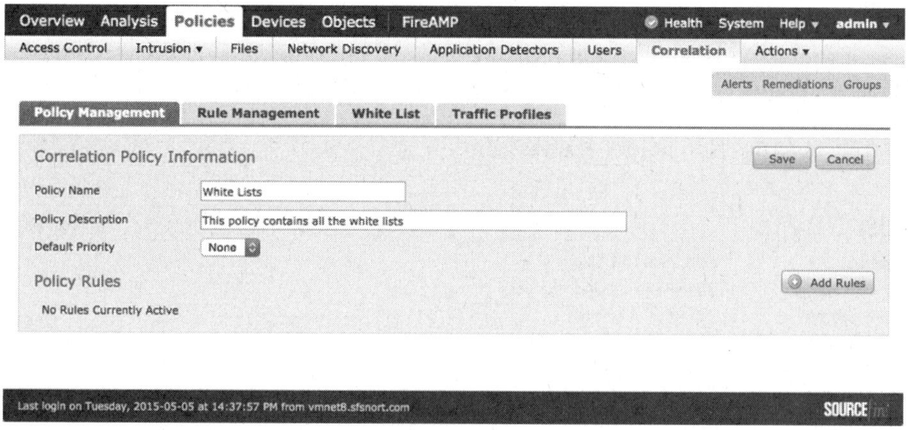

Clicking the Add Rules button brings up the list of rules and white lists that we've created. We can then follow the same procedure for a correlation rule to assign a response. Finally, save and activate the new correlation policy.

When a white list is added to an active correlation policy, the host(s) in that IP range will be evaluated in relation to the white list. They will be classified in one of three categories.

Compliant Valid targets that are compliant with the white list

Non-Compliant Valid targets that violate the white list

Not Evaluated Invalid targets and hosts that have not yet been evaluated

This will be shown in the host profile via a new host attribute with the same name as the white list. You can view all the non-compliant hosts by navigating to Analysis ➤ Correlation ➤ White List Violations as shown in Figure 11.34.

FIGURE 11.34   White list violations

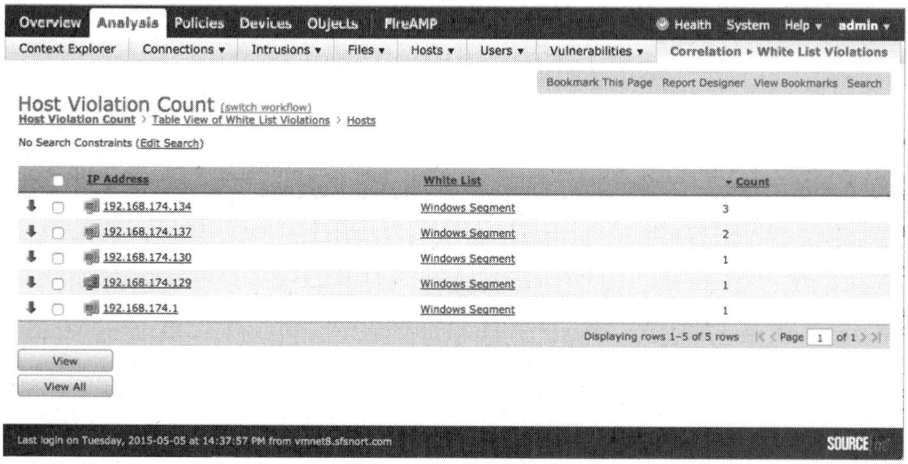

The default workflow shows the host IP addresses with the white list and a violation count for each. Clicking the computer icon for a specific host will bring up the host profile. In Figure 11.35, you can see that this host has an unauthorized SMTP client, by the black circle next to the SMTP application protocol near the bottom. Note, at the very bottom, the Windows Segment host attribute indicating that this host is non-compliant.

FIGURE 11.35   Non-compliant host entry

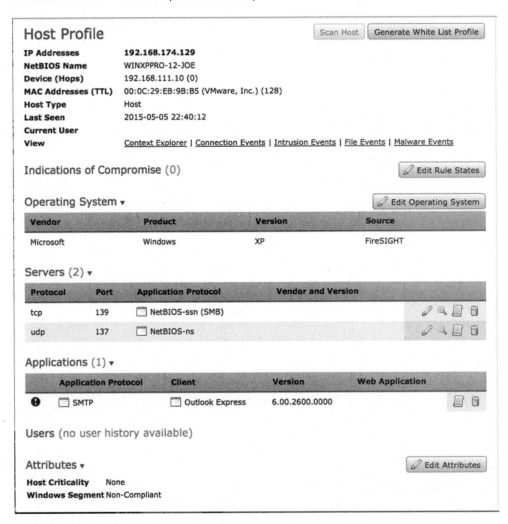

Finally, when a discovery event representing a white list violation occurs, a special type of event is triggered, known as a white list event. These events only occur after a white list has been created and then enabled in a correlation policy. From this point forward, any discovery of an non-compliant application, OS, or protocol will generate a white list event—in addition to executing whatever response(s) were configured in the policy. These events can be found by navigating to Analysis ➤ Correlation ➤ White List Events as shown in Figure 11.36.

FIGURE 11.36   White List Events page

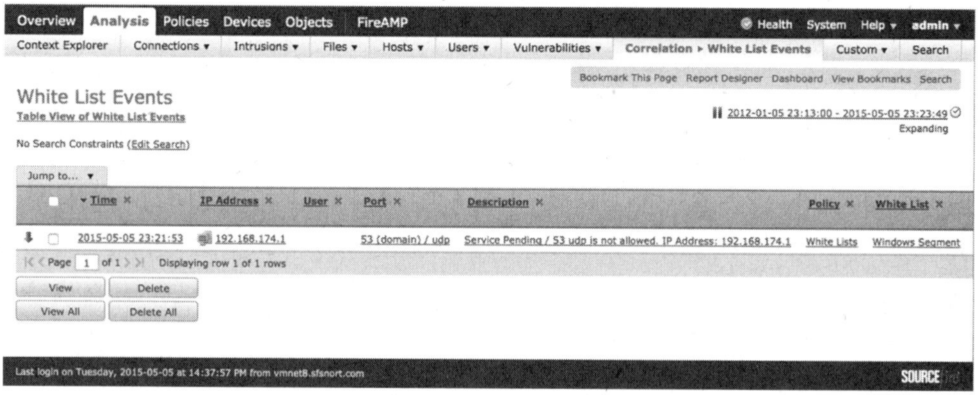

White lists can be a powerful feature to provide visibility to unauthorized software or operating systems. However, if white lists are used on a dynamic network segment, you may find a large number of non-compliant hosts and numerous white list events. This can be addressed in two ways:

Limit white lists to "static" network segments. For example, apply your white lists only to critical hosts that do not change on a normal basis. By using a detailed host profile with your white list, you can be alerted to many software changes on the host(s).

Limit the number of attributes in your host profile. If you use a white list covering a large number of more dynamic hosts, you can limit the list to just one or two areas. For example, just specify the operating system(s) allowed, but do not specify applications, protocols, or services. This way, your hosts will only be non-compliant if they are running an unauthorized operating system.

The bottom line is to try to avoid too much noise (unnecessary alerting) in your white lists. These unnecessary alerts may reduce the effectiveness of this feature.

Traffic Profiles

The last correlation feature is traffic profiles. You can think of a *traffic profile* as a "baseline" of activity. The profile defines the criteria for the baseline, such as IP address, application protocol, transport protocol, and so on. Then, once activated, the profile collects a number of data points about the traffic over the profile period. Once the profile is built, you can add it to a correlation rule and specify the deviation that would cause the rule to trigger. Last, you add the rule to a correlation policy and select an appropriate response.

You start out at the same place we have for all the correlation features: by navigating to Policies ➢ Correlation. From here, click the Traffic Profiles tab to view existing profiles. By default, this screen is blank, as shown in Figure 11.37.

FIGURE 11.37   Traffic profile list

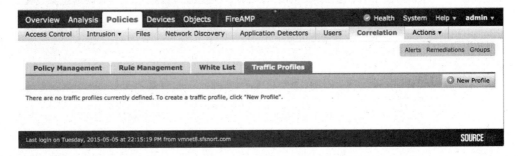

To begin, click the New Profile link on the right. This loads the profile configuration screen shown in Figure 11.38.

FIGURE 11.38   Traffic profile configuration

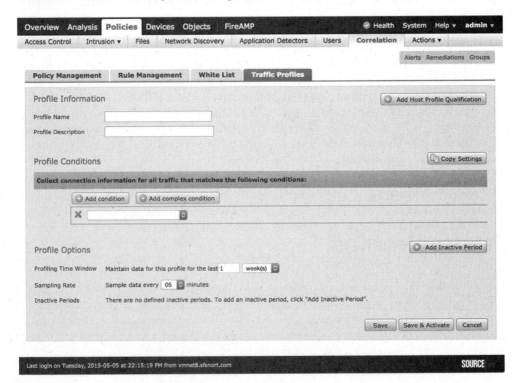

The Profile Information section contains the profile name and an optional description.

Moving down, you have the Profile Conditions section. Here you will specify the type of traffic you want to profile. If you have already set up some conditions you want to build upon, you can click the Copy Settings button to copy from an existing profile.

Entering profile conditions is similar to what you've already seen for a correlation rule. We are simply defining the conditions for the connection to be included in this profile.

It is important to note that traffic profiles are built from connection events. You must be logging connections for the hosts/applications specified in your traffic profile for this feature to work. Also, these must be "end of connection" events. If you find your traffic profiles are empty, it may be because your Access Control policy is not configured to log connections.

Add conditions as necessary to limit your profile to the desired traffic. In the example shown in Figure 11.39, we are collecting HTTP traffic in the DMZ portion of the network.

FIGURE 11.39 Traffic profile example

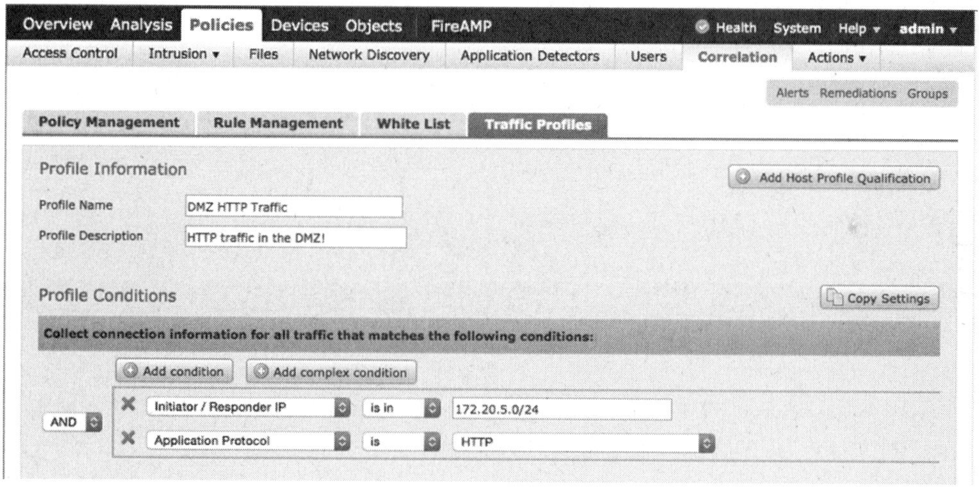

The last section is Profile Options (shown later in Figure 11.40). This is where we determine how long to collect data for the profile as well as some other parameters. The duration to maintain the data is called the *profiling time window, or PTW*. This can range from hours to days to weeks. The default PTW is 1 week, since most traffic patterns generally repeat on a weekly basis.

Once you select a PTW, next comes the sampling rate. The default sampling rate is every 5 minutes, but you can change that to up to 60 minutes in 5-minute increments.

The combination of PTW and *sampling rate* will yield a number of data points in your profile. Keep in mind that this is a statistical sample of data, so a small number of data points will not yield a very meaningful sample. The rule of thumb is that your traffic profile should have at least 100 data points. The number of data points can be calculated with the following formula:

PTW/samplingrate = Datapoints

FIGURE 11.40   Completed traffic profile example

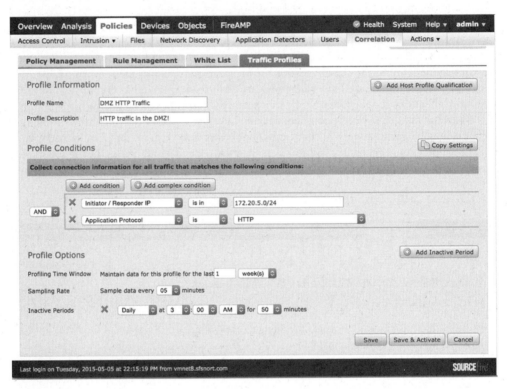

For example, if your PTW was 1 day (24 hrs) and your sampling rate was one sample every 60 minutes (1 hr), the number of data points would be

$$24/1 = 24 \text{datapoints}$$

This is not sufficient to provide a reliable sample. By increasing the time window or decreasing the minutes in the sampling rate, you can increase the total samples to make the profile more effective.

Another option when creating the profile is inactive periods. This is one or more periods during which the profile does not collect data. This might be helpful to ignore traffic spikes during known periods such as backups. Profiling this traffic will likely cause spikes in the profile and potentially trigger a violation when you add this to a correlation rule. To ignore these known periods of high traffic, you can add one or more inactive periods to your profile.

You can also create your profile without any inactive periods and then review the traffic statistics later and add inactive periods as needed.

The completed traffic profile example is shown in Figure 11.40. It will profile traffic data as follows:

- It will profile all HTTP traffic in the 172.20.5.0/24 network.

- The profile will gather data for 1 week with samples every 5 minutes.

- The profile will not gather data daily at 3:00 a.m. for 50 minutes during the nightly backup. (It is unlikely that HTTP would actually be used as the backup protocol, but this is just an example.)

When you are finished with the profile, click either the Save or Save & Activate button. The former will save the profile so it's ready to be activated later, while the latter will save and begin collecting traffic data immediately.

Clicking the Save button returns you to the screen shown in Figure 11.41. Note that the switch icon to the right shows that the profile is inactive. Remember to click the switch to activate the profile when you are ready to begin collecting data.

FIGURE 11.41   Updated traffic profile list

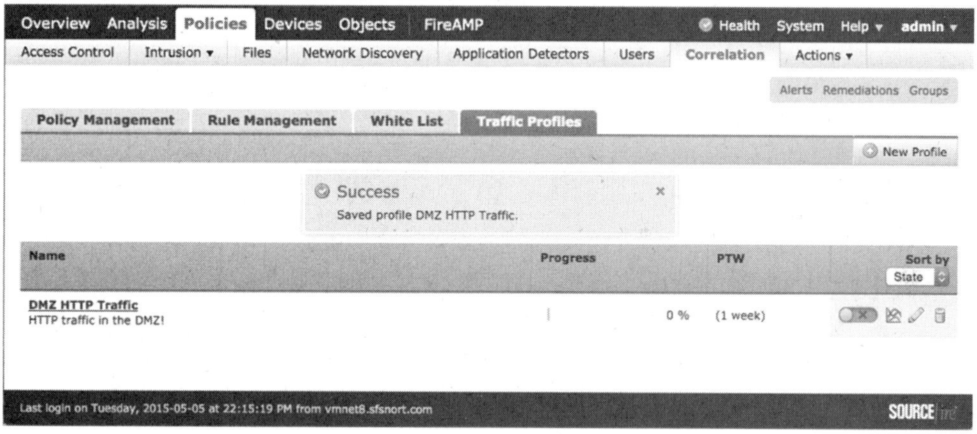

The Progress column contains a percentage bar that indicates the completeness of the traffic profile. Once the profile is activated, this bar will reach 100 percent at the end of the profile's PTW. You can also view the data collected by a traffic profile by clicking the graph icon to the right of the switch. Initially, this graph will be empty, but over time, as your profile collects traffic information, it will appear in this graph. Figure 11.42 shows a completed traffic profile.

Now that you have one or more traffic profiles, they must be added to a correlation policy to be of any use. Traffic profiles can't be added directly to a policy; you must first create rules that will trigger for certain profile conditions.

Returning to the Rule Management tab, we will again create a correlation rule as explained previously. However, this time we will select the option for "a traffic profile changes" from the drop-down. Once it's selected, we get another drop-down listing all the available profiles. From here, we can create the rule as with previous rules. Figure 11.43 shows the available criteria for a traffic profile rule.

FIGURE 11.42 Traffic profile graph

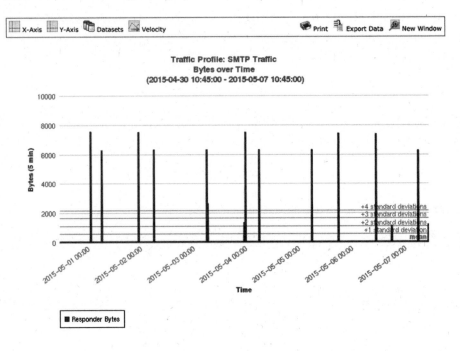

FIGURE 11.43 Correlation rule criteria

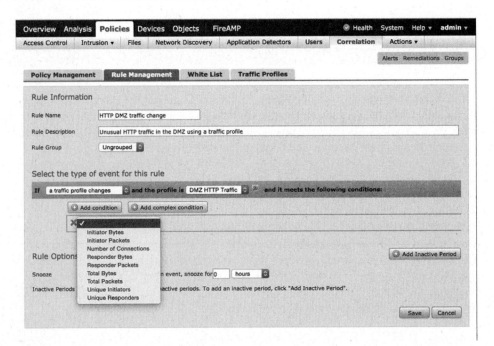

As you can see in the figure, the following data points are collected during a traffic sample:

- Initiator Bytes
- Initiator Packets
- Number of Connections
- Responder Bytes
- Responder Packets
- Total Bytes
- Total Packets
- Unique Initiators
- Unique Responders

Using the default 5-minute interval means we are collecting all this data for each traffic profile every 5 minutes.

In our rule example, we can select one or more of these counters to cause the rule to trigger. Creating a useful rule requires that we have some idea about what is "normal" for this profile. This is where the graph previously shown in Figure 11.42 comes in. Armed with this information, you can see what a "normal" week looks like for HTTP traffic in the DMZ. You then write your rule to detect unusual activity—however you define it.

In Figure 11.44, we have finished our rule, which is looking for a significant increase in the number of connections or the number of unique initiators.

FIGURE 11.44   Completed correlation rule

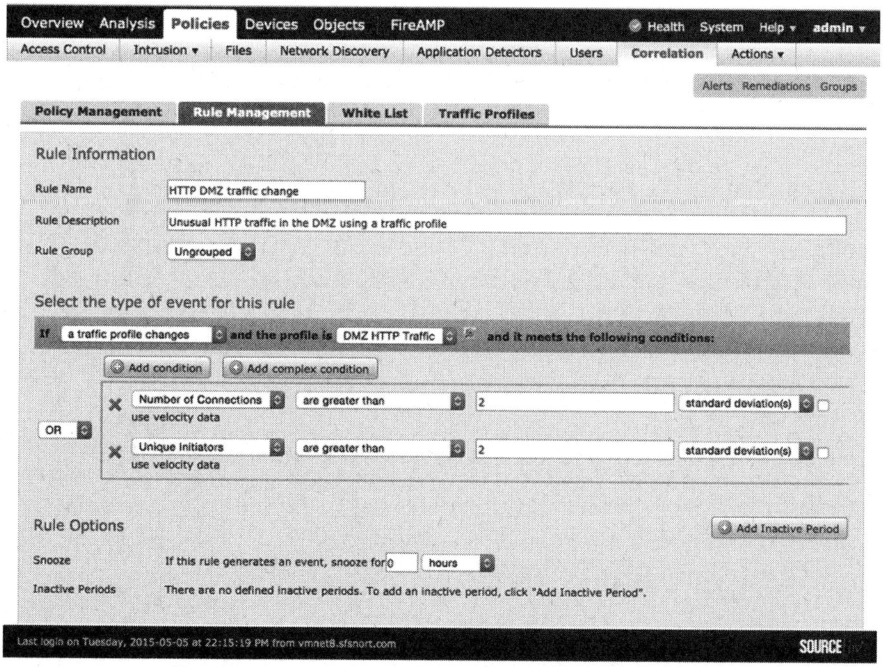

From here, it is simply a matter of creating a correlation policy or adding the rule to an existing policy and selecting the appropriate response. Since we covered that previously, we won't repeat those steps here.

One last note about traffic profiles. When a traffic profile is created, it does not stay static. This is a "sliding" window of time updated continuously. This means a seven-day traffic profile will always show the previous seven days, not just the first seven days after it was activated. This provides flexibility to the profile, allowing it to adjust to the growth of your network. By using a rule criterion such as a data point that is two standard deviations above the average, you can detect unusual spikes in traffic while still allowing the profile to be continuously updated.

Summary

In this chapter, we discussed correlation policy—an often overlooked but very useful feature of the FireSIGHT System. We looked at correlation rules, white lists, and traffic profiles—all of which can be used to detect malicious or unauthorized activity. We also covered responses such as alerts and remediations, which can allow the Defense Center to take an action in response to an event.

Hands-on Lab

In this lab, we will cover creating and implementing a sample correlation rule to detect a large HTTP flow for a specific host.

Perhaps we have a sensitive web server that should only serve small pages with limited graphics. We determine that all HTTP responses should be under 10MB. If we detect an HTTP response exceeding 10MB, we know that is not normal and may be an indication of malicious activity.

Prerequisites

- The access control policy must configure connection logging for the host(s) in question. Without connection events, our traffic rule will not work.

- An existing alert is configured for us to use in response to this rule. It could be SNMP, syslog, email or even a custom response.

Steps

1. Navigate to Policies ➤ Correlation and click the Rule Management tab.
2. Click the Create Rule link.
3. Give your rule a name and optional description.
4. In the event type drop-down select "a connection event occurs."

5. Click the first rule condition drop-down and select "Responder IP."

6. Leave the second condition at the default "is" and enter the IP address of your web server.

7. Click the Add Condition button to add a second condition to your rule.

8. Change the logical operator on the left to AND.

9. Click the second rule condition drop-down and select Responder Bytes.

10. Change the second condition to "are greater than" and enter **10000000** (note - you cannot use commas, so count your zeros!).

11. Click the Add Condition button again to add a third condition.

12. For this condition, select Application Protocol, and then select "is" and HTTP from the drop-down list.

13. Click the Save button to save your rule.

14. Click the Policy Management tab.

15. Click Create Policy.

16. Give your policy a name (something like Unusual Traffic) and, optionally, a description.

17. Click the Add Rules button.

18. Check the box next to your new rule and click the Add button.

19. Click the red Responses flag to the right of your rule.

20. Double-click one or more responses from the Unassigned Responses list at the bottom to move them up to the Assigned Responses box, and then click the Update button.

21. Click the Save button to save your new policy.

22. Back at the Policy Management tab, click the switch icon to the right of the rule to activate your new policy.

23. Test by using your favorite web browser or wget to download a file larger than 10MB from your web server.

You should see a connection event, correlation event, and whatever notification response you selected. Remember that your rule is based on a connection event, so if you are troubleshooting, this is the first thing to consider. Is your Access Control policy configured to log connections?

Exam Essentials

Know the three evaluation values of a white list.

- Compliant: valid targets that are compliant with the white list
- Non-Compliant: valid targets that violate the white list
- Not Evaluated: invalid targets and hosts that have not yet been evaluated

Know what happens when a correlation rule matches an event.   The Defense Center logs a correlation event and initiates any configured responses.

Know the types of alerts the system can generate when a correlation rule is triggered.   When a rule is triggered, the system can log a correlation event to the database and generate SNMP, syslog, or email alerts.

Know the names of the built-in remediation modules:

- Cisco IOS Null Route
- Cisco PIX Shun
- Nmap remediation
- Set attribute value

Review Questions

You can find the answers in Appendix A.

1. Which of the following options is an example of what you can do using correlation policy?

   A. Alert when a non-compliant operating system is detected.

   B. Block unencrypted connections to a host.

   C. Generate an alert when a host triggers multiple IPS events in a short period.

   D. Detect brute force login attempts on the Defense Center.

2. Which of the following are possible host white list values?

   A. Compliant

   B. Non-compliant

   C. Not-evaluated

   D. All of the above

3. What does a white list attribute of Compliant mean?

   A. The host is not a white list target.

   B. The host does not have any white list violations.

   C. The host has not been compromised.

   D. The host is not on a monitored network.

4. What is the result when network traffic matching a correlation rule is detected?

   A. The device generates a correlation event.

   B. The connection is terminated.

   C. The Defense Center generates a correlation event.

   D. A white list event is generated, and the connection traffic is captured.

5. Which of the following lists the valid types of built-in alerts the Defense Center can generate in a correlation policy?

   A. Database logging, SMTP, PCAP, SNMP

   B. SMTP, SNMP, syslog, database logging

   C. SNMP, email, syslog, SMS

   D. Database logging, SNMP, SSH, SMTP

6. Which of the following is *not* a default remediation module?

   A. Cisco IOS Null Route

   B. Cisco PIX Shun

   C. Custom Email

   D. Set Attribute Value

7. How can the number of data points collected during a traffic profile be determined?

    A. This setting is automatic and cannot be configured.

    B. By dividing the packets per second by the profile window.

    C. By counting the spikes in the traffic profile graph.

    D. By multiplying the profiling time window (PTW) by the sampling rate.

8. When creating a new traffic profile, what are the default PTW and sampling rate?

    A. 1 week, 5 minutes

    B. 1 week, 1 hour

    C. 24 hours, 5 minutes

    D. 24 hours, 30 minutes

9. Which of the following is *not* a valid method for creating a custom remediation?

    A. Perl script

    B. Shell script

    C. Precompiled, statically linked C program

    D. Custom DLL

10. Which event types are valid for inclusion in a correlation rule?

    A. User event

    B. Health event

    C. Evasion event

    D. Audit event

Chapter 12

Advanced IPS Policy Settings

THE SSFIPS EXAM TOPICS COVERED IN THIS CHAPTER INCLUDE THE FOLLOWING:

✓ **12.1 Describe the features and settings of Application layer preprocessors**

✓ **12.2 Describe the features and settings of Network and Transport layer preprocessors**

✓ **12.3 Describe the features and settings for specific threat detections in the advanced section of IPS polices**

✓ **12.4 Understand the benefits of the detection enhancements and performance settings in the intrusion policy editor**

It's the perfect time to introduce you to some essential advanced IPS policy settings, and coming up, we'll survey important Application layer *preprocessor* settings, Network and Transport layer preprocessors, and specific threat detection preprocessors. We'll also talk about the significant advantages gained via detection enhancements and performance settings.

By the end of this chapter, you'll possess solid insight into how dramatically advanced policy configurations impact network inspection.

To find up-to-the-minute updates for this chapter, please see www.lammle .com/firepower or the book's web page at www.sybex.com.

Advanced Settings

In addition to the IPS policies, rules, FireSIGHT Recommendations, and layers you're now familiar with, there's another group of advanced configuration settings that have a major effect on how the device inspects traffic by controlling the preprocessors. Knowing how to manipulate these settings gives you power to control the vital tasks that preprocessors are responsible for, like data normalization—fragmentation reassembly, data stream reassembly, and removing ambiguities in protocols. Preprocessors also report protocol anomalies and search for specific threats in ways that are often too complex for standard rules.

The advanced settings fall into these eight categories (Figure 12.1):

- Application Layer Preprocessors
- SCADA Preprocessors
- Transport/Network Layer Preprocessors
- Specific Threat Detection
- Detection Enhancement
- Intrusion Rule Thresholds
- Performance Settings
- External Responses

FIGURE 12.1   Advanced Settings

Edit Policy: Demo_IPS Policy

Policy Information	Advanced Settings			< Back
Rules	**Application Layer Preprocessors**			
FireSIGHT Recommendations	DCE/RPC Configuration	⦿ Enabled ○ Disabled		✎ Edit
⊟ Advanced Settings	DNS Configuration	⦿ Enabled ○ Disabled		✎ Edit
Back Orifice Detection	FTP and Telnet Configuration	⦿ Enabled ○ Disabled		✎ Edit
Checksum Verification	HTTP Configuration	⦿ Enabled ○ Disabled		✎ Edit
DCE/RPC Configuration	Sun RPC Configuration	⦿ Enabled ○ Disabled		✎ Edit
DNS Configuration	SIP Configuration	○ Enabled ⦿ Disabled		
Event Queue Configuration	GTP Command Channel Configuration	⦿ Enabled ○ Disabled		✎ Edit
FTP and Telnet Configuration	IMAP Configuration	○ Enabled ⦿ Disabled		
Global Rule Thresholding	POP Configuration	○ Enabled ⦿ Disabled		
GTP Command Channel Conf	SMTP Configuration	⦿ Enabled ○ Disabled		✎ Edit
HTTP Configuration	SSH Configuration	⦿ Enabled ○ Disabled		✎ Edit
IP Defragmentation	SSL Configuration	⦿ Enabled ○ Disabled		✎ Edit
Latency-Based Packet Handli	**SCADA Preprocessors**			
Latency-Based Rule Handling	Modbus Configuration	○ Enabled ⦿ Disabled		
Packet Decoding	DNP3 Configuration	○ Enabled ⦿ Disabled		
Performance Statistics Config	**Transport/Network Layer Preprocessors**			
Regular Expression Limits	Checksum Verification	⦿ Enabled ○ Disabled		✎ Edit
Rule Processing Configuration	Detection Settings	○ Enabled ⦿ Disabled		
SMTP Configuration	Inline Normalization	○ Enabled ⦿ Disabled		
SSH Configuration				
SSL Configuration				
Sun RPC Configuration				
TCP Stream Configuration				
UDP Stream Configuration				
⊕ Policy Layers				

Each one of these categories has an array of settings that determine how they will inspect the specific protocol layers. The preprocessors are largely preconfigured from the *Talos* team and usually don't need to be modified, but situations definitely crop up when your inspections could really benefit from some fine-tuning.

Just so you know what to expect, we won't be covering each and every setting. Rest assured, we'll cover the major items, but if you want details on a specific setting that we haven't highlighted, consult the *FireSIGHT System User Guide*.

With that said, to access the advanced settings, open your IPS policy, select Advanced Settings in the navigation pane, and click the plus icon (+) to expand the section. On the navigation pane, you'll see a list of all the enabled categories. On the detail pane, you find all the categories and if they're enabled or not.

Don't be freaked out by the fact that some categories are not enabled by default. One reason is that there aren't any IPS rules enabled that leverage the disabled preprocessors. If an IPS rule requires a particular preprocessor, you'll be alerted when you save the policy, so no worries!

Preprocessor Alerting

Preprocessors have the ability to alert based on conditions such as when anomalies or detected threats are discovered, and you can control the specific things they'll alert on with preprocessor rules. Access these fine-tuning rules via a link inside the individual preprocessors or in the rule section of the preprocessor using the filters.

To get to the *preprocessor rules*, just click the link shown in Figure 12.2.

FIGURE 12.2   Preprocessor rule link

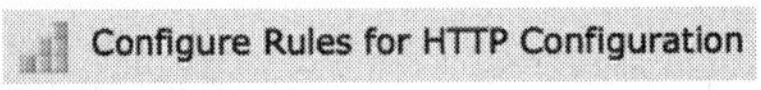

The rules can be enabled and disabled just as any other IPS rules can, but keep in mind that doing this only impacts alerting and does nothing to control the underlying preprocessor function.

Application Layer Preprocessors

Application layer preprocessors have lots of different capabilities. They can perform data *normalization* and data extraction as well as promptly alert you to anomalies in the protocols. The following preprocessors are in this section:

- DCE/RPC Configuration
- DNS Configuration
- FTP and Telnet Configuration
- HTTP Configuration
- Sun RPC Configuration
- SIP Configuration
- GTP Command Channel Configuration
- IMAP Configuration
- POP Configuration
- SMTP Configuration
- SSH Configuration
- SSL Configuration

Out of this group, the HTTP Configuration preprocessor is definitely one of the more important ones in the system due to the ubiquitous nature of the protocol. The HTTP protocol contains header and body data that bad guys use to exploit weaknesses in browsers and servers. In addition, there are different encodings, compressed data, and even obfuscation techniques that can be leveraged inside of HTTP. The preprocessor can really help the IPS to see past all of these things by leveraging normalization techniques.

To gain access to the available settings, click the Edit button on the left side of the interface by HTTP Configuration, or choose HTTP Configuration from the navigation pane. The settings will be broken out based on global settings and targets.

Global Settings

The global settings specify what the system will look for as a whole, and it offers four options, as shown in Figure 12.3:

Detect Anomalous HTTP Servers: This option generates an IPS alert if the system detects HTTP traffic occurring over nonspecified HTTP ports. Keep in mind that this isn't necessary if you're leveraging FireSIGHT.

Detect HTTP Proxy Servers: Generates an alert when proxied traffic is seen on the network. If you have legitimate proxies, they would need to be defined in the Targets section, and the box Allow HTTP Proxy Use would need to be checked as well.

Maximum Compressed Data Depth: This specifies how much compressed data should be read and decompressed from the HTTP data stream. This one is important because today's web servers often compress data being sent across the network and if we don't decompress the data, it can't be properly interpreted. The valid values range from 1 to 65535 bytes.

Maximum Decompressed Data Depth: Specifies how much data is to be normalized from the decompressed data.

FIGURE 12.3   HTTP Configuration global settings

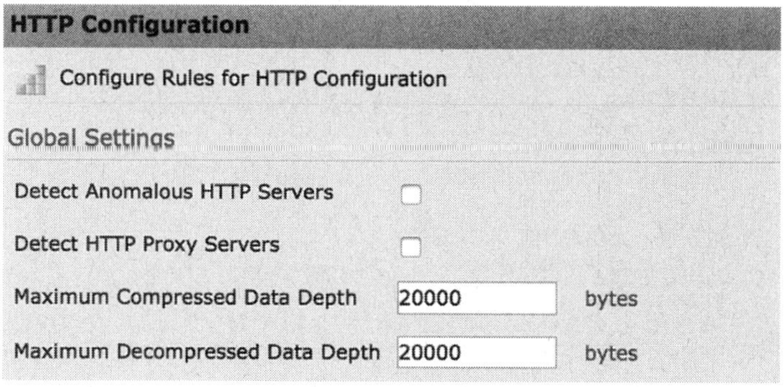

The most interesting of these options are the ones dealing with compression. It can be pretty tempting to place these at their maximum values, but doing so often comes with a performance penalty. Think about the vast amount of web traffic traversing your network... Do you really need to decompress all of it? And if you want that to happen, is your device properly equipped to handle that amount of processing?

The default setting for this is found in Connectivity Over Security. The Balanced Security and Connectivity polices are set to 1460 and 2920 for maximum compressed data depth and maximum decompressed data depth. This allows the system to look into the first packet of the HTTP session and see what's happening. As for the Security Over Connectivity policy, the numbers are set to 20000 each, allowing for a look deeper into the session's data stream. All of this works to give us greater visibility, but always remember that there may be a trade-off when it comes to performance!

Targets

The Targets section allows you to customize inspection to your environment by allowing you to specify individual servers, lists of servers, or subnets and have various parameters set according to the needs of those systems. There's also a default setting that applies to anything that's not actually specified as a target, which allows you to enable deeper inspection on one server or segment versus another. To add a target, just click the plus icon (+) next to Servers. This is shown in the upper left of Figure 12.4.

FIGURE 12.4 HTTP Configuration targets

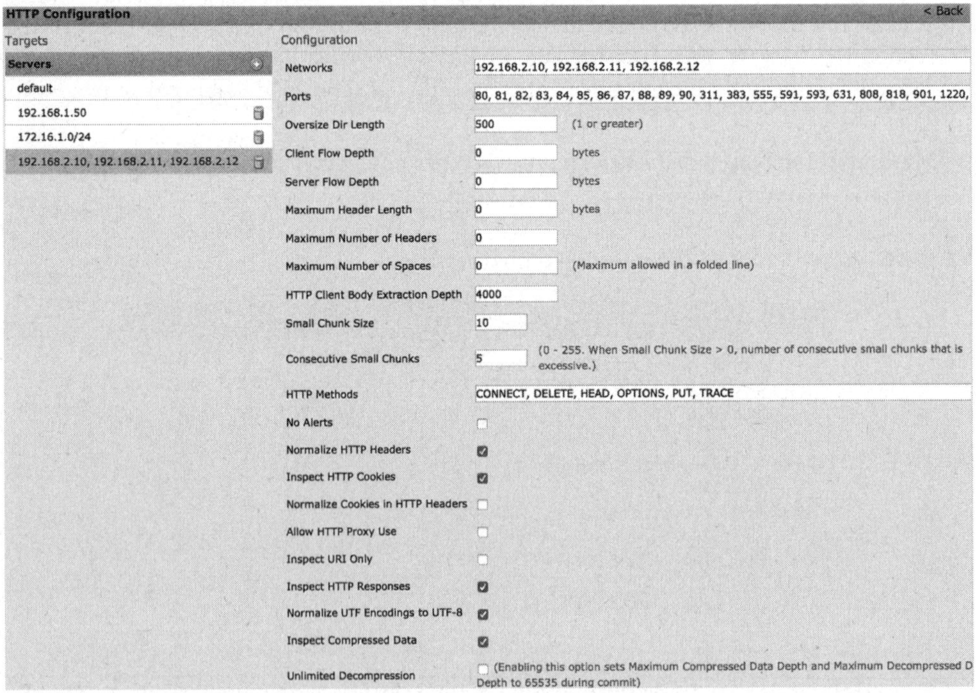

You can improve the performance of the systems by specifying targets and adjusting the settings based on inspection needs. Here's a list of items you can check out and adjust if needed:

Client Flow Depth: Delimits how many bytes of traffic from the client to the server you want to normalize. There are three choices of valid values: -1 to disable inspection completely, a number of bytes between 1 to 1460, or 0 to cause all bytes to be inspected. And again, though tempting, opting to have all bytes inspected can have an ugly impact on performance!

Server Flow Depth: How many bytes to normalize from the server to the client. The valid values are: -1 to disable inspection, 1–65535 bytes, or 0 to specify all bytes.

HTTP Client Body Extraction Depth: How many bytes of message body to extract from HTTP sessions. You would use this with the rule keyword: http_client_body. The valid values are -1 to disable, a value from 1 to 65495, or 0 to inspect the entire client body.

Inspect HTTP Responses: This setting enables the decoding, normalizing, and extracting of the header fields in the HTTP responses. The extracted fields can then be leveraged by the IPS rules.

Normalize HTTP Headers: Allows for decoding and normalization of HTTP headers.

Inspect Compressed Data: This setting tells the system to decompress compressed data streams.

Unlimited Decompression: Overrides the Maximum Compressed Data Depth and Maximum Decompressed Data Depth settings. When Unlimited Decompression is enabled, the value is set to 65535.

These can be really great tools for customizing the level of inspection carried out for the HTTP protocol on the network. We understand that it can be hard to resist the temptation to enable the maximum for all of them, but we're not kidding when we tell you about the performance issues doing that would cause on your device. By far, the better strategy is to customize the settings on a per-host, per-subnet, or list-of-hosts basis. This way, you can prioritize and enable stronger inspection on your high-value/high-risk hosts while preserving valuable system resources by setting a lower level of inspection on others.

There's one more thing we need to cover in the Targets section—the Profile setting, which enables the decoding of encodings commonly used by different types of web servers. This one is key because it allows you to quickly configure the preprocessor for your different web server types. Your Profile choices as shown in Figure 12.5 are as follows:

FIGURE 12.5 HTTP Configuration targets continued

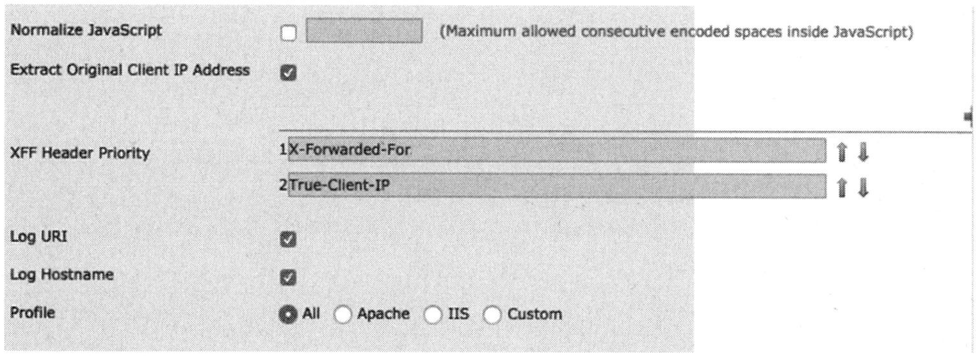

All: Permits the decoding of most common encoding types.

Apache: Used to decode the encodings found in Apache web servers.

IIS: Used for decoding types of encodings commonly found in Microsoft Internet Information Server (IIS).

Custom: Allows you to customize the types of decoding you want to implement.

SCADA Preprocessors

Don't be fooled—just because there are two Supervisory Control and Data Acquisition (SCADA) preprocessors (Figure 12.6), DNP3 and MODBUS, the IPS can certainly inspect other SCADA protocols too. In fact, the IPS can inspect all layers of packets from the Network layer up through the Application layer regardless of the protocols! The preprocessors are just there to make decoding the protocols easier. Still, keep in mind that if you implement any of the rule options that leverage the preprocessors' decoding, make sure to enable the preprocessors themselves.

FIGURE 12.6   SCADA preprocessors

Transport/Network Layer Preprocessors

Transport and *Network layer* preprocessors handle the low-level reassembly of traffic and are considered essential building blocks of detection. This is because if the lower protocol layers cannot be rebuilt properly, there's little hope in interpreting the upper layers!

Here's a list of the preprocessors in this section (also shown in Figure 12.7):

- Checksum Verification
- Detection Settings
- Inline Normalization
- IP Defragmentation
- Packet Decoding
- TCP Stream Configuration
- UDP Stream Configuration

FIGURE 12.7   Transport/Network layer preprocessors

Transport/Network Layer Preprocessors

Checksum Verification	⦿ Enabled ○ Disabled		🖉 Edit
Detection Settings	○ Enabled ⦿ Disabled		
Inline Normalization	⦿ Enabled ○ Disabled		🖉 Edit
IP Defragmentation	⦿ Enabled ○ Disabled		🖉 Edit
Packet Decoding	⦿ Enabled ○ Disabled		🖉 Edit
TCP Stream Configuration	⦿ Enabled ○ Disabled		🖉 Edit
UDP Stream Configuration	⦿ Enabled ○ Disabled		🖉 Edit

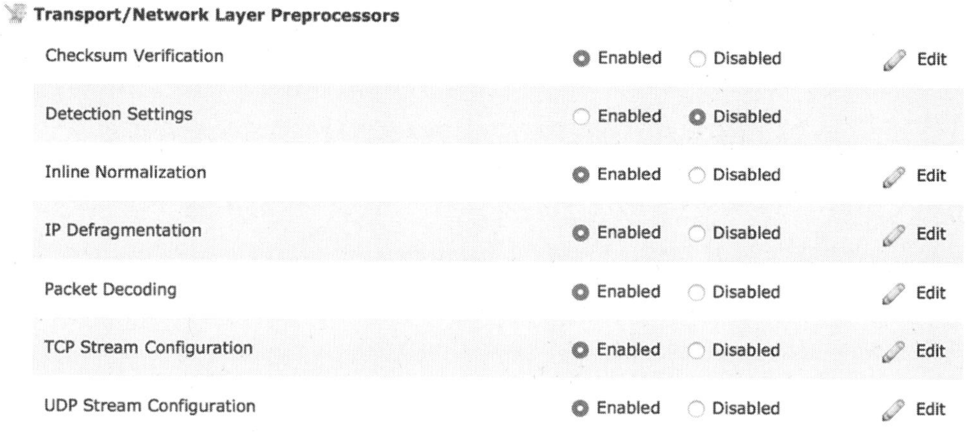

We're going to keep focus upon a few of these that are key, beginning with Inline Normalization.

Inline Normalization

This preprocessor is designed to function when you are deployed inline and your IPS policy has the blocking feature enabled. Its purpose is to remove deviations in IP, TCP, and ICMP protocol standards. When this is enabled, you can pick and choose the types of normalization to enable for the protocols (see Figure 12.8). Some of the important settings in here include the following:

Minimum TTL: Allows you to designate the minimum *Time to Live (TTL)* of a packet traversing the device. It means that if a given TTL is less than the specified value, the TTL will be reset to the Reset TTL value below.

Reset TTL: Specifies the TTL value.

Normalize IPv4: Enables normalization of IPv4 traffic. The default normalizations will set all option fields to 1 (No Operation), clear the TOS field, and shorten packets that exceed the Total Length field value.

Normalize IPv6: Modifies the Option Type Text fields in IPv6 traffic to 0.

Normalize ICMPv4: This will clear the Code field when an ICMPv4 ping is seen.

Normalize ICMPv6: Will clear the Code field when an ICMPv6 ping is seen.

Normalize TCP: Enabling this feature will clear the following fields: Reserved, Options, Urgent Pointer (if the control bit isn't set), and it will block additional SYNs that don't match the original SYN sequence number. It will also drop packets that are retransmissions of previously dropped packets, along with a number of anomalies identified by the TCP Stream preprocessor.

Again, we highly recommend that you enable this preprocessor if your device is inline because the normalizations can protect against a legion of generic threats and anomalies!

FIGURE 12.8 Inline Normalization

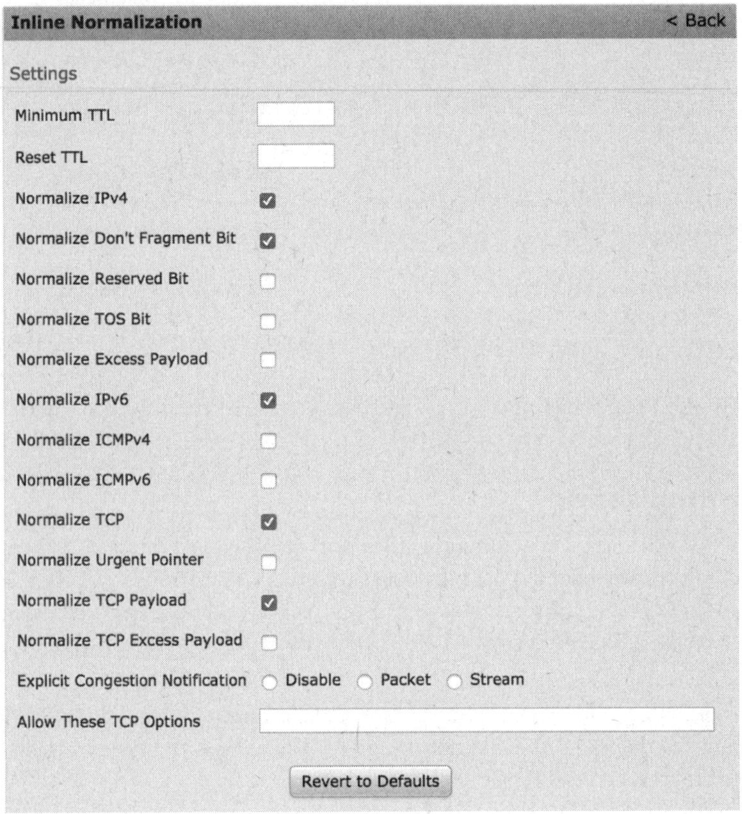

IP Defragmentation

IP fragmentation attacks and evasions have been around for quite a while. Attackers rely on various methods of overlapping offsets, small fragments, and vulnerable IP stacks to sneak their exploits by undetected and sometimes even to actually deploy them.

The IP Defragmentation preprocessor, shown in Figure 12.9, gives the IPS power to normalize data based on the observed traffic. It can also reassemble the information just as the targeted host would, referred to as host-based reassembly. A huge advantage to this technique is that it ensures more accurate detection and reassembly for the higher-layer protocols.

The default settings are pretty good for the preprocessor, but you still can turn on the rules for alerting purposes if you want. The system predominantly leverages this preprocessor for reassembly not alerting.

FIGURE 12.9   IP Defragmentation

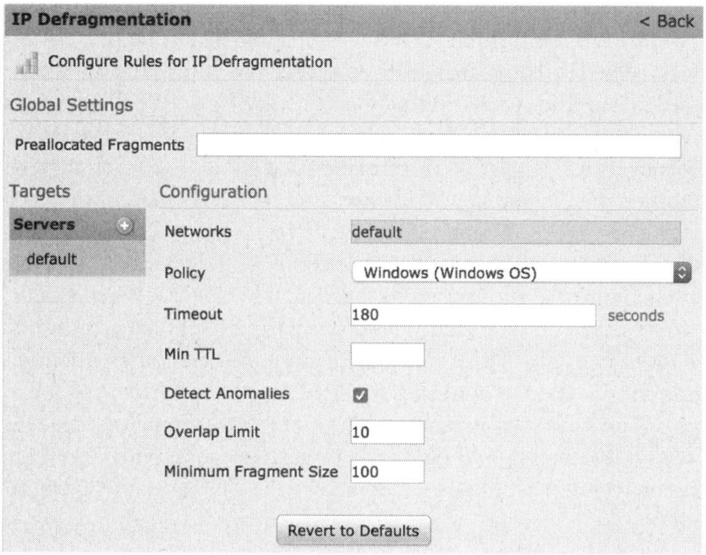

Even so, we really need to spend some time on the Servers section. Just as with the HTTP Configuration preprocessor, you can customize the system to interpret data based on specific IP addresses, lists, or subnets. An important part of the server configuration is deciding on these policy types:

- BSD (AIX, FreeBSD, HP-UX B.10.20, IRIX)
- BSD-Right (HP JetDirect)
- First (HP-UX 11.00, MacOS)
- Linux (Linux, OpenBSD)
- Last (Cisco IOS)
- Solaris (Solaris OS, SunOS)
- Windows (Windows OS)

This list represents the OS reassembly types available to the preprocessor. Choosing the appropriate method for a particular IP or subnet improves the accuracy of reassembly during evasion attempts. It can be a huge and horrifying task to input each and every one of your hosts into the settings here, so it's best to choose the dominant OS type per subnet. No worries—you can still spotlight your high-value/high-risk systems individually.

If you're inline, there's an even better alternative: Allow the inline normalization preprocessor to deal with the evasions. And even if you can't enable inline normalization, there's another setting called Adaptive Profiles that we'll cover in a bit, which allows FireSIGHT to automatically pass the fragmentation reassembly method on to the device for any networks covered by the discovery policy.

TCP Stream Configuration

The TCP Stream Configuration has lots of functions, but the two primary ones are to maintain session state and reassemble TCP data streams. The state of TCP communication sessions is critical to the IPS because its rules leverage the Snort rule keyword, "flow." The flow keyword allows the rule writer to specify conditions like flow: to_server, established, which indicates that subsequent rule conditions should only be matched when viewing a packet that is part of an established session moving to server from client. When flow and other state-based keywords are used, the IPS's detection gets increasingly specific by avoiding numerous potential false positives.

The other role of this preprocessor is to rebuild the TCP data streams, which allows the IPS to examine session traffic as opposed to individual packets. A huge benefit to this is that the rules can be based on data that would normally be split across multiple packets, matching that data to one rule. This single rule examines the data stream and can even be used to look at half the session, examining the flow to_client or to_server, enabling more targeted detection. The TCP session reassembly can even be target based, meaning that the stream can be rebuilt just as it would be on the targeted system, which really helps defeat certain TCP evasion techniques. Figure 12.10 shows the TCP Stream Configuration dialog.

FIGURE 12.10 TCP Stream Configuration

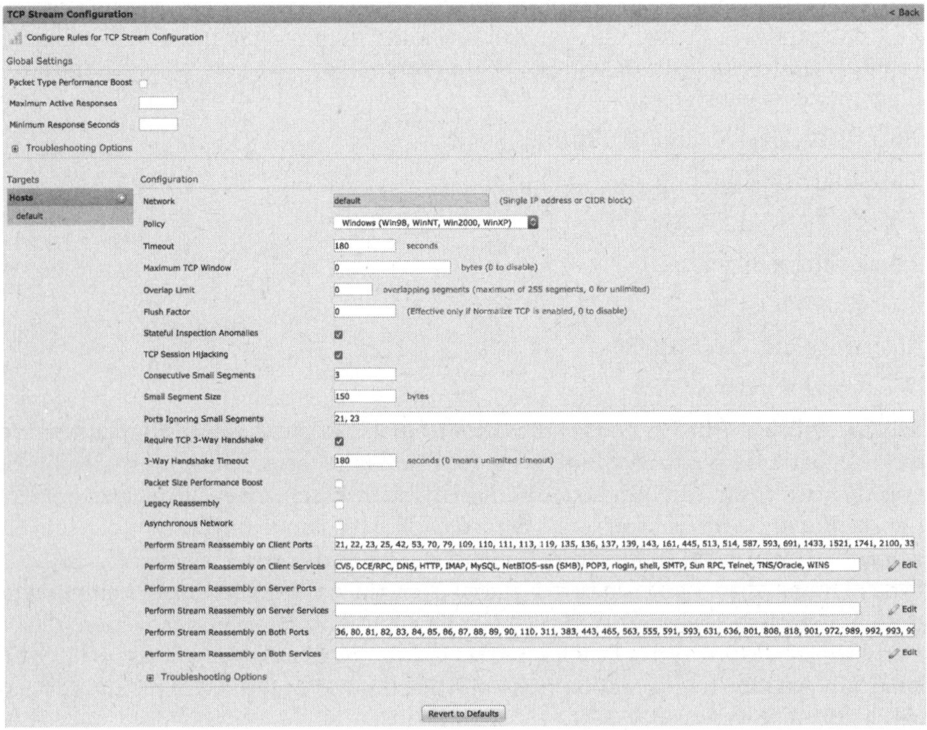

You can add to the hosts list to specific reassembly types by OS in the settings of the preprocessor. The reassembly types are referred to as policies. The available policies are shown in Figure 12.11.

FIGURE 12.11   IP defragmentation

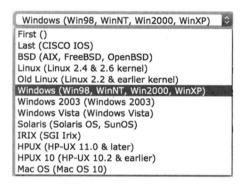

As you did with the IP Fragmentation preprocessor, you can specify hosts based on an IP, a list, or a subnet, and again, the inline normalization preprocessor boosts efficiency by weeding out malicious TCP packets. You can also use Adaptive Profiles to automatically pass the OS information from the host profile to the managed device.

Another really interesting setting is the Asynchronous Network check box. If your device is deployed in an asynchronous environment, be sure to enable this feature. The setting Require TCP 3-Way Handshake should be disabled in these environments.

The Stream Reassembly section lets you designate the ports to perform stream reassembly on. Client Ports specifies that you want to reassemble traffic moving from the client to the destination port specified, and Server Ports means you want to reassemble traffic moving from a server to a client originating from the ports specified. The setting Both Ports is directing the reassembly of traffic both to and from the clients and servers. The default ports that are listed are a "who's who" of common TCP application protocols.

If Adaptive Profiles is enabled, you can also specify based on the service names. This way, FireSIGHT (the Defense Center) can pass the information to the IPS (the devices) about services running on nonstandard ports. Here's another place where it's tempting to specify all ports, but just don't give in and do that! The performance implications could seriously haunt your decision. So only reassemble the traffic you need to.

Specific Threat Detection

Not all preprocessors handle data normalization or reassembly. As their name implies, those populating the Specific Threat Detection section handle specific network threats or attacks. If you enable these preprocessors, be sure to turn on the corresponding alert rules. The four Specific Threat Detection categories, as shown in Figure 12.12, are as follows:

Back Orifice Detection: Make all the jokes you want and more, just remember that this fends off attacks by looking for the Back Orifice magic cookie, which is contained in an XOR UDP packet. Again, get it out of your system—let the funnies flow!

Portscan Detection: Effective, but not nearly as entertaining, this feature detects *portscans*, port sweeps, decoy portscans and distributed portscans. The system will show summary data about any of these attacks in the event analysis.

Rate-Based Attack Prevention: This option allows rate-based filtering for things like SYN packets or connections and can be used as a denial of service (DoS) prevention tool.

Sensitive Data Detection: Allows for detection of sensitive data on the network, including things like credit card numbers, social security numbers, US phone numbers, and email addresses. You get to specify the protocols to inspect and the number of instances to detect before an alert is generated. You can even write your own detections by leveraging a lightweight regular expressions syntax.

FIGURE 12.12   Specific Threat Detection preprocessors

Detection Enhancement

The only item in Detection Enhancement is Adaptive Profiles, which gives FireSIGHT the ability to pass information to the IPS in terms of the particular IP fragmentation and TCP stream reassembly technique to use. The information is updated by default every 60 minutes based on the Attribute Update Interval in the preprocessor settings. Before opting to use Adaptive Profiles, you've got to enable them in your IPS policy as well as having discovery enabled on your network. You can specify the networks you want to leverage the adaptive settings for in Adaptive Profiles Settings, or you can leave the default value of 0.0.0.0/0, which would enable adaptive profiles for all monitored networks. Figure 12.13 shows the Adaptive Profiles Settings options.

FIGURE 12.13   Adaptive Profiles Settings

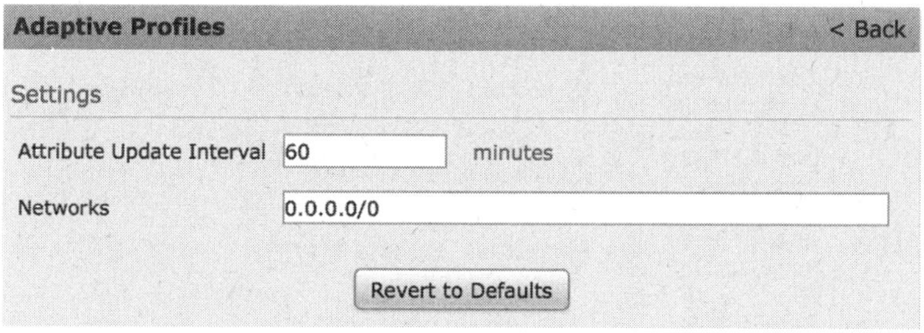

Adaptive Profiles	< Back

Settings

Attribute Update Interval `60`   minutes

Networks `0.0.0.0/0`

[Revert to Defaults]

Intrusion Rule Thresholds

It is good to know is that there's a default threshold in place for your IPS events. This works like the event filtering we talked about back in Chapter 3, "IPS Policy Management," except that instead of a per-rule basis, this one applies across the board. You can edit the global rule threshold to view the settings, as shown in Figure 12.14.

FIGURE 12.14   Global Rule Thresholding Settings

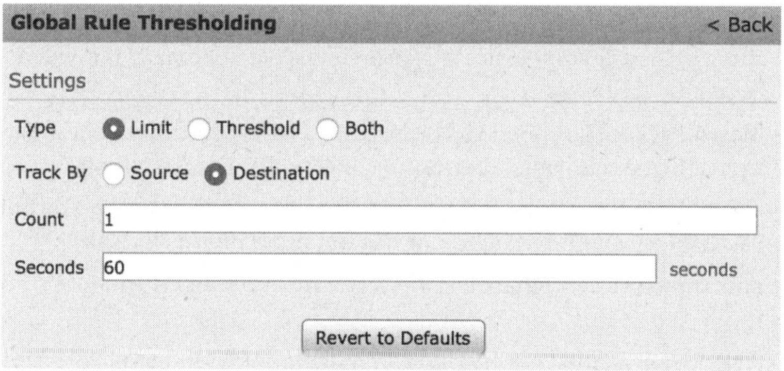

Global Rule Thresholding	< Back

Settings

Type   ● Limit   ○ Threshold   ○ Both

Track By   ○ Source ● Destination

Count   `1`

Seconds   `60`   seconds

[Revert to Defaults]

The limit is set so that you see only one event every 60 seconds provided that subsequent events are of the same kind and going to the same destination, which is good because it prevents the database from being filled with duplicate event information. You can adjust the settings or even disable the global thresholding feature all together.

Performance Settings

The Performance Settings section (Figure 12.15) contains a group of settings that control the inner workings of the detection engine. For the most part, you don't want to modify the settings unless directed by the Cisco TAC.

FIGURE 12.15   Performance Settings

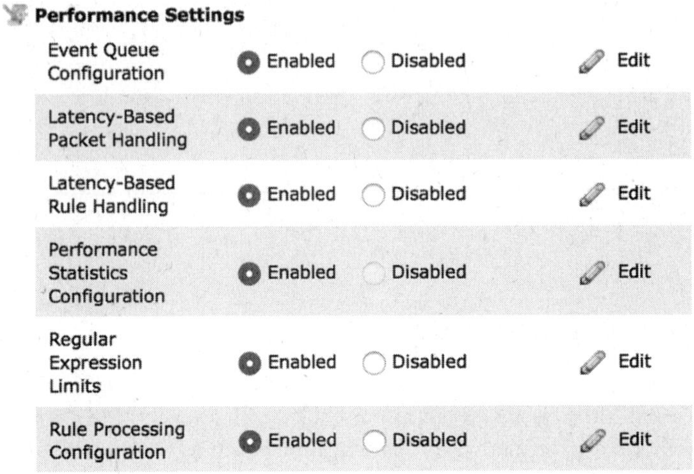

We're still going to cover them so you're aware of them just in case. The following settings are available:

Event Queue Configuration: Specifies how many packets to insert into the event queue. There's also a setting that indicates whether to inspect content in individual packets or within the rebuilt data stream.

Latency-Based Packet Handling: This is used as a safety measure in case the IPS is delayed inspecting an individual packet. We'll get into more detail on this soon.

Latency-Based Rule Handling: Use this setting to prevent a poorly performing rule from impacting inspection on the device. Again, more on this in a bit.

Performance Statistics Configuration: Indicates how often performance statistics are collected.

Regular Expression Limits: Limits the search depth and number of recursions performed by the regular expression engine.

Rule Processing Configuration: Specifies how many matches and alerts can be generated for traffic. This allows multiple rules to fire for matching traffic.

Latency-Based Packet Handling

As we just mentioned, the Latency-Based Packet Handling setting is a mechanism to ensure that the system processes packets in a timely manner. Problems do arise when a packet in a stream takes an excessive amount of time to process—other data stacked in the queue could eventually be dropped from inspection if things take too long!

Latency-Based Packet Handling gives the device the ability to measure the time it takes to process a packet through the system and if a time-out interval is exceeded, the packet will stop being inspected. You can enable a rule that will allow the system to alert if the conditions are met for doing that.

Here are the minimum values based on network speed:

- 1 Gbps = 100 μs
- 100 Mbps = 250 μs
- 5 Mbps = 1000 μs

In the real world, you would actually want to come up with your own numbers based on the average number of packets per second and average time per packet. It would also be a really good idea to add a time buffer into your calculation. Figure 12.16 shows the configuration dialog.

FIGURE 12.16   Latency-Based Packet Handling

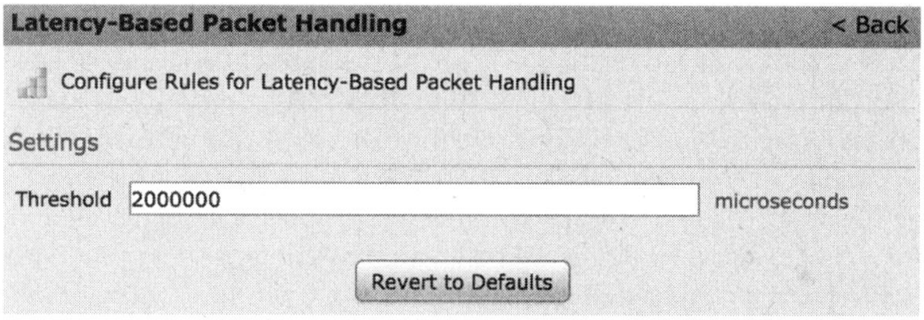

Latency-Based Rule Handling

Latency-Based Rule Handling essentially measures the time it takes to process individual rules. It's similar to the packet handling we already covered in that it allows the system to monitor itself for signs that inspection isn't happening as it should. If a rule fails to process traffic in an efficient manner a certain number of times in a row, that rule can be automatically disabled by the system. The system will also re-enable the rule after a time-out expires. This preprocessor includes rules that can be enabled to generate events when rules are disabled and re-enabled.

The settings let you configure these three things (Figure 12.17):

Threshold: Specifies the time allowed for a rule to process a packet.

Consecutive Threshold Violations Before Suspending Rule: How many times in a row an individual rule must exceed the threshold value.

Suspension Time: How long a rule will be disabled.

Here are the recommendations for Minimum Threshold:

- 1 Gbps = 500 μs
- 100 Mbps = 1250 μs
- 5 Mbps = 5000 μs

FIGURE 12.17   Latency-Based Rule Handling

Latency-Based Rule Handling		< Back
Configure Rules for Latency-Based Rule Handling		
Settings		
Threshold	513	microseconds
Consecutive Threshold Violations Before Suspending Rule	3	count
Suspension Time	30	seconds
	Revert to Defaults	

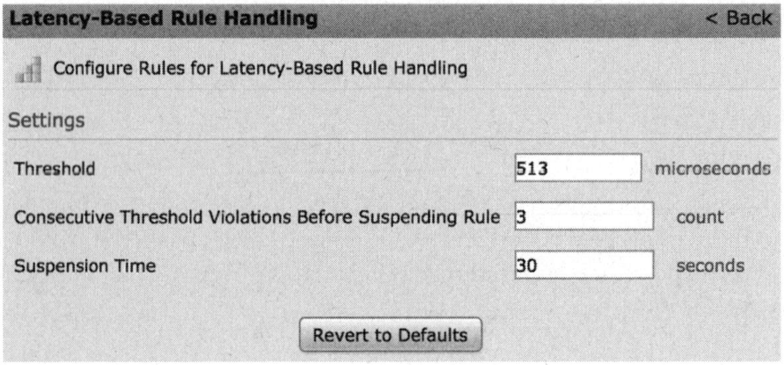

External Responses

The last section in the advanced settings is home to the external responses, SNMP Alerting and Syslog Alerting, shown in Figure 12.18. With SNMP Alerting, you need to specify the setting to communicate to an SNMP server (v2 or v3). You would then enable the alerts on the individual rule in the rule section.

For Syslog Alerting, you must specify the syslog server, the alerting level, and severity to report. The syslog output would then send an alert anytime an IPS event triggered. The alert originates from the managed device.

FIGURE 12.18   External Responses

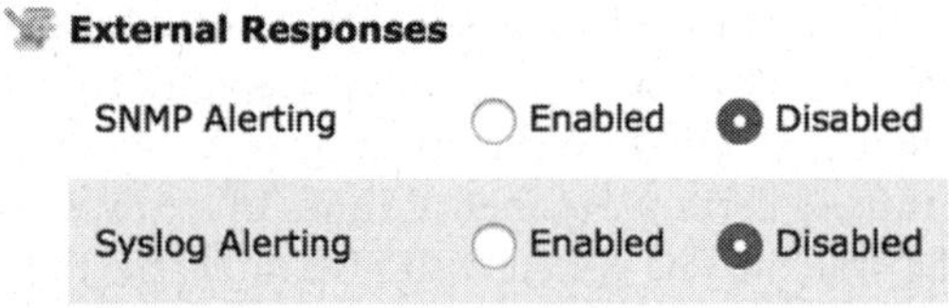

External Responses		
SNMP Alerting	○ Enabled	● Disabled
Syslog Alerting	○ Enabled	● Disabled

Summary

In this chapter, we covered the all-important advanced settings of the intrusion policy.

We described what preprocessors are and how they are used by the system. We also toured the advanced settings themselves, going into detail on the following items:

- HTTP Configuration
- Inline Normalization
- IP Defragmentation
- TCP Stream Configuration

- Adaptive Profiles
- Latency-Based Packet/Rule Handling

Hands-on Lab

In this section, you will go through the following three labs:

Hands-on Lab 12.1: Modifying the HTTP Configuration Preprocessor

Hands-on Lab 12.2: Enabling Inline Normalization

Hands-on Lab 12.3: Demonstrating the Validation of Preprocessor Settings on Policy Commit

Hands-on Lab 12.1: Modifying the HTTP Configuration Preprocessor

In this lab, you will modify the HTTP Configuration settings in several ways. First you will add a host to the configuration and modify inspection properties for the host. Then you will modify how one of the preprocessor rules alerts.

1. From the main menu, navigate to Policies ➢ Intrusion ➢ Intrusion Policy.

2. Find the previously created policy called Demo IPS Policy and click the edit icon.

3. In the navigation pane, select Advanced Settings. This will expand the advanced settings in the detail pane.

4. Navigate to the HTTP Configuration section and click Edit.

5. In the Servers section, hit the plus icon (+) to add a server to the configuration.

6. In the Add Target dialog box, type **192.168.2.25**. This will represent a web server that your device is protecting.

7. Since this is our web server, we know that it is only running web services on port 80. Remove all ports other than 80 from the port list for the newly added server.

8. Scroll to the bottom of the configuration settings and select the IIS profile. This will examine HTTP traffic, enabling the decodings that are common to IIS.

9. Scroll back to the top of the settings and click the link Configure Rules For HTTP Configuration. This opens the rules for the policy, filtering on the ones available to the HTTP preprocessor.

10. In the list of rules, find the one titled HI_CLIENT_OVERSIZE_DIR. This is a rule that will trigger when web requests exceed 500 characters (as configured by the setting Oversize Dir Length). While this could indicate a buffer overflow attempt, in today's web traffic, it is not uncommon for the active content found on popular pages to redirect to sites with the requests routinely exceeding the length, creating false positives if this is enabled on a user segment.

11. Disable the rule HI_CLIENT_OVERSIZE_DIR.

12. Click the Policy Information link in the navigation pane (notice the icon indicating that settings have changed).

13. Click Commit Changes and confirm the dialogs.

Hands-on Lab 12.2: Enabling Inline Normalization

In this lab, you will enable the inline normalization settings for your device.

1. Open the IPS policy called Demo IPS Policy in the policy editor.

2. Select Advanced Settings in the navigation pane.

3. Scroll down in the details pane to Transport/Network Layer Preprocessors.

4. Find Inline Normalization in this section and click the Enabled radial button.

5. Once it's enabled, click the edit icon for Inline Normalization.

6. Check the box for Normalize Excess Payload.

7. Scroll down in the details pane to Transport/Network Layer Preprocessors.

8. Click the Policy Information link in the navigation pane. (Notice the icon indicating that settings have changed.)

9. Click Commit Changes and confirm the dialogs.

Hands-on Lab 12.3: Demonstrating the Validation of Preprocessor Settings on Policy Commit

In this lab, you will witness the validation that the system does while committing polices. If a preprocessor is required for the policy to function properly and that preprocessor is disabled, the validation will cause the preprocessor to be enabled.

1. Open the IPS policy named Demo IPS Policy in the policy editor.

2. Select Advanced Settings in the navigation pane.

3. Scroll down in the details pane to Application Layer Preprocessors.

4. Find DCE/RPC Configuration in this section and click the Disabled radial button.

5. Click the Policy Information link in the navigation pane. (Notice the icon indicating that settings have changed.)

6. Click Commit Changes and OK on the Description of Changes dialog box.

7. Notice the warning dialog that appears.

8. Click OK to commit.

9. Once the policy is committed, edit the same policy again.

10. Notice that the DCE/RPC Configuration was re-enabled.

11. Click Discard Changes under Policy Information to return to the policy list.

12. Click the Apply Policy check mark.

Exam Essentials

Understand the functions of the Application layer preprocessors.   The Application layer preprocessors normalize data and look for anomalies. The preprocessors can be tuned to the specific environment they are in. Preprocessors can generate alerts by themselves if the corresponding rules are enabled. Otherwise, the normalized traffic is sent to be processed against the IPS rules.

Describe the Network and Transport layer preprocessor functions.   Network and Transport layer preprocessors perform the low-level reassembly to handle IP fragments and TCP stream reassembly. These also allow for target-based reassembly so the managed device can put the packets back together just like the target operating system. If you are deployed inline, Cisco recommends the inline normalization preprocessor.

Describe the features of the specific threat preprocessors.   The specific threat preprocessors include items like Back Orifice detection, port scan detection, and sensitive data detection. The port scan detection can identify port scans, port sweeps, decoy port scans, and distributed port scans. The sensitive data detection preprocessor can be customized for user-defined data using a lightweight PCRE implementation.

Understand the performance settings.   The performance settings in the advanced IPS section allow you to tune the system in terms of how traffic is processed. These should be adjusted under the guidance of TAC. Latency-based packet handling and latency-based rule handling can control what the device does should it become overwhelmed with events or in special detection cases.

Review Questions

You can find the answers in Appendix A.

1. Which preprocessor section would cover packet fragmentation reassembly?
   A. Application Layer Preprocessors
   B. SCADA Preprocessors
   C. Transport/Network Layer Preprocessors
   D. Specific Threat Detection

2. The Application Layer Preprocessor for HTTP allows for what to be normalized?
   A. Applications, SQL, and Perl
   B. Headers, cookies, and UTF encodings
   C. Bodies, cookies, and SQL scripts
   D. Request Byte, Response Byte, and Body Byte

3. If you are deployed inline, the Inline Normalization preprocessor can eliminate the need to configure specific TCP reassembly policies. If you are in a passive deployment, what could you do to automate the policy selection for TCP normalization?
   A. Enable Adaptive Profiles.
   B. Enable Passive Normalization.
   C. Enable Active Reassembly.
   D. You can only automate this in inline deployments.

4. The Targets section of the HTTP Configuration allows the administrator to do what?
   A. Redirect network threats to a black hole
   B. Control inspection on a per-host or subnet basis
   C. Configure inspection for all HTTP traffic
   D. Designate whether or not to enable target discovery

5. What is the setting that prevents a flood of events from overwhelming the FSM database?
   A. Global Rule Thresholding
   B. Database Overflow Protection
   C. Event Queue Configuration
   D. Event Filtering

6. In the advanced settings, what type of external responses are allowed?
   A. SMTP and Estreamer
   B. SNMP and Estreamer
   C. SMTP and Syslog
   D. SNMP and Syslog

7. Which feature enables the system to disable poorly performing rules?

   A. Latency-Based Packet Handling

   B. Latency-Based Rule Handling

   C. Automatic Application Bypass

   D. Rule Thresholding

8. Under Specific Threat Detection, what are the available preprocessors?

   A. SynFlood Detection, PortScan Detection, Rate-Based Attack Prevention, and PII Protection

   B. Back Orifice Detection, Portscan Detection, SCADA Protection, and Sensitive Data Detection.

   C. SynFlood Detection, PortScan Detection, PII Detection, and SCADA Protection

   D. Back Orifice Detection, Portscan Detection, Rate-Based Attack Prevention, and Sensitive Data Detection.

9. What types of PII are looked for in the Sensitive Data Detection preprocessor?

   A. US phone numbers, social security numbers, credit card numbers, and email addresses

   B. US phone numbers, social security numbers, credit card numbers, and US bank account numbers

   C. Phone numbers, social security numbers, credit card numbers, and physical addresses

   D. US phone numbers, social security numbers, account numbers, and email addresses

10. Inline Normalization can prevent network threats by performing what functions?

   A. Inline Normalization enables IPS blocking.

   B. Inline Normalization sends traffic to the IP and TCP preprocessors.

   C. Inline Normalization removes deviations in IP, TCP, and ICMP protocol standards.

   D. Inline Normalization cannot stop threats.

Chapter

13

Creating Snort Rules

THE SSFIPS EXAM TOPICS COVERED IN THIS CHAPTER INCLUDE THE FOLLOWING:

✓ **9.1   Be familiar with the options used to create Snort rules inside the Cisco NGIPS**

In this chapter, we're going to focus exclusively on the fundamentals of Snort rules, detailing their structure, syntax, and options. We'll also explore how Snort performs rule optimization for better performance and show you how rule matching takes place internally.

The core of the FireSIGHT System's intrusion detection capability is the IPS detection engine, which includes the preprocessor and the IPS rule base. Once the IPS engine initializes, the rule structures initialize and begin building decision trees by grouping rules based on things like destination ports. The system uses these rules as a yardstick to measure packets sent to it and determine their fate accordingly.

We're going hit the ground running and open this chapter by diving right into rule structure and syntax. After that, we'll go deeper into exploring basic rule options and the many ways they're used. From there, we'll move on to configuring and creating Snort rules using the Rule Editor in the system GUI. We'll wrap up things up by demonstrating how to import an existing rule as well as how to verify it within the system.

To find up-to-the-minute updates for this chapter, please see www.lammle .com/firepower or the book's web page at www.sybex.com.

Overview of Snort Rules

A Snort intrusion rule comprises keywords calling for actions like looking for and detecting attempts to exploit vulnerabilities on your network. These goals are achieved via analyzing network traffic to detect whether network packets match the conditions specified in the rule.

So the system essentially compares incoming packets against the conditions specified in each rule, and if the packet data matches criteria, the rule triggers. What happens next depends on whether the rule is an alert rule or a pass rule. If an alert rule has been triggered, it will generate an intrusion event. A pass rule will cause the traffic to be ignored. And of course we'll remind you that you can view and evaluate intrusion events from the FireSIGHT Management Center (FMC).

Each rule has two logical sections: the rule header and the rule body. The body is made up of keywords and arguments that establish the criteria that must be met to trigger an alert. It includes event messages and the patterns a packet must match to trigger the rule as well as guidance on which part of the packet the IPS engine should inspect.

To get a picture of this, let's take a look at a rule, and then break it down and talk about it piece-by-piece.

Header:

```
alert tcp $EXTERNAL_NET any -> $HTTP_SERVERS $HTTP_PORTS
```

Body:

```
(msg:"POLICY-OTHER Adobe ColdFusion admin interface access attempt";
flow:to_server,established; content:"/CFIDE/administrator"; fast_pattern:only;
http_uri; metadata:policy balanced-ips drop, policy connectivity-ips
drop, policy security-ips drop, service http; reference:bugtraq,57330;
reference:cve,2013-0632; reference:url,www.adobe.com/support/security/
advisories/apsa13-01.html; classtype:policy-violation; sid:25975; rev:2; )
```

Let's start with the rule header pieces.

Rule Headers

The rule header section details exactly how to match traffic based on these factors:

- The rule's action or type
- The protocol
- The source and destination IP addresses and netmasks
- The directional operator that indicates the flow of traffic from source to destination
- The source and destination ports

Figure 13.1 illustrates the rule header, the parameters, and the arguments, which combined, structure the rule header.

FIGURE 13.1   Snort rule header

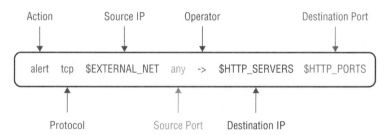

The following list describes each item in the rule header shown in Figure 13.1:

- Action `alert` directs an event to be generated when the rule is triggered.
- Protocol `tcp` runs the rule against TCP traffic only.
- Source IP `$EXTERNAL_NET` will test traffic coming from any host that is not on your internal network.

- Source port any will test traffic coming from any port on the originating host.

- Operator -> will run the rule against external traffic destined for the web servers in your network.

- Destination IP $HTTP_SERVERS will run the rule against traffic to be delivered to any host that is a specified web server in your internal network.

- Destination port $HTTP_PORTS will run the rule against traffic delivered to an HTTP port in your internal network.

Check out Figure 13.1 again. Did you notice that we used variables instead of IP addresses? It's not that we can't use IP addresses; it's that if we do, and those addresses ever change, we'd have to go to each rule and change the headers. That's a really tedious job that everyone wants to avoid, and if we go with variables, all we have to do is head straight to the configuration file and change the variable IP addresses—nice!

Rule Actions

Looking at Figure 13.1 again, you can see that a rule's first parameter specifies the action the system takes when a packet triggers a rule. Don't forget that you only have two rule actions when using the managed device in IPS or Monitor only mode:

Alert: Log the event and send an alert message.

Pass: Ignore the packet and pass it.

However, since most of our installations would have our managed devices deployed as inline, we actually have three rule states for each rule that can be configured:

Generate events: When a rule triggers, send a console alert.

Drop & Generate events: This option will block packets and send a console alert.

Disabled: A disabled rule is not matched against packets. You would set a rule to disabled to optimize your managed device's performance or to reduce false positives.

 These same three options are available when configuring a passive environment. The difference in the passive is that an event will be created when a rule is triggered instead of packets being actively dropped.

Protocols

In the second field of the rule header, you get to choose the protocol you want to measure the packet against and execute the rule. You can call out the following protocols by name:

- TCP
- UDP
- ICMP
- IP

Beware—just don't implement a rule listing IP as the protocol in the rule header. If you do that, you're saying that all traffic must be scrutinized even if you're just looking for TCP traffic! We're not saying you won't see rules with IP in the header because you will. It's just more efficient to use ICMP, UDP, or TCP in the header.

You can even write a rule using a different protocol than the four we listed here. To do that, you need to use the IP protocol label from 0 to 255, and to find the protocol values, simply Google for IP protocol field values.

Source and Destination IPs

Okay, so after you've taken care of the protocol field, you still have to deal with your source IP addresses. This is important because the destination IP address is also right there in the very header that the rule is set up to inspect. This is where using variables instead of IP addresses comes in really handy, because when you're dealing with variables, you don't have to statically configure IP addresses for each rule. If you do decide to go with addressing, understand that you just can't use a hostname or FQDN—it's either IP addresses or variables!

Anyway, when it comes time to configure source and destination IP addresses, you'll get to configure the following:

- You can use the keyword any so that the rule will test all addresses.

- You can specify a single unicast address.

- You can create a list of IP addresses for the rule to check by enclosing the IP addresses in brackets ([]) and separating them by commas with no spaces. Example: [172.16.10.1,172.16.10.20]

- Use a CIDR block to specify a subnet. Example: 172.16.16.0/20

- You can tell a rule not to check an address with the bang (!) character. Example: !172.16.10.100

- You can use a variable, just as we showed in Figure 13.1. These are defined in the snort.conf file; however, there is no way to look at this file from the FMC GUI. The built-in variables can, however, be seen when looking at the default variable.

Source and Destination Ports

The source and destination IP addresses found in the rule header we just talked about aren't alone in there. They're joined by the source and destination port number fields, which are also specified within the header. These are the numbers/protocols you'll find at the Transport layer, and by specifying port numbers, you can restrict the rule inspection to ports originating to and from a given destination. You also gain a lot more granularity than you would get by just creating a rule that specifies IP addresses. Also, going with the variable route empowers your rule to be more efficient while reducing the amount of false positives returned. This actually makes the rule more specific and stops it from triggering on a packet whose port numbers don't really indicate suspicious behavior.

Here are some of the ways you can list the source and destination port:

- Use the keyword any so that the rule will test all port numbers.

- Specify a single port number.

- Specify a range of ports using a dash (-). Example: `80-443`

- Just as with IP addresses, exclude with the bang (!). Example: `!80`

- List multiple ports with the comma (,) and port ranges. Example: `[21, 23, 80-110]`

- Use the variables as we demonstrated back in Figure 13.1, which are defined in the `snort.conf` file.

Specifying Direction

Speaking of Figure 13.1, let's take a quick trip back there. Can you see that there's a directional operator between the source IP address and port number and the destination IP address and port number?

The directional operator in the rule header predictably allows you to specify the direction that the packet must travel for the rule to trigger against it. If you want the rule to trigger when a packet traverses from the source to destination IP address and port numbers, use the directional operator `->`, just as shown in Figure 13.1.

And if you want to have a rule trigger against all traffic traversing between source and destination IP addresses and ports, use the `<>` directional operator.

The Rule Body

The body is the where the Snort rule's real power resides. There, you can create a rule that will command drilling into a packet to get down to its content and trigger on malicious or suspicious activity!

As for convention, the rule body must adhere to a very specific syntax, and the entire body is enclosed in parentheses. Rule options end with a semicolon. An option is structured with a keyword followed by a colon, which is followed by an argument. If there are multiple arguments, separate them with commas.

To harness the rule body's raw power, use the content keyword to have the rule trigger on a content string like this:

```
content:"root"; nocase;
```

In this example, the rule will trigger if it finds the string "root"—and yes, of course, it's case insensitive!

Keep in mind that a rule can have multiple content references. Also important is to remember that multiple content references are treated as an AND, not an OR. Here's an example:

```
content:"username:"; nocase; content:"password:"; nocase;
```

In this example, both username and password content conditions must be met for the rule to trigger. If only one of the content conditions matches up, the rule won't trigger.

Snort rules allow you to combine multiple, compatible keywords plus their attributes, called arguments, which tell the detection engine how to evaluate packets and thoroughly test the packet. Because you can string any number of compatible keywords together and combine them to create rules, you can get intensely specific. As an added benefit, this extraordinary ability protects you from receiving false positive alerts too.

So let's move on and talk more about all these keywords and arguments we use when creating a rule now.

Defining the Event Message

When a rule is triggered you can get yourself some very meaningful text displayed along with the event each time it's triggered via the msg keyword. Here's an example:

```
alert tcp any any -> $HOME_NET 21 (content:"root"; nocase; msg:"Bad FTP!";
sid:1000000;)
```

This rule requires an alert to be triggered whenever a TCP packet from any source IP addresses using any source port number is transmitted to $HOME_NET with destination port 21 and a content string that equals root. The message in the alert will say "Bad FTP!" This gives you relevant, meaningful context and insight into the reason the event occurred without having to memorize legions of Snort ID (sid) numbers! You can use any alphanumeric string up to 255 characters as the event message.

Content Matches

As we demonstrated earlier, the content keyword is used to specify exactly what you want detected in a packet. The detection engine searches the packet for that string—as an example, bin/sh. You can enter whatever it is that you want to match with either an ASCII string or hexadecimal content, but remember that the hexadecimal message is always surrounded by the pipe character |.

By using the content keyword, we can match content using the following:

- ASCII test: bin/sh

- Hexadecimal (binary byte code): |40D7 B1EE FFFF|

- A combination of Hex and ASCII: |40D7 B1EE FFFF|/bin/sh

Notice that those hexadecimal characters are enclosed within the pipe symbols. The spaces within the pipes are ignored by the detection engine but are often used to improve readability in the rule. Understand that you can't use spaces in the ASCII section of the content.

Also understand that you can use as many content keywords as you want in a rule. If you do this, it indicates that multiple content matches must be found in the packet for the rule to trigger. And remember, it's always an AND; never an OR! You can also exclude content from being searched with the bang (!) character.

Constraining Content Matches

Being able to filter the location and case sensitivity of content searches is a great way to hone security. We do that with options appended with the content keyword. As an example, we can easily make the detection engine ignore the case of an ASCII string with the nocase option:

```
content:"root"; nocase;
```

Here, we told the detection engine to look for root but to ignore case so it will still trigger if it sees any other variation of the term, like Root, ROOT, or RooT, for example.

And now that you know how to ignore the content case sensitivity, let's go deeper into how to make the detection engine begin looking for our specified content at the precise location we want it to using something called *offset*.

Starting at byte 0, the offset starts counting at the precise point where you've specified that the detection engine should begin looking. So, if you dictate an offset of 6, the detection engine will start at 0 and skip to the 6th byte before it will begin looking for the content. Now, why on Earth would you want to do this? Because you've been given the heads up that there's an attack eminently headed your way that has a packet in it with the word "World" starting in the 6th byte, that's why! To fend off the attack, your rule would look like this:

```
content:"World"; offset:6;
```

▪ Figure 13.2 illustrates how the offset works.

FIGURE 13.2   Constraining content matches

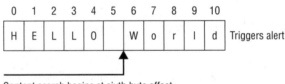

Content search begins at sixth byte offset.

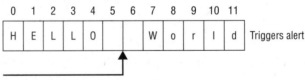

Content search begins at sixth byte offset.

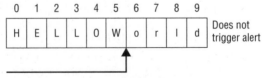

Content search begins at sixth byte offset.

Look at Figure 13.2 again... see those three packets, all including the content "World"? Well, only the first two packet examples will trigger an alert because in them, the content

"World" started at the sixth byte or even further down the packet. The first packet has "World" starting at its sixth byte and the second one has "World" in its seventh byte, which will also trigger because we instructed the counting to start at the sixth byte and the seventh byte is past that. To clarify, the detection engine will start looking for the content "World" at the sixth byte and continue until the end of the packet. The third example has "World" starting at the fifth byte, so clearly it won't trigger an event.

But what if we wanted to be even more specific? Let's say we've got intel that the attack's content is definitely located on the sixth byte—nowhere else—so we want to exclude all other locations within incoming packets? This is where the depth option comes in. Let's take a look.

Depth is the precision tool you use for telling the detection engine exactly how many bytes to read. In our last example, the second packet triggered an alert because the content "World" was somewhere from the sixth byte to the end of the packet. But if we use depth and do this:

```
content:"World"; offset:6; depth:5;
```

Then we've told the detection engine to start at the sixth byte, count only five bytes, then stop, meaning our second example in Figure 13.2 wouldn't match and wouldn't trigger an alert.

Another very cool tool is distance. We use this keyword to tell the detection engine to find an additional match beyond the first one that will occur a specified number of bytes after the last content match. Figure 13.3 gives you an example.

FIGURE 13.3   Distance

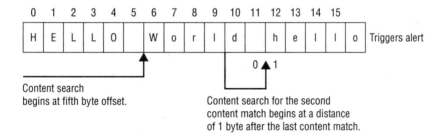

And the rule body we would use to make everything in Figure 13.3 happen would look like this:

```
content:"World"; offset:6; depth:5; \
content:"hello"; distance:1;
```

Translated, this basically says, "If content "World" matches starting at the sixth byte, then look for content "hello" with a distance of 1 byte (starting at zero) from the end of the first content match, 5 bytes long, (a depth of 5)." The slash (\) is in there because we put the rule on two lines. The rules about the rules tell us that a rule must only be on one line—unless you use that slash!

A third trick we can use is within. This keyword says that the next content match has to show up within the specified number of bytes after the end of the last content match, plus the distance value. If we want to make that happen, our rule would need to be updated to look like this:

```
content:"World"; offset:6; depth:5; \
content:"hello"; distance:1; within:5;
```

Okay, so before adding within to the mix, our rule dictated, "If content "World" matches starting at the sixth byte, then look for content "hello" with a distance of 1 byte (starting at zero) from the end of the first content match, which was 5 bytes long (depth of 5)." Our rule still directs that to happen; only now, it gets even more specific by telling the detection engine that the content "hello" has to be within 5 bytes after the end of the last content match, plus the value of the distance keyword. And if all this happens, trigger an alert—phew!

Server Flow

The flow keyword determines the direction of traffic flow that the rule will be applied to. Here's our list of possibilities:

to_client: This triggers on server responses.

to_server: This triggers on client responses.

from_client: This triggers on client responses.

from_server: This triggers on server responses.

At first glance, you're probably thinking this list looks a little redundant, right? After all, since from_server and to_client mean the same thing and to_server and from_client mean the same thing, why do we need all of them? The answer is because they're essentially two opportunities to write things in, giving you two extra ways to add context and readability to your rule. Still, in most cases, the only ones you'll use are to_client and to_server.

You can also use these two arguments to describe state-related flows:

established: This argument means that the rule will only trigger when the packet is part of an established TCP connection.

stateless: This argument means the rule can trigger regardless of the state of the TCP connection.

So, established means that we only want to match packets that have established a full, three-way handshake. If we want to match packets on a TCP stream that didn't establish a three-way handshake, then we would go with the stateless argument.

Way back at the beginning of the chapter, we showed an example that had the following in the beginning of the rule body:

```
(msg:"POLICY-OTHER Adobe ColdFusion admin interface access attempt";
flow:to_server,established; [output cut]
```

This rule would only trigger if the data flowing *to the server* had *established* the three-way handshake.

Furthermore, we could apply these two arguments if it matters to us whether the TCP stream is rebuilt or not:

no_stream: This will not trigger when a stream is rebuilt.

only_stream: This will trigger only when a stream is rebuilt.

Just so you know, people don't use no_stream and only_stream all that much, but it's still good to know they're available just in case you need them.

Snort ID Option

When a Snort rule triggers, the alert output will display the Snort ID. This really helps categorize the events and alerts because rules use unique numbers. For example, your custom-created rules will have Snort ID numbers greater than 1,000,000, but default Snort rules, as well as those that default to the detection engine, will have ID numbers below 1,000,000. Here's the syntax:

```
sid:<ID_VALUE>;
```

Later on in this chapter, we'll create a custom Snort rule using the FireSIGHT System's graphical interface and you'll see firsthand that the system creates the Snort ID for you. We'll also come up with a custom rule and import it into the system. Whenever you create custom rules, always record the Snort ID for reference!

Rule Revision Number

Always increment the rule revision number whenever you change a Snort rule so you'll remember that the rule has been edited. Rule revision numbers will show up in the alert output when triggered. Here's a look at the syntax:

```
rev:<REVISION_VALUE>;
```

If you use the graphical interface, it will number the revision number for you—something we'll demonstrate soon.

Metadata

When you want a rule to trigger on service information, you can use the metadata keyword. The metadata keyword is also a great way to provide information to Snort. This metadata keyword is used to provide information to the administrator regarding the type of malicious traffic, the rule number, and the version of the rule. This can all be critical information in trying to decipher what has actually taken place in your network and the management of your rules.

Here's an example of triggering a rule based on HTTP traffic:

```
alert tcp $EXTERNAL_NET any -> $HOME_NET 80 \
(msg: "Alert on web traffic"; sid: 1000001; \
```

```
rev: 1; metadata: service http; \
classtype:misc-activity;)
```

The metadata keyword with the service argument is required when writing rules for specific services like HTTP, HTTPS, SMTP, SNMP, and so on.

Here's what the correct usage of the metadata keyword using multiple services looks like:

```
metadata: service <service ID>, service <service ID>;
```

You've got to use the service identifier when writing rules for identifying services in your rule because if you don't, your rules might not trigger when you need them to!

Table 13.1 presents the service IDs you can use with FireSIGHT.

TABLE 13.1   Metadata service IDs

Service	Service	Service	Service
dcerpc	dns	finger	ftp
ftp-data	http	Imap	isakmo
netbios_dgm	netbios-ns	netbios-ssn	nntp
oracle	pop2	Pop3	smtp
ssh	telnet	tftp	x11

If you need to use any service in your rules that's not defined here, you've got to contact Cisco TAC.

There's one last feature you need to know about before we get into talking about flags: You can use the metadata argument to force an impact flag to appear with an event if the custom rule you created triggers. This hardcodes the impact flag for the rule and is done using the following:

```
metadata: impact_flag red;
```

Flags

Within the TCP header are various flags, and the flags keyword is used to check whether specific TCP flags are enabled in the TCP header or not. Table 13.2 shows the flags.

TABLE 13.2   TCP flags

Flag	Flag	Flag
F: Fin	S: SYN	R: RST
P: PSH	A: ACK	U: URG
C: CWR - Congestion Window Reduced (MSB in TCP Flags byte)	E: ECE - ECN-Echo (If SYN, then ECN capable. Else, CE flag in IP header is set.)	0: No flags set

And the format looks like this:

```
Flags: [! | * | +]<FSRPAU120>[,<FSRPAU120>];
```

If you want to get even more detailed, you can use the following modifiers to change the match criteria:

+: Match on the specified flag plus any others.

*: Match if any of the specified bits are set.

!: Match is the specified bits are not set.

Here's an example:

```
alert tcp any any -> any any (flags:SA,CE; msg:"syn+ack packet; sid 1000010;)
```

This rule would only alert if the SYN and ACK bits were set regardless of the state of the reserved bits because after the comma, the C and E flags were set to ignore. Since there aren't any other flags there in the ignore portion of the rule, an alert still wouldn't happen even if any other flag was set somewhere else.

File_Data

The file_data keyword is used in a lot of the default rules created by Cisco (rules with numbers below 1,000,000). It's a tool for looking in the data portion of the packets in the responses from HTTP, SMTP, POP or IMAP servers.

The file_data keyword really does come in handy because it saves you from having to examine the entire payload body for content, when you only want to search for content in the response body. With it, you can scour responses from an HTTP server for certain data.

Here's an example for you:

```
alert tcp any any -> any any(msg:"FILE DATA"; file_data; content:"goo";)
```

So, in this rule, we'll only look for "goo" in the payload body of packets coming from the server, skipping over the headers.

Now take a look at this one:

```
alert tcp any any -> any any(msg:"FILE DATA"; file_data; content:"goo";
pkt_data; content:"bar";)
```

The pkt_data keyword prior to content:"bar" means that the rule will look for "bar" starting at the first byte of the payload rather than at the beginning of the response body.

Fast_Pattern

The fast_pattern matching engine is used to quickly determine which rules a packet would qualify for further inspection against. It works by queuing the rules at the beginning of the detection engine startup that have the keyword content in them.

Fast_pattern is a little piece of code you'll find at the beginning of the detection engine, as shown in Figure 13.4.

FIGURE 13.4 Fast_Pattern

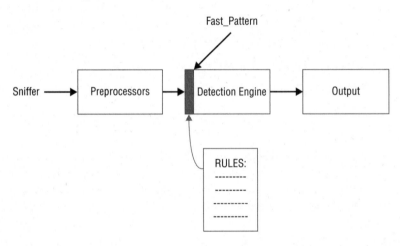

When the Snort process loads, it goes through the rules. Each rule that has a content keyword is loaded into the fast_pattern matching engine. So, any packet that comes in is first checked to see if it matches in the fast_pattern matching engine. If there aren't any pieces of content found in the packet, it won't be processed any further. The fast_pattern matching engine comes in handy for eliminating packets so they won't hang around to be processed against rules that they will never match. Though this may seem to be overhead, it can significantly reduce the number of rules that need to be evaluated and therefore increases performance. The better the content used for the fast_pattern matcher, the less likely the rule will needlessly be evaluated.

If there happen to be two content keywords in a rule, then it will load the longest one. So if, for example, you want to prioritize "goo", you want it to be loaded into the fast_pattern matcher. You would make sure that happens with the fast_pattern keyword like this:

```
content:"goo"; content "food";
type="note"
content: "goo"; fast_pattern;
```

Here, because the keyword "food" is longer, it would have been loaded into the FP matching engine instead of "goo" by default. We got around that by using the fast_pattern keyword in a rule to direct which content should be sent to the fast_pattern code, which in this case is "goo" instead of "food".

> The fast_pattern modifier can be used with negated contents only if those contents are not modified with offset, depth, distance, or within.

Flowbits

If you want to set tags that can be referenced in subsequent rules, then the flowbits rule option is for you. By using this option, you're basically assigning state names to sessions. The system can detect and alert on attacks that occur within multiple packets in a single session by looking at subsequent packets. For example, if you have an exploit delivered in a PDF file, flowbits can be used to monitor a session and determine that a PDF has been seen in the session and set a flowbit if true. Then, a second rule that monitors the state of the flowbit can check subsequent packets of the session (or the file data) to see if the exploit condition exists.

The tags created by the flowbits option can also be used to track the state of conditions in a given connection. If things change during that connection, you can alter the status of a previously set flowbit to maintain user awareness of the tags you're tracking.

The following output shows the flowbit command and the various options available to be used along with it, which we'll define below the output:

```
flowbits: [set | unset | toggle | isset, reset, noalert] [,<STATE_NAME>]
[,<GROUP_NAME>];
```

set: Sets the specified state for the current flows.

setx: Sets the specified states for the current flow and clears other states in the group.

unset: Unsets the specified state for the current flow.

toggle: Sets the specified state if the state is unset and unsets the state if it's set.

isset: Checks if the specified state is set.

isnotset: Checks if the specified state is not set.

noalert: Will cause the rule to not generate an alert, regardless of the rest of the detection options.

reset: Resets all states on a given flow.

state_name: Used to uniquely identify the flowbit when the flowbit is set. This name is basically just a text string a user specifies (it can include periods, underscores, or dashes) that can be used by other rules when testing the flowbit.

group_name: Another text string that can include periods, underscores or dashes, this will group multiple flowbits together when possible. False positives can result based on the multiple flowbit associations being made. Since only one flowbit can be active at a time when associated to a group, using this option will cause one flowbit to become unset when another becomes active.

Byte_Jump/Test/Extract

The following arguments allow us to create more efficient rules by beefing up the Snort rules with the ability to find information within a packet when we don't know the location beforehand. These arguments can unearth stuff by looking at other information in the packet. Let's take a look at our three options.

Byte_Jump   The byte_jump argument allows us to move the inspection pointer from the configured number and find the value of those bytes, allowing us to skip data that's considered irrelevant in the packet.

Byte_Test   The byte_test option allows us to read bits and bytes and understand if they are less than, greater than, equal, or not equal to our specified value. This is typically used for determining if a packet has more data than an allowed buffer size for a given protocol.

Byte_Extract   The byte_extract option enables us to dissect a packet down into a series of bytes and create a variable that describes the resulting value, which can also be used somewhere else in the same rule. For example, if we extract the data field of the packet, instead of having to use the depth or within arguments, we can go with the variable created by the byte_extract option as an alternative.

Writing Rules

You may never find yourself actually having to write a Snort rule with the Cisco FireSIGHT System because it comes with plenty of default rules that are sufficient for many installations. And if that weren't enough, Cisco is busy updating the rules daily to cover the latest threats to your network.

Still, since you *can* write rules, why not have at it? Let's say you just happened to discover a zero-day attack... One must be prepared, right? Plus, writing rules is a productive way to have a little fun!

Here's a list of basic questions and guidelines that you should go through prior to writing a rule to be certain you're creating an efficient rule that's actually needed on your system. Let's go through this step-by-step:

1. Make sure you clearly identify the problem and understand if what you're dealing with really requires a new rule.

2. Capture the data from the suspected problem and make sure you can reproduce the problem. You can use using Snort, WinDump, or TCPDump to capture the traffic.

3. After you've captured the data, pay attention to any constraints in the network protocol that was captured too. For example, identify the protocol used with the traffic, the ports, and if it always originates from a specific network.

4. Make sure you can identify the traffic characteristics that the rule will generate an event against. For example, which identifiers will call out the traffic in question, and does the packet content have identifying strings? Also, do these factors always appear in the same place?

5. Once you gather all the information from steps 1 through 4, write a rule, using variables instead of static IP addresses whenever possible.

6. Verify your rule by implementing it and ensuring that it captures the suspicious traffic you were after in the first place.

Okay, now that you've got the basics down, let's build a rule using the GUI.

Using the System GUI to Build a Rule

The FireSIGHT graphical interface provides an easy-to-use rule building menu to help you write Snort rules. This interface allows you to build, edit, and import rules from the interface.

To gain access to the graphical rule builder, enter Policies ➢ Intrusion ➢ Rule Editor, as shown in Figure 13.5

FIGURE 13.5   Getting to the FireSIGHT graphical rule builder

Once you've chosen Rule Editor, choose Create Rule on the right side of the following screen, as shown in Figure 13.6.

FIGURE 13.6   Creating a rule

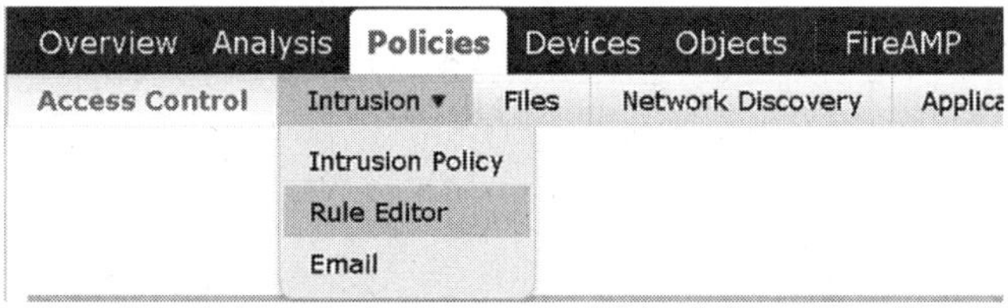

Looking again at the right side of Figure 13.6, you can see where you can delete local rules, import rules and create rules. Click the Create Rule button and you'll be taken to the screen shown in Figure 13.7, where a sample rule has already been configured and shown in the figure.

FIGURE 13.7   FireSIGHT graphical rule builder

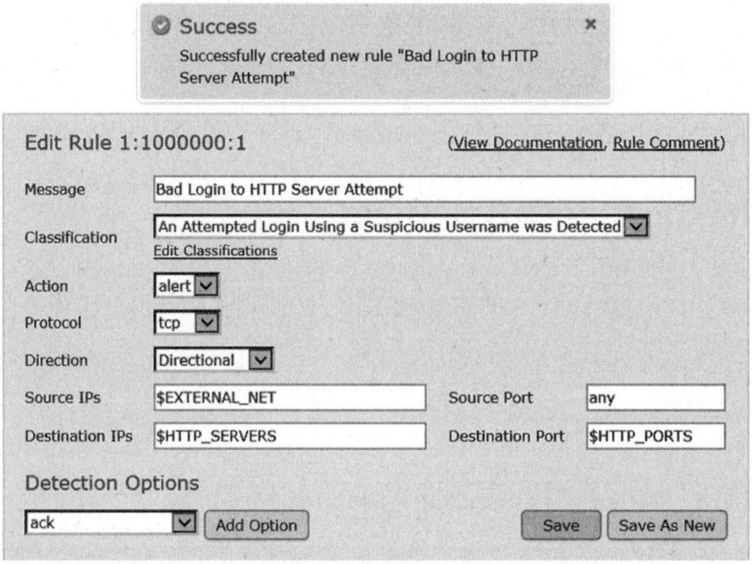

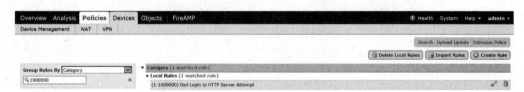

From here you can easily construct new rules by simply filling in the fields with the information you want and clicking Save. Notice that it saved the rule with a message that I used and that it also created rule 1000000.

Now, if you go back to Policies ➢ Intrusion ➢ Rule Editor, as shown in Figure 13.8, you can see we searched for Snort rule 1000000. From this screen we can edit or delete the rule. The 1000000:1 tells us this is revision 1 of the rule.

FIGURE 13.8   Finding your rule in the system

Don't forget! By default, the new rule is not active in any intrusion policy. Remember to edit an intrusion policy, set the new rule to Generate Events or Drop And Generate Events, then commit the policy changes and ensure that the Access Control policy on the test sensor has a rule that calls for the test traffic to be inspected by the intrusion policy where we just activated the rule.

You can import a rule you created in a text editor by clicking the Import Rules button. When you do that, you'll get the screen shown in Figure 13.9.

FIGURE 13.9 Importing a rule

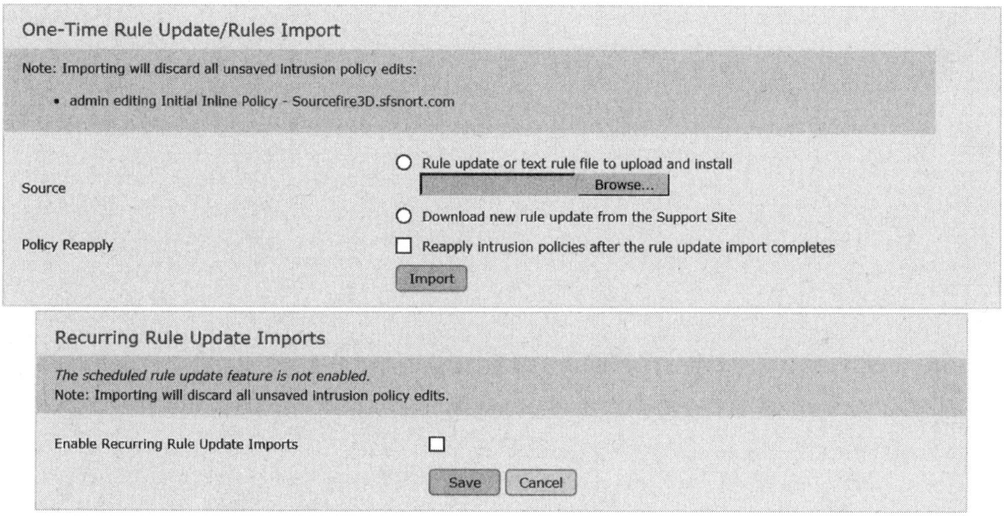

From this screen, you can import a rule, download a rule update from the Support Site, and even reapply the IPS policy after the rule update import completes. On the second part of the screen, you can schedule rule update imports, which will enable them to happen on a recurring basis.

Summary

This chapter began by providing you with an understanding of rule structure and rule syntax and then moved on to some basic rule options and arguments and covered how and when they're used.

We finished up by configuring and creating Snort rules using the Rule Editor in the system GUI, learning how to verify the rule in the system, and then finding out how to import an existing rule into the system.

Exam Essentials

Understand the rule header.   The rule header section details exactly how to match traffic based on the following factors:

- The rule's action or type
- The protocol
- The source and destination IP addresses and netmasks
- The directional operator that indicates the flow of traffic from source to destination
- The source and destination ports

Remember what the rule body includes.   The rule body comprises keywords and arguments that establish the criteria that must be met to trigger an alert. It includes event messages and the patterns a packet must match to trigger the rule as well as guidance on which part of the packet the IPS engine should inspect.

Review Questions

You can find the answers in Appendix A.

1. What are the two logical sections that make up a rule?
   A. Header and footer
   B. Header and body
   C. Message and body
   D. Content and body

2. If you want to set tags that can be referenced in subsequent rules, which argument do you use?
   A. msg
   B. fast_pattern
   C. byte_jump
   D. flowbits

3. Which argument allows us to skip data in the packet that is considered irrelevant to the inspection?
   A. fast_pattern
   B. flowbits
   C. byte_jump
   D. byte_extract

4. Which keyword or argument is used to quickly determine which rules a packet would qualify for further inspection by queuing the rules at the beginning of the detection engine that have the keyword content in them?
   A. fast_pattern
   B. flowbits
   C. cache
   D. byte_test

5. When you want a rule to trigger on service information instead of just IP and port information, what keyword can you can use?
   A. flowbits
   B. metadata
   C. fast_pattern
   D. file_data

6. Which of the following is *not* in the rule header?
   A. IP source/destination address
   B. Port source/destination address

    C. Metadata

    D. Directional operator

7. Which keyword is used to look in the data portion of the packets in the responses from HTTP, SMTP, POP, or IMAP servers?

    A. `file_data`

    B. `metadata`

    C. `detection_filter`

    D. `flowbits`

8. Which keyword is used to reduce the number of logged alerts for noisy rules?

    A. `byte_count`

    B. `metadata`

    C. `detection_filter`

    D. `file_data`

Chapter

14

FireSIGHT v5.4 Facts and Features

Last, but definitely not least, this key chapter covers the new features in FireSIGHT System v5.4 that launched in February 2015. Don't be fooled when you hear people refer to this release as a "point" upgrade because that's a serious understatement. Version 5.4 is a major-league upgrade with substantial new capabilities.

In addition to all the bright new features, the user interface has been updated significantly, rearranging where we make important changes. The settings themselves remain largely unchanged from previous versions but they've been moved in the user interface.

As of this writing, the SSFIPS test doesn't yet present questions on version 5.4, but we wouldn't be surprised if Cisco updated the exam and peppered it with a few questions about new features before the next major release. Version 6.X is currently slated to arrive late 2015, and of course, Cisco just might wait to modify the exam until after the new version hits. Either way, the exam isn't why we've included this chapter. Our first priority is to make sure you're familiar enough with version 5.4 to be completely capable of utilizing all of its cool new features. Being equipped to face down some 5.4-related questions in case they show up on the exam is just icing on the cake!

To find up-to-the-minute updates for this chapter, please see www.lammle.com/firepower or the book's web page at www.sybex.com.

Branding

As the product evolves further into the Cisco fold, we're actually witnessing the original Sourcefire brand's extinction. This process is apparent right from the start at the login page displayed in Figure 14.1.

See that? The Sourcefire logo in the top left has been replaced with Cisco's Golden Gate Bridge, also the favicon on the browser tab is now the Cisco logo. What's more, the Cisco TAC support numbers are placed right there alongside the legacy Sourcefire numbers. A search of the 5.4 Help reveals but a few lingering references to Sourcefire, and many of these actually refer back to the old support site: support.sourcefire.com, shuttered in late May 2015. Even after logging in, we're greeted with the Cisco logo in the lower right corner of each page, exactly where the old Sourcefire logo used to be! So, yes… these moves present sound evidence that we can expect these things to become part of the Sourcefire fossil record at some point instead of being included in future versions of the FireSIGHT System. With all this in mind, let's heed the writing on the wall and explore what's new and improved in version 5.4 now.

FIGURE 14.1   5.4 Login screen

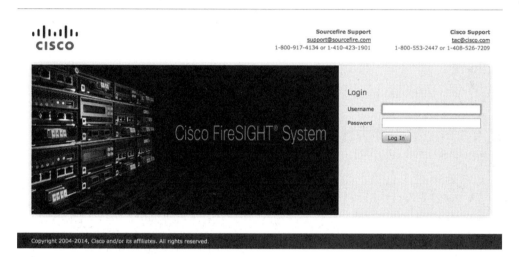

Simplified IPS Policy

We'll start with briefly calling out the simplified intrusion policy. Over the years, the designers of the Sourcefire System have continually updated the interface to make the complex mission of configuring Snort easier. This is no easy task. There are numerous knobs to turn in the IPS policy, and back in the day each Snort configuration item didn't even come linked with a hierarchy or any other kind of simplified way of viewing them. It took a while for the advanced settings in the intrusion policy to get moved into their own area, complete with a more user-friendly view for those who didn't need to dig into the gory details of preprocessor settings!

With the genesis of 5.4, Cisco has taken this arrangement a step further by pulling almost all of the advanced settings out of the intrusion policy, making the policy pretty much just Snort rules now. Where previous versions had nearly three dozen items under Advanced Settings, this version has only four, as shown in Figure 14.2.

And as you can see, only the Rules, Policy Layers, and FireSIGHT Recommendations sections remain unchanged.

FIGURE 14.2 5.4 IPS Advanced Settings

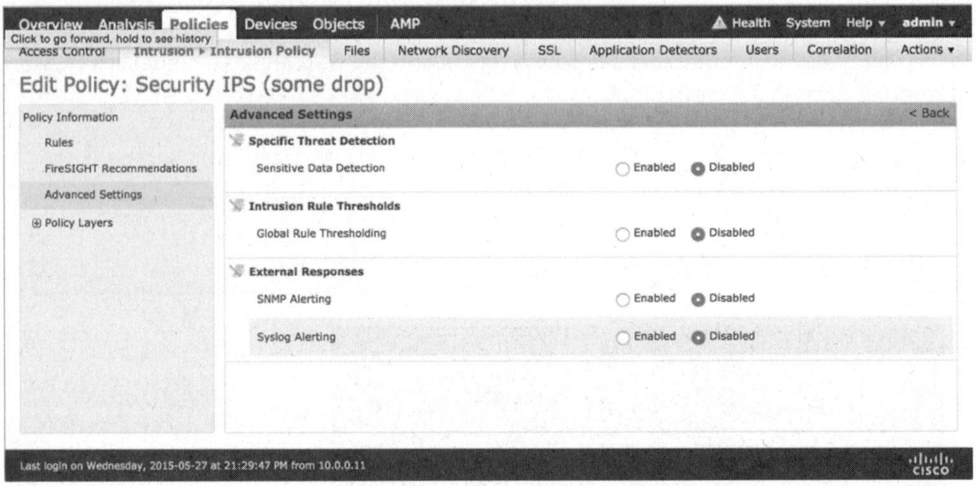

Network Analysis Policy

So do we lose a whole bunch of control because most of the advanced settings have been removed from the intrusion policy? Of course not! All of those settings have simply relocated to different places in the user interface, and one of these new locales just happens to be under a totally new policy called the network analysis policy. Yes, you read that right—as if we didn't have enough policies already, version 5.4 has added two brand-new ones: SSL and network analysis.

The design on the interface seems to just scream that the network analysis policy was meant to be hard to find. There's not even a menu item for it! But people still may need to get to it, and when you do, you'll have to do a little digging. A little direction will help… One way to navigate to this policy is to sneak in by first viewing the IPS policies at Policies ➢ Intrusion ➢ Intrusion Policy. From this page, you can see a Network Analysis Policy link in the upper right. Another way to find the Network Analysis Policy link is when you're viewing the main Access Control Policy list at Policies ➢ Access Control. Maybe Cisco will stop hiding this in future iterations, but for now, it's still curiously absent from the main Policies menu.

Anyway, click on the Network Analysis Policy link to get to the Network Analysis Policy list shown in Figure 14.3.

You've accessed the standard policy management interface with its Report, Edit, and Delete icons for each policy as well as the compare button above.

If you upgrade to 5.4 from a previous version, the system will automatically create a network analysis policy for each of your existing IPS policies. The advanced settings within each earlier intrusion policy will be included in the corresponding network analysis policy.

FIGURE 14.3   5.4 Network Analysis Policy list

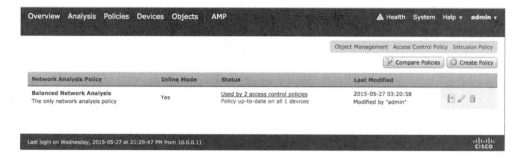

When you create a new network analysis policy, it will bring up a similar dialog to the one presented during IPS policy creation (Figure 14.4). The Name and Description fields are standard. The dialog box also includes an Inline Mode check box. Checking the Inline Mode box allows preprocessors such as Inline Normalization to make changes to packets or drop them.

FIGURE 14.4   5.4 Network analysis policy creation

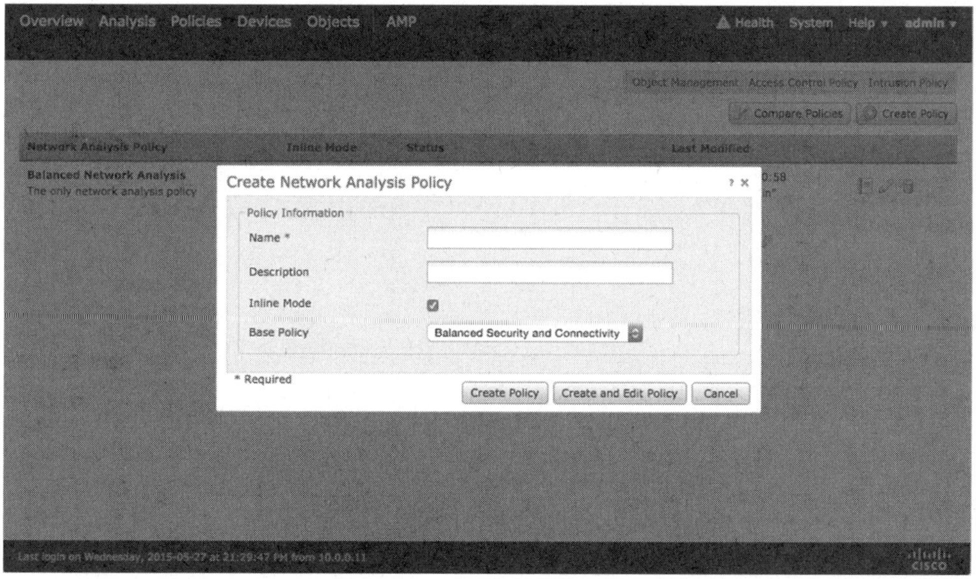

The Base Policy drop-down list (Figure 14.5) allows you to pick any of the Cisco standard base policies or a custom network analysis policy. Just so you know, layers work the same way in network analysis as they do in intrusion policy.

FIGURE 14.5 5.4 Network analysis base policy

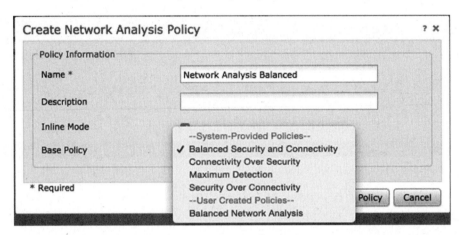

The network analysis policy main configuration page (Figure 14.6) looks like someone cut out part of the intrusion policy and moved it here. That's because they did. This nice, familiar view includes Policy Layers plus all those AWOL advanced settings from the intrusion policy configuration.

FIGURE 14.6 Edit network analysis policy

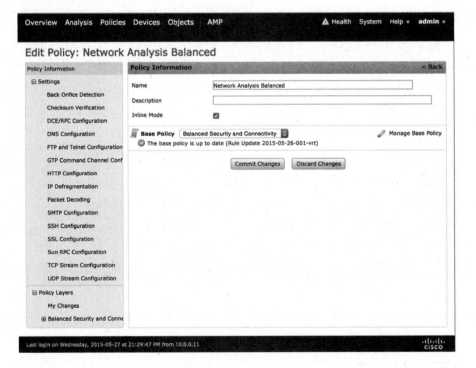

Why Network Analysis?

So moving all those advanced settings into another policy is really just a handy way to simplify intrusion policy editing, right? Definitely, but there's more to it than that. The other big important reason for doing this has to do with the way Snort performs preprocessing. Both the IPS and network analysis policies analyze traffic and are invoked by the access control policy. Traffic is processed first according to the network analysis policy (preprocessors) and then by the intrusion policy (Snort rules). By separating the two policies, we can apply the preprocessor normalization and detection features to traffic separately from the IPS rules! We'll tell you exactly how that works by exploring access control policy next.

Access Control Policy

To implement powerful features like network analysis and SSL decryption, the access control policy was updated in version 5.4. Most of the changes can be found on the Advanced tab while editing a policy. Figure 14.7 shows the new Advanced tab.

FIGURE 14.7   Access Control advanced settings

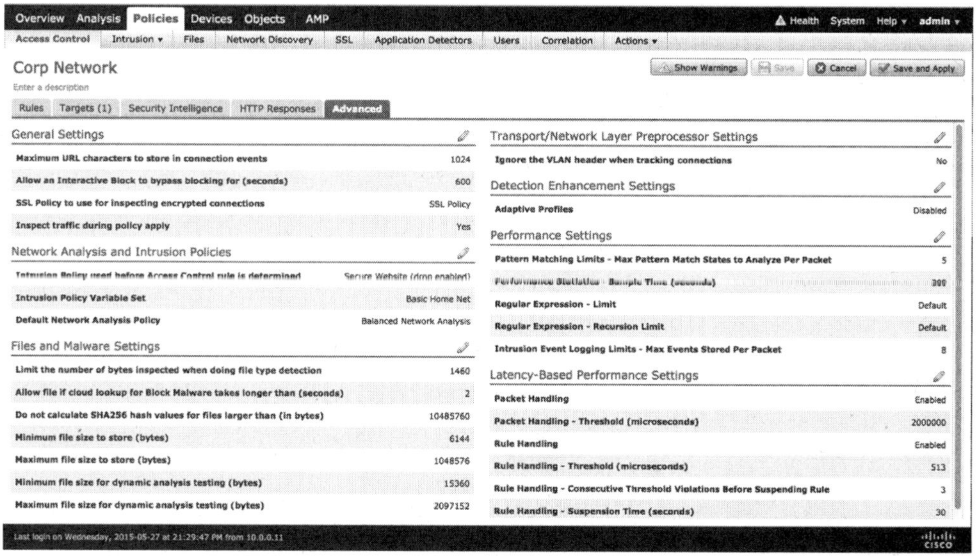

Wow—there's a lot more settings on this screen than in previous versions, so let's take a look at each of these sections and see what's new!

General Settings

Clicking the pencil icon by General Settings will load the dialog box shown in Figure 14.8.

FIGURE 14.8   General Settings

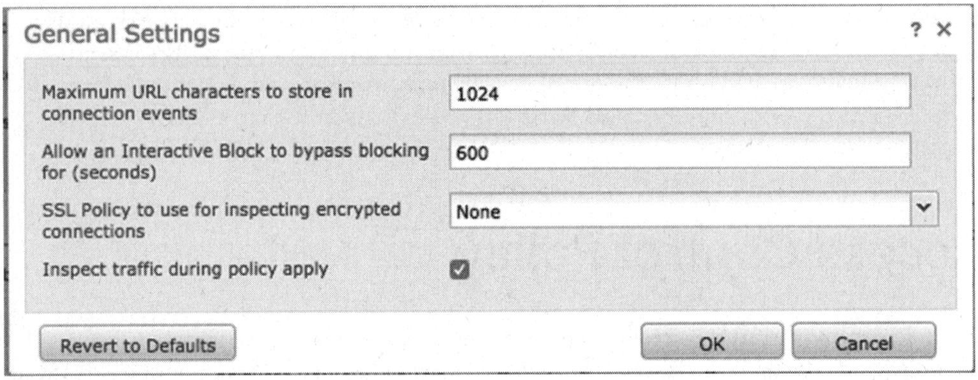

There are two new items we should talk about here: SSL Policy To Use For Inspecting Encrypted Connections and Inspect Traffic During Policy Apply.

SSL Policy To Use For Inspecting Encrypted Connections   As you might expect, this is what you need to set for inspecting encrypted connections. It's pretty straightforward—you just choose how you want to decrypt SSL. Leaving the default value of None in place disables SSL decryption.

Inspect Traffic During Policy Apply   This setting actually resuscitates a feature from version 4.X. The setting has to do with whether or not the device will continue to process traffic with the current Access Control policy while it's loading the new one when in inline mode.

If the box is unchecked, an inline IPS system will allow uninspected traffic to pass while the new policy is loading. If you leave it in its checked, default state, the system won't allow any uninspected traffic to pass during a policy apply. Now, according to the system Help, sticking with that default can result in a "brief disruption" of traffic during a policy apply. This is a huge hint—if you like connectivity just a little bit more than security, you should uncheck this box.

Network Analysis and Intrusion Policies

The Network Analysis and Intrusion Policies section pictured in Figure 14.9 is totally new to version 5.4:

Let's talk about all the settings here.

FIGURE 14.9   Network Analysis and Intrusion Policies

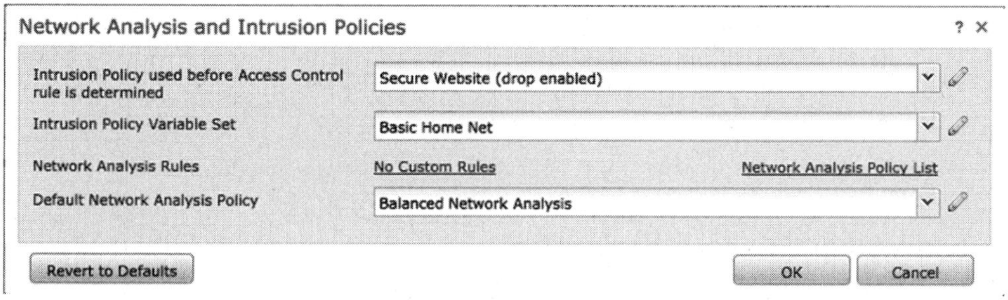

Intrusion Policy Used Before Access Control Rule Is Determined   Sometimes the system has to process a few packets and allow them to pass before it can determine which Access Control rule applies to the connection. For instance, if a rule is designed to block a particular URL, the packets preceding the URL must be allowed. This handy little setting allows you to choose an intrusion policy to inspect that allowed traffic until the proper Access Control rule is settled on.

Intrusion Policy Variable Set   This simply refers to the variable set used with the intrusion policy specified above.

Network Analysis Rules   There are two links under this heading. Opting for the one on the right called Network Analysis Policy List simply takes you to the list of network analysis policies.

Clicking No Custom Rules loads the dialog box shown in Figure 14.10.

FIGURE 14.10   Network analysis custom rules

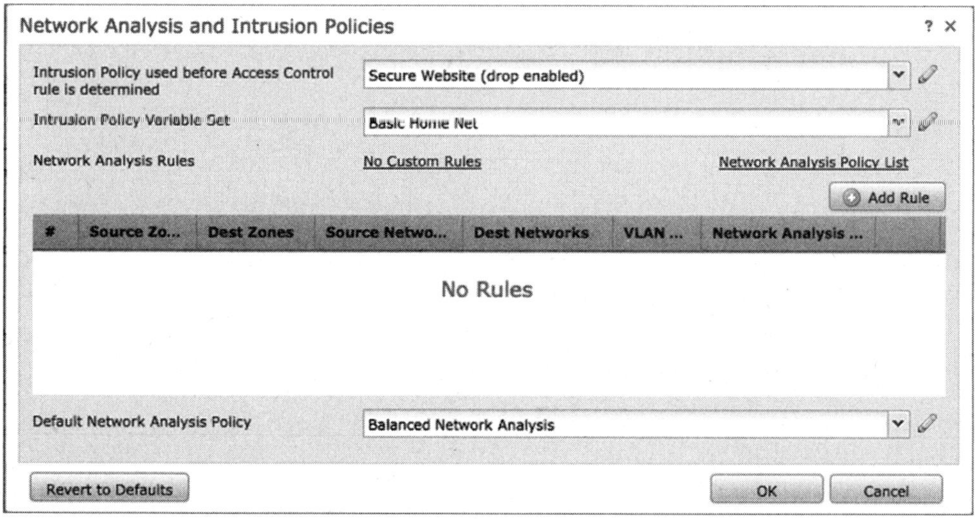

Here's where you can create custom rules to direct traffic to specific network analysis policies. Traffic can be selected based on zone, IP, VLAN ID, or a combination of these. Predictably, once rules are created, the link changes from No Custom Rules to displaying the number of custom rules that have been created. The same created rule count will also be displayed back on the Advanced tab under the Network Analysis and Intrusion Policies section.

Default Network Analysis Policy   This determines which Network Analysis Policy to implement if there aren't any custom rules or if none of the custom rules match the traffic flow.

Files and Malware Settings

These settings are unchanged from version 5.3.

Transport/Network Layer Preprocessor Settings

At first glance it looks like this section only has one item in it... Not so fast! As usual, clicking that pencil reveals more—in this case, the dialog box shown in Figure 14.11

FIGURE 14.11   Transport/Network Layer Preprocessor Settings

Transport/Network Layer Preprocessor Settings	? ✕
Ignore the VLAN header when tracking connections	☐
Maximum Active Responses	No Limit
Minimum Response Seconds	No Limit
Troubleshooting Options	▲
Session Termination Logging Threshold	1048576
Revert to Defaults	OK Cancel

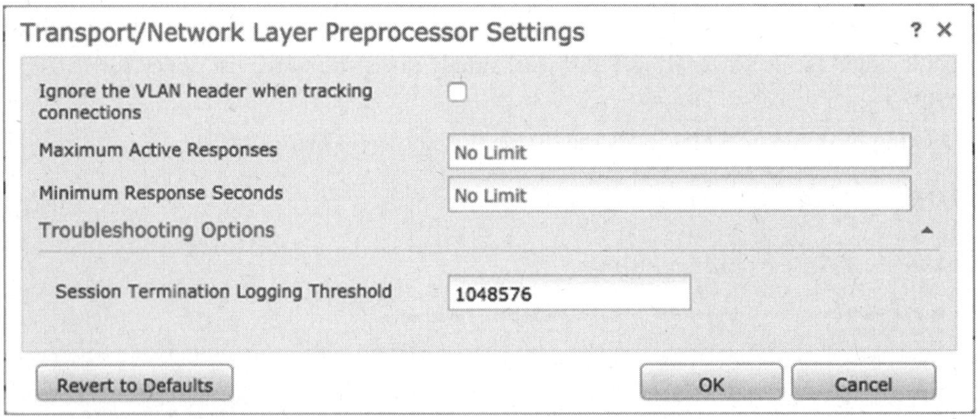

You probably noticed that these settings aren't really new. They're transplanted from the intrusion policy advanced view and are also unchanged from their Version 5.3 counterparts.

Detection Enhancement Settings

Clicking the pencil by this item reveals the configuration dialog box shown in Figure 14.12.
These settings are also transplants from the intrusion policy in previous versions. They work the same way as well.

FIGURE 14.12   Detection Enhancement Settings

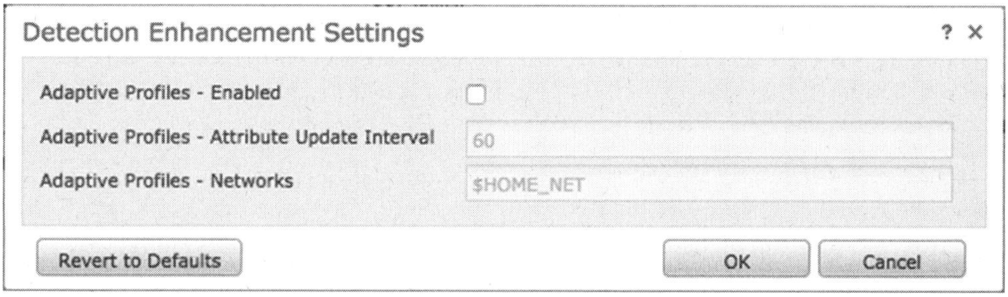

Performance/Latency Settings

Again, clicking the pencil icons by Performance Settings or Latency-Based Performance Settings loads the corresponding configuration dialog. And just as it was with the last few settings, these are also version 5.3 intrusion policy transplants with their functionality remaining unchanged for the most part. The only thing that's different is that they can once again be disabled if desired.

SSL Inspection

A major difference between versions 5.3 and 5.4 has to do with SSL decryption. Starting with v5.4, Cisco supports decryption and inspection of SSL and TLS traffic through the Series 3 FirePOWER hardware devices. This new inspection capacity can be used to carry out some important tasks like verifying if traffic is genuine based on the inspection of certificates and discerning if traffic is coming from and headed to valid sources. V5.4 can also decrypt traffic to make way for IPS inspection. The types of encryption supported are SSL v3 and TLS v1.0, v1.1, and v1.2.

The task of traffic decryption can be handled in several ways, with one scenario focused on the traffic coming into your network. By loading a server's private encryption key into the Defense Center, you can decrypt the traffic and perform full IPS and file inspection.

Another traffic decryption method is the re-sign option for inspecting outbound SSL traffic. It works like this: A user makes a request to a site. Based on your SSL policy, the managed device intercepts the request and issues a provided certificate to initiate a session with the user. The device itself then establishes an encrypted session with the original target. To prevent the user from getting certificate mismatch errors in their browser, you would sign the device certificate using a certificate authority trusted by your users' web browsers.

SSL Objects

SSL policy controls which traffic to decrypt and what action to take if traffic cannot be decrypted. This is used in conjunction with IPS, file and access control polices you configured earlier. In addition, there are new object types added to support SSL rules. Three object types were added in v5.4:

> Private keys that are uploaded to the Defense Center manager are encrypted with a randomly generated key before they are stored.

Cipher Suite List   You can choose from the ciphers populating this list and use them as matching criteria in your rules, but you can't add to the list of the ciphers—only Cisco can do that! But you still get to create your own object that can comprise all of the Cisco predefined types, or just subsets of the ones you want to highlight. This is shown in Figure 14.13.

FIGURE 14.13   Creating a cipher suite list

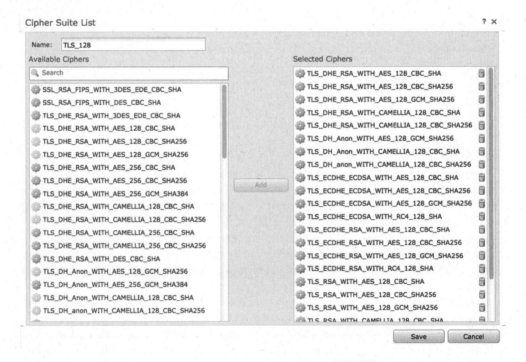

Distinguished Name   We can also create distinguished name objects (Figure 14.14) to deploy in rules where the DN in the certificates used during session negotiation matches the DN of the site users are visiting. This is great for simply controlling the traffic to and from specific websites. It also comes in handy when you want to sort the things you want to decrypt from stuff you don't. There are four factors you can specify during DN object creation:

- Country Code (C)
- Common Name (CN)
- Organization (O)
- Organizational Unit (OU)

FIGURE 14.14   Creating a distinguished name object

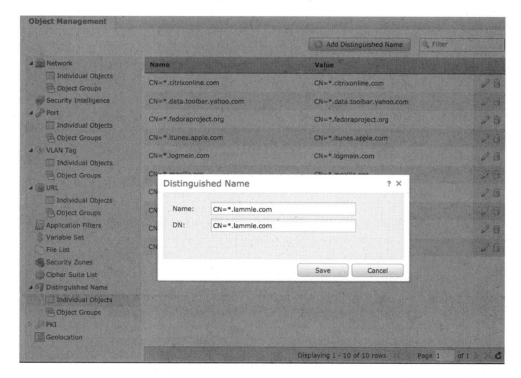

The fields other than Country Code can contain up to 64 characters. The use of wildcards such as * is supported, but only in a specific field. For example, `CN="*ammle.com"` would match `lammle.com` but *not* `www.lammle.com` or `lammle.co.com`.

You can also create a DN object group—a collection of individual DN objects for use in rules, as shown in Figure 14.15.

FIGURE 14.15 Distinguished name object group

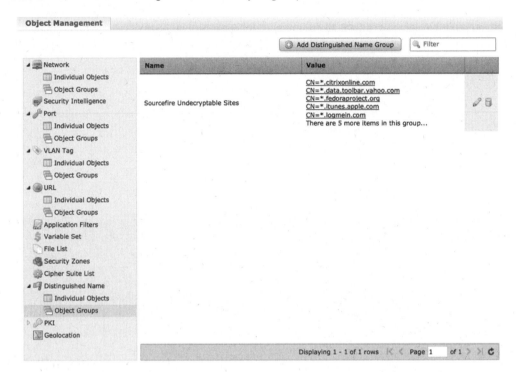

PKI These objects allow you to add public key certificates and private keys for your SSL inspection. Under this section, there are four items you can add:

Internal CAs These are made up of a certificate and private key and used to inspect incoming traffic as well as to resign out going traffic.

Trusted CA Comprising the public certificate of an external certificate authority or one in a chain of trust, trusted CAs are used for matching traffic.

External Certs These contain the public certificate for a site and are also used for matching traffic.

Internal Certs Comprising a certificate and private key and used to inspect incoming traffic.

Another option is to add group objects for the above types of objects. And just so you know, there's already a number of trusted CAs in the system for our convenience. Check out Figure 14.16.

FIGURE 14.16 Trusted CA objects

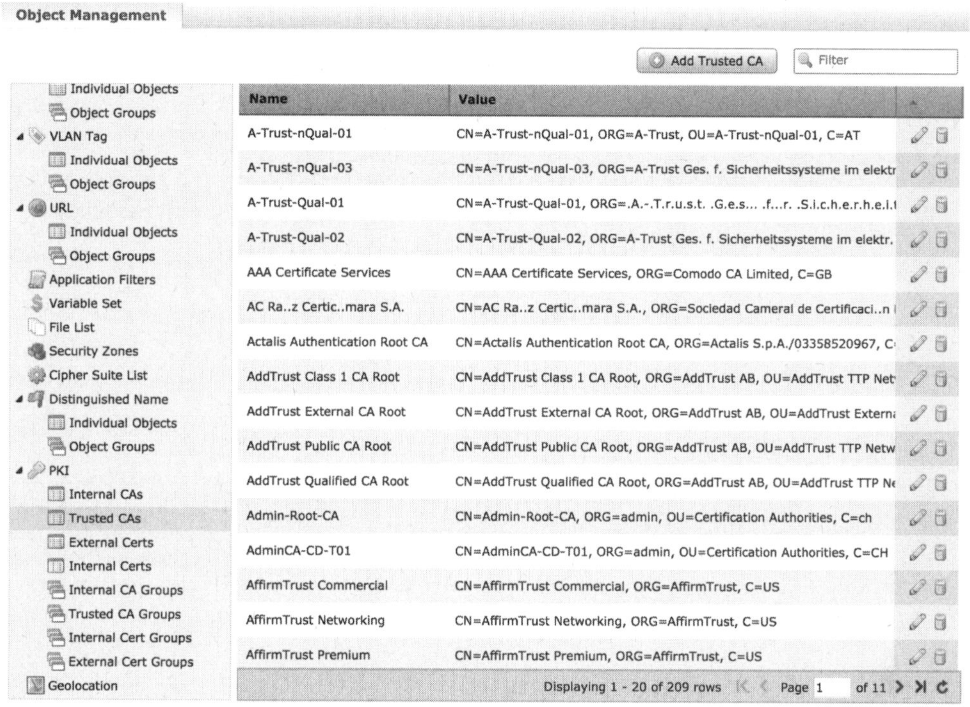

SSL Policies

So, to control the SSL activity, you need to leverage the new SSL policy. This works in conjunction with the Access Control policy. You must specify the SSL policy in the advanced tab of the Access Control policy. Once you do, your traffic is then evaluated by both. Know that the SSL policy must be created from scratch, and the option to do that is found under the SSL Policy tab as seen in Figure 14.17.

FIGURE 14.17 SSL Policy tab

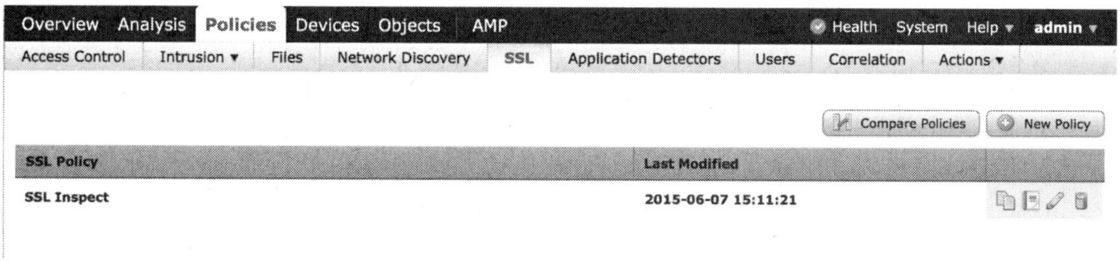

Once you've created an SSL policy, you can add rules specifying the actions to take based on an array of conditions, similar to creating an AC policy. The SSL policy offers these three tabs, shown in Figure 14.18:

Rules—Here's where you would place the specific rules for controlling the SSL traffic.

Trusted CA Certificates—Allows you to add trusted certificate authorities from a pre-built list. You can also add to the list.

Undecryptable Actions—Allows you to determine what will happen if the system can't decrypt the traffic under certain conditions. Your choices are to inherit the default action for the policy, Do Not Decrypt, Block, or Block With Reset.

FIGURE 14.18   SSL policy

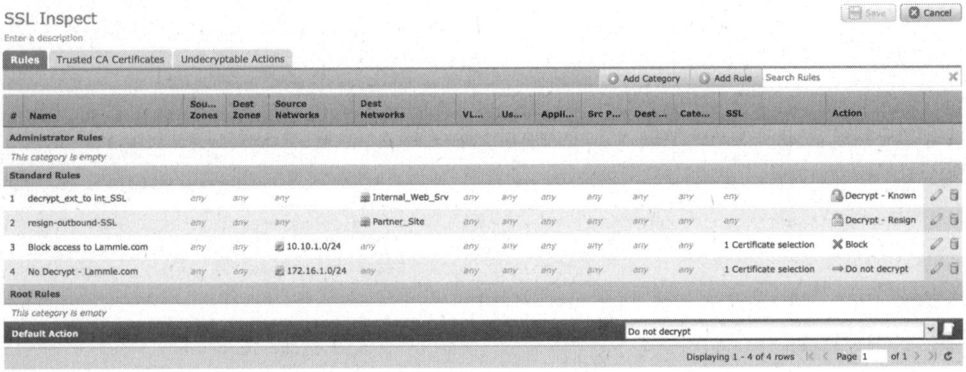

SSL INSPECT RULES

When adding an SSL rule (like the one shown in 14.19), you can apply the following six actions:

Decrypt – Resign This will decrypt the traffic and re-sign with the specified key from a CA.

Decrypt – Known Key This will decrypt the traffic with the private key of the target server.

Do Not Decrypt This allows the traffic to pass through without performing any decryption.

Block This is the same as in the access control policy.

Block With Reset This is the same as in the access control policy.

Monitor Allows the traffic to be tracked, but takes no further action. In an SSL policy, traffic will be evaluated against subsequent rules until there's a match.

FIGURE 14.19   SSL rule

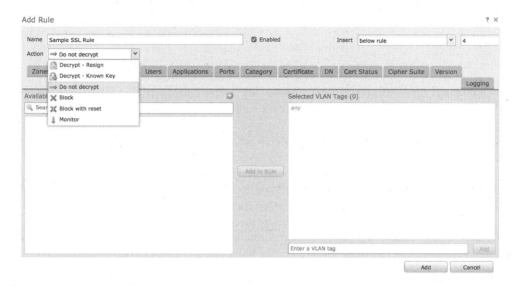

As far as matching criteria goes, we get to enjoy all the same options that we had before with AC rules, plus five additional features:

Certificate: Allows us to specify a certificate to be used by a server to negotiate an SSL session.

DN: The DN of the certificate used to negotiate a session.

Cert Status: The status of the certificate being passed—revoked, self-signed, valid, expired, etc.

Cipher Suite: Which ciphers to match.

Version: The encryption version to look for. Supported versions include: SSLv3, TLS v1.0, TLS v1.1, and TLS v1.2.

There are a couple of parameters needed when you're adding decrypt rules that will tell the system exactly how you want it to handle the task. When going with Decrypt – Known Key (Figure 14.20), you've got to specify the certificate to use to decrypt, which is something you added through the objects.

FIGURE 14.20   Decrypt – Known Key

When opting for Decrypt – Resign (Figure 14.21), you need to specify the key to re-sign the traffic with and indicate that's what you want to happen by checking the box.

FIGURE 14.21   Decrypt – Resign

Understand that when you're using these rules, you're basically telling the system what to do with SSL traffic, so tread thoughtfully here because your choices can have a not-so-subtle impact on the system's overall performance. Again, it's really tempting to take no chances whatsoever, go all in, and decrypt absolutely everything you can! That's probably a very bad idea and rarely, if ever, necessary. Instead, proceed by implementing a wise, strategic decryption approach that targets specific factors that are likely sources of trouble in your particular environment. At this writing, performance values haven't yet been published, but any individual implementation is bound to have a direct impact. So choose carefully—there are many variables impacting performance, including traffic throughput, intrusion policy, discovery policy, number of sessions to decrypt, and so on. It's difficult to quantify the direct impact that SSL inspection will have in a given environment, but one thing is for sure—there's certain to be one!

New Rule Keywords

Now, we're going to talk about two new important Snort rule keywords that were added as part of this update: `file_type` and `protected_content`.

File_type

This new keyword gives rule writers the ability to identify the type of file a given rule should apply to. Snort recognizes "magic patterns" to determine the file type, which are actually unmagical but distinctive byte values that specific files with similar formats have in common. For example, all GIF files will begin with the fixed value GIF followed by the version (87a or 89a).

File type identification was previously achieved via flowbit rules, but it required a whole crew of rules to detect various file types.

The process is a lot cleaner using the `file_type` keyword instead because now you can write rules that only evaluate packets if they're pieces of a certain kind of file. The syntax looks like

```
file_type: <FILE_TYPE>;
where FILE_TYPE is <TYPE>[·<VERSION>][|<FILE_TYPE>]
```

Here are a few examples:

- Detecting a PDF document:
  ```
  file_type:PDF;
  ```

- Detecting a specific PDF version:
  ```
  file_type:PDF,1.6;
  ```

- Detecting multiple PDF versions:
  ```
  file_type:PDF,1.6,1.7;
  ```

Protected_content

The `protected_content` option is designed to allow searching for content in a packet without having to spell out that content in a rule. This comes in particularly handy when you want to search for sensitive text while hiding it from anyone else with access to the rule. It's helpful if you're looking for things like passwords you've used.

The way it works is elegantly simple: Just enter the hash value of the string you're hunting instead of the content itself, using an MD5, SHA256, or SHA512 hash to specify your secret content.

The syntax for this keyword is

```
protected_content:[!]"<content hash>"; length:orig_len[;
hash:md5|sha256|sha512];
```

It's vital to remember that unlike a simple content check, this keyword must contain a `length` parameter. This is because Snort hashes the specified bytes in the packet and compares them to the hash in the rule. So you can't search through an entire packet using the `protected_content` keyword. Doing so would be too computationally expensive, requiring numerous hash operations on each packet!

Here's an example for you—the following rule is set to find the string "HTTP" at offset 10 in the packet:

```
alert tcp any any <> any 80 (msg:"MD5 Alert";
protected_content:"293C9EA246FF9985DC6F62A650F78986"; hash:md5; offset:10;
length:4; sid:1000005;)
```

Platform Enhancements

Version 5.4 also offers some sweet new benefits like VMware Tools Support, which means we can now use VMware Tools with FireSIGHT virtual appliances for improved manageability.

Also new is VMXnet3 support on virtual appliances, interface types that pave the way for high-speed interfaces up to 10 Gbps on virtual appliances.

Three other platform enhancements are as follows:

- The new Multiple Management Interfaces feature permits the configuration of multiple management interfaces on Defense Centers. This lets us split event traffic and management traffic between two interfaces if we want to.

- LACP Support arms devices to take part in Link Aggregation Control Protocol (LACP) negotiation and aggregate multiple links in switched or routed mode.

- Defense Center 2000 and Defense Center 4000 replace the DC1500 and DC3500, respectively. They're both based on the Cisco UCS (Unified Computing System) platform, but the DC4000 provides more than double the performance of the DC3500.

International Enhancements

As our world becomes more globalized, the ability to fine-tune security to meet the realities of a more complex and multifaceted marketplace is becoming increasingly important for all of us. Features like Unicode support strengthen the system with the capacity to display the names of files detected via malware detection, file detection, and FireAMP file events. It supports the display of non-Western characters, including those that are double-byte encoded.

Employing geolocation and Security Intelligence in correlation rules lets us create correlation rules based on geolocation and Security Intelligence data. For example, this allows admins to alert on an Impact 1 intrusion event from a particular country if desired.

Support for FireAMP private cloud fortifies the Defense Center to connect to a FireAMP private cloud instead of a public cloud. This requires the installation of the private cloud virtual appliance.

Minor Changes

Here's a list of refinements that may not be quite as impressive, but they're still important enough for us to tell you about them:

- The list of performance graphs on the Intrusion Event Graphs page (Overview ➤ Summary ➤ Intrusion Event Graphs) has been significantly expanded.

- Expanded IoC support now allows dynamic, data driven updates. Also, as new FireAMP Connector IoCs become available, they'll be automatically supported by the Defense Center.

- User logins can now be detected over FTP, HTTP, and MDNS protocols.

- The User Statistics dashboard is now called Access Controlled User Statistics. The widgets are the same, only the name has changed.

- Inline normalization is automatically enabled when you create a network analysis policy with inline mode enabled. This only applies to new policies—the setting isn't modified in policies if upgrading from 5.3.

- We can now configure LDAP authentication to use Common Access Cards (CACs) and allow users to log in to the system directly using the card.

Summary

Version 5.4 of the FireSIGHT System brings an awesome bounty of new and updated features to the Cisco NGIPS. Even though this information isn't on the current SSFIPS exam yet, we were excited enough about all the new version's powerful new features that we just had to fill you in and tell you all about them. We hope you've had fun during this preview and that we've equipped you with enough of the details to hit the ground running with v5.4!

Appendix

Answers to Review Questions

Chapter 1

1. B

Virtual appliances can be deployed passively or inline but do not support switched or routed interfaces.

2. A

Both Defense Center and device appliances use the default login of **admin/Sourcefire**.

3. D

Options A, B, and C are methods available for configuring an appliance management IP address.

4. B

The Control license enables application control functionality, allowing the device to become an NGFW. Options A and B would also be a correct answer because a Control license requires a Protect license.

5. A

A Malware license requires that a Protect license be enabled on the device.

6. C

A VPN license requires both the Protect and Control licenses to be enabled on the device.

Chapter 2

1. D

Each of these methods is supported for populating custom file lists.

2. A

Only option A contains the string matching the object. Note that option B is a secure protocol, so the URL will not match regardless.

3. C

Network objects can contain IP addresses, CIDR blocks, or a mixture of both.

4. A

Valid security zone types are inline, passive, routed, switched, and ASA.

5. B

Application types include application protocol, web application, and client.

6. C

Security zones can be configured in either Objects ➢ Object Management or Devices ➢ Device Management.

7. A

These two Security Intelligence lists are only populated by right-clicking on an IP address in an analysis view. Editing the object only allows removing addresses from the lists.

8. D

Options A, B, and C are true regarding the Default Set.

9. D

VLAN tag objects cannot contain comma-separated lists of VLAN IDs.

10. B

Business relevance is the likelihood that an application will be relevant to your business versus used for recreation. Low business relevance means time spent using the application will likely not be productive to the business. A weaker argument could also be made for risk because a high-risk application could host malware and therefore impact productivity.

Chapter 3

1. B

Balanced Security and Connectivity is a well-performing policy in terms of latency and security.

2. C

Policy layers allow for multiple configurations. The configurations can be shared across IPS policies.

3. A

When you modify your policy, an icon will appear in the user interface by the Policy Information section indicating that the policy should be saved. When you click in the Policy Information section, the Commit Changes button will appear at the bottom.

4. D

The rule states are Disable (to turn the rule off), Generate Events (to send an alert to the DC), and Drop and Generate Events (to send an event to the DC and drop the traffic).

5. A

Rule thresholding allows you to control the number of alerts based on either the source or destination IP address.

6. D

The default layers of a policy include the My Changes layer and the base policy layer. If FireSIGHT recommendations have been generated, they will appear above the base policy layer.

7. C

The default rule overhead setting is Medium.

8. B

Policies are exported in a binary format. They can be imported into another FSM assuming they are on the same software version.

9. D

Reports can be generated to document all the settings of the policy. The reports are saved as PDF files.

10. A

The Drop When Inline check box controls whether or not the IPS rules drop traffic or not. The rules in the policy have an option to drop and alert if the traffic is found.

Chapter 4

1. A

These alerts are sent from the device.

2. A

Allow rules are used to let traffic pass while inspecting via IPS/file policies.

3. D

Interactive Block will return an HTTP response page allowing the user to click Continue and bypass the block if desired.

4. D

Addresses can be added to the global blacklist and whitelist by right-clicking on an IP in an event view or clicking a graph in the Context Explorer.

5. D

For source ports, only TCP and UDP are allowed. For destination ports, many additional IP protocols can be selected.

6. D

The default is to store 1024 URL characters; this is configurable on the Advanced tab.

7. D

While this could be done with an Interactive Block rule (C), doing so would also allow the user to override the block if desired.

8. C

Only the Monitor rule action does not provide for any trusting, blocking, or inspection of traffic.

9. C

You can select one or more existing objects, enter IP addresses. or even add objects on-the-fly.

10. A

You can apply an Access Control policy to as many devices as you want, but only one policy can be deployed per device.

Chapter 5

1. B

When you configure the discovery policy, you would limit the IP addresses monitored to prevent the system from using all the discovery licenses. If not, the policy does not limit the discovery and you will record information about hosts outside of your network that are probably not relevant to your security.

2. C

Active Directory logins are read via an agent installed on a Windows host. This agent would connect to the AD server and read the security logs.

3. C

Both IPv4 and IPv6 addresses can be used. The default discovery networks are 0.0.0.0/0 and its IPv6 equivalent ::/0

4. D

The two built-in attributes are notes and host criticality.

5. A

The discovery component of FireSIGHT enables the system to collect information on hosts (including applications, services, and OS identification), connections (including flow information), and users (user ID and login information).

6. D

The host profile displays all information about a host. It can be accessed by clicking on the computer icon next to an IP address, by drilling into a network map, or by drilling into Analysis ➤ Hosts.

7. B

To view the summary of your traffic, you can go to Overview ➤ Dashboard ➤ Connection Summary. Alternately, you can go to Overview ➤ Summary ➤ Connection Summary.

8. B

The LDAP-specific parameters are base DN, base filter, user name, and password / confirm password. The UI access attribute is part of the attribute mapping configuration.

9. D

User discovery can take place for the following protocols: AIM, IMAP, LDAP, Oracle, POP3, SIP, and Active Directory.

10. A

The attributes that can be user-defined are text, URL, list, and integer attributes. Creating a whitelist will also insert an attribute.

Chapter 6

1. A

Events by Priority and Classification is the default intrusion workflow.

2. B

The expanding time window starts at a fixed point and always stops at Now. This causes it to constantly grow.

3. D

Clicking on a source IP address loads the next workflow page with just the packet(s) from that source IP. If the workflow has a table view, the packet view page always follows.

4. B

Flexible searches with multiple search criteria is a feature of the Context Explorer.

5. C

Impact 2 indicates the source or destination host is in the network map and is running a server application on the port.

6. B

Because a suppression only suppresses the event output, if used for a drop rule in an inline configuration, the rule will continue to silently drop matching traffic.

7. C

Thresholds can be set on rules to prevent them from alerting until they match a select number of packets.

8. B

Multiple packets are downloaded as zip archives, single packets are in libpcap format.

9. D

Copying is used to copy event data for use in the incident management function.

10. B

False positives are to be expected. A critical part of tuning is locating and eliminating false positives as much as possible.

Chapter 7

1. D

From the Network Trajectory Page search text box, you can search for a file by SHA-256 hash, filename, or host IP.

2. A

All of the options are elements in this context box except SHA-256.

3. D

Spero analysis involves evaluating hundreds of file attributes, including headers, DLLs called, and other metadata.

4. A

Malware inspection for POP3 is only supported for file downloads.

5. D

File and malware inspection are controlled by the file policy.

6. D

From the Network Trajectory Page search text box, you can search for a file by SHA-256 hash, filename, or host IP.

7. B

While you can get there eventually from the Files dashboard, the fastest way is via the Context Explorer.

8. C

File policy is applied to traffic via an Allow, Interactive Block, or Interactive Block with Reset rule in the Access Control policy.

9. D

Dispositions returned from the cloud are clean, unknown, and malware.

10. A

Dynamic Analysis is the only method that requires uploading the actual file to the cloud for analysis. It often takes 10 minutes or more because the file must be executed. Files are uploaded directly from the device, and only MSEXE file types are supported.

Chapter 8

1. C

User Preferences allow individuals to change their password and set default workflows, time zone preferences, and default home screens.

2. B

The database settings under System Configuration allow the administrator to enable external database connectivity.

3. A

When enabled, Change Reconciliation will email a report every 24 hours showing any change that has taken place within the FSM's configuration.

4. B

If these storage options are enabled, you can store backups and reports remotely. The protocols that are supported are NFS, SMB, and SSH.

5. C

The language preferences are limited to US English and Japanese.

6. D

The time preferences can be set in the system policy. The available options are manually from system settings, NTP from an NTP server, or NTP from the Defense Center.

7. B

Health policies are set to run every 5 minutes by default. This can be changed in the health policy.

8. D

The red would indicate that a Critical threshold has been met in a health policy.

9. A

The Blacklist tab allows you to set up exclusions to health checks. You can blacklist an entire device or individual counters.

10. A

With Health Monitor alerts, you can send email, SNMP traps, and syslog messages. These will allow you to get immediate notification in case your console is not being monitored 24/7.

Chapter 9

1. E

When you choose to configure permission escalation, all user roles are available to escalate to. Choose the user role that matches the rights that the user needs when escalating.

2. B

Out of the options listed, only the backup server configuration is optional when configuring an authentication object.

3. A

Network Admins can review, modify, and apply device configurations as well as review and modify access control policies.

4. B

Security Approvers can view and apply, but not create, configuration and policy changes.

5. C

Security Analysts can review, analyze, and delete intrusion, discovery, user activity, connection, correlation, and network change events. They can review, analyze, and (when applicable) delete hosts, host attributes, services, vulnerabilities, and client applications. Security Analysts can also generate reports and view health events (but not delete or modify health events).

6. D

Security Analysts (Read Only) have all the same rights as Security Analysts, except that they cannot delete events.

7. B

To set up a user so the user can escalate its permissions, from the User Management screen, click the User Roles tab and then click Configure Permission Escalation; then choose the user role the user will have its permissions escalated to.

8. B

The LDAP-Specific Parameters configuration are Base DN, Base Filter, User Name, and Password / Confirm Password. The UI access attribute is part of the Attribute Mapping configuration.

9. D

To create users, from the main menu, navigate to System ➤ Local ➤ User Management. From this screen, you can create users in the local database or have them authenticate externally.

10. A

Access Admins can view and modify access control and file policies but cannot apply their policy changes. Administrators can set up the appliance's network configuration, manage user accounts and Collective Security Intelligence cloud connections, and configure system policies and system settings. Users with the Administrator role have all rights and privileges of all other roles (with the exception of lesser, restricted versions of those privileges).

Chapter 10

1. D

Both the FireSIGHT Manager and the managed devices have a default IP address of 192.168.45.45. It can be used to initially connect to the devices for configuration.

2. C

The built-in password for the managed device and FireSIGHT Manager is Sourcefire. These should be changed when you first set up your devices.

3. B

Stacking allows a device to be connected to a similar device type to increase inspection throughput. This is done with a special stacking module that allows the resources of the systems (CPU and memory) to be shared. This does not give you additional inspection ports.

4. D

The three VPN types supported by FireSIGHT are point-to-point (PTP), star, and mesh.

5. A

Dynamic is a many-to-many translation where you would specify a source network, a translated network address, and a destination network for the traffic. The ports would stay the same across the translation.

6. D

The passive interface allows the interface to be used in a read-only manner for detection.

7. B

The registration key is a passphrase used to authenticate the FSM to the managed device for the initial connection. Once the connection has been established, authorization is handled via certificates.

8. C

Inline interface sets can be configured to fail-open to allow network traffic to flow in the event of a hardware failure. This would require the device to have the supported fail-open netmods.

9. D

Automatic Application Bypass terminates the IPS inspection process if traffic takes an excessive amount of time to make it through the device (bypass threshold). It will generate a troubleshooting file and a health alert and restart inspection within 10 minutes.

10. A

A managed device can participate in RIP and OSPF environments.

Chapter 11

1. A

A white list can be created to define compliant host characteristics, including operating system(s). By adding this white list to a correlation policy and configuring a response, you can be alerted when a non-compliant OS is detected.

2. D

All of the options are possible values for a host white list attribute.

3. B

If a host is compliant with the white list, the list will show as Compliant in the host profile.

4. C

When a correlation rule triggers, the Defense Center generates a correlation event (and also initiates the responses specified in the correlation policy).

5. B

The possible response types in a correlation policy are SMTP, SNMP, syslog, database logging, and custom remediation. Note that database logging always occurs, and a custom remediation can be scripted to do virtually anything—thus the "built-in" stipulation.

6. C

The default remediation modules are as follows:

- Cisco IOS Null Route
- Cisco PIX Shun
- Nmap Remediation
- Set Attribute Value

7.   D

The number of data points in a traffic profile is determined by multiplying the PTW by the sampling rate. Cisco recommends that a traffic profile contain at least 100 data points.

8.   A

The default PTW is 1 week, and the default sampling rate is every 5 minutes.

9.   D

All of the options are valid except D, custom DLL. The Defense Center is a Linux platform (no DLLs).

10.   A

Correlation rules can use the following event types:

Intrusion

Discovery

Connection

User

Host input

Traffic profile change

Malware

Chapter 12

1.   C

The IP Defragmentation preprocessor in the Transport/Network Layer Preprocessors handles IP fragmentation reassembly.

2.   B

The normalizations performed by the HTTP preprocessor include HTTP headers, cookies in headers, UTF encodings, and JavaScript.

3.   A

Adaptive Profiles allows FireSIGHT to pass OS information to the IPS for the purpose of IP fragmentation and TCP stream reassembly.

4.   B

The Targets section allows the administrator to add hosts, networks, or lists of hosts where they can customize HTTP inspection for the individual entries.

5.   A

Global Rule Thresholding is enabled by default to prevent the database from being filled with duplicate event information. The limit is set so that you see only one event every 60 seconds provided subsequent events are of the same kind and going to the same destination.

6. D

The external responses alerting available from the IPS device are Syslog and SNMP. When syslogging is enabled, all events are sent. For SNMP, the servers are configured in the advanced settings and the alerting is enabled on the individual rules.

7. B

Latency-Based Rule Handling allows the administrator to set a threshold based on the time to process the rule against traffic. If the threshold is exceeded a specified number of times in a row, the rule will be automatically disabled.

8. D

The Specific Threat Detection preprocessors include the following: Back Orifice Detection, Portscan Detection, Rate-Based Attack Prevention, and Sensitive Data Detection.

9. A

The built-in checks for the Sensitive Data Detection preprocessor include US phone numbers, social security numbers, credit card numbers, and email addresses.

10. C

Inline Normalization's purpose is to remove deviations in IP, TCP, and ICMP protocol standards. When this feature is enabled, you can pick and choose what types of normalizations to enable for the specific protocols.

Chapter 13

1. B

The two logical pieces that make up the rule are the header and the body.

2. D

By looking at subsequent packets in a session, the system can detect and alert on attacks that occur within multiple packets in a single session.

3. C

The byte_jump argument allows us to move the inspection pointer from the configured number and find the value of those bytes. This allows us to skip data in the packet that is considered irrelevant to the inspection.

4. A

Fast_pattern is a little piece of code found at the beginning of the detection engine and is used to quickly determine which rules a packet would qualify for further inspection by queuing the rules at the beginning of the detection engine startup that have the keyword content in them.

5. B

When you want a rule trigger on service information instead of just IP and port information, you can use the metadata keyword.

6. C

The rule header consists of rule action, protocol, IP source/destination address, port source/destination address, and directional operator.

7. A

The file_data keyword is used in a lot of the rules created by Cisco (rules numbered below 1000000) and is used to look in the data portion of the packets in the responses from HTTP, SMTP, POP, or IMAP servers.

8. C

The detection_filter sets a rate that, when exceeded, can generate an event. Unless the source or destination host exceeds this detection_filter rate, then the event won't be generated. This is used to reduce the number of logged alerts for noisy rules.

Index

Note to the Reader: Throughout this index boldfaced page numbers indicate primary discussions of a topic. Italicized page numbers indicate illustrations.

Free Online Learning Environment

Register on Sybex.com to gain access to the free online interactive learning environment and test bank to help you study for your Securing Cisco Networks with Sourcefire Intrusion Prevention System certification. The online test bank includes:

Assessment Test to help you focus your study to specific objectives

Chapter Tests to reinforce what you learned

Practice Exams to test your knowledge of the material

Electronic Flashcards to reinforce your learning and provide last-minute

test prep before the exam

Searchable Glossary gives you instant access to the key terms you'll need

to know for the exam

Go to `http://sybextestbanks.wiley.com` to register and gain access to this comprehensive study tool package.